Culture Front

Culture Front

Representing Jews in Eastern Europe

EDITED BY BENJAMIN NATHANS
AND GABRIELLA SAFRAN

PENN

University of Pennsylvania Press

Philadelphia

Publication of this volume was assisted by a grant from the Martin D. Gruss Endowment Fund of the Center for Advanced Judaic Studies, University of Pennsylvania.

Published by
University of Pennsylvania Press
Philadelphia, Pennsylvania 19104–4112

Printed in the United States of America on acid-free paper

10 9 8 7 6 5 4 3 2 1

A Cataloging-in-Publication record is available from the Library of Congress
ISBN-13: 978-0-8122-4055-9
ISBN-10: 0-8122-4055-3

In memory of John Doyle Klier, 1944–2007
Scholar, teacher, friend

Contents

Preface

This volume originated in the 2002–3 academic year of study at the Center for Advanced Judaic Studies of the University of Pennsylvania, organized around the topic of East European Jewry. Benjamin Nathans of the University of Pennsylvania was the primary force in proposing the program, running its weekly seminars, and planning the concluding conference. We are all indebted to him and to his editorial partner, Gabriella Safran of Stanford University, one of our visiting fellows for the year, for conceptualizing the book at hand and for bringing it to completion.

The twenty scholars in residence at the Center for all or part of the year included many of the major senior figures along with some of the most interesting younger people working on the history, arts, and culture of the Jews of Eastern Europe. The group was, as always, an international one, with fellows from North America, Israel, and Europe, east and west. Most were historians, though there was significant representation by scholars of Yiddish, Hebrew, and Russian literature. The formal weekly seminars were supplemented by smaller reading groups, including one focusing on Yiddish literature and run entirely in that language.

Some sixty years after the Jewish communities of Eastern Europe were almost eradicated by the Holocaust, the study of their culture and history is thriving, and we all came to realize that the activities of the Center represented a celebration of this renaissance. Our scholarly exchanges, and the book that emerged from them, provide ample testimony to the field's renewed vitality. I am most appreciative of all who participated in our year-long project and especially of those who have agreed to have their essays appear in this volume.

David B. Ruderman
Joseph Meyerhoff Professor of Modern Jewish History
Ella Darivoff Director, Center for Advanced Judaic Studies
University of Pennsylvania

Introduction
A New Look at East European Jewish Culture

Benjamin Nathans and Gabriella Safran

For most of the last four centuries, East European Jewry constituted the deep reservoir of Jewish civilization, the most important repository and generator of Jewish culture and the inspiration for the Russian Jewish historian Simon Dubnov's influential theory of "hegemonic centers" in Jewish history. Among the Jews of Poland, Lithuania, Galicia, European Russia, Romania, and Ukraine—the broad swath of territory between the Baltic and the Black Seas, known since the Enlightenment as "Eastern Europe"—there developed many of the currents that transformed modern Jewish (and not only Jewish) life. From the ranks of East European Jewry emerged mass movements of religious awakening (most visibly, though not exclusively, under the rubric of Hasidism), of revolutionary change (via various forms of socialism), and of national redemption (Zionism and Autonomism). In Eastern Europe, Jews produced a print culture in Jewish languages (Yiddish and Hebrew) without equal in the modern history of their diaspora. From East European Jews and their offspring arose the dominant Jewish centers of the twentieth century in Israel and North America, the lion's share of their political and cultural elites, as well as their characteristic forms of public life.

That East European Jews should have come to occupy the forward ranks of Jewish history was by no means a foregone conclusion. On the contrary, influential nineteenth-century writers like the German Jewish historian Heinrich Graetz routinely referred to "the demoralized and barbarous state" of their counterparts in Eastern Europe, aligning the Jews with the Enlightenment's larger mental map of Europe as divided into a "civilized" West and a "barbarous" East.[1] The "Ostjuden," the "Eastern Jews" whose backwardness was occasionally recast by fin-de-siècle observers as a form of Jewish authenticity, remained icons of primitivism, their "easternness" refracted through an orientalizing gaze.

It is thus one of the paradoxes of Jewish history in Europe that, as Gershon Hundert has recently argued, a kind of precocious modernity emerged precisely among Jewish communities long regarded as anchors of tradition.[2] Such a paradox cannot be dissolved simply by appealing to a dialectical model whereby particularly immobile traditions generate unusually radical attempts to break free of them. For with its increasing diffusion of printed texts, its social antagonisms, and its extraordinary demographic vitality, tradition in Jewish Eastern Europe was anything but immobile. Nor can the paradox be understood simply as a response to especially inhospitable surroundings, for despite the well-known flashpoints of collective violence visited upon East European Jews across the centuries, we still know relatively little about the consequences of that violence and even less about the *longue durée* of nonviolent relations between Jews and the gentile societies in whose midst they lived.

Paradoxes invite intellectual ferment. So too does the opening of long-inaccessible archives. With the collapse of Communist governments across the Soviet bloc at the end of the 1980s, an extraordinary range of historical documents relating to the history of East European Jewry became available to scholars around the world. And scholars themselves became more accessible to each other across what had been the Iron Curtain of postwar Europe. Inspired by these developments and by the sense that new ways of thinking about East European Jewry were taking shape, in 2002 the leaders of the Center for Advanced Judaic Studies at the University of Pennsylvania decided to convene a year-long seminar on the theme of "Jewish History and Culture in Eastern Europe, 1600–2000." Several dozen scholars from North America, Europe, and Israel converged in Philadelphia with a shared ambition: to pool their expertise in the disciplines of history, literature, religious studies, folklore, and allied fields in order to take stock of the cumulative insights contained in the new scholarship. In the uniquely hospitable setting of the CAJS, a dialogue took shape among scholars, disciplines, and texts. Our year together culminated in a conference in May 2003, the annual Martin Gruss Colloquium, which allowed us to add distinguished colleagues from Eastern Europe and elsewhere to the conversation. From the year-long seminar and the Gruss Colloquium emerged the present volume.

Several broad debates structured the work of the seminar over the course of the year. Have the motifs of crisis and catastrophe unjustifiably monopolized the interpretation of East European Jewish history and culture? Have scholars fully come to terms with Salo Baron's influential critique of the "lachrymose conception" of the Jewish past—the notion that gentile persecution and Jewish suffering have been the shaping forces of Jewish history? How else might we analyze the friction and violence of Jewish life in Eastern Europe? Did the Jews of Eastern Europe constitute worlds unto themselves, or did they display affinities with, or adaptations to, the surrounding Slavic societies? In what ways can we speak of East European Jews as a coherent entity across numerous social upheavals and shifting political boundaries, which made Jews subjects, and occasionally citizens, of a wide range of states and empires, from the Poland of the magnates to the Soviet Union of the commissars? How can we account for the emergence of Jewish political and cultural modernism in an allegedly backward setting, and how did that modernism navigate the chasms within the Jewish world between high and low, haves and have-nots?

The historians, literary critics, and social scientists in the group brought different skills to the analysis of these questions. In the course of our weekly seminars, participants examined East European Jews as subalterns, soldiers, readers, constituents of public opinion, members of a multi-ethnic intelligentsia, and more. Discussions brought into focus unfamiliar dimensions in the biographies of writers such as S. Y. Abramovitch (Mendele Moykher Sforim), Shloyme Rappoport (S. An-sky), and Isaac Babel. Other seminars explored the legacy of East European Jewish historians and literary scholars such as Salo Baron, Simon Dubnov, Meir Viner, and Emanuel Ringelblum, as well as the origins of the YIVO Institute for Jewish Research, established in interwar Vilna as the embodiment of historical self-consciousness among the Jews of Eastern Europe. Thus the seminar gave participants, among other things, a chance to scrutinize some of the earliest fashioners of the East European Jewish past and thereby to reflect more deeply on our own enterprise.

If the distinctiveness of East European Jewry is to be found in its combination of religious traditionalism and precocious quests for collective self-emancipation, then the present volume offers fresh insights into that distinctiveness by paying special attention to its cultural expression. Our turn to culture partakes of the humanities' larger shift in interest toward cultural history but also stems from a more local sense of saturation in the study of Jewish politics writ large. To put it differently, the articles gathered in the present volume take up problems of power and identity at the level not of platforms, parties, and parliaments but of the production and consumption of cultural goods. They do so, moreover, across a broad range of textual genres in Jewish and non-Jewish languages, produced and consumed by Jews as well as their Slavic neighbors. As its title suggests, the present volume not only puts culture at the forefront of analysis but treats verbal artistry itself as a kind of frontier through which Jews and Slavs represented, experienced, and negotiated with themselves and each other. We by no means wish to limit our work to the Bolshevik vision of a "cultural front," a militant campaign to instrumentalize culture for political purposes—though such episodes too figure in the pages that follow. Rather, we aim to illuminate the evolving forms and functions of cultural representation and their significance across nearly four centuries of East European Jewish history.

There is a certain historical logic in highlighting the role of culture in the lives of East European Jews. The eighteenth-century distinction between "West" and "East" in the European imagination was grounded in the notion of civilization, the apex of a hierarchy of phases of human development known as "progress," whose shining example was to be found in France and England. "Civilization," as the anthropologist Marshall Sahlins has observed, "was not pluralizable: it did not refer to the distinctive modes of existence of different societies but to the ideal order of human society in general." It was precisely in the eastern half of Europe that the contrary concept of culture was born, both as a defense of particularism in the face of the global pretensions of civilization and as a form of compensation for the absence of nation-states. The idea of culture as "a distinctive mode of experience and existence," notes Sahlins, "emerged in a relatively underdeveloped region, and as an expression of . . . comparative backwardness, or of its nationalist demands."[3] In the essays collected in this volume, the various guises of culture—chronicles, polemics, plays, novels, poetry, autobiographies, translations, museum pieces—provide portals through which to examine competing claims concerning East European Jews' place on the continuum of backwardness and progress.

Despite our reservations regarding the lachrymose conception of the Jewish past, acts of traumatic violence—the Cossack massacres of the mid-seventeenth century and the Holocaust of the mid-twentieth—nonetheless form the bookends of our collection. In both cases, however, the focus is on the afterlife of violence: not its causes or its perpetrators or even its victims so much as its interpreters. Part I of the present volume, "Violence and Civility," engages a pair of defining markers of the continuum of backwardness and progress. In "Jewish Literary Responses to the Events of 1648–1649 and the Creation of a Polish-Jewish Consciousness," Adam Teller shows how an episode of mass violence helped crystallize a distinct East European Jewish identity—distinct not just from gentile neighbors but also from other branches of Ashkenazic Jewry. Well before the massacres by Cossack forces under the leadership of Bogdan Chmielnicki, Jews living in the Polish-Lithuanian lands regarded themselves as more fortunate than their counterparts in Western Europe, enjoying greater security and autonomy as well as more distinguished centers of learning. While the massacres represented a severe blow to this self-image, Teller marshals evidence from numerous Jewish chronicles of the violence in order to argue that Polish-Lithuanian Jews emerged from the ordeal more inclined than ever to see themselves as members of a new and distinct Jewish society, linked to the sacred biblical past but not destined simply to reenact earlier archetypes of suffering and martyrdom.

In an especially attentive reading of the most famous of those chronicles, Natan of Hannover's *Yavein Metsulah* (Abyss of despair), Teller explores the tension between, on the one hand, the desire to represent the events of 1648 as the product of immediate historical antecedents and, on the other, the need to cast those events as inevitable (and hence ahistorical) fulfillments of biblical prophecy. Historical specificity can be found, inter alia, in Hannover's unusual sensitivity to the complex multi-confessional configurations of violence, involving Orthodox Christians and Catholics as well as Jews, and in the virtual absence of links to earlier, medieval episodes of mass anti-Jewish violence and Jewish martyrdom. Ultimately, Teller argues, the image that emerged from 1648—of East European Jewry as a historically distinct "holy community"—itself became an archetype for future generations of Polish and Russian Jews seeking to make sense of violence in their own time. In this manner, the cultural meanings extracted from mass violence were as historically significant as its social and demographic consequences.

A century after the Chmielnicki massacres became an unintended crucible of East European Jewish identity, plans emerged to consciously transform that identity in the name of a new ideal: civility, the antithesis of violence. In "'Civil Christians': Debates on the Reform of the Jews in Poland, 1789–1830," Marcin Wodziński shows how Polish reformers initially found common ground with a small band of Jewish maskilim, followers of the Jewish Enlightenment (Haskalah), in an attempt to curb rabbinical authority and to combat what was construed as superstition in Jewish life. What began as a series of proposed reforms of institutions and customs, however, metamorphosed into a "civilizing mission" aimed at turning Jews into model or "civil" Christians. For Polish reformers, themselves increasingly cast as backward vis-à-vis other Europeans, an enlightened form of Christianity constituted the highest stage of the civilizing process. Wodziński explains the metamorphosis as a function of Poland's own traumatic dismemberment at the end of the eighteenth century, resulting in the loss of statehood and the search for a cultural, as opposed to political, form of nationhood. As the ideal of making Jews useful to state and society gave way to the deeper mission of making them "civilized," a fissure opened up between the limited maskilic agenda of social integration and Polish reformers' hopes that Judaism would yield entirely to Christian civilization. Both sides of this debate, Wodzinski argues, failed to recognize the growing chasm between them (though for different reasons), thus laying the groundwork for the profound deterioration of Polish-Jewish relations at the beginning of the twentieth century, in the age of mass politics.

In Part II, "Mirrors of Popular Culture," Alyssa Quint, Eugenia Prokop-Janiec, and Michael Steinlauf reexamine texts that may in the past have seemed at once too formulaic and poorly crafted to be taken seriously by literary critics and too evidently fictional to attract the attention of historians. They base their analysis on two assumptions: first, that popular culture *matters* no less than high culture, even when it is imitative or ideologically crude and panders to the perceived taste of the market; and second, that lowbrow works are as capable as highbrow ones of containing complex, self-contradictory meanings. These scholars employ a literary-sociological approach that attends not only to literary form but also to time, place, writer, audience, medium, literary institutions, linguistic codes, and how all those elements were in flux. All three essays reflect on the cultural implications and byproducts of the processes of contact and conflict between Jews and non-Jews that Teller and Wodzinski investigate. The authors trace what happened when Yiddish writers borrowed secular, European literary forms, when Polish writers described Jewish characters who were in the process of adopting Polish culture, and when both Jewish and Polish writers wanted Jewish audiences to buy tickets to watch Polish-language theatrical depictions of Jewish life.

In "The Botched Kiss and the Beginnings of the Yiddish Stage," Alyssa Quint provides a new twist on the best-studied model for a narrative depiction of contact between Jews and non-Jews: the familiar Haskalah story line of a Jew's journey away from tradition and toward secular education and enlightenment. She investigates two of the early comedies of the founder of the Yiddish theater, Avrom Goldfaden (1840–1909): *Aunt Sosya*, written in 1869 for private readings in drawing rooms, and *Bontshe the Wick-Layer*, written in 1875 for the newly (albeit briefly) legalized Yiddish stage. As Quint shows, Goldfaden struggled to marry the Yiddish language to the comedic form, which tends to depict the triumph of young lovers over the conservative society of their elders. The botched kiss scene at the center of each play symbolizes, according to Quint, the difficulty of performing comedy, particularly the romantic plot elements, in Yiddish. Although critics of Goldfaden in the past have dismissed his early comedies as immature and derivative, Quint probes that derivativeness to find the tensions in his worldview, concluding that while the earlier *Aunt Sosya* remains faithful to the Haskalah form in its denigration of tradition and celebration of secular education, the slightly later *Bontshe* already reveals nostalgia for Jewish ways and even hesitation about the maskilic project.

Even as Goldfaden and his fellow maskilim pushed for change in East European Jewish culture, they responded to change, despite themselves, with some unease. *Bontshe* dramatizes the unhappy coexistence of differ-

ent literary institutions in a scene on a split stage where the young heroine reads love letters as her grandmother reads the *Tsenerene* (a Yiddish
adaptation of Bible stories): Odele responds ecstatically to her lover,
"Yes, I am yours, my dear!" as Bontshe repeats, "And she understood
that she was naked and she sewed fig leaves and she gave her husband
[the fruit] so he may also eat from the Tree of Knowledge." Will the
promise of modern romance make up for the loss of innocence? Goldfaden's play, as Quint argues, cannot say. But with the comic juxtaposition
of his two female readers, he uses a popular literary medium to juxtapose a variety of possible answers.

Eugenia Prokop-Janiec, in "The Polish Popular Novel and Jewish Modernization at the End of the Nineteenth and Beginning of the Twentieth
Centuries," moves the action forward to the 1890s. She draws on debates
in cultural theory about national identity and its connections to culture,
including popular literature, which she calls "a significant tool for building a national 'imagined community' and negotiating its identity and
borders." She looks at a time when some Jews were growing wealthy and
adopting Polish ways, sometimes even converting to Catholicism and
marrying Poles. Against this background of boundaries seemingly being
blurred or erased, she shows how they were in fact reinscribed and made
stronger, a process both depicted in and accomplished by means of the
literature Prokop-Janiec discusses. She pays careful attention to the
details of popular novels (by Poles and Jews) that describe such acculturation, pausing to explore the ways in which depictions of faces, characters, and settings can encode Jewish or Polish identity. For example, in
Marian Gawalewicz's 1892 novel *Mechesy* (Baptized Jews), a Jew buys an
old Polish manor house and redecorates it in a gaudy way to show off
his wealth; his Polish, non-Jewish daughter-in-law redecorates it again to
make the house "more modest, but also more dignified"—and, evidently, more Polish. This chapter brings together a wide assortment of
novels and stories by Polish and Jewish writers with a host of different
political opinions who all participate in the cultural project of reinscrib-
ing boundaries.

Michael Steinlauf's "Cul-de-Sac: The 'Inner Life of Jews' on the Fin-
de-Siècle Polish Stage" looks at a series of plays on Jewish themes performed in Polish for heavily Jewish audiences in Warsaw summer garden
theaters. This trend began in 1897 with the fantastic success of Gabriela
Zapolska's *Malka Szwarcenkopf*, a play depicting the doomed love of two
urban, "modern" Jews who have moved intellectually and emotionally
out of the world of tradition but remain trapped by its expectations. The
author of the play, a brilliant but scandalous Polish actress, was sympathetic to Jews but thoroughly ignorant about them, and her play was full
of howling inaccuracies. (Zapolska's director had asked a local Jewish

marshelik, a wedding jester, for help with the Hebrew text of the engagement, and the man, "convinced that in the theater they wanted to mock
the engagement ceremony, in place of the real text gave a parody consisting of curses and cheap jokes.") Nonetheless, thousands of Jews,
wearing Polish-style clothes or Hasidic *kapotes*, attended nightly. When
the season ended, producers desperately tried to repeat this success,
staging Jewish-themed plays by Zapolska, other Polish writers, and Jewish
writers such as Wilhelm Feldman, but unsuccessfully. By turning his
attention to this episode of Warsaw theatrical history, Steinlauf recap-
tures some of the strangeness of a moment when Jews paid money to go
to the theater to laugh at (as he argues) Polish misrepresentations of
Jewish life on stage and simultaneously to cry at the fate of urban heroes
with whom, it seems, they identified in spite of the errors. Steinlauf
shows that acculturation does not go hand-in-hand with sympathy or
understanding, nor do these processes proceed in a linear, evolutionary
way. Rather, the cultural contact suggested by the first Zapolska production cannot be made to speak neatly for increasing polonization of Jews
or increasing Polish knowledge about Jews: cultural products—
including pop culture ones—can be shared, but they can mean different
things for different sections of their audience and different groups
among their producers.

While Quint, Prokop-Janiec, and Steinlauf assert that popular culture
can be complexly political, the chapters in Part III, "Politics and Aesthetics," probe what was often the complexly apolitical stance of highbrow
literature. Jonathan Frankel's work on Yosef Haim Brenner, Hamutal
Bar-Yosef's essay on Haim Nahman Bialik, Kenneth Moss's discussion
of Yiddish and Hebrew programs for the translation of an international
literary canon, and Kathryn Hellerstein's investigation of four Yiddish
writers' revisions of the Esther story all consider the connections (and
sometimes lack of connection) between writers' politics and the literary
imperatives they followed in their work. They present Jewish writers as
readers who did not themselves seek out explicit political messages in
literary texts and did not wish to produce literary texts that sounded anything like political propaganda.

Thus Frankel's Brenner, in "Yosef Haim Brenner, the 'Half-Intelligentsia' and Russian-Jewish Politics, 1899–1908," emerges as a political animal sewn uncomfortably into the same skin as a literary aesthete. In
Brenner's second novel, *Misaviv lanekudah* (Circling the point), his
writer-protagonist insists that to write a story in which the pogroms of
1881–82 transform a Jewish character neatly from a revolutionary who
works alongside Russians into a Zionist would be "a sin," the mark of
"tendentious" (and therefore bad) prose. On the one hand, Frankel
observes, Brenner accepted the Russian and Hebrew traditions of the

poet-as-prophet, the idea that writers need to voice the needs and thoughts of their nations and also to guide them, and, on the other hand, he believed that in order to take themselves seriously as artists, writers need to understand art as a separate sphere and create works that respond to their own creative will, rather than to any political (or market-driven) imperatives. This impasse may have led Brenner to make the artistic choices he did in the spare, bleak Hebrew novellas for which he became famous, whose characters voice contradictory viewpoints, none apparently coinciding with the agenda of Brenner himself. Nonetheless, Frankel disagrees with the critics who see Brenner as so politically protean that his ideology cannot be defined at all; rather, Frankel locates fundamental consistencies in Brenner's commitments—to Hebraism, to Jewish political self-assertion, and ultimately to Zionism—and insists on their seriousness.

The national and ideological import of the works of Bialik, the iconic founder of modern Hebrew poetry, would seem far more incontrovertible than Brenner's. In "Recreating Jewish Identity in Haim Nahman Bialik's Poems: The Russian Context," Hamutal Bar-Yosef searches behind the icon for the sources and the significance of Bialik's construction of Jewishness. She argues that key aspects of Bialik's depiction of the Jews and Jewish culture are borrowed from the Russian high culture that Bialik knew well (from depictions of Russianness in Tolstoy, Dostoevsky, Pushkin, and Solov'ev), though she makes it clear that Bialik did not import Russian concepts wholesale but rather engaged in a complex negotiation with them. Bar-Yosef does not trace Bialik's encounters with individual Russian works (which she, reasonably enough, takes for granted) but looks for broad themes and shared images in the Russian canon and in Bialik's poems. She depicts Bialik as a reader of Russian literature, particularly highbrow literature, and she sees him envisioning the Jews in that image (as people who study, whether in the traditional study house or elsewhere—something quite distant from the middlebrow reader or theatergoer at the center of the previous set of chapters). One of the elements of Bialik's work that seems to have been borrowed from the Russians is what emerges at the center of Frankel's article on Brenner: the tension between poetry imagined as an expression of the political convictions of the national poet versus poetry as an expression of the individual feelings of the artist. As Bar-Yosef demonstrates, the dichotomy was neither simple nor paralyzing: Bialik could obey the call of the national writer, creating works that spoke to the demands of the nation, while simultaneously basing his image of the nation on the picture of the solitary writer, silently attuned to his own inner world.

Whereas Frankel and Bar-Yosef investigate the experiences and texts of individual writers, Kenneth Moss, in "Not *The Dybbuk* but *Don Quixote*:

Translation, Deparochialization, and Nationalism in Jewish Culture, 1917–1919," turns his attention to the literary institutions that brought writers' work to readers. He looks carefully at an endeavor that occupied the energy and thoughts of both Hebrew and Yiddish publishers and critics in the first decades of the twentieth century, especially during the years of revolutionary upheaval: projects to translate all (or a representative sample) of the world (meaning Western) literary canon into Hebrew or Yiddish, in order to make contemporary Jewish writing less parochial, less nationally specific, and thereby, paradoxically, to strengthen it. These critics belonged to different political camps, but they were united in their enthusiasm for the translation project—and their insistence that their project, and literature in general, perforce belong to a cultural sphere by its nature apolitical, possessed of its own goals that should not be entwined with politics. As Moss stresses, this was not so much an attempt to educate or influence readers who were seen as members of the Jewish masses as it was an attempt to educate readers envisioned as potential writers. Of all the elements of literary sociology, the emphasis for the translation enthusiasts Moss studies was on code, meaning language: by having world literature translated into Hebrew or Yiddish, they imagined that those Jewish codes themselves would be strengthened and endowed with new capabilities, made equal to other European languages.

Bar-Yosef shows that in a sense, Bialik was already doing what Moss claims the Hebrew and Yiddish critics wanted other writers to do—to create in a Jewish language but with full cultural literacy in European literatures. Nonetheless, Bialik was not perceived by critics during the revolutionary era as doing what they wished Jewish writers would do: in spite of his broad cultural literacy and his linguistic inventiveness, he filled his works with Jewish images, creating something far too parochial, too thematically (rather than just linguistically) Jewish for their taste. Brenner would seem to do a far better job performing the task that these critics set. But for all these writers, whether Moss's literary critics or the playwrights and novelists examined by Quint, Prokop-Janiec, and Steinlauf, the politics of culture cannot be neatly aligned with the politics of nation (or state).

Kathryn Hellerstein, in "Beyond the *Purim-shpil*: Reinventing the Scroll of Esther in Modern Yiddish Poems," picks up where Moss leaves off. If critics argued in 1917–19 that Jewish writers, in order to reconcile the individualist stance of the writer with the obligation of a Jewish writer to serve the people, must write in Jewish languages but with non-Jewish thematics, then Hellerstein looks at the reflections of these same conflicting demands in the work of four interwar Yiddish poets. She shifts the focus from the rhetoric of literary institutions toward literary texts themselves and uses the tools of close reading to consider four poems (or three poems and one poem cycle) based on the biblical story of Esther and on the holiday of Purim, when that story is read aloud. The Esther story, as Hellerstein notes, offers ideal material for this task, since it thematizes the force of beauty and a single voice (a woman's at that) rather than the strength of community. Purim celebrations centered around the Esther story can be seen as similarly subversive of community and tradition. As Hellerstein shows, her four poets—Moyshe Broderzon, Miriam Ulinover, Roza Yakubovitsh, and the best-known among them, Itzik Manger—each draw on the Esther story to situate a speaker in uneasy relation to a Jewish community which at times they feel they must represent and at other times they know they do not. Hellerstein makes it clear that her poets, in citing the Esther story, defamiliarize it profoundly: they show it in a new light and thereby remove its liturgical aura. At the same time, they reveal their loss of faith that a single voice—or prayer—might rescue a people. Individual art has been liberated, but the enemies of the Jews are unmoved. Unlike earlier Yiddish poets who had produced new liturgical or paraliturgical pieces on the model of the Esther story, the interwar Yiddish poets create "an unsacred parody of a sacred fantasy of Jewish triumph over adversity."

The concept of a literary or cultural sphere that exists at one remove from politics not only was the fantasy of some of these writers but also is realized in many of the writings that our contributors examine. Modern though they are, they adhere to a Jewish literary tradition of deep and self-conscious intertextuality; they are dense with allusions, in dialogue with people long dead, who lived and wrote on the other side of political or cultural barriers. Thus these texts both demand and reward careful analysis from varied disciplinary perspectives. The contributors to this volume periodically step out of the realms in which they were trained (as literary critics or historians) in order to bring together different modes of textual analysis. They locate the texts in literary time and space (where, as in Manger's poems, the biblical Esther can fall in love with a basting stitcher who belongs to a radical tailors' union, part of the Jewish labor movement of the early twentieth century) as well as political time and space (where the tensions between the time and space of the biblical scroll [Megillah] and that of interwar Poland matter and inform the discussion). By combining these analytic modes, they—and we—hope to cast new light on the historical experience of East European Jewry.

In the final section, "Memory Projects," chapters by Marcus Moseley and Jeffrey Shandler probe the tension among different ways of narrating familiar Jewish stories—and how those stories sound different in our own time. In "Revealing and Concealing the Soviet Jewish Self: The Desk-Drawer Memoirs of Meir Viner," Moseley moves the focus east to the Soviet Union and forward to the late 1930s, when Viner, a Yiddish literary critic who had immigrated to the Soviet Union in 1926 to enjoy the state support for Yiddish there, found himself writing texts that emerged from entirely contradictory ideologies. On the one hand, as a critic he voiced the dictates of the Soviet state, sharply criticizing writing that in any way celebrated Jewish "bourgeois" tradition, folklore, religion, anything that privileged individual Jewish lives, the memories of individuals, the autobiographical details of their past. On the other hand, during the late 1930s, at the height of Stalinist terror, he wrote his own autobiography, in which he described his grandfather and his childhood friends in the same nostalgic language he had condemned in other writers. He wrote these memoirs, as they say in Russian, "for the drawer" rather than for publication, but they were published nonetheless after his (and Stalin's) death, in the late 1960s. In our current post-Soviet era, when many long-dormant memoirs of this sort have emerged from the drawer, critics and historians have analyzed the tightrope that their authors walked between the ideological mandate that valued not individual experience but the experience of the masses, and the very individualistic urge to write an autobiography, between the approved Soviet models for writing a canonically socialist life, and the real details of memory and experience. Moseley reads Viner's autobiography closely against some of his critical pieces, benefiting from recent trends in Russian literary criticism while situating Viner in a specifically Jewish/Yiddish context and noting the ways in which his self-censored autobiography draws on the specifically Jewish traditions of life-writing that he inherited from writers such as Sholem Aleichem and Abramovitch.

Viner faced both ideological and logistical problems as a writer. Even before the Holocaust, increasing Jewish acculturation in Europe and the United States led to a diminishing audience for Yiddish culture. The cultural institutions necessary to support Yiddish literature were for a time stronger in the Soviet Union, where they enjoyed state support, than anywhere else. But once a Yiddish writer benefited from those institutions, he or she had to accept the accompanying ideological strictures that limited what one could write and for whom. The result was Viner's memoir "for the drawer": a work meant for no present or living audience. Whereas some of our contributors apply the literary critical apparatus developed for highbrow literature to popular culture, texts meant above all to appeal to the market, Moseley takes the opposite tack by analyzing a work that demonstratively does not care about appealing to anyone. His chapter introduces the problem of a culture that outlives its consumers. The texts produced by such a culture, it seems, must work to construct new readers or fantasize a community of the future that will one day read the writing that, for the present, dare not speak its name.

This is a primary theme of Jeffrey Shandler's "The Shtetl Subjunctive: Yaffa Eliach's Living History Museum." He discusses a different attempt to memorialize the details of memory and experience: the proposal by a historian of Jewish Eastern Europe to create a full-scale ongoing reenactment of her native town, Eyshishok (Lithuania), which began construction in June 2003 in Rishon le-Tsiyon, Israel. This planned theme park would offer visitors to Israel the chance to experience life in a shtetl, including such experiences as praying in a synagogue, attending a Yiddish theater performance, and going to a meeting of a Zionist youth group. Shandler details the plans for the Eyshishok museum and pays special attention to the ways in which it privileges certain interpretations or facets of the past over others. For instance, he probes the decision not to represent the one-sixth of the population of Eyshishok that was Christian, and he observes that "there will . . . be minyanim . . . worshipping in the synagogues—but will there also be a band of Jewish socialist revolutionaries, who will come along to disrupt them?" He notes that the idea of inviting visitors to the museum to celebrate their own life-cycle events there—including events such as the bat mitzvah, a ceremony marking a girl's coming of age that would not have been celebrated in the historical Eyshishok—points toward another moment of disjuncture between the historical evidence and the plans for reenactment.

One might read Eliach's plan as a response to the same question that Viner faced: how does one produce modern secular culture that engages the Jewish past, when the audience and the cultural institutions of the Jewish past have changed or vanished? With the diminishing body of readers who can grasp references to East European Jewish daily life, Eliach proposes to create such an audience by educating them in her museum. Indeed, she hopes to invite her visitors to study—children in a *heder*, adults in a yeshiva—so as to master the required information. Like the subjects of other chapters, from Goldfaden to Bialik to Manger, Eliach thematizes the changes in cultural institutions in her own work, as well as the political changes that accompanied and sometimes motivated them. One topic that Shandler does not address in much detail is the place of the Holocaust in Eliach's reconstruction. On the one hand, Eliach declares that her plan was inspired precisely as a response to the well-known images of the Holocaust—piles of corpses, emaciated survivors—and by an urge to create something that would tell audiences about the life of East European Jews before that cataclysmic event. On the other hand, her project is justified by the Holocaust, without which the project of reconstructing the shtetl would seem more quixotic and less necessary.

The present volume thus takes readers on a journey through the cultural history of East European Jewry whose culmination is a project of hyper-realism, delivering its subjects into the realm of the virtual. One might juxtapose Eliach's "living history" Shtetl Museum with Natan of Hannover's "Yavein Metsulah," another memory project with which this volume began. Both authors were survivors of the cataclysmic violence that inspired their work, and both projects suggest the centrality of violence in the construction of East European Jewish memory. Both Hannover and Eliach felt compelled to commemorate not only the violence but also the vibrant Jewish life that preceded it—and, with greater or lesser displacement, survived it as well. In this sense, the essays collected here do not displace the lachrymose conception of the Jewish past; instead they contextualize and interrogate it in the under-explored terrain of cultural production. In so doing, they remind us that Jews in Eastern Europe sustained and were sustained by a remarkable range of cultural expression, in which desires and aspirations as well as fears and contradictions found their voice.

* * *

We would like to express our gratitude, first of all, to our contributors and to all those who gathered at the University of Pennsylvania's Center for Advanced Judaic Studies in the 2002–3 academic year to think and write about East European Jewish history and culture. The conversations begun there have continued to enrich our lives and work. We thank David Ruderman, director of the CAJS, and staff members Sheila Allen, Bonnie Blankenship, Samuel Cardillo, Natalie Dohrmann, Etty Lassman, and Elsie Stern for all their help during that year. We are likewise grateful to Arthur Kiron, CAJS librarian and curator of Penn's Judaica collections, as well as library staff members Josef Gulka, Seth Jerchower, and Judith Leifer for their tireless assistance with research questions large and small. Jerry Singerman, our editor at the University of Pennsylvania Press, and Erica Ginsburg, our project editor, made the production of this volume as painless as such a task can possibly be. The Lucius N. Littauer Foundation generously supported the translation of Marcin Wodziński's article into English. Finally, we both thank our families for their support and patience.

BN and GS

Notes

1. Heinrich Graetz, *History of the Jews* (Philadelphia, 1949), 5:394; Larry Wolff, *Inventing Eastern Europe: The Map of Civilization on the Mind of the Enlightenment* (Stanford, 1994).

2. Gershon Hundert, *Jews in Poland-Lithuania in the Eighteenth Century: A Genealogy of Modernity* (Berkeley, 2004).

3. Marshall Sahlins, *How "Natives" Think: About Captain Cook, For Example* (Chicago, 1995), 10–12.

Part I
Violence and Civility

Chapter 1
Jewish Literary Responses to the Events of 1648–1649 and the Creation of a Polish-Jewish Consciousness

ADAM TELLER

The massive attacks on the Jewish communities in the southeastern regions of the Polish-Lithuanian Commonwealth that accompanied the Cossack rebellion of 1648 came as a terrible shock to the Jewish world.[1] Though the exact extent of the loss of life is still in question, a recent study has argued that some 30 percent of the Jews in Ukraine died in the uprising.[2] Jewish communities, both in the immediate vicinity and in distant countries, obviously needed to come to terms with and explain a tragedy of such proportions. This was done in various ways. On the most practical level, Jews organized to provide relief to prisoners, refugees, and families of victims.[3] The Council of Four Lands proclaimed a formal fast day for Polish-Lithuanian Jewry, and newly composed liturgical poetry was recited in synagogues.[4] In addition, a number of authors published accounts of the tragedy for both contemporary and future audiences.[5] On a more informal level, survivors often wrote of their experiences without publishing them or told stories of what had transpired, which in many cases would become local legends.[6]

Thus it would seem that the events of 1648 came to form part of the Jewish collective memory, particularly in Eastern Europe. So well were they remembered that the Chmielnicki massacres became identified in the East European mentality as the archetype of anti-Jewish violence over the centuries. Following the waves of pogroms in the western borderlands of the Russian Empire in 1881–84, 1903–6, and 1919–20, Jewish writers such as Simon Dubnov, Yehuda Leib Peretz, and Sholem Asch all used the memory of the Chmielnicki massacres in one way or another in order to make sense of the events.[7]

From the range of contemporary materials written about the massacres, one text in particular stands out as the basis for many of the retell-ings and reworkings of the events by the Jews of Eastern Europe. It is the chronicle *Yavein Metsulah* (Abyss of despair), written by Natan Notte Hannover from Zaslaw and published in Venice in 1653. Its popularity seems to have been based on a number of factors: a simple prose style, a clear chronological framework, and a penetrating analysis of the massacres' causes.[8] However, though this work's highly individual nature is widely noted, most treatments of the Jewish literature written in the wake of 1648 tend to treat it all together as a single, largely uniform body of work as far as its approach to the events is concerned.[9] In order better to understand the breadth of responses to the events, this study takes a more differentiated view of the texts.

The discussion here is largely confined to the works themselves and their immediate impact following their publication in the 1650s. This early stage is significant because, as will become clear, accounts of the Chmielnicki massacres significantly influenced the development of a specific Polish Jewish identity in the early modern period. This identity had begun to develop with the massive move of Ashkenazic Jews from the German lands to Eastern Europe in the late Middle Ages and blossomed in the framework of the Polish-Lithuanian Commonwealth. This was due, among other things, to the Jews' huge success in penetrating the Polish economy, their creation of stable and (largely) efficient social structures as well as their feeling of superiority over their surroundings and their deep-seated sense of "chosenness."[10] The goal here, then, is to focus on the Jewish responses to the events of 1648 as another of the elements that made up East European Jewish identity in the early modern period and to evaluate the ways in which they influenced its development.

This chapter, therefore, opens with a discussion of the processes of identity formation among the Jews of Poland in the century and a half preceding the events of 1648. It will then examine the different ways in which contemporary authors dealt with the events themselves, devoting special attention to Natan Notte Hannover and *Yavein Metsulah*. It will conclude with a discussion of how the various conceptualizations of the events affected the development of a Polish Jewish identity in the wake of the massacres.

Polish-Lithuanian Jewry: Toward a New Identity

The development of a new Jewish civilization in Eastern Europe from which the Polish-Lithuanian Jewish identity sprang started during the Middle Ages. When the German rabbi Moshe Mintz took up the rabbinate of Poznan in the late fifteenth century, he noted that the customs there (particularly with regard to marriage documents, *ketubot*) were quite different from those he was used to in Ashkenaz.[11] There followed a further process of social and cultural differentiation in the sixteenth century, when the Jewish center in Poland-Lithuania began to grow rapidly and became one of the largest and most important in the Jewish world of the day. The conditions of life in Poland-Lithuania, and particularly relations with non-Jewish society, were perceived to be quite different from those in other European countries. In a famous letter, the Cracow rabbi Moshe Isserles wrote to one of his pupils: "Though I thought that you would stay in Germany to be a rabbi and a teacher in one of the communities, perhaps it is preferable [to eat] a dry crust in peace here . . . where the hatred of us is not as great as in Germany."[12] In his apologetic work *Hizzuk Ha'emuna* (Strengthening the faith), the Karaite doctor Isaac of Troki went further: "In those three kingdoms [Spain, France, and England] . . . they spilled the blood of many Jews with false accusations, decrees, and forced conversions, until [finally] they expelled the Jews from their lands . . . [This is] not so in the other countries where the Jews live . . . [and the rulers] support the Jews with privileges to allow them to live there in peace and tranquility."[13]

Though this very positive view of the Jews' new and improved situation in Poland-Lithuania was often tempered with skepticism and fears that it would not last, sixteenth-century Polish-Lithuanian Jewry soon became a demographically expanding, self-confident, and prosperous community, largely on the basis of contacts with the magnate estate owners.[14] The novelty of this situation was so pronounced that when reading the stories of the book of Exodus, some Jews no longer identified with the enslaved Children of Israel but saw themselves in the role of the Egyptian enslavers. This was, of course, quite apt in the setting of Ukraine, where Jewish leaseholders ran entire estates and had peasants perform feudal labor obligations for them.[15] Rabbi Feivish of Cracow admonished such leaseholders that "when the Jews were enslaved in Egypt they took care not to work on the Sabbath. How much the more so now *when we are not the slaves but the masters*, should we take care to keep the Sabbath day holy."[16]

The sense of a break with the past also began to be felt in the realm of Jewish cultural development, though here it was a much slower and more hesitant process. On the very basic level of language, Polish-Lithuanian Jews continued to speak their ancestral tongue, a Jewish German dialect, while the influence of their new surroundings was felt through the increased penetration of slavisms into their speech, which would eventually transform medieval Judeo-German into the Yiddish language of Eastern Europe.[17] This meant that in their contacts with the Jews of the German lands (from where they, as Ashkenazic Jews, had sprung), they could immediately sense their different cultural development.[18] In terms of community organization, too, the Cracow Jewish leadership recognized that while their communal life was to some extent based upon the traditions of Jewish social organization they had received from their forefathers, of equal importance in its constitution was the new legal status the Jews enjoyed in Poland.[19]

This duality also affected halakhic development in the sixteenth century. The great codifier Moshe Isserles seems to have understood that, by his day, the Polish Jewish community had undergone rapid changes in its structure as well as its legal status and that the halakhic system that had been appropriate for the Ashkenazic communities of the Middle Ages needed to be updated.[20] Though he argued in the introduction to his commentary on the *Shulkhan Arukh* that he was following the Ashkenazic tradition (Hebrew, *minhag*) of Central European Jewry, when Isserles actually came to codify the *minhag*, he gave clear preference to the customs of Polish Jews (and was criticized for it, to no avail, by rabbis outside Poland).[21] Poland-Lithuania's new place in the Jewish world soon began to be felt in the yeshiva realm, too: the Polish and Lithuanian academies developed a new syllabus and pedagogical method (called *pilpul*) and attracted a growing number of students from Poland-Lithuania and from abroad.[22] Thus, in the realms of social, economic, and cultural life, there seems to have been a feeling, sometimes openly expressed, that Polish Jewry was a new phenomenon which, in many ways, superseded the medieval Ashkenazic world and its traditions.[23]

Old and New in the Jewish Responses to 1648

The events of 1648 must therefore have come as a shattering blow to Polish-Lithuanian Jewry with their newfound self-confidence. Many of the chroniclers noted that it had also been a year of messianic expectations, dashed in the sea of violence that overtook the Jewish communities.[24] While this was undoubtedly the case, the feeling of a reversal of fortune that the story of messianic disappointment expressed may well have gone beyond the circle of mystics who foretold the end of days, and touched Jewish society as a whole. From a situation of economic strength and security the Jews were plunged into weakness, defenselessness, and self-doubt.[25] While scholars are now divided as to the long-term social and economic effects of the uprising—within a relatively short time after the catastrophe, the Jews managed not only to reestablish themselves but to grow in numbers and economic strength—the feelings of shock, uncertainty, and powerlessness engendered by the events tempered the collective responses of Polish-Lithuanian Jewry to the catastrophe that had overtaken them.[26]

As mentioned above, the Jews marked the events in two major ways:

through the composition and recital of special prayers on a specially instituted fast day (as well as on the traditional fast days of the Ninth of Av and Yom Kippur), and by means of historical chronicles. Though most studies of this literature have tended to treat both prayers and chronicles as a largely unified body of material, it would seem that these two kinds of memorials worked in different ways.

The first of these ways can be seen in the nature of the date chosen by the leaders of Polish Jewry for the special day of fasting and remembrance for the victims of the Chmielnicki massacres. They picked the Hebrew date of 20 Sivan, the day on which the great massacre of the Jews in the Ukrainian town of Niemirow had started. As one of the Hebrew chroniclers, Joshua Schussberg, explained: "The evil ones unsheathed their sword in that town and it was the beginning of the catastrophe, and one always follows the beginning. Just like with the fast of the 9th of Av—even though most of the Temple was burnt on the 10th, we fast on the 9th."[27] In fact, the slaughter of Jews in Ukraine seems to have started some time before the Niemirow massacre, so the choice of date was predicated by something else.[28] In this case it seems to have been the fact that 20 Sivan was already recognized as a fast day: it had been set by the great French rabbi, Rabbenu Tam, to commemorate the victims of the medieval blood libel at Blois in 1171.[29] The message was that the suffering of Ukrainian Jews was not something entirely new but formed just the latest link in the long line of Jewish suffering going back to the Middle Ages and beyond.

The idea that the suffering of 1648 was nothing new in Jewish history was most clearly expressed in the works of the famous Rabbi Yom Tov Lipman Heller, rabbi of Cracow in the 1640s and early 1650s.[30] When asked to write a special penitentiary prayer in the wake of the massacres, he initially refused, arguing that the religious poetry written in the wake of the Crusades was quite good enough to be used in the new circumstances.[31] Later, he changed his mind and decided to add a few new stanzas of his own to one of the older poems. This does not seem to have satisfied his congregants, who continued to press him to write a complete poem, which he did in 1651. He opened the poem with the Hebrew words "Eleh ezkera" ("These I shall remember"), which is a common opening for martyrological prayers. The text itself identified the Cossacks and the Tatars as Amalek, the Jewish people's archetypal enemy first identified in Exodus 17. In terms of its actual content, the poem mentioned only the date of the massacres (5408), the treaty between the Cossacks and the Tatars, the fact that the rebellion broke out during an interregnum, and the massacre in Niemirow. The rest of the poem was full of descriptions of the atrocities perpetrated on the Jews with few details of time and place.[32]

An examination of the other liturgical poetry written in the wake of the massacres reveals that Heller's composition was not unusual in this regard.[33] The authors of these poems generally mentioned a few historical details (often, though not always, the same as those chosen by Heller) but expounded largely on atrocities and suffering for which no immediate historical context or explanation was given. For those who had genuine knowledge of the events, these poems must have acted as a reminder of what had actually happened, but for those who did not (Jews outside Poland and later generations), the descriptions imparted little detailed understanding. Of course, giving historical knowledge in the modern sense was not the poems' goal. They aimed to call the Jewish people to penitence by reminding them of their sufferings, and in this regard, what had happened in 1648 was not significantly different from what had come before. The poems therefore created a stylized account of events that would allow the memory of the massacres to be merged into a broader popular memory of Jewish suffering.

Thus, it would seem that the penitentiary prayers recited on 20 Sivan, 9 Av, and Yom Kippur were less concerned to reflect the specific events of 1648 than to present them in a way that would allow them to form part of the continuum of Jewish suffering stretching back into the distant past. They therefore created what might be termed an "empty memory," that is, a memory of an event whose real historical details were, at best, blurred and, at worst, nonexistent.[34] This may have had the effect of moving the events of 1648 into the realm of myth and turning the helpless victims into leading actors in the cosmic drama in which the Jewish people played out their fate. However, in terms of the memories of the massacres themselves, it would seem that these penitentiary prayers did not so much preserve them as cause most of the specific historical details to be forgotten.

The tension between the desire to remember what actually happened in 1648 and the need to collapse the events into a broader memory of Jewish suffering seems to have been felt by Rabbi Shabtai Hakohen, the leading Lithuanian rabbinic authority, who composed special penitentiary prayers for 20 Sivan. To the edition of his prayers published in 1651 he added a special introduction, in the form of a short historical chronicle, called *Megilat Eifah* (Scroll of darkness) in which he gave specific historical details of the massacres.[35]

A similar response may be found in the work *Petah Tshuvah* by Gabriel Schussberg.[36] This was a hybrid work, primarily written as a penitentiary prayer to be recited on Yom Kippur and 20 Sivan, but including a detailed commentary by the author explaining the historical background to the events described in the poetry.[37] The reason for this structure was precisely the fact that the Hebrew style of the *piyyut* left very little room for detailed descriptions of what had actually happened to the Jews of Ukraine.[38] By writing the poem with the commentary, Schussberg was able to infuse the classical genre of the penitentiary prayer with more specific content with which his audience could identify, even though the format broke up the narrative line of the description and made the task of retelling the events quite complex.

The trend of emphasizing the particular events of 1648 over the generalities of Jewish suffering is more clearly seen in other chronicles. Though *Tsa'ar Bat Rabim* (The suffering of many) by Abraham ben Shmuel Ashkenazy opened with a short elegy for Polish Jewry, it eschewed the genre of synagogal poetry.[39] Along the same lines, *Tsok Ha'itim* (In terrible times) by Meir ben Shmuel of Szczebrzeszyn was written in verse (or rhymed prose), but it does not seem to have been intended for recital in synagogue.[40] The authors of these chronicles were clearly interested in preserving the memory of the specific events of 1648 and so devoted most of their effort to composing a reasonably clear and coherent narrative account of what happened. The author of *Tit Hayeven* (Deep mire) took this approach to its logical conclusion, simply presenting a list of the various communities destroyed in the uprising together with the number of dead in each place.[41] Thus, the chronicles presented a specifically Polish Jewish memory, in which the Jews' connections to the past were played down in favor of their own historic experience.

It is worth noting that the potential of a single author to foster a collective memory only really developed with the invention and spread of printing. This meant that the seventeenth-century chronicles could expect the kind of broad audience they needed to form a general memory; medieval chronicles, which were largely confined to manuscript and not annually recited in synagogue, could only have had a much more limited effect. Some of the seventeenth-century authors seem to have been aware of this aspect of their work. In his introduction to *Tsok Ha'itim*, Meir of Szczebrzeszyn wrote: "I composed this scroll in order that [the events of 1648] should not ever be forgotten by us or by our descendants. All those who have the fear of God in their hearts should not harden them and should not worry about the pennies, but should buy [it]."[42] Considerations of sale and distribution were relatively new in this period, but the seventeenth-century authors were already aware just how powerful an instrument the printing press was for influencing the development of Jewish culture.[43]

On one issue, however, the authors of the chronicles did not deviate far from the traditional penitentiary prayers: the ways in which they explained the theological significance of the events. Since the prayers collapsed the memory of the events into the continuum of Jewish catastrophe stretching back to the destruction of the Temple, they were able to rely on the traditional assumption that the Jewish people were being punished for their sins, sins that also remained the same over history. Thus, the prayers needed to give no specific explanations of the sins for which the Jews were being held to account. Moreover, it was a traditional convention that the Jews' suffering had expiated their sinfulness and given them holy status.[44]

In the chronicle with which he introduced his penitentiary prayers, Shabtai Hakohen achieved the same effect by identifying the specific events of 1648 that he described with the past sufferings of the Jewish people. Thus, twice in the course of his short *Megilat Eifah* he mentioned the fact that the massacre of Niemirow happened on the same day as the blood libel at Blois; he compared the devastation in Ukraine to the destruction of the Temple; and, perhaps most significant, he used the metaphor of the binding of Isaac (the *Akedah*), so popular in the medieval chronicles of Jewish martyrdom during the Crusades.[45] Thus, even as he tried to preserve a specific memory of the events of 1648, Shabtai Hakohen retained in his text their connection with the continuum of Jewish martyrdom by identifying them typologically with catastrophes from the Jewish past.[46] Once the events were connected with the past in this way, there was no need to explain precisely what the Jews' sins were in the present. Moreover, whatever their sins had been, the Jews' sufferings had already cleansed them of guilt.

The typological connection was used differently by Meir of Szczebrzeszyn in *Tsok Ha'itim*. He compared Polish-Lithuanian Jewry to Nadav and Avihu, the sons of Aaron, who were burned alive by God's anger when they offered "alien fire" as a sacrifice.[47] His explanation: "Of course [the choice of] Nadav and Avihu is because they were burnt in the fire and condemned by burning and the Name of Heaven was thus sanctified by them."[48] Thus, whatever the sins of Polish-Lithuanian Jewry might have been, their deaths, like those of Nadav and Avihu, had expiated them.[49]

Schussberg's *Petah Tshuvah* (Gateway of repentance) had a more sophisticated approach to this issue: Polish Jewry was destroyed, he claimed, like the Second Temple, on account of the Jews' pointless hatred of each other (Heb., *sinat hinam*). He gave this explanation in light of social tensions and immorality within the Polish-Lithuanian Jewish community, pointing the finger at both the learned judges in the great communities and the ignorant *arendarze* in the countryside.[50] In both cases, however, the significance of events was understood by comparing the specific episodes of 1648 with stories from the past.

The use of typological descriptions to allow an interpretation of events could lead to a certain degree of tension within the texts. This may be seen in a Yiddish "historical song" describing the events of 1648, published the same year.[51] In one verse, the author, Yosef ben Elazar Lipman Ashkenazi from Kremsier in Moravia, wrote, "Their souls [those of the martyred Polish-Lithuanian rabbis] will certainly rest with [those of] other pious men// The Ten Martyrs of the Kingdom who perished as martyrs." A few verses later, he continued, "Who has heard of such deeds in ancient times/ Treating people so cruelly?"[52] Thus the events were, at one and the same time, typologically connected to the Jewish past and yet wholly new. It was this tension that allowed the authors of the chronicles to express their feeling that their experience was unique while not cutting themselves off from the flow of Jewish history.

It should be emphasized, however, that none of the chronicles mentioned the great suicidal martyrdom of the Jews during the first crusade of 1096. The date chosen for the fast, 20 Sivan, commemorated a blood libel that occurred nearly eighty years after those horrendous events and that did not lead to the same acts of self-immolation. The reticence about drawing comparisons does not seem to have been a result of ignorance: Rabbi Yom Tov Lipman Heller and the other authors of penitentiary prayers were able to place the events of 1648 after 1096 in the continuum of Jewish memory.[53] If the chronicles failed to mention them, it seems to have been a matter of choice: the seventeenth-century chroniclers did not find any relevance in the events of the eleventh century.[54]

Various scholars have noted the different concepts of martyrdom (Heb., *kiddush Hashem*) exhibited by the Jews on these two occasions: in a classic study, Jacob Katz argued that the very concept had changed between 1096 and 1648, while Edward Fram analyzed the contrasting religious background to the events as the reason for the differences between them.[55] However, the phenomenon under discussion here is not socio-religious but literary. Whatever the differences in concepts of martyrdom or patterns of behavior may have been, they alone did not prevent the seventeenth-century chroniclers from referring to the events of the eleventh century for comparison or context. In fact, with the exception of Shabtai Hakohen in the introduction to his penitentiary prayers, the chroniclers did not refer directly to any of the sufferings of the Jews in medieval Ashkenaz beyond noting the double significance of the fast of 20 Sivan.[56] In their eyes, the experiences of Polish-Lithuanian Jewry seem to have constituted a new phenomenon, which, though integrated into the general flow of Jewish history, represented a break with their immediate past.

Yavein Metsulah: Structure and Message

Yavein Metsulah demonstrates a rather more complex approach to the events of 1648. The text itself is reasonably short: twenty-two closely printed quarto pages in the first edition. Following an author's foreword and a brief introductory paragraph, the work is divided into fifteen sections, the first fourteen of which describe individual events or massacres. The different sections are of varying lengths and levels of detail. Not all the events they describe are directly connected to the Chmielnicki uprising, nor is Jewish suffering the main focus of every section (though obviously it is extremely prominent throughout the work).

The final section of the book is headed: "And now I shall describe the practices of the Kingdom of Poland which completely [followed] the way of justice and righteousness."[57] The two and a half pages that comprise this section contain a description of the internal workings of Jewish society in Poland and are therefore of quite a different nature from the rest of the work. Thus, in order to understand the impact of *Yavein Metsulah,* it is important to see how all the different sections fit together as a whole to create the image of 1648 that Hannover wanted to present to his readers.

In order to achieve this, I focus on one aspect of *Yavein Metsulah,* namely the different narrative strategies employed in the text. Most analyses of the work until today have tended to evaluate its significance as a historical source by looking at the veracity and accuracy of its reporting.[58] However, simple *reportage* was not the only way in which authors of historical chronicles were able to transmit messages to their readership. The way the historical narrative was structured could be no less important a tool in this endeavor.[59] Here, then, I examine the nature of Hannover's narrative in order to understand more clearly the message he wanted to convey. In addition, I identify the different chronological frameworks used in the text in order to understand how the author situated the events he was describing in the general sweep of Jewish history.

The key to understanding the narrative strategy of *Yavein Metsulah* is to be found in the author's foreword. There he explained his reasons for writing the book. The Jews having witnessed the wrath of God visited on Polish Jewry, he wrote:

All this was foreseen by King David, may he rest in peace, when he prophesied the joining of the Tatars and the Greeks [i.e., Ukrainians] to destroy His chosen Israel in the year 5408. In their usual fashion, the Greeks offered the Jews the following ultimatum: he that wishes to remain alive must convert and publicly renounce Israel and God.[60] The Jews, however, did not listen, but stretched out their necks to be killed as martyrs. . . . This book may thus be a chronicle for future generations to retell. . . . I have dwelt at length on the causes of the disaster and . . . also on the days on which the great massacres happened, so that everyone can work out the day on which his father or mother died and observe the memorial properly.[61]

The purpose of the chronicle is therefore twofold: to help survivors mourn their lost relatives and to explain to future generations how Polish Jewry died as martyrs. Martyrdom is therefore the central theme of this text and is here given an unambiguous definition. It is the choice of death over conversion to Christianity.[62]

Hannover's chronicle reveals an outlook similar to that of Jewish historiography of the sixteenth century.[63] He was not entirely unaware of this since he chose to open his work with a quotation from the chronicle *Tsemah David* (Shoot of David), by the late sixteenth- and early seventeenth-century Prague Jewish humanist scholar David Gans.[64] This choice of reference is all the more prominent since it is the only source Hannover mentions by name. In the section following the quotation, Hannover examines in some detail the political, social, and economic contexts of the rebellion. He explains its outbreak against the background of the religious, ethnic, and economic tensions in Ukraine, soberly assessing too the Jews' own role.[65] He is able to reach an astonishing degree of relativity in his outlook when he describes the peasants' degradation in being ruled by "the most despised people"—meaning the Jews. Though all the other chronicles speak briefly of the political background (such as the agreement reached by the Cossacks and the Tatars), Hannover is the only author to use an extensive and very detailed description of developments in the non-Jewish world to explain events.

Like most of the other chroniclers, Hannover puts special weight on Polish-Jewish relations as a factor influencing the Jews' fate. Though he is alone in his willingness to sympathize to a certain extent with the fate of the Ukrainian peasants (whom he identified with the suffering Children of Israel in their Egyptian captivity), he is in agreement with the general view that the Poles (whom, he notes, also suffered grievously in the rebellion) were the Jews' natural allies.[66] While he does not gloss over cases of Polish treachery toward the Jews, such as at Tulczyn, he states openly that it was only the Jews' relations with the Polish magnates and the latter's help for them which enabled them to survive.[67]

In terms of his theological view, Hannover chooses to see the massacres as a fulfillment of a biblical prophecy. This moves him away from the typological approach to historical understanding, since in this view the prophet has foreseen a single concrete event (or in this case, set of events), which has come to pass. The connection between past and present is therefore linear. This is quite unlike the circular pattern typical of the typological approach, which sees historical events as repeating themselves according to a pre-determined pattern. The use of prophecy also serves Hannover by allowing him to shift the focus from the divine to the human. He makes a number of comments in the course of the text to show that the pattern of events is following Divine dictates: "All the communities repented sincerely, but it did not avail, for the evil decree had already been sealed";[68] "Had not God spared us one [nobleman] we would all have perished."[69] However, these remarks are few in number so that, on the whole, God remains in the background and is rarely seen directing events. This means that while the actors in the story are still basically fulfilling God's program as prophesied by King David, the way they do so, their motivations, and the unfolding pattern of events are largely described without reference to God; they thus take on a distinctly human aspect. It is precisely this aspect of events that most interests Hannover in *Yavein Metsulah,* and he devotes most of his text to examining it.[70]

The narrative structure of *Yavein Metsulah* is not simply chronological, for the author employs an episodic framework, with each section named after one massacre or another.[71] It is within these individual sections that Hannover builds his picture of the Jews' place in the 1648 rebellion in order to explain what happened to them. An examination of the first four sections dealing with 1648 shows that each depicts a different aspect of their fate.[72] The first includes a detailed scene with the Jews of Pohrebicze and Zywotow, who chose to go into captivity with the Tatars[73] rather than face the threat of conversion or death; the second deals with the Jews of Niemirow who were murdered without being given the option to convert; the third deals with the Jews of Tulczyn who were martyred rather than converting; and the fourth includes a description of the Jews of Zaslaw who fled before the enemy and became refugees.[74] There is no attempt here to show a unified picture: each community is presented as being faced with a different situation and reacting in a different way.

What is noticeable in these narratives is that most of the Jews did not martyr themselves in the "classic" way Hannover described in his introduction. The reasons for this are given in his retelling of the two central stories of 1648—the massacres in Niemirow and Tulczyn—where he gives his explanation of the nature of *kiddush Hashem* in the events he describes. Since these two massacres came to represent the whole of the 1648 uprising for the Jews, Hannover devotes considerable attention to them. Thus, in order to understand his message, the stories should be examined in detail.

The following is a brief account of Hannover's narrative concerning events in Niemirow. After coming to an agreement with the local burghers, the Cossack forces tricked the Jews into letting them into town by

pretending to be Poles and flying a Polish flag. Once inside they insti-
gated a huge massacre of the Jewish community. The communal rabbi,
Yehiel Michel, who had previously preached a sermon in the synagogue
exhorting his congregation to martyr themselves rather than convert,
joined in the general flight from the troops, surviving the ensuing
slaughter. He was captured by a soldier but pleaded for his life and eventually ransomed himself. He then tried to flee to the cemetery with his
mother but was attacked by a Ukrainian shoemaker. His mother offered
her life for his, but the shoemaker refused, killing first the rabbi and
then the mother. The rabbi was brought to burial by his widow. The
scene ends with two stories of Jewish maidens who tricked their Cossack
captors, preferring martyrdom to forced marriage.[75]

This tale presents a complex framework for understanding Jewish
martyrdom in 1648. Clearly, a rabbi who preaches martyrdom and then
flees, ransoms himself, is protected by his mother, and is finally killed by
a shoemaker does not cut a heroic figure.[76] However, the point seems
clear: the rabbi is genuinely prepared to martyr himself rather than convert but is faced with a different reality: not a crusading army of Christ,
but a Cossack army and a vicious mob driven by socioeconomic motives
as much as by a desire for religious confrontation. At no stage in the
story is the rabbi (or the other Jews of the community) even given the
choice to convert in order to save himself, so he has no possibility of
becoming a martyr. This view also explains why Hannover emphasized
the maidens' martyrdom at the end of the story.[77] He was showing that
when faced with a genuine religious threat (i.e., the marriage sacra-
ment), the Jews, in this case the maidens, were prepared to die rather
than succumb.

The Tulczyn narrative has a different tone. After coming to an agreement with the Cossacks to save themselves by sacrificing the Jews, the
local nobles tricked the Jews into disarming. Then the Cossacks entered
the town and took all the Jews' property, leaving them alive. The rabbi
exhorted the Jews to martyr themselves if necessary but expressed the
hope that they would be able to be ransomed. However, the Cossacks
presented the Jews with a clear choice: convert or die. The Jews chose
martyrdom. The scene ends with the Cossacks reneging on their deal
with the Polish noble governor of the town, raping his wife and daughter
and then murdering them together with him.[78]

This narrative is discussed by Fram, in a paper comparing Hannover's
story with the testimony of eyewitnesses preserved in rabbinic responsa
in order to reconstruct the actual course of events. His conclusion is that
Hannover did not just report events at Tulczyn but reworked the story,
even using materials from another example of martyrdom (in Gomel)
in order to create the literary effect he thought would best convey his

message.[79] In Hannover's retelling, the Jews seem to be faced with a situation where there is no immediate massacre and they might be able to ransom themselves. However, once again there is a reversal of fortune and the Jews are not given the chance to purchase their freedom. Instead, they are faced with the "classic" martyr's choice—and in that situation remain true to their faith. Finally, Hannover emphasizes the treacherous nature of the Cossacks and the common fate they planned for the Jews and the Polish nobles.

At closer inspection, the two narratives of Jewish martyrdom in Niemirow and Tulczyn seem to have a similar structure.[80] It may be summarized as follows:

1. The Jews are betrayed by trickery.
2. The rabbi tells the community how it should behave.
3. The opposite happens.
4. Those who tricked the Jews are tricked in return.

It is noteworthy that while the narrative structure is the same in both cases, the details of each story are quite different—sometimes even opposite. In Niemirow the Jews are tricked by the Cossacks, in Tulczyn by the nobles; in Niemirow the rabbi preaches martyrdom, in Tulczyn the rabbi hopes for ransom; in Niemirow the Jews are massacred with no possibility of martyring themselves, in Tulczyn they are unable to ransom themselves but must chose martyrdom; in Niemirow the Cossacks are finally tricked by Jews (the maidens who martyr themselves), in Tulczyn the nobles are tricked by the Cossacks. The message here seems to be that the reality of the massacres was not at all stable but rather a confusing kaleidoscope of different loyalties, alliances, and situations. No single response applied to all conditions. There is, however, one element that is constant in both narratives: when they were genuinely faced with the choice of converting or being killed, the Jews steadfastly chose martyrdom. This was the case both in Tulczyn, where the whole community chose to die, and in Niemirow, where it was the Jewish women who became martyrs.

In fact, the portrayal of women in *Yavein Metsulah* is quite noteworthy. In the other chronicles, women are portrayed in three main contexts: as the victims of the most brutal violence (with much emphasis laid on the Cossacks' mutilation of their wombs and children), as the victims of rape and "forced marriage," and as individuals who saved themselves by converting to Christianity.[81] Beyond the element of *reportage* in these stories, the emphasis laid upon women's experiences would seem to indicate that they had a deeper significance. Meir of Szczebrzeszyn wrote: "[The Ukrainians] slashed the bellies of pregnant women and mocked them, saying 'Where is their God?' "[82] The attack on the Jewish women is therefore an attack on the natural (Divine) order of society.[83] Gabriel Schussberg also discussed cases of rape and murder: "[The Ukrainians] tortured, raped, and defiled [the Jewish women] and after their defilement murdered them, saying that the Daughters of Israel are not decent or worthy to receive their seed." Here, the Jewish women have become a symbol of purity and are defiled by the attackers sexually and religiously.[84] One of the few exceptions to this rather stereotypical use of female figures is a story told in *Tsok Ha'itim* of a Jewish maiden in Niemirow who chooses martyrdom over forced marriage before a priest by jumping into the river.[85]

These elements are not lacking in *Yavein Metsulah*. Hannover gives a highly detailed description of the vile attacks on and rapes of Jewish women in the first section dealing with 1648.[86] He also mentions the women in connection with the conversions to Christianity, though he is careful to make them secondary to the men in this regard.[87] In the Niemirow narrative, however, he gives the women quite different roles. He uses the character of the rabbi's mother in a scene where she pleads for her son's life with the murderous Ukrainian. Next, he introduces the figure of the rabbi's wife who gives her husband a Jewish burial. Finally, he picks up on the story of the Jewish maiden who martyred herself by jumping into the river and adds another story about a Jewish maiden who tricks her Cossack captor into shooting her before their marriage.[88] These are four stories of women who are not simply passive victims but who take a hand in deciding their own fate.[89]

On a symbolic level, these female characters seem to balance out the more common stereotypes found in the other chronicles. In place of the Jewish mothers who are portrayed just as mutilated bodies, the rabbi's mother actively pleads for her son. In place of the Jewish women who are defiled, the rabbi's wife purifies her husband's body for burial; and in place of the women who are raped and forcibly married, the two Jewish maidens actively martyr themselves. Once again, Hannover seems to be saying that the complex reality of 1648 cannot be reduced to simple or stereotypical formulas. Moreover, in the context of the events in Niemirow, where Jews were not given a chance to choose martyrdom, it was the maidens who fulfilled this role and so stood in for the community as a whole.[90] These are not messages that Hannover states directly in his lucid style of reporting; they are literary statements made through his choice of materials, emphasis, and narrative structure.

In terms of the concepts of time used in the text, Hannover is quite strict in the chronological framework he employs. Though, as we have seen, he divides the story into various episodes, he is the most careful of all the chroniclers to ensure that his narrative flows chronologically. He also has the broadest range, starting at the end of the sixteenth century and ending in 1652. Another important aspect of his writing is his insistence on dating at least some of the events described. In his introduction, he states that this was to help those who had lost family members to determine the exact date of death for purposes of mourning. However, the inclusion of dates also gives the text as a whole a sense of reliability and strengthens the impression that it is simple *reportage*.

Hannover's concept of the massacres as fulfilling biblical prophecy, which he discusses at length in his foreword to the text, is also of great significance in his use of time because it strengthens his linear view of chronological progression. As discussed above, it permits him to view the events of his own day as being significantly connected to the Jews' past (since they were prophesied in it) without being a *repetition* of previous experience, because the prophecy dealt specifically with what would happen in 1648. In fact, Hannover seems somewhat reluctant to adopt the typological view of history and generally avoids presenting the massacres as being some kind of restatement of previous events.[91] Moreover, though he discusses the date of 20 Sivan twice in the text, once as the date of the Niemirow massacre and once as the date of the general fast, he does not even mention the fact that it also commemorated a medieval blood libel.[92] For him, the idea that the events of 1648 were fulfilling ancient prophecy seems to have allowed them to be understood as unique and not to be submerged in the old litany of Jewish suffering.

It was in this light that Hannover had to deal with the Jews' responsibility for the catastrophe. Here he is at his most traditional, insisting that the Jews were indeed being punished for their sins. "Would the Holy One Blessed Be He dispense judgment without it being justified?" he asks.[93] However, he is unwilling to lay the blame on the Polish Jews themselves. Instead, he quotes the saying from the Talmud to the effect that the righteous in each age are punished for the sins of the generation.[94] As Mintz has shown, a similar device was used in the wake of the massacres of the First Crusade in order to show that the destruction caused was not the result of sin, but was a kind of Divine compliment—the idea being that it was the righteous in every generation who were chosen to suffer.[95] However, Hannover subtly manipulates this concept. Starting from the idea that it was the righteous of the age who were punished, he goes on in the final section of the book to identify Polish Jewry as a whole with the righteous group and so to suggest that they were all being punished for some unspecified sins committed by others. There could perhaps be no greater message of consolation for his suffering compatriots than that.

In the final section, where he describes the inner life of Polish Jewry, Hannover abruptly abandons his strict chronological framework. He bases his description of his society around the six foundations of the world presented in the mishnaic tractate *Pirkei Avot* (Ethics of the fathers): Torah, Service, Charity, Truth, Justice, and Peace. The text is therefore not chronologically connected to the rest of the narrative but presents the world of Polish Jewry as based on eternal Jewish values. Hannover was not the first author to organize a text according to these concepts, but his choice to do so at the end of his chronicle is quite striking, for it seems to remove the subject of discussion from the very flow of history. Though this section is cast in the form of an elegy for a lost world and written in the past tense, it was clear to the author in 1652 that much of Polish Jewry had not been significantly harmed, and that their cultural and institutional life continued strongly.[96] The text itself reads as a lively description of a very vital society.

The significance of this section, therefore, is quite ahistorical. By removing the text from his book's chronological framework, the author seems to make Polish Jewish society timeless. In addition, by organizing his description around the values from *Pirkei Avot*, he imparts to it a kind of holiness, making it almost eternal. The text seems to create here a myth of Polish Jewish society as something above and beyond the vicissitudes of a very cruel reality. If the world of Polish Jews is eternal, it hints, then it must survive the present troubles—a message of hope to Polish Jewry; and if it has survived, then it must be based on Judaism's eternal values—a message of pride for future generations. In this combination, it would seem, lies an important source of the popularity of *Yavein Metsulah* with Polish Jews over the years.

It is now possible to juxtapose Hannover's portrayal of events with his uses of time in order to understand how the memory of the massacres he created could affect the development of Polish-Jewish identity. In its presentation of events, *Yavein Metsulah* emphasizes the highly individual nature of this society and its experiences, which it implicitly views as different and separate from those of the Jewish past. In addition, by placing the mythical portrayal of Polish Jewish society after the description of the terrible events of 1648, the text seems to suggest that the existence of that society, renewed after the massacres, is somehow the very apotheosis of the Jews' sufferings. Thus, by working against the chronological framework of the book and emphasizing the novelty of the Jews' situation in Poland during the massacres, and then following this with a description of all that had previously been best in Polish Jewish life, *Yavein Metsulah* managed paradoxically to transform one of the most destructive outbursts in Jewish history into a foundational experience for Polish Jewry. Its optimistic ending—with Jewish society seeming to outlive the disaster (a feeling that must have grown stronger as Jewish society did indeed recover and develop)—became a message of consolation for later generations of East European Jews who fell victims to violence. Moreover, Polish Jews reading this text not only learned of the course of events, but in their complex portrayal could identify a picture of their entire world. Hannover's conceptual framework encompassed their social and economic life as well as their relations, both positive and negative, with their surroundings. He describes the confusing array of forces and different demands facing the Jews in 1648 as well as their different responses to them, showing that the classical concept of martyrdom was not always relevant in the specific circumstances that arose. However, he takes care to emphasize the Jews' willingness to martyr themselves when occasion demanded and so ensures that their most exalted values find expression in his work. The final section gives an idealized portrayal of Poland's Jewish institutions, rounding off a full portrait of Polish Jewish life.

In fact, Hannover's text might be said to have created a picture of the Polish Jewish world in which the Jews' experiences from different aspects of their reality were integrated into a single conceptual framework. According to the sociologists Berger and Luckman, it is this kind of "overarching universe of meaning" that stands at the basis of group consciousness and so gives legitimacy to any society.[97] It was, therefore, in its complex narrative portrayal of Polish Jewish life in all its contexts that *Yavein Metsulah* succeeded in creating such a symbolic universe and so made its contribution to the development of Polish Jewish identity.[98] As we have seen, this was an identity already in the process of formation during the early part of the seventeenth century. However, after the survivors had understood and interpreted the events of 1648 along the lines laid down in *Yavein Metsulah,* Polish Jewry could more easily see themselves, and be seen by other Jews, as a clearly defined collectivity with a particular identity of its own.[99]

Conclusion: Polish Jewish Identity Following 1648

Yavein Metsulah proved to be the most popular of the chronicles written after 1648, appearing in both Hebrew and Yiddish translation no fewer than eight times before 1800.[100] Of the other chronicles, only *Tsok Ha'i- tim* was reprinted during this period (twice in the 1650s, one of these a plagiarized copy).[101] The sensational "historical poem" in Yiddish describing the massacres appears to have been reprinted in 1648 soon after its initial publication.[102] The only chronicle to rival *Yavein Metsulah* in terms of distribution was Shabtai Hakohen's *Megilat Eifah*, which served as the introduction to his penitentiary prayers for 20 Sivan. This was because it was later included as an appendix in reprints of the popular historical work *Shevet Yehudah* (The tribe of Judah), which appeared in six Hebrew or Yiddish versions before 1800.[103]

The significance of these two texts' popularity for the development of Polish Jewish identity lies in the different forms of memory they preserved. *Megilat Eifah*, in its connection with the recital of penitentiary prayers and its typological view of events, created a memory that was less specifically Polish-Jewish and more generally Ashkenazic in nature, while *Yavein Metsulah*, with its more strictly linear chronological framework, tended to break the links with the immediate Ashkenazic past and so create a rather more specifically Polish memory.[104] What is surprising in the co-existence of these two memories is less the existence of a rabbinic tradition emphasizing the continuity of Jewish life, but rather the popularity of *Yavein Metsulah*'s emphasis on a local, Polish memory. Here, it would seem, the new center of Jewish life in Eastern Europe was staking its claim to be an independent entity with characteristics and identity all its own.

However, I would like to suggest that the popularity of these two texts is evidence for the existence of not one but two separate, partly overlapping strands of Jewish identity among early modern Polish Jewry. The first of these was a conservative and traditionalist strand that saw Polish Jewish life as just another link in the chain of Jewish history. The second was a newer, popular strand of Jewish identity, which sprang up with the development of the new center of Jewish life in the sixteenth and seventeenth centuries and saw Polish Jewish society as a unique phenomenon that broke with the Jewish past in significant ways. Though there was obviously some tension between them, these two strands of Jewish identity seem to have existed side by side in East European Jewry over the centuries, as evidenced by the continued popularity of both *Yavein Metsulah* and *Megilat Eifah* until the Holocaust.[105]

However, with the passage of time, the events of 1648 receded into the past and the two types of memory seem to have partially merged. In paradoxical fashion, *Yavein Metsulah*'s break with the typology of previous Jewish suffering allowed the events it described to become themselves archetypes for anti-Jewish violence in Eastern Europe. This was the reason why they were continually referenced by generation after generation of East European Jews trying to make sense of violent events in their own time.[106] Thus, while the barbarous events of 1648, described so graphically in *Yavein Metsulah*, may have been little more than a minor interruption of long-term Jewish demographic, social, and economic development, they were of fundamental importance for the newly evolving consciousness and identity of Polish Jewry.[107]

Notes

1. For descriptions of the massacres, see M. Balaban, "The Great War" (Hebrew), in *The House of Israel in Poland* (Jerusalem, 1948), 1:81–90; M. Balaban, *Historia i literatura żydowska* (Lwow-Warszawa-Krakow, 1925), 3:262–64; S. Dubnow, *A History of the Jewish People* (Tel Aviv, 1958), 7:9–15 (Hebrew). A great deal has been written about the Chmielnicki uprising and the fate of the Jews. See the extensive bibliography in Joel Raba's massive historiographical study: J. Raba, *Between Remembrance and Denial: The Fate of the Jews in the Wars of the Polish Commonwealth During the Mid-Seventeenth Century as Shown in Contemporary Writings and Historical Research* (Boulder and New York, 1995). Since the publication of Raba's study, a collection of papers entitled *Gezeirot Ta"h: Jews, Cossacks, Poles and Peasants in 1648 Ukraine* has been published by the journal *Jewish History*. See *Jewish History* 17, no. 2 (2003): 105–255. On some of the military aspects of the Jews' participation in the uprising (as well as other campaigns), see J. Goldberg, "The Jews Face the Enemies of the Polish-Lithuanian Commonwealth" (Hebrew), in J. Goldberg, *Jewish Society in the Polish-Lithuanian Commonwealth* (Jerusalem, 1999), 277–88. The Chmielnicki uprising began in the spring of 1648 and lasted on and off until 1654. In the Jewish collective memory, it is the events of the summer and fall of 1648 that characterize the uprising as a whole, so it is known to Jews as "Gezeirot Tah ve'Tat"—"The Evil Decrees of 5408–09." This is because they straddled the Jewish New Year of 5409, which was in the fall of 1648. For ease of reference here, I shall refer to the uprising as a whole as the 1648 uprising.

2. S. Stampfer, "What Actually Happened to the Jews of the Ukraine in 1648?" *Jewish History* 17, no. 2 (2003): 207–27. Though the thrust of Stampfer's article is to scale down estimates of the actual number of deaths, his research also shows that earlier estimates of the Jewish population in the Ukraine were exaggerated. Thus, even if the absolute number of victims needs to be reduced further, as Stampfer suggests, the proportion of those lost still remains at about 30 percent of the total. These are, of course, huge losses in relative terms.

3. I. Halperin, *Jews and Judaism in Eastern Europe* (Hebrew) (Jerusalem, 1968), 212–62; D. Carpi, "The Work of the Padua Community for the Jews of Poland During and After the Persecutions of 1648–1660" (Hebrew), *Gal-Ed* 18 (2002): 57–72.

4. See the extensive collection of sources in Y. Gurland, *On the History of the Decrees against Israel* (Hebrew), 7 vols. (Przemysl-Krakow-Odessa, 1887–92) (reprinted in one volume, Jerusalem, 1972).

5. I. Zinberg, *A History of Jewish Literature*, trans. B. Martin (Cincinnati and New York, 1975), 6:121–31; B. Weinryb, "The Hebrew Chronicles on Bohdan Khmel'nyts'kyi and the Cossack-Polish War," *Harvard Ukrainian Studies* 1 (1977): 153–77.

6. Ch. Shmeruk, "Yiddish Literature and Collective Memory: The Case of the Chmielnicki Massacres," *Polin* 5 (1990): 173–83; H. Bar-Itzhak, *Jewish Poland: Legends of Origin. Ethnopoetics and Legendary Chronicles* (Detroit, 2001), 136, 149–50; G. Bacon and M. Rosman, "A 'Chosen' Community in Distress: Polish Jewry after Ta"h Ve'Ta"t" (Hebrew), in *The Concept of Chosenness in Jewish and General History*, ed. Sh. Almog and M. Heyd (Jerusalem, 1991), 207–18.

7. See Shmeruk, "Yiddish Literature," and G. Bacon, "'The House of Hannover': Gezeirot Tah in Modern Jewish Historical Writing," *Jewish History* 17, no. 2 (2003): 179–206. Cf. A. Mintz, *Hurban: Responses to Catastrophe in Hebrew Litera-*

ture (New York, 1984), 103–5 and elsewhere; D. Roskies, *Against the Apocalypse: Responses to Catastrophe in Modern Jewish Culture* (Cambridge, Mass., 1984), 48–49 and elsewhere.

8. N. Hannover, *Yavein Metsulah* (Venice, 1653). This first edition of this text has been reproduced in *The Stories of the Decrees in 5408 and 5409* (Hebrew) (Jerusalem, 1982). For an English translation, see N. Hannover, *Abyss of Despair (Yeven Metsulah): The Famous 17th Century Chronicle Depicting Life in Russia and Poland During the Chmielnicki Massacres of 1648–1649,* trans. A. Mesch (New Brunswick, N.J. and London, 1983). On Hannover and his book, see Y. Shatzki, "An Historical-Critical Introduction to Nathan Notte Hannover's 'Yavein Metsulah'" (Yiddish), in *Gezeires Ta"h* (Vilna, 1938), 9–159; Y. Izraelson, "Nathan Notte Hannover's Life and Literary Activity" (Yiddish), *Historishe Shriften fun YIVO* 1 (1926): 1–26 (reprinted in Shatzki, "Historical-Critical Introduction," 87–120); R. Michael, *Jewish Historical Writing from the Renaissance to the Modern Age* (Hebrew) (Jerusalem, 1993), 83–85; Raba, *Between Remembrance and Denial,* 37–70; E. Fram, "Creating a Tale of Martyrdom in Tulczyn, 1648," in *Jewish History and Jewish Memory: Essays in Honor of Yosef Haim Yerushalmi,* ed. E. Carlebach, J. Efron, and D. Myers (Hanover, N.H., 1998), 89–112.

9. Weinryb, "Hebrew Chronicles on Bohdan Khmel'nyts'kyi"; Raba, *Between Remembrance and Denial,* 37–70; Zinberg, *History of Jewish Literature.*

10. G. Hundert, *Jews in Poland-Lithuania in the Eighteenth Century* (Berkeley, 2004), 4. I am here taking an approach slightly different from that of Weinryb, "Hebrew Chronicles on Bohdan Khmel'nyts'kyi," 176–77, who argued that *Yavein Metsulah* and the other chronicles reflected the attitudes of their time. While this is undoubtedly partially true, I am more interested here in seeing how Hannover's chronicle might have *influenced* the development of Jewish attitudes and identity following 1648.

11. M. Mintz, *The Responsa of Rabbi M. Mintz* (Hebrew) (Salonica, 1802), no. 109, quoted in I. Yuval, *Scholars in Their Time: The Religious Leadership of German Jewry in the Late Middle Ages* (Hebrew) (Jerusalem, 1988), 320–21.

12. M. Issereles, *Responsa* (Hebrew), ed. A. Siev (Jerusalem, 1970), 417, no. 95.

13. Isaac of Troki, *Hizzuk Ha'emunah* (Hebrew) (Ashdod, 1970), part 1, chap. 46.

14. On the Jews' place in Polish society, see J. Goldberg, "On the Attitude of Polish Society Toward the Jews" (Hebrew), in J. Goldberg, *Jewish Society in the Polish-Lithuanian Commonwealth* (Jerusalem, 1999), 9–79. Cf. M. Rosman, "Jewish Perceptions of Insecurity and Powerlessness in 16th–18th Century Poland," *Polin* 1 (1986): 19–27; M. Rosman, "A Minority Views the Majority: Jewish Attitudes towards the Polish-Lithuanian Commonwealth and Interaction with Poles," *Polin* 4 (1989): 31–41.

15. S. Ettinger, "The Jews' Role in the Colonization of the Ukraine, 1569–1648" (Hebrew), *Tsiyon* 21 (1956): 107–42.

16. I. Halperin, ed., *Acta Congressus Generalis Judaeorum Regni Poloniae (1580–1764)* (Jerusalem, 1945), 497. The emphasis in the text is my own. See also H. H. Ben Sasson, "Statutes for the Enforcement of the Observance of Shabbat in Poland and Their Social and Economic Significance" (Hebrew), *Tsiyon* 21 (1956): 183–206.

17. I am here following the developmental scheme laid down in J. Baumgarten, *Le Yiddish: Histoire d'une langue errante* (Paris 2002), pp. 55–109 and esp. 113–16.

18. Cf. Ch. Shmeruk, "An Outline of Yiddish Literature in Poland and Lithuania until the Decrees of 1648–1649" (Hebrew), in *Yiddish Literature in Poland* (Jerusalem, 1981), 13–73, esp. 14–25.

19. "Our leaders should not be appointed without the agreement of the *Seniores, Boni Viri*, and Communal Representatives [i.e., members of the Community Council] and according to our Holy Torah and also to the privileges which we have from the Kings and all the ministers and governors." Quoted in M. Balaban, "Die Krakauer Judengemeinde-Ordnung von 1595 und ihre Nachtraege," *Jahrbuch der juedisch-literarischen Gesellschaft* 10 (1912): 296–360; 11 (1916): 88–114. Quotation from 10 (1912): 309.

20. E. Reiner, "The Rise of an Urban Community: Some Insights on the Transition from the Medieval Ashkenazi to the 16th Century Jewish Community in Poland," *Kwartalnik Historii Zydow* 3–207 (September 2003): 363–72, esp. 367.

21. Since the Shulkhan Arukh was a codification of the Halakhah according to Sephardic minhag, Isserles' commentary adapted it to the Ashkenazic environment by adding a layer of explanatory notes, which effectively codified Ashkenazic minhag. For an analysis of this project and its significance, see J. Davis, "The Reception of the Shulhan Arukh and the Formation of Ashkenazic Jewish Identity," *AJS Review* 26 (2002): 251–76.

22. E. Reiner, "The Yeshivas of Poland and Ashkenaz during the Sixteenth and Seventeenth Centuries: Historical Developments" (Hebrew), in *Keminhag Ashkenaz U'Polin: Studies in Jewish Culture in Honour of Chone Shmeruk*, ed. I. Bartal, E. Mendelsohn, and Ch. Turniansky (Jerusalem, 1993), 9–80; Ch. Shmeruk, "Young Men from Germany at the Polish Yeshivas" (Hebrew), in *The Call for a Prophet*, ed. I. Bartal, E. Mendelsohn, and Ch. Turniansky (Jerusalem, 1999), 3–17.

23. Elhanan Reiner has argued: "Sixteenth-century literature not infrequently expresses awareness of the essential real difference between the Ashkenazi Jewish community, faithful to Ashkenazi tradition as it had developed since the 10th century, and the new Polish community, whose self-image fluctuated between its links with the old Ashkenazi community and its identification as a young community with its own, independent traditions." Reiner, "Rise of an Urban Community," 367.

24. All the chronicles mention the fact that this was a year of messianic expectations, based on the fact that the numerical value of the Hebrew word "this" or "that" was the same as the value of that year in the Jewish calendar, i.e., 408. Any verse in the Bible that expresses an expectation that the Messiah would come in this or that year could therefore be interpreted as referring to 408 (1648). See, e.g., Rabbi Shabtai Hakohen's use of Leviticus 16:3 for this purpose. Shabtai Hakohen, *Megilat Eifah*, in S. Aben Verga, *Liber Schevet Jehuda* (Hebrew), ed. M. Wiener (Hannover, 1855), 1:139.

25. Cf. Abraham ben Shmuel Ashkenazy, *Tsa'ar Bat Rabim* (Hebrew), ed. B. Friedberg (Lwow, 1905), 14. "The Jews fled the Ukraine, but they did not flee in the daytime when all could see, rather the faithful fled like a slave who flees his master when everyone is asleep, from a fine abode to a poor abode."

26. For modern views that the long-term effects of the massacres were not as significant as previously thought, see Hundert, *Jews in Poland-Lithuania*, 15; J. Israel, *European Jewry in the Age of Mercantilism, 1550–1750* (Oxford, 1989): 120–21, 152–53; M. Rosman, "The Image of Polish Jewry as a Center of Torah Study after the Decrees of 1648–1649" (Hebrew), *Tsiyon* 51 (1986): 435–48; M. Nadav, "The Community of Pinsk in the Period from the Decrees of 1648–1649 until

the Treaty of Andruszow (1648–1667)'' (Hebrew), *Tsiyon* 31 (1966): 153–96. Recent studies of the Jews' relations with the Polish magnates have shown just how well they were able to reconstruct their lives in the decades after 1648: M. Rosman, *The Lords' Jews: Magnate-Jewish Relations in the Polish-Lithuanian Commonwealth During the 18th Century* (Cambridge, Mass., 1990); G. Hundert, *The Jews in a Polish Private Town: The Case of Opatow in the Eighteenth Century* (Baltimore, 1992); A. Teller, *Money, Power, and Influence: The Jews on the Radziwill Estates in the 18th Century* (Hebrew) (Jerusalem, 2005).

27. Gabriel Schussberg, *Petah Tshuvah* (Hebrew) (Amsterdam, 1651), 4a.

28. On the earlier massacres, see N. Hannover, *Yavein Metsulah* (Hebrew) (Venice, 1653), 2b. Since the original is unpaginated, the pagination is my own.

29. Cf. the discussion in Y. Yerushalmi, *Zakhor: Jewish History and Jewish Memory* (New York, 1989), 48–52. The fact that this date was chosen by Polish Jews, however, does not necessarily mean that the fast instituted by Rabbeinu Tam had been observed consistently over the centuries.

30. On Yom Tov Lipman Heller, see J. Davis, *Yom-Tov Lipman Heller: Portrait of a Seventeenth-Century Rabbi* (Oxford, 2004). On his responses to the events of 1648, see pp. 205–18.

31. For the story of their composition, see the printer's introduction to Lipman Heller's penitentiary prayers for 20 Sivan, published in Cracow in 1650–51. The text was reprinted by A. M. Haberman, "Piyyutim and Poems by Rabbi Yom Tov Lipman Heller" (Hebrew), in *In Honor of Yom Tov: Essays and Studies*, ed. Y. Hacohen Fishman (Jerusalem, 1956), 125–45 (here, 125–28).

32. Ibid., 136–38.

33. The largest collection of this literature is to be found in Gurland's *On the History of the Decrees against Israel.*

34. Yerushalmi, *Zakhor*, 43, comments on this kind of memory: "We may safely assume, for example, that what was 'remembered' had little or nothing to do with historical knowledge in any sense that we would assign to such a phrase."

35. This text has been reprinted many times. I use here the version included as an appendix to M. Wiener's edition: S. Aben Verga, *Liber Schevet Jehuda* (Hebrew), ed. M. Wiener (Hannover, 1855), 1:134–39.

36. See Schussberg, *Petah Tshuvah*, 4a.

37. Zinberg, *History of Jewish Literature*, 129, mistakenly states that this text is a commentary on the book of Lamentations. This is not the case: the *piyyut* is an original composition based on various biblical verses.

38. In his study of the literature of this period, Elboim points out that the commentary was perhaps the most popular form of literary composition. Interestingly, here Schussberg composed both the original poem and the commentary to it. See J. Elboim, *Openness and Insularity: Late Sixteenth Century Jewish Literature in Poland and Ashkenaz* (Hebrew) (Jerusalem, 1990), 82.

39. Abraham ben Shmuel Ashkenazy, *Tsa'ar Bat Rabim*. In 1648 two editions were published of a poem in Yiddish dealing with these events, which the author called an "elegy" (Heb., *kinah*), suggesting that it was meant for recital in synagogue. It is published in M. Weinreich, *Pictures from Jewish Literary History* (Yiddish) (Vilna, 1928), 198–211. However, in reality, this composition had much more in common with the genre of cheap pamphlets with news in poem form of some sensational event published in Yiddish for a mass audience. In the historical literature, these poems are called "historical songs" and are invaluable historical sources. See M. Erik, *The History of Yiddish Literature from the Earliest*

Times until the Period of the Haskalah (Yiddish) (Warsaw, 1928), 384–91; Ch. Turni-ansky, "Yiddish 'Historical Songs' as Sources for the History of the Jews in Pre-Partition Poland," *Polin* 4 (1989): 42–52.

40. In his introduction, Meir of Szczebrzeszyn encourages his audience to buy his book and "read it always, particularly 'in the straits' [the days of mourn-ing leading up to 9 Av] and on 20 Sivan." Meir of Szczebrzeszyn, *Tsok Ha'itim* (Cracow, 1650). This seems to be a description of personal reading rather than recitation.

41. Cf. E. Zimmer, "The Persecutions of 1096 as Reflected in Medieval and Modern Minhag Books" (Hebrew), in *Facing the Cross: The Persecutions of 1096 in History and Historiography*, ed. Y.-T. Assis et al. (Jerusalem, 2000), 157–70. Zimmer (162, esp. n. 20) explains that in some communities outside the area of the Rhine, the prayers that memorialized the massacres of the Jews during and after the First Crusade in 1096 did not mention the victims by name but by commu-nity, with the numbers of dead given for each one. This may have influenced the very dry style of *Tit Hayeven*.

42. See above, n. 40.

43. Elhanan Reiner, "A Biography of an Agent of Culture: Eleazar Altschul of Prague and His Literary Activity," in *Schoepferische Momente des Europaeischen Judentums in der fruehen Neuzeit*, ed. M. Graetz (Heidelberg, 2000), 230–47; Reiner, "The Ashkenazi Elite at the Beginning of the Early Modern Era: Manu-script versus Printed Book," *Polin* 10 (1997): 85–98.

44. Cf. Mintz, *Hurban*, 63.

45. See above, n. 35.

46. In his opening section, Shabtai Hakohen quotes the verse "and cut down all the stragglers in the rear of you" (Deuteronomy 25:18), which refers to the nation of Amalek, Israel's archetypal enemy. This strengthens the typological connection of this text with previous accounts of Jewish catastrophe.

47. Leviticus 10:1–3.

48. See above, n. 40.

49. This is a reference to Midrash Vayikra Rabba 20:12: "Said Rabbi Hiya son of Rabbi Abba, 'Aaron's two sons [Nadav and Avihu] died on 1 Nissan.' And why does he mention their death on Yom Kippur if not to teach that just as Yom Kippur expiates our sins, so the death of righteous men expiates."

50. Schussberg, *Petah Tshuvah*, 4b, 5b.

51. See M. Weinreich, *Pictures from Jewish Literary History* (Yiddish) (Vilna, 1928), 198–211.

52. Ibid., 201, 203, verses 13 and 27.

53. See above, n. 30.

54. S. Schwarzfuchs, "The Place of the Crusades in Jewish History" (Hebrew), in *Culture and Society in Medieval Jewry: Studies Dedicated to the Memory of Haim Hillel Ben-Sasson* , ed. M. Ben-Sasson, R. Bonfil, and J. Hacker (Jerusalem, 1989), 251–67; Zimmer, "The Persecutions of 1096," 157–70.

55. J. Katz, "Between 1096 and 1648," in *Festschrift for Yitzhak Baer on His Sev-entieth Birthday* (Hebrew), ed. S. Ettinger et al. (Jerusalem, 1960), 318–37; E. Fram, "Between 1096 and 1648: A Re-examination" (Hebrew), *Tsiyon* 61 (1996): 159–83. See also the continuation of their polemic: J. Katz, "More on 'Between 1096 and 1648'" (Hebrew), *Tsiyon* 62 (1997): 23–29; E. Fram, "Still Nothing Between 1096 and 1648" (Hebrew), *Tsiyon* 62 (1997): 31–46. Though Katz cogently criticized Fram's readings of various rabbinic texts, he was unable satis-factorily to answer Fram's central point—that the differences between the Jewish

responses to the two waves of violence were caused not by internal developments in rabbinic thought but by the essential differences in the situations in which the Jews found themselves. Katz himself admitted that since he did not know Polish, he did not have access to all the sources when he wrote his paper about the events of 1648. Katz, "More on 'Between 1096 and 1648,'" 23.

56. In fact, of the chronicles, only *Megilat Eifah* and *Tsok Ha'itim* mention the blood libel at Blois.

57. Hannover, *Yavein Metsulah*, 9b.

58. Cf. n. 8 above, esp. Shatzki, "Historical-Critical Introduction." 9–25. An important exception here is Fram's paper, "Creating a Tale of Martyrdom." However, despite Fram's success in revealing some of the literary strategies employed by Hannover in composing this account, I disagree with his conclusion (97) that Hannover's aim was to show that all those who died in 1648 were "classic" martyrs. A broader examination of *Yavein Metsulah* seems to me to lead to a different conclusion. See below.

59. Cf. J. Cohen, "The Decrees of 1096: The Events and the Accusations— Stories of Martyrdom in Their Cultural and Social Context" (Hebrew), *Tsiyon* 59 (1994): 169–208.

60. Here Hannover is using a popular midrashic quotation that the Greek kingdom ordered the Jews to renounce their religion or face death. Cf. Bereshit Rabba 2, 16, 44; Shemot Rabba 15; Vayikra Rabba 13, 15. The use of language here is a play on words since, for Hannover, "Greek" was the term generally used for the Ukrainians who followed the Orthodox Christian rite (though, of course, in reality they followed the Russian and not the Greek rite). In fact, this is one of the relatively few occasions where Hannover draws a typological parallel between the experiences of Polish Jews and those of previous generations (i.e., just as the Jews of the Second Temple period were threatened by "Greeks," so was Polish Jewry). It should be noted, however, that he sets this typological usage in the context of his general argument that the events of 1648 were simply fulfilling King David's prophecy. The connection between a prophecy and its fulfillment is linear and denotes a one-off event that has been foreseen. This is quite different from the typological approach that sees history repeating itself time after time following a set pattern. The tension here remains unresolved. See below.

61. Above, n. 8, "Foreword." See also the discussion in D. Roskies, ed., *The Literature of Destruction: Jewish Responses to Catastrophe* (Philadelphia, 1989), 111–13.

62. On various concepts of martyrdom that can be found in this period, see the polemic between Katz and Fram (above, n. 54). It is important to remember that the popular use of the term *kiddush Hashem* in this period could cover Jews who had been killed by non-Jews for any reason. Cf. Fram, "Re-examination," 180. Against this background, Hannover's insistence on the "classic" definition of the term is noteworthy.

63. On this body of literature as a whole, see M. Kohn, "Jewish Historiography and Jewish Self-Understanding in the Period of the Renaissance and Reformation" (Ph.D. diss., University of California, Los Angeles, 1979). Cf. A. Funkenstein, *Perceptions of Jewish History* (Berkeley, 1993), 208–19. Funkenstein (219) claims that in the writings of the famous Italian renaissance Jewish historian, Azariah de Rossi, "we look in vain for traces of the most enduring and significant achievement of humanistic historical thought, namely the clear articulated realization . . . that historical events can only be comprehended if one

reconstructs the full historical context in which they were embedded, a context which endows them with meaning." Traces of such an approach, though not fully articulated, may be found in *Yavein Metsulah.* See below.

64. Cf. M. Breuer, "Modernism and Traditionalism in Sixteenth-Century Jewish Historiography: A Study of David Gans' Tzemah David," in *Jewish Thought in the Sixteenth Century,* ed. B. Cooperman (Cambridge, Mass., 1983), 49–88.

65. Hannover, *Yavein Metsulah,* 1a.

66. Interestingly, Hannover's analysis of the socioeconomic background to the events of 1648 is very closely paralleled by the first of the Cossack chronicles decribing the uprising. It is known as the "Eyewitness Chronicle" and seems to have been composed about a generation after *Yavein Metsulah,* in the last third of the seventeenth century. See Z. Kohut, "The Khmelnytsky Uprising, the Image of the Jews, and the Shaping of Ukrainian Historical Memory," *Jewish History* 17, no. 2 (2003): 141–63, esp. 145–46.

67. Hannover, *Yavein Metsulah,* 3a.

68. Ibid., 5a.

69. Ibid., 2b. The reference here is to the magnate Jarema Wisniowiecki, who was venerated by the Jews as the Polish nobleman who had done the most to help them and save them from the massacres.

70. I am here in agreement with A. Melamed, who states in his study of sixteenth and seventeenth century perceptions of Jewish history by Italian Jews: "The very fact that in addition to Divine Providence, some of them (i.e., Italian Jewish historians) gave also natural and rational explanations to historical occurences marks a new, definitely 'non-medieval' step in the development of Jewish historiography." A. Melamed, "The Perception of Jewish History in Italian Jewish Thought of the Sixteenth and Seventeenth Centuries: A Re-Examination," *Italia Judaica* 2 (1986): 139–70. Though in later years Hannover became very influenced by mystical thought, there is little evidence of mysticism in *Yavein Metsulah.* He makes some use of gematriah (numerology) in his foreword, but this was a very populist form of mysticism and no sign of a serious mystical trend. Cf. G. Scholem, "The Sabbathean Movement in Poland" (Hebrew), in *The House of Israel in Poland,* ed. I. Halperin (Jerusalem, 1956), 2:36. The rest of the book exhibits no mystical tendencies beyond the platitudinous prayer for the speedy arrival of the Messiah. Hannover, *Yavein Metsulah,* 10b.

71. There is an interesting parallel here with Ibn Verga's popular chronicle *Shevet Yehudah,* which had a similar episodic structure. By Hannover's time, this chronicle was also available in Yiddish translation. See M. Stanislawski, "The Yiddish Shevet Yehudah: A Study in the 'Ashkenization' of a Spanish-Jewish Classic," in *Jewish History and Jewish Memory,* 134–49.

72. The importance of these sections is that in addition to describing atrocities committed against Jews, they also give detailed descriptions of complex situations that developed in individual communities and, through the use of direct speech, reveal the Jews' motivations. Their significance within the text may be seen in the fact that these four sections take up more than five of the book's twenty pages.

73. These were forces, largely from the Crimean peninsula, that made their living from banditry. It had been the Cossacks' traditional role to defend the Polish-Lithuanian commonwealth from their depredations, so the Cossack-Tatar agreement was a major blow to Polish foreign policy. Unlike the Cossacks and Ukrainians, the Tatars were Moslems with no marked religious animus toward the Jews. Their main interest seems to have been taking captives for eventual ransom. See Halperin, *Jews and Judaism,* 212–49.

74. Hannover, *Yavein Metsulah*, 2b-5b. Hannover writes the fourth of these sections in the first person since he was an eyewitness of and a participant in the events.

75. Ibid., 3b.

76. These are details that appear only in *Yavein Metsulah*. The rabbi's death together with his mother appears elsewhere, but the story of the sermon dealing with martyrdom and the mother's attempt to save her son are not to be found in any of the other chronicles.

77. Here, too, Hannover not only puts in the story from *Tsok Ha'itim*, he adds another story of his own. It is impossible to say whether he had a source for this second tale or invented it himself; however, he obviously chose to include it to strengthen the section dealing with maidens' martyrdom.

78. Hannover, *Yavein Metsulah*, 3b-4b. This ends the great scene of martyrdom, though the section as a whole continues with further descriptions of the combat between the Poles and the Cossacks.

79. Fram, "Creating a Tale," 89–97.

80. I am indebted to my graduate student, Ella Shpolansky-Glickson, for pointing out to me the parallels in these stories. See E. Shpolansky-Glickson, "Historical Writing in Hebrew Following the Massacres of 1648–1649" (Hebrew) (M.A. thesis, University of Haifa, 2000).

81. Meir of Szczebrzeszyn, *Tsok Ha'itim*, 2b. Cf. the historical poem in Yididsh about the massacres (above, n. 39), 203. In verse 31, an account of Jewish women being raped is followed immediately by their conversion to Christianity, with no mention of men in this context at all.

82. Meir of Szczebrzeszyn, *Tsok Ha'itim*, 2a.

83. On this theme in the contemporary writing on 1648, see N. Yakovenko, "The Events of 1648–1649: Contemporary Events and the Problem of Verification," *Jewish History* 17, no. 2 (2003): 165–78.

84. Schussberg, *Petah Tshuvah*, 8b.

85. Meir of Szczebrzeszyn, *Tsok Ha'itim*, 1b.

86. Hannover, *Yavein Metsulah*, 2b.

87. After describing the brutal attacks on the women, Hannover discusses the sufferings of the Polish clergy, and only then adds: "Thus, west of the Dnieper several thousand Jewish people perished and several hundred were forced to convert" (ibid., 2b). In his discussion of the permission granted by the king for Jews converted by force to return to Judaism, Hannover mentions the return of women forcibly married by Cossacks but only after he has mentioned the men who had been forced to convert (ibid., 8b-9a). This should be compared with the verse in *Tsok Ha'itim*: "Many women renounced the religion/ And pleaded with the Ukrainians who had chosen them./ Many Jews [i.e., men] broke the covenant./ They did not keep God's law/ they transgressed God's orders/ and the Jews who were forced [to convert] were still careful/ but they did not give up their lives/ they alone remained alive." Meir of Szczebrzeszyn, *Tsok Ha'itim*, 2b.

88. These stories do not appear in any of the other chronicles. Whether or not they are based on eyewitness reports, Hannover chose to include them and structured them into his narrative in a certain way. That he felt a certain amount of freedom in so doing is shown in Fram's study. Fram, "Creating a Tale," 89–97.

89. For a description of the portrayal of women in the Crusade narratives as active in their opposition to the Christian forces, see S. Gershenzon and J. Lit-

man, "The Bloody 'Hands of Compassionate Women': Portrayals of Heroic Women in the Hebrew Crusade Chronicles," in *Crisis and Reaction: The Hero in Jewish History*, ed. M. Mor (Omaha, 1995), 73–91. I here take issue with their evaluation (83) of the passive role of women in *Yavein Metsulah*. For a different approach to the portrayal of women in the Crusade chronicles, see A. Grossman, *Pious and Rebellious: Jewish Women in Europe in the Middle Ages* (Hebrew) (Jerusalem, 2001), 346–72.

90. This is not to claim that Hannover tried to portray women in an especially positive light throughout the chronicle. In his section dealing with the massacre at Narol, he brings eyewitness evidence that women survivors had kept themselves alive by resorting to cannibalism. Hannover, *Yavein Metsulah*, 7a.

91. Though see n. 60 above.

92. Hannover, *Yavein Metsulah*, 3b, 9a.

93. Ibid., 9b. He is quoting from the Babylonian Talmud, Berakhot 5b.

94. Hannover, *Yavein Metsulah*, 9b. The quotation is from the Babylonian Talmud, Shabbat 33b.

95. Mintz, *Hurban*, 6, 104.

96. Hannover discusses the reconstruction of Jewish life after 1648, describing the policies of the Council of Four Lands to deal with the social crisis that had been caused and explaining that the Jews returned to many places from which they had fled. He then goes on to describe further attacks on them and the creation of more refugees in the early 1650s. Hannover, *Yavein Metsulah*, 8a–9a. On the reconstruction of Jewish society after the massacres, see M. Rosman, "Dubno in the Wake of Khmel'nyts'kyi," *Jewish History* 17, no. 2 (2003): 239–55, and Nadav, "Community of Pinsk," 153–96.

97. P. Berger and T. Luckman, *The Social Construction of Reality: A Treatise in the Sociology of Knowledge* (Harmondsworth, 1984), 110–46.

98. Cf. J. Le Goff, *History and Memory* (New York, 1992), 128–52. Cf. also Bar-Yitzhak, *Jewish Poland*, 160.

99. G. Hundert, *The Jews in a Polish Private Town: The Case of Opatow in the 18th Century* (Baltimore, 1992), 36.

100. Ch. Friedberg, *Bet Eked Sepharim: Bibliographical Lexicon* (Tel Aviv, 1951–56), 2:420, no. 400.

101. Ibid., 3:868, no. 142. Cf. J. Gurland, *On the History of the Decrees against Israel* (Cracow, 1890), 3–6. Interestingly, though the first of edition of *Yavein Metsulah* was published in Venice and that of *Tsok Ha'itim* in Cracow, the latter book seems to have been more popular in the Sefardic world. Its second edition was published in Salonika (1652) and its third, a plagiarized edition, in Venice (1656). All subsequent editions of *Yavein Metsulah* until the twentieth century were published in the Ashkenazic world. A sign of the popularity of *Tsok Ha'itim* among Sefardim in the seventeenth century may be seen in the story of Shabtai's Zvi's meeting with Polish rabbis in 1666, where he points to *Tsok Ha'itim* as his source of knowledge for the events of 1648. See J. Barnai, *Sabbatheanism: Social Aspects* (Hebrew) (Jerusalem, 2000), 60.

102. See Turniansky, "Yiddish 'Historical Songs.'"

103. On the Yiddish translations of *Shevet Yehudah*, see M. Stanislawski, "The Yiddish Shevet Yehudah," 134–49.

104. The other chronicles discussed here each finds its own place on the scale between the traditionalism of *Megilat Eifah* and the individualism of *Yavein Metsulah*.

105. Y. Fichman, "Foreword," in N. Hannover, *Yavein Metsulah* (Hebrew) (Tel Aviv, 1945), 5–14. This is not to argue that the responses to the events of 1648 were the sole, or even the most important, element in the identity of East European Jews. They formed just one of a multitude of strands that were woven together to make up a complex and multi-faceted identity.

106. Above, n. 6.

107. For the social and economic significance of the events of 1648, see above, n. 26. See also G. Hundert, "Poland: Paradisus Judaeorum," *Journal of Jewish Studies* 48 (1997): 335–48, esp. 345.

Chapter 2

"Civil Christians": Debates on the Reform of the Jews in Poland, 1789–1830

MARCIN WODZIŃSKI

Translated from the Polish by Claire Rosenson

Much has already been written in both Polish and Jewish historical literature about the efforts to reform the Jewish community on Polish lands at the end of the eighteenth century and in the early decades of the nineteenth century. However, as a rule, the treatment of this subject has not moved beyond the reconstruction of facts; only the reforms that took place during the period of the Four-Year Sejm (1788–92), and especially their political and social context, have been somewhat better researched. Moreover, the debates that took place during the Four-Year Sejm and the reforms that were undertaken later in the Duchy of Warsaw (1807–13) and during the constitutional period of the Kingdom of Poland (1815–30) have generally been discussed independently of each other. In this way the basic continuity of the reform process and the proportionality of its elements have been lost.[1] This is all the more surprising since many of the participants in the "Jewish debate" in the Kingdom of Poland were the very politicians and journalists who had debated the reform of the Jews at the time of the Four-Year Sejm; legislation put forward in the Congress Kingdom concerning the Jews was clearly connected to the proposals of that Sejm. The result of this state of research is rather paradoxical. Considering our relatively reliable knowledge of the facts concerning the debates of that period, as well as of the drafts publicized, the arguments put forward, and the social and political contexts, it is surprising that so little is known about the nature of the reform plans, their significant evolution, their primary goals, and above all what, according to the reformers, the reformed Jewish community was to look like.

Equally unsatisfactory, it seems, is the state of knowledge about the primary ideological camps in those "Jewish debates." Traditional historiography has seen two camps on the Polish (Christian) side:[2] the enlightened reformers who were favorably disposed toward the Jews and backward obscurantists who were hostile to them. Among the Jews, it identified the maskilim who favored reform and the traditionalists who opposed change.[3] Modern historians have cast doubt on these classifications, demonstrating that such black-and-white divisions do not reflect the actual views of the participants and in fact say more about the ideology of the classifying historian than about the phenomenon described. In reality, very few of the writers and politicians of that time took the step of rejecting Enlightenment rhetoric; except for extreme cases, it is difficult to find examples of participants in the debate who did not pretend to the title of "enlightened reformer," if only in a very conservative version of the term.[4] On the other hand, the so-called good reformers and the so-called anti-Semites criticized the real and supposed faults of the Jewish community with equal harshness. The differences between them were often of a technical and not an ideological nature: the former saw the granting of rights to Jews as a necessary condition of successful reform, while the latter wanted to confer these rights only after reform had been carried out, as a reward for the acceptance of reform. Thus the difference did not concern the general diagnosis or the established goal of the reform or the general ideological framework. Likewise, the divisions on the Jewish side were not entirely explicit, and it was not always clear to which of the two sides someone belonged. While supporting modernization, the maskilim expressed numerous reservations about the proposed changes, just as the so-called traditionalists were not opposed a priori to grand transformations—and some even actively supported them. Among the participants in the debate who are difficult to classify are Herszel Jozefowicz, the rabbi of Chełm, to whom conservative views are usually ascribed only because he was a rabbi,[5] or the *mitnaged* Solomon Z. Posner, a talmudist and land owner who was known for promoting the social integration and economic transformation of the Jewish population.[6] The difference between these "progressive *mitnagedim*" and the conservative maskilim, of whom the best example is the Polish writer and mathematician Abraham Stern, was not always obvious.[7]

Rather than a readable but false division into four camps, with two on each side, what we are dealing with here is an entire range of views. It seems disingenuous to arrange them according to a homogeneous scheme. Therefore, in the present study I propose to analyze the general categories around which the entire "Jewish debate" was centered and in light of which the opinions of politicians who appeared to belong to opposing groups were, surprisingly often, identical. Although this will not resolve the question of the eventual existence of divisions and groupings within the circles that were drafting the reform of the Polish state, it will at least allow us to describe the most important common tendencies in all or almost all of public opinion of that time without unnecessary value judgments. The present study puts an emphasis on these common tendencies and elements because in my opinion the tool to understanding the actual meaning of the debates, on both the Jewish and Polish sides, lies beyond all these petty differentiations. In fact, all the debates about particular customs, educational practices, or moral values were essentially informed by general Enlightenment concepts of what culture is and how it should be represented. In the following pages I demonstrate how these normative views of culture were conceptualized in categories of civil Christians and civilizing process and how the meanings attributed to the notions of civilization and culture developed together with the sociocultural contexts of pre-partitioned and post-partitioned Poland.

Diagnosis

In order to correctly understand the proposals for the regulation of the situation of the Jews in Poland, we must first consider what Polish proponents of reform perceived as the sources of Jewish shortcomings, where and how they wanted to combat them, and what they wanted to change. The diagnoses varied. Some pointed to legal discrimination; others spoke of the inappropriate system of education. But the basic assumption was always that Jewish society had degenerated socially, economically, and even morally due primarily to customs and beliefs that, "under the guise of religion," had acquired the sanction of inviolable religious laws. In short, the degradations of Judaism were the source of the evil.

One of the sources of this conception, it seems, was the old anti-Semitic prejudice that found the sources of the supposed errors, including the practice of alleged ritual murder, in "Judaism laid bare."[8] However, it seems unfair to accuse all reformers of holding anti-Semitic stereotypes, since many of them renounced such views and were highly critical of openly anti-Semitic publications.[9] Alongside the traditional anti-Semitic prejudices there existed another, significantly more important source of the Polish reformers' criticism of the beliefs and practices of Judaism: contemporary publications by liberal reformers in France, Austria, and the German lands, as well as publications by maskilim in Germany, France, and ultimately Poland. Obvious and oft-cited examples include the proposals of the Prussian official and Enlightenment writer Christian Wilhelm von Dohm, publications by Henri Gregoire, a liberal advocate of Jewish emancipation in France, and the articles of toleration issued by the Austrian emperor Joseph II. The role of *Haska-*

lah publications was also important and, I believe, underestimated. The writings of the eighteenth-century Polish maskilim Menahem Mendel Lefin Satanower and Jacques Calmanson can serve as examples, as can works published outside Poland, including those of the Paris-based Polish Jew Zalkind Hurwicz or the Jewish philosopher and Lithuanian maskil Solomon Maimon. In 1792, Lefin published draft legislation for the reform of Jewish society that had been prepared for the Four-Year Sejm's Deputation for the Discussion of Proposed Reforms of the Jews. Calmanson's work—published in 1796, but also prepared during the period of the Four-Year Sejm—included a broad study of the beliefs and customs of Polish Jews in addition to a proposal for reform. These two texts, like many others, cemented the clearly articulated conviction that the success of the reform depended on ridding Judaism of deformations that had arisen within it. Lefin distinguished two streams in the religion of the Jews: the rationalist, best represented by the medieval philosopher Moses Maimonides and the alleged founder of the Jewish Enlightenment, Moses Mendelssohn, and the mystical, based on the *Zohar*, with Hasidism as its contemporary incarnation. The state should oppose the mystical stream with all its power, Lefin argued, since it represented the degeneration of a religion of reason based on the Talmud and was in conflict with the basic tenets of Judaism.[10] Likewise, Calmanson justified the necessity of reform by the existence of "Jewish sects that have spread through former Poland." The religion, cleansed of the fanaticism represented by the Hasidim and the Frankists, would revive the customs and morality of the Jews and return to its previous form—which according to Calmanson resembled the Enlightenment ideal of natural religion.[11]

Jewish voices were important to Polish proponents of reform because they came to serve as a reliable verification of the accuracy of the Polish reformers' diagnosis: since the Jews themselves—at least some Jews—recognize that their community is in need of change, the deterioration of this population must be very advanced, and since the Jews themselves see the sources of that deterioration in the degeneration of Judaism, then this diagnosis is surely correct.

However, on this matter there was a certain fundamental difference between Polish and Jewish reformers. Calmanson and Lefin, following the example of other *Haskalah* modernizers, laid out precisely which elements of contemporary Judaism they considered part of the inviolable foundation of the true Mosaic religion and which beliefs and customs they believed were pollutions of it. For both of them, the religion based on the Bible and the Talmud (though read critically) was the true religion, and sectarianism, fanaticism, and mystical belief were deformations of it. Christian reformers seemingly accepted the differentiation between that which constituted the inviolable religion and everything that had incorrectly come under that term and therefore was subject to reform. However, they did not feel obligated in the least to accept the particular categorizations made by the maskilim. The reformers themselves were to be the arbiters of what belonged to the first category and what to the second. In fact, these categorizations underwent in the period under discussion a very significant evolution, which was indicative of the entire transformation in the reform projects and the conceptions of the place of the Jewish people in Poland. In the early phase of the debate, the distinguishing criterion was the social significance of particular beliefs and practices. Mateusz Butrymowicz, the deputy from Pinsk to the Four-Year Sejm who was the first to propose the reform of the Jews in Poland, wrote: "The secular government can neither correct nor change religion, but it can and should distinguish what has incorrectly come under its rubric." In contemporary Judaism Butrymowicz distinguished dogma, which was inviolable, from "ceremonies, or their rites," which were to be modified. The division was thus made, at least formally, between cultural ideas, which were to remain intact, and the social practices they generated. Among the "ceremonies" that were to be subject to reform he listed the Jewish holidays, the laws of *kashrut*, and the practice of resting on the Sabbath. Butrymowicz proposed that a Sanhedrin should be convened to reduce the number of "the Jewish holidays, which are not so much the observance of holidays as criminal idleness," and to give Jews permission to eat non-kosher foods; the rabbis would also grant to Jews serving in the military and Jewish public servants permission to carry out their duties on Saturdays.[12] Such reforms targeted practices of wide social importance, a fact that, in the reformers' minds, served as their justification. In Butrymowicz's opinion, such reforms would in no way violate the principles of Judaism. Curiously, the author was able to list the Jewish "ceremonies" that he felt did not belong to the essence of Judaism, but he did not devote a single word to characterizing the inviolable foundation that supposedly was not subject to reform. It could be that this foundation simply was not the focus of his interest because it lay beyond the area of reform; but it seems likely, too, that this omission was dictated by the ignorance that was so characteristic of Polish proposals for reform. Butrymowicz did not bother to define the phenomena described; what belonged to reformable "ceremony" was determined by whether he considered the custom socially harmful, or even inconvenient, rather than by any actual understanding of its religious significance. Ultimately, however, what really mattered was not only the social significance of the customs in question but also the reformers' stereotypes about them. The persistence of attempts to abrogate the laws of *kashrut* (the social consequences of which were minimal) becomes understandable only when we recognize that refusal to share a common meal was, according to Polish custom, a great offense. Butrymowicz, like other Polish reformers, must simply have felt personally insulted by the (abstract) refusal of the Jews to share meals with them, the more so as the (abstract) Jew who was refusing was a person of lower status and, in Butrymowicz's sensibility, lower in every regard. The refusal to share a common meal thus violated both the Enlightenment conception of equality (which the abstract Jew questioned) and the aristocratic conception of honor and social order.

Conceptions of the division between healthy and unhealthy elements of Jewish belief were present in later proposals as well. Stanislaw Potocki, the well-known Mason and anti-clericalist, was the Minister of Religious Faiths and Public Education in the early years of the Kingdom of Poland and therefore officially responsible for, among other things, the reform of the Jews. Justifying the Jewish policy of the European states, he wrote, "The solicitude of today's governments for [the Jews] is not aimed at subverting their faith, but rather the terrible and anti-social superstitions that they have incorporated into that faith."[13] Despite the seeming convergence with Butrymowicz's views, a fundamental evolution had taken place here, and it laid out the direction of change in the Jewish debate from the end of the eighteenth century to the beginning of the nineteenth. Whereas Butrymowicz differentiated belief from practice—that is, ideas, values, and myths from their cultural representations—in the views of later reformers the boundary lay between the even more abstract "true religion" and morality. Reform proposals sought not only to transform customs but also to reconstruct the entire system of norms and values, the ideas generating cultural practices. This shift from moderate plans for social reforms to a radical call for a deep transformation of the entire Jewish culture emerged after 1795, but it found clearest expression only after 1815. These views were formulated most fully by Stanisław Staszic, a distinguished author and politician of the Polish Enlightenment who was actively engaged in planning for the reform of the Jews in Poland, and who was in effect the author of the "Jewish policy" of the constitutional period in the Kingdom of Poland.[14] Staszic had spent several years studying in Paris, and as a result he had an excellent knowledge of French Enlightenment literature. He drew on this knowledge extensively in formulating his views on, among other things, the "Jewish question." Following anti-talmudic conceptions of the French ecclesiastical historian Claude Fleury and his successors, Staszic accepted that the perfect Jewish religion of the biblical period had been damaged by the false influence of the Talmud, which had nothing to do with the true Mosaic religion.[15] The differentiation between good Mosaism and bad Judaism introduced here allowed for unlimited criticism of the latter. In 1816 he wrote:

We should say the Jewish religion and not the Mosaic religion, because the current belief of that population is not Mosaic; Moses did not give and did not know
any Talmuds, and he couldn't even have understood them. All of today's teaching of faith is based on the Talmuds, and that is the main source of its damage
. . . to Jewish morality. Moses speaks in his Books only of peoples who do not
believe in God, who take the rivers, mountains, trees, and stones for Gods; on
the contrary the religion of the talmudists, and thus of today's Jews, speaks of
Christians, that Christians do not believe in God, that they are the godless idola-
ters about which Moses speaks in the Old Testament, and on which after all the
entire Christian religion is grounded. With such a false though religious image
of Christianity, the morality of the Jews with regard to the Christians is false and
harmful.[16]

Thus according to Staszic the Talmud was a source of Jewish separatism,
anti-Christian prejudice, and dual morality. He argued that "the religion
of today's Jews must be cleansed of Talmuds," which in essence would
mean the rejection of the entire post-biblical tradition of Judaism. Staszic's program therefore called for the replacement of Judaism with a
new religion, called Mosaism and based on the Five Books of Moses. The
state was to grant the Jews a new religion and to prevent this new religion
from becoming a basis for Jewish separatism and fanaticism, as they
believed Judaism had been.

Central to Staszic's criticism of Judaism was the assumption that talmudic beliefs were the source of Jewish separatism, and that this separatism was in turn the source of all the Jews' misfortunes. The author
repeatedly stressed that religion could not give the Jewish people—or
anyone else—the right to create institutions independent of the state;
such institutions would serve autonomous goals that might not be in
accord with the intentions of the state. The new Jewish religion should
therefore be a private religion in the strict sense of the word. Though
the ideologists of the Enlightenment formulated the postulate of private
status for all religions, their attitude toward Judaism and toward Christian denominations was only formally equal. Staszic asserted that since
Judaism was to be a private religion, and since Jews could join any non-
Jewish organization, the creation of such institutions as the *kahal* or
brotherhoods from which Christians were excluded could not be
allowed. It did not enter Staszic's head that virtually all contemporary
organizations refused Jews the right of membership, and the assertion
that a Jew could join any non-Jewish organization (even after the
reform) was simply absurd. Imagine a Jew in a parish rosary circle, or
any other equivalent of a Jewish psalm brotherhood. For Staszic the former was not an institution at all, while the latter was a harmful one. Thus
it is difficult to speak of equal treatment of the faiths. But this does not
mean that Staszic failed to understand the reality of his day; quite the
opposite. The problem was that Staszic—like the majority of ideologists

of the Enlightenment—did not accept the existence in the state of institutions of a confessional character, and the Jews were the only estate (or quasi-estate) in the former Commonwealth whose separateness was defined by religion. The attack on Judaism was thus a criticism of estate forms of national organizations, especially based on confessional stratifications. However, Staszic's criticism affected not only social institutions of Judaism. His attacks on the Talmud and Judaism based on the talmudic tradition led him to negate the entire Jewish system of norms and values. Consequently, in his numerous projects and administrative regulations, Staszic constantly endeavored to eradicate not only Jewish social organization, but also any traces of Jewish cultural distinctiveness, be it Jewish educational practices, literature, ethical values, norms and patterns of family life, or food customs.[17]

Polish reformers from Butrymowicz through Staszic and Potocki agreed that the cause of the Polish Jews' difficulties and the social problems connected with them was Judaism, and that therefore Judaism needed to be "returned to the original purity which had been darkened by the superstitions of the Talmud."[18] In radical versions, characteristic for the later phase, Judaism was to be replaced by a new "Mosaic religion." A new religion was not only to be purged, but first and foremost to become purely private, since the reformers were not interested in religion so much as its social implications. Religion was a subject of consideration because it was believed to be a decisive factor in shaping characteristics of Jewish society; thus changing Judaism equaled transforming its social manifestations. In time, however, the diagnoses radicalized the reform and new goals were set for it.

What Are "Civil Christians"?

The Polish reformers' declarations on the goals of the reform were surprisingly concordant, just as their declarations on the diagnosis of the problem had been. The goal of the reform program, as it was generally formulated in the early stages of the debate, was to "mold the Polish Jews into citizens useful to the country."[19] This assertion only seemed trite. It not only used a set phrase expressing the utilitarianism of Enlightenment ideology, but demonstrated that the reform was undertaken with an eye to the Polish and not the Jewish subjects of the state, and, further, that the beneficiaries of the reform would be the state and the non-Jewish part of Polish society; the Jewish community would not necessarily benefit. The only politician to mention "the happiness of the million [Jewish] people" in the debates of the Four-Year Sejm was Scipione Piattoli, an Italian Catholic priest who was secretary to King Stanislaw Augustus and an enthusiast of the reform of the Jews of Europe.[20]

At the other end of the spectrum stood those who during later debates emphasized the one-sidedness of the advantage for non-Jewish society as a virtue of their proposals, and even expressed concern that the improvement of their legal and educational situation would provide the Jews with the means for exploiting the Polish people more effectively.[21] Debating the founding of the Warsaw Rabbinical School in 1818, members of the Council of State of the Kingdom of Poland agreed that it was necessary to proceed cautiously with the reform of the Jews so that "the lessons would not strengthen a harmful corporation," and so that instead of changing the Jews, the process of civilizing them would not give them yet another instrument for cheating Christians.[22] Here, too, Staszic went the farthest in advancing his particular program. He wrote of the Jews: "They have a superior family arrangement, and they surpass us in the establishment of the authority of fathers and husbands and in the arrangement of marriages. . . . If we cannot in the present degree of our associations likewise change, improve, and perfect those elements in our nation, then we must try to shake them among the Jewish race as well."[23] Even if these views were not widespread, they illustrate clearly the one-sidedness of the benefit of the planned process and its primary goal. We should explain here that Staszic and other Polish statesmen lost sleep over the Jews' "superior family arrangement," not because of a disinterested dislike of Jews, but because, as they believed, it aided more rapid Jewish demographic expansion. This in turn was considered the main reason for the transformation of the Jewish population in Poland into a "privileged estate," for Jewish separatism, and for its gradual achievement of independence from the rest of society.[24] Radical critics, among them the popular writer Julian Ursyn Niemcewicz, stirred public opinion with frightening talk of the "Jewification" of the country or the transformation of Poland into "Judaeo-Polonia." This was most indicative of the later phase of the reform plans, in which the formulation about Jews as "citizens useful to the country" lost its popularity. In new projects the reformers claimed Jews should be industrious, obedient to the orders of the state, honest, clean, but above all identical to the surrounding Christian population in every way except for religion. Kajetan Koźmian, a member of the Council of State and writer of the late Enlightenment, put it most concisely. Commenting on draft legislation on the Jews in 1816, he characterized the goal of the proposed reforms as follows: "to transform the Jews from useless and harmful members of society into good citizens attached to their country, to give them more light—namely, the morality that they lack; in a word, to make of them *civil Christians*, that is, people who for their neighbors, for the monarchy, for the country, would acquire Christian sensibilities."[25]

Other authors also wrote about the "surrogate Christians," that is, the

Jews who "in custom and lifestyle" would be identical to Christians.[26] These declarations should not be interpreted, as they sometimes have been, as expressions of crypto-missionary aspirations. When politicians believed that the final result of the proposed reform of the Jews should be their conversion en masse, they were not ashamed to express such opinions openly.[27] However, in the debates under discussion, both in the last years of the Polish-Lithuanian Commonwealth and in the period of the Kingdom of Poland, voices of this type were rare. One prominent representative of the "missionary" option was a distinguished politician and a close associate to Tsar Alexander I, Adam J. Czartoryski, who nevertheless belonged to the minority.[28] The decisive majority opposed missionary activities and emphasized that a condition of the success of the reform was full religious tolerance, and although some of them supported the conversion of individual Jews to the Christian faith, they fought bitterly against the linkage of that mission with general plans for the reform of the Jews. Stanisław Staszic was representative of the reformers holding this attitude when he rejected a suggestion for support of missionary activity with an observation that "although European empires promote Christianity, it is not their aim to force anybody to accept Christianity."[29] It is worth repeating in this context that in the constitutional period (1815–30), it was precisely the views of Staszic that shaped the "Jewish policy" of the Congress Kingdom.

The Frankist obsession, which was alive throughout the period under discussion, also contributed to the dislike on the part of numerous writers and politicians for missionary efforts. The specter of converts who seemingly accepted Christianity but who worked to infiltrate Christian society, take advantage of it, conquer it, and eventually destroy it had existed since the conversion of Jacob Frank's followers to Catholicism in the mid-eighteenth century.[30] For the first time in the history of the Polish mentality, Jews (albeit converts) became the protagonists in a conspiracy theory of history, taking over that function from the recently liquidated Jesuit order.[31] Proposals for the mass conversion of Jews were therefore decidedly unpopular.

It is also worth remembering that for the majority of those Polish reformers who were true to Enlightenment ideology, the concept of "Christianity" had nothing at all to do with religion. In the view of many, Christianity was simply the best of the known forms of social organization and the highest form of culture, and therefore "the civil Christian" was the ideal being, one who accepted the culture and morality of the Christian world without the unnecessary (and, in the opinion of the radicals, harmful) ballast of religious beliefs. The Jew, transformed into a "civil Christian," was thus to be the ideal creature of enlightened reforms and the ideal subject of the enlightened state, one who abandoned the talmudic system of social-cultural organization in favor of a more advanced one.

As for the details, it was agreed above all that this imagined, enlightened Jewish community would renounce the external markers of its separateness, take on Polish attire and the Polish language, and abandon its judicial and administrative separateness. There was even discussion of whether the rabbinate should be completely dismantled or merely have its sphere of competence limited to strictly religious matters; likewise, there was the question of whether the *kahal* should be preserved, and if so, in what form. Regardless of the answers given in these writings, it was agreed that the final result should be the annihilation of the Jewish religious-estate structure; that is, of the infamous *status in statu*. According to the drafters of the proposals, the Jews were also to submit to the Polish educational system; they were to be removed from the system of *propinacja* (the licensing of alcohol sales) and directed toward "useful" activities. Likewise, the practices of marrying early and burying the dead quickly were to be prohibited, as were the use of expensive fabrics and kosher food. However, according to the reformers, the most important task was to force the Jews to accept not only Christian customs, but also Christian norms of morality: "For as there is one God, there is only one morality."[32] Of course, in the conception of the enlightened men, Christian morality was the same as natural, universal morality. The Jew thus should not differ from his Christian neighbor in profession, language, attire, or even customs and morality; the only difference allowed was the difference in beliefs—on the condition, of course, that these beliefs (rather than a religion) would not require external expression, and would therefore remain strictly private.

What Does It Mean to Civilize?

All of this sounds like a program of total assimilation. This accusation has often been made against Polish reformers, particularly in nationalist-oriented Jewish historiography. It appears to be justified, since Polish reformers stated the goal of totally "remaking the Jews into Poles" repeatedly and without mincing words, while liberal proposals to leave the Jews a certain margin of religious and cultural separateness were isolated and unpopular.[33] However, for at least two reasons, it would be a mistake to write off the reformers' intentions as a program of total assimilation. First, the very term "assimilation" is loaded (particularly in its Hebrew version—*hitbolelut*); it is not merely descriptive but contains a value judgment. Second, and most important, the projected reforms were not just about assimilation itself. As the terminology used in those

"Jewish debates" clearly demonstrates, they went significantly beyond that.

In publications from the period of the Four-Year Sejm, the terms used most often in reference to the plans for changing the situation of the Jews were "reform," "improvement," and sometimes "refinement." The term "assimilation" did not appear and in fact was in principle unknown until the second half of the nineteenth century.[34] The concepts of "reform" or "improvement" were not loaded in principle and could signify any change in the situation of the Jewish community. But around 1815 a new term appeared in the debate—one that was, in my opinion, indicative of the fundamental change between the first and second phases of the discussion of the situation of the Jewish population in Poland. That term was "civilization."[35] At the turn of the century this concept was still nebulous and weakly grounded in the Polish language; its international career began only at the end of the eighteenth century as the influences of French Enlightenment thinking took hold. From the French *civilité*, the term had been popularized by Erasmus of Rotterdam and for several centuries denoted politeness or norms of behavior as codified by the courts and courtiers' culture.[36] However, by the end of the eighteenth century the term assumed a new meaning. Initially, the term was so imprecise in Polish that the meanings of the verb "to civilize," that is, to refine, to polish, were often spliced with the adjective "civil," in the sense of civic or citizen (as opposed to clerical or military).[37] The concept of the "civil Christians" could thus embrace both "secular Christians" and those who were "civilized into Christians." Despite this lack of clarity, the concept of "civilization" soon became a permanent part of the public debate. "Civilization" was usually understood as a concept near to "culture," broadly conceived, and in principle stood in for it since the term "culture" appeared in public debate in Poland only several decades later. But at the same time, "civilization" contained the essential concepts of progress and the hierarchy of various civilizations, and thus involved a clear value judgment. This was consistent with the development of the term in other European languages. Despite remarkable differences between French and German uses of the term, each contained a distinct colonialist ideology of the superior "civilization" of European elites that was to be transferred to and inculcated in both "lower" social groups within the same society and in "lower" societies.[38] "To civilize" meant to raise from a demeaning state of barbarism and cultural primitivism to the "higher," better, and above all more modern culture, and "civilization" was "modern and progressive culture."[39] On the highest rung of the hierarchy was of course the enlightened civilization of Western Europe. Arguments over civilization and civilizing progress were not the exclusive property of the Jewish debate in Poland; quite the contrary. Such debates have taken place and continue to take place today in many countries that are subject to the influence of Western society (especially American cultural imperialism). In Poland at the beginning of the nineteenth century, the major debate over "civilization" concerned not the Jews but above all the Poles. Nevertheless, this term turned out to be particularly convenient in reference to the reform of the Jewish population as well and quickly became a permanent part of it. The concept of the "civilizing of the Jewish people" emphasized that despite its delay in this area, Poland was and always had been part of the Christian civilization of the West, while the Jews remained outside of this civilization and thus on a lower developmental level. In part, aside from the obvious compensatory function, this thinking provided an excuse for the difficulties of Polish society as a whole— which was forced to struggle with such wild and backward elements within its midst.

It seems that it was Stanisław Staszic who introduced the concept of civilizing to the debate on the reform of the Jews. Staszic wrote often about "the civilization of Christian associations" (that is, of the social organizations of Christian societies) as well as about the soothing and enlightening effects of "civilization."[40] The concept soon became widespread and, I believe, is the best indicator of the character of the second stage of the debate on Jewish reforms in Poland. The appearance of the concept of the "civilizing" of the Jewish people in the years 1815–1830 was not coincidental. During the Four-Year Sejm, after the Sejm had undertaken the task of state reform, the guiding concepts of reform proposals were state and society. The fall of the Polish-Lithuanian commonwealth in 1795 and a series of violent political changes in the years following led to the general reformulation of the conceptual categories of public discourse in nineteenth-century Poland. In place of the state and the "political nation," the nation defined by its spirit and culture became the primary category in Polish literature. Society became a rather nebulous category, grounded more in the cultural life of the nation than in state structures.[41] Of course the nation was still an open category, much closer to a community of culture than a community of blood, and in this sense early-nineteenth-century conceptions of nation were more connected to the old Enlightenment conception of society than to the views of nationalists at the end of that century. Nevertheless, the change that took place at the turn of the nineteenth century in the categories used to describe the world was radical and widely felt. For this reason the old assumption that the Jews needed to become "citizens useful to the country" was turning out to be insufficient. As we have observed above, around the turn of the century reformers shifted their interest from Judaism as a source of social organization to "Talmudism" as a basis of Jewish culture as a whole. After 1795 the Jews were not only supposed to accept sociopolitical reform, but were in addition to "become civilized"; that is, they were to cast off the outdated Jewish culture and to accept without reservation the "higher" and "modern" Polish culture. Polish reformers assumed that "Jewish civilization," which embraced such varied problems as language, morality and customs, forms of social organization, and cultural life, was a wild, primitive culture that was giving way to the enlightened culture of Europe and was therefore condemned to utter destruction. Moreover, according to this conception, the backwardness of the Jewish population was causing a delay in the civilizing process of Polish society as a whole; therefore the only way for Jews to become "citizens useful to the country" was to renounce Jewish culture and accept Polish culture. This was typical cultural imperialism. The alleged cultural inferiority of the Jews was used to justify every use of coercion against them: the proposed actions were "only seemingly harsh for the Jews, and in reality will be most beneficial for them."[42] The reform was thus to be not only a total linguistic, cultural, structural, and national assimilation, but was also to raise the Jews from their primitive state. Characteristically, Polish public opinion accepted this view, which was so hostile to the Jewish tradition, precisely at the time when it was itself struggling with an analogous conflict between the progress of civilization as defined by the Western model and the defense of traditions and native cultural patterns.

One way or another, the need to "civilize" the Jewish people became the main postulate of the Polish reformers after 1815. The proposals called for the displacement of the Hebrew and Yiddish languages, a ban on the publication and distribution of books promoting traditional rabbinical culture, support for publications in Polish promoting Polish culture, support for secular education, and the promotion of norms of behavior characteristic of the Christian majority.

The most complete proposal for reform was prepared by the Jewish ("Starozakonny"—lit. "Old Testament") committee, a state institution established in 1825 precisely for the task of "civilizing the Jewish people."[43] The committee perfectly illustrated the direction of the "civilizing" policy undertaken by the government of the Kingdom of Poland in the constitutional period. Luigi Chiarini, priest, professor at Warsaw University, and one of the prominent ideologues of nineteenth-century anti-Semitism, gave the committee's proposals their final shape.[44] However, Chiarini's anti-Semitism should not lead us to conclude that his views exclusively informed the committee's draft proposals. First of all, Chiarini was not solely responsible for committee policy. Maskilic circles were consulted on many of his proposals, and on numerous points Chiarini's views converged with those of the dominant Polish reformers including, among others, Staszic, who was active in planning the committee. Thus, despite Chiarini's anti-Jewish phobia, his proposals and rhetoric remained within the Enlightenment mainstream of the debate. One could even say that it was precisely his Enlightenment proposals for reform taken to the extreme that constituted his main contribution to the development of the "rationalist" anti-Semitism of the nineteenth century.

According to the committee, the reform was to be divided into two parts: temporary reform and radical (i.e., ultimate) reform. The concept of the two stages of reform was probably taken from Jacques Calmanson, who had proposed very similar stages.[45] The goal of the first stage was to be the immediate limitation of the harmfulness of the Jewish people, and the goal of the second stage was to be the enactment of deep moral and cultural reform. Its basic instruments were to be the following:

1. the Rabbinical School and elementary schools for Jewish children;
2. a moral treatise, to be drawn up by well-known Israelites, which would use quotations from Jewish religious texts to bring the Jews closer to Christian "pure morality";
3. the translation of the Talmud into French for the purpose of conclusively discrediting all of its superstitions and fairy tales;
4. a course on Hebrew antiquities to be taught at Warsaw University in order to educate Christian specialists in the field of Jewish culture;
5. the establishment of a committee for the censorship of Hebrew books and periodicals, and the subordination of the only permitted Jewish publishing house in the kingdom to this committee, which would support the cause of propagating the moral reform of the Jews.

Most of the planned institutions did in fact come into being, and some of them had existed before establishment of the committee. The Rabbinical School was the most famous of these, established the following year (its creation approved in 1818); the education of the spiritual leadership was considered a high priority.[46] Chiarini personally chaired the Department of Hebrew Antiquities at Warsaw University and began the translation of the Babylonian Talmud into French, but above all he took pains to extract financial gains from this enormous project. The plan was to entrust Abraham Stern, the most famous of the Polish maskilim, with the preparation of the treatise on morality, but when he refused the task was given to Abraham Buchner, a teacher at the Rabbinical School and a prolific maskilic author.[47] Elementary schools for children of the Jewish faith came into existence in 1820. The government very actively promoted the publication of works in Polish at least as early as the beginning of the 1820s, when government agencies ordered the publication of catechisms for the Jewish faith and prayerbooks and textbooks for Jewish schools.[48] Another important element of the government's educational plan was the sponsoring of the Polish Jewish weekly *Dostrzegacz Nadwiślański* (Observer on the Vistula, 1823–24), the first and for a long time the only Jewish newspaper in Eastern Europe, published by Antoni Eisenbaum, a radical modernizer and later director of the Rabbinical School. The Censorship Committee came into existence in 1822, though in point of fact it had always existed. The censorship of Hebrew books involved both the supervision of current publishing efforts, which hindered the publication of certain types of rabbinical literature (particularly mystical), and the supervision of public and private Jewish libraries in Poland. As a result of this enormous undertaking, thousands of books that the authorities considered contrary to "the civilized spirit of European societies" were removed from circulation,[49] and the Congress Kingdom became one of the leading centers of Haskalah publication, luring authors primarily from Russia.[50] The "radical reform," as planned by the committee, attempted to transform a wide range of aspects of Jewish culture, most notably replacement of Yiddish and Hebrew with Polish (and, partially, German); entire eradication of the Talmud and vast fields of Jewish religious literature from elementary education, rabbinical training and popular use; propagation of "pure Christian morality" through new publications, school textbooks, moral treatises, and the Jewish press (quite an innovative enterprise in Eastern Europe); and introduction of secular knowledge to the curriculum of the elementary education.

Among the arguments raised when the Jewish Committee was dissolved in the mid-1830s was that virtually all of the committee's actions, particularly in the area of so-called radical reform, had been ineffective.[51] However, it is important to note that the criticism concerned only the effectiveness of the activities undertaken, and not their designated goal of "civilizing" the Jews. This concept remained the most lasting element in the Polish vision of Jewish society, even after the government withdrew its planned reforms of the Jewish people (or anyone else) after the collapse of the revolution in 1831. Jewish society continued to be viewed as existing on a lower cultural level and thus in need of "civilizing"; that is, it needed to be raised from the level of Jewish culture to the level of Polish culture. "Civilizing" thus replaced reform. The committee expressed this view clearly in its first report in 1826:

The only way to accomplish a thorough and lasting reform of the Jewish [*starozakonny*] people is through the spread of pure moral and religious enlightenment.

... All mechanisms and regulations, though they may be correct in and of themselves, will not bring lasting benefit, because, acting only on the ill effects, they
cannot destroy the nucleus itself. . . . Given this state of affairs, we must think
not of the organization of the Jews [*starozakonnych*], but above all of their radical
improvement.[52]

Traditional historiography has correctly indicated that in time, the
demand for the Jews to "civilize themselves" became a useful justification for the disadvantageous political-legal position of the Jewish population and the petrification of the reigning social order.[53] It seems,
however, that the ill will of the ruling circles and their social subsidiaries
cannot explain everything here. We must keep in mind that this process
had a more general character; it did not concern the Jews alone and it
was not limited to the abandonment of plans for political reform. The
change that was taking place at the time in the basic conceptions of
political discourse made the conceptions of the Four-Year Sejm and the
political journalism of the Stanislavian period appear increasingly outdated. In the public debate of the late Enlightenment, which is to say
the period after the fall of the Polish-Lithuanian state, emphasis shifted
ever more clearly from the category of the state to the category of the
nation. After 1815 romantic literature accelerated the process of the
maturation of the modern category of nation. The divorce of the nation
from the state became increasingly obvious. Many politicians active in
the administration of the Kingdom of Poland did not identify completely with the state that they ran, and in social perception there existed
a chasm between the state and the nation. This tendency manifested
itself in the early years of the Kingdom's existence even among politicians who were enthusiastic about its founding, and deepened with every
dramatic political crisis. A natural consequence was the neglect of the
plans aimed at integrating the Jewish community into state institutions
and the cultivation of those aspects of integration that brought that community closer to "Polishness," the Polish nation, and society conceived
of as a "community of Poles." The reform thus lost its political-legal
character and became increasingly a matter of identity and culture.
After 1815 the debates were about how the reformed Jewish culture was
to look and no longer about its social role.

Jewish Perspectives

As has frequently been observed, Polish and Jewish conceptions of the
reform of the Jewish people had very similar sources, remained closely
connected, and constantly influenced each other. They cited, disputed,
and agreed with each other, and a significant portion of the publications
and drafts arose as part of a direct polemic. Polish public opinion paid

such lively attention to Jewish pronouncements (which does not mean that it understood them) that some Polish writers published under Jewish pseudonyms when expressing their opinions on matters not directly connected with the "Jewish question" in order to attract greater attention from readers.[54]

Moreover, for Jewish proponents of modernization, universal European Enlightenment and its East European variant provided not just a necessary ideological context, but also very important institutional and personal support. Limiting ourselves to just the most spectacular examples, we could mention that one of the most important East European maskilim of the eighteenth century, Menahem Mendel Lefin, owed his success above all to the support of the Polish enlightened reformer and aristocrat Adam Kazimierz Czartoryski.[55] Abraham Jakub Stern, the most influential of the Polish maskilim of the first half of the nineteenth century, had a similar relationship with his patron Stanisław Staszic.[56] In the constitutional period of the Kingdom of Poland (1815–30) these relationships became institutionalized outright when almost all the leaders of the Polish Haskalah found employment in institutions directed by reformers of the Polish state.

This relationship was not one-sided, however. The existence of the maskilim was essential for Polish proponents of reform, too. The maskilim served them as a source of information about a reformed community, as the allies (and in the eyes of their opponents, collaborators) needed for this type of social reform, and above all as confirmation that such reform was possible. The writer and liberal politician Julian Ursyn Niemcewicz, who otherwise evaluated the Jewish community rather pessimistically, referred often to the maskilim he knew—including, for example, Abraham Stern and Jacques Calmanson—as models of behavior for all of Jewish society. The line of argumentation was as follows: if Stern and other maskilim could submit themselves to reform with such good results, then others can as well.[57] This type of thinking about enlightened Jews as proof of the reformability of Jewish society as a whole was present in Enlightenment conceptions throughout Europe, and the universal "proof" was the example of the best-known German maskil, Moses Mendelssohn.[58]

The superficial—and essentially formal—convergence of the Polish and Jewish reform programs also determined the frequency of mutual references and the patency of connections. Above all the two sides agreed that reform was necessary, that the situation of the Jewish population was bad. They agreed that the areas requiring reform were the superstitiousness of the Jewish population and its anti-Christian prejudices, the unhealthy professional structure, the lack of secular education, and the low level of cultural, linguistic, and social integration.

Moreover, both the Polish and the Jewish reformers saw the deformations of Jewish social life as the cause of this state of affairs. They were also in agreement in blaming (though with different degrees of intensity) the unhealthy political-legal situation for pushing the Jews to these pathologies. Questions of the autonomy of the *kahal*; the scope of the spiritual leaders' authority; differences in attire, language, and customs; economic and social problems arising from the concentration of Jews in brokerage, commerce, and some handicrafts; educational programs; and access to the political-legal structure were all debated with equal interest by Polish and Jewish modernizers, and the various reforms proposed for solving them were often similar to each other. The closeness and ideological kinship thus did not raise any doubts among either the interested parties or later historians.[59]

Yet behind these apparent similarities lay much greater differences. The origins of the conflict lay in the heart of the plans for the transformation of the Jews, that is, in the attitude toward religion as a source of Jewish culture. Outwardly, there was much in this area that united the maskilim and the Polish reformers. Both sides accepted that Judaism had become contaminated by pseudo-religious superstitions and thus was in need of reform. Some of the maskilim even accepted the differentiation between Mosaism and Judaism (or between Mosaism and Talmudism) and built their program of cleansing the religion—like Staszic and Chiarini—on the postulate of returning to the Bible and rejecting the Talmud.[60] And although radical anti-talmudic views existed only at the margins of the Polish Haskalah, criticism of various forms of traditional Judaism and the customs connected with it was widespread enough among the maskilim that it could serve as an area of understanding, however fragile, with the Polish reformers. The maskilim did, in fact, accept the far-reaching criticism of religious institutions (particularly the position of the rabbi, the *kahal*, the religious brotherhoods, and the practice of *herem*) and the need for their transformation. Some even agreed to a moral purging, provided that it would affect only the fanatical branches within Judaism. The discord arose around the question of how deep this transformation was to be, who was to direct it, and, above all, what the outcome would be. Moreover, the discord broadened in time, when the visions developed by Polish reformers changed from a conception of social integration to a concept of "civilizing" Jews into "civil Christians," that is, into the Jew who would be distinguished from his Polish and Christian neighbors only by his beliefs. The new Mosaic religion was to be entirely private and free of ritual to the extent possible, with organized religion limited to a minimum.

All this was in sharp opposition to the basic assumptions of the ideology of the Haskalah and the maskilic vision of the new Jewish culture.

To put it as succinctly as possible, this was a conflict between marginalization and rebirth. The maskilim did not agree to the total criticism of the rabbinical tradition and the rejection of the Talmud and religious law. They carefully distinguished between the role of the dominant institutions and organizations of religious life and the role of religion itself and of reformed religious institutions. While they agreed that the unlimited power of the *kahal* was an evil to be fought against resolutely, they did not agree with plans to liquidate all forms of collective religious life and religious institutions, and the very concept of Mosaism as a private religion was completely alien to them. Though they often struggled against the abuses of the rabbinate, they sought to rebuild that institution, even going so far as to get involved in the activities of the Warsaw Rabbinical School.[61] The most conservative of the Polish maskilim, like Abraham Stern, were particularly fierce defenders of the traditions of Judaism. Jacob Tugendhold, censor of Hebrew books and prolific maskilic writer, admitted that "recalcitrant idols of fanaticism are stirring and testing the clear waters of the essence of my religion, which was drawn by the holy patriarchs,"[62] but at the same time he rejected all accusations against Judaism as such and the pretensions of the Polish reformers to interfere in Jewish ritual law.[63] He approved of the plan for reform but insisted that it must happen "without the least offense to our religious laws."[64] This theme reappeared in virtually all of Tugendhold's and Stern's later statements. The evolution of Polish public opinion and its concepts significantly distanced Polish projects from the program of the Haskalah.

It is essential to note that these and similar opinions of the Polish maskilim were published in Polish, and therefore served a polemical purpose; they were clearly directed to the Polish reader because publications directed at the Jews alone would surely have appeared in Yiddish or perhaps Hebrew. At times these opinions took the form of apologetics. The fact that the proponents of the Haskalah resorted relatively frequently to polemics and apologetics demonstrates they were aware that the Polish public (including the reformers) had only rudimentary knowledge of the beliefs and practices of Judaism, and that even much of that was false. Thus a condition for the success of reform was the correction of fictitious ideas in order to shape a correct and positive image of Judaism. The educational project became so important that in a certain sense it replaced the truly deep polemics the maskilim avoided throughout the period.

A good example can be found in the Polish and Jewish voices on Hasidism. Anti-Hasidic statements in the press were sometimes offered as proof of the deterioration of the Jewish community and as examples of the Haskalah criticisms of these degenerations. Hasidism represented the worst features of Judaism, according to the Polish authors. However, without an understanding of the context and basic function of the anti-Hasidic Haskalah texts, these writers tended to absolutize the criticism and demonization of Hasidism and, secondarily, of the Jewish world as a whole.[65] Thus the effects of the anti-Hasidic criticisms in polemical writings aimed at a Polish audience (that is, published in Polish, German, or French) were the opposite of what the authors had intended. Many maskilim were aware of this problem. In order to avoid such damages they attempted to mute internal Jewish conflicts, so that they would not feed harmful stereotypes,[66] and they made a conscious effort to influence Polish writers and politicians concerned with Jewish issues, whether through personal contacts or conciliatory public exchanges. Open criticism of the views of the Polish reformers was rare and probably hesitant, out of concern that a favorably inclined journalist or politician might be offended. Maskilim were also unlikely to criticize Polish reforms openly because their alliance with the Polish government and opinion leaders was too valuable, for three reasons. First, the symbiosis with the state institutions meant that there was a real chance to enact the programs of the Haskalah and to influence the "Jewish policy" of the government in the direction that the maskilim desired. Second, the alliance with the government strengthened the position of the maskilim in their conflicts within the Jewish community. Finally, since drawing closer to Christian society was one of the primary watchwords of the Haskalah, the maskilim had to believe in the good will of at least a part of that society. Those within Polish society who desired the integration of the Jewish population were natural partners, particularly if they were connected through Enlightenment ideology. Likewise, we must not forget that criticism of the proposals presented by government institutions was hindered by censorship.[67] A genuinely heated debate thus developed only around those proposals whose anti-Jewish attitudes were obvious and that were perceived as direct threats to Jewish society.

The rarity of such violent disagreements does not prove, however, that Jewish proponents of modernization were unaware of their differences of opinion with the Polish reformers. On the contrary, their deep desire for rapprochement and harmony in no way hid from the maskilim the fact that these proposals were fundamentally different. The earliest Jewish reaction known to us from the time of the Four-Year Sejm, the response of Rabbi Herszl Jozefowicz of Chełm to Butrymowicz's pamphlet, is proof that there was awareness of the differences. If the maskilim missed something essential, it was not the differences themselves but the possible consequences that could result (and eventually did result) from those differences if they were passed over in silence.

Thus it seems that the seeds of conflict between the Polish and Jewish reformers were present in the earliest reform proposals from the time of the Four-Year Sejm. However, it does not appear that these differences were insurmountable or that they made the crisis in Polish-Jewish relations at the end of the nineteenth and greater part of the twentieth centuries inevitable. They resulted rather from the evolution in political discourse that occurred at the turn of the nineteenth century. The proposals from the time of the Four-Year Sejm made social integration a top priority, and although Polish reformers intended to accomplish it through the radical reform of Judaism and its institutions, it still seemed possible to reconcile these demands with the program of the Haskalah. The situation changed with the fall of the Polish-Lithuanian commonwealth. It was at this time that the plans for reform demanded not only that the Jews be made into "citizens useful to the country" but also that they be "civilized." The far-reaching consequences of this assumption turned out to be in deep conflict with the ideas of the Haskalah. Haskalah programs, though they aimed at modernization and social integration with the surrounding Christian population, were not identical with the assimilationist tendency, the desire to completely abandon the world of Jewish values. In essence it was the opposite. In addition to the programs aimed at fighting the external markers of separateness, adapting mentally and professionally to the conditions of the external world, and struggling against attitudes unfriendly to Christians, an equally important—if not the most important—element of the Haskalah program was the defense of Jewish identity and distinct Jewish culture through the strengthening of the position of religion and religious values. Religion and the things connected with it—the Bible, the Hebrew language, and the historical tradition—were thus to be the primary instruments of the reformulation of Jewish culture and of Jewish identity generated from this new culture.[68] In essence these assumptions expressed the most basic contradiction in the programs of the two groups. When Tugendhold or Eisenbaum used the term "civilization,"[69] the same term that the Polish reformers used, they had in mind changes that would lead to social and economic integration, to the Jews' assimilation of the technical achievements of modern civilization, and at the same time to the cultural and religious revitalization of the Jewish people. The social distance separating the Poles and the Jews was to decrease or simply disappear, but at the same time Jewish collective identity was to grow stronger and the reformed culture was to ground these internal Jewish connections. Thus for the maskilim, "civilizing" was akin to the concept of social and economic integration (as Staszic, too, sometimes understood it), rather than to the idea of raising the Jews from a state of barbarism and abandoning their cultural distinctiveness; they did not consider Jewish culture (referring of course to its ideal form, not the contemporary rabbinical culture) uncivilized at all. So even if the maskilim agreed with the diagnosis that Jewish society was civilizationally delayed and in need of reform, their answer to the question "What kind of civilization do the Jews need?" would have been completely different from that of the Polish reformers. The "civilization" was to be "modern" and akin to "the arrangement of European societies," but above all it was to be "Jewish." This signified a disagreement with the basic assumptions of the Polish reform proposals. Nevertheless, this conflict never found expression in the general debate between Polish and Jewish reformers.

Conclusions

The growing distance between the Polish and Jewish reformers was long ignored by both groups, though for entirely different reasons. Herszel Jozefowicz, the rabbi of Chelm, put it accurately when he wrote: "The gentlemen should not bother with trifles, such as we, the lowest, are in their eyes . . . for we are not worthy of it."[70] Toning down Jozefowicz's derisive tone somewhat, it should be said rather that the Polish reformers did not see the Jews as a subject but only as an object of reform, and so they did not take into account in their proposals the opinion of the community to be reformed. While they readily and often made use of the expertise of educated Jews, the role of these Jews was limited to opinions and appeals. Politicians who were particularly hostile to the Jews even indicated that representatives of the Jewish people should not play too great a role in drafting reforms because they might distort them.[71] However, for the Jewish reformers the maintenance of the illusion of a common goal was a *sine qua non* of their entire program and of the success of their alliance with the institutions of government. The desire for idyllic harmony was so strong that it led them to paper over certain obvious differences. Moreover, advancing social integration and linguistic assimilation could lead both sides to hope that the existing differences could be overcome with time. For this reason, the moment of greatest triumph for the idea of integration had to become the beginning of the crisis in Polish-Jewish relations that took the form of an eruption of anti-Semitism in the 1880s. From that moment it became ever more obvious that even if the dominant community fulfilled the requirements considered essential for the deep assimilation of the minority, this goal would not necessarily be achieved. In 1861–63 the Jews of the Kingdom of Poland achieved formal equality, public opinion of all stripes spoke of Jews downright enthusiastically, and declarations of brotherhood were widespread.[72] Moreover, actions followed declarations: representatives of the Jewish population were allowed to join prestigious social organizations and were represented on citizens' social committees and even in state institutions, including the official Council of State and the insurgent government. It appears that the rapprochement of Polish and Jewish circles was voluntary and sincere on both sides, and that the "brotherhood" arose from the solidaristic ideals that were strong and widespread at the time. But on the Polish side this process aroused the rather widespread expectation that with the "Polish-Jewish brotherhood" would come the Jewish assimilation that Polish reformers had been planning for more than seventy years. According to this expectation, the Jews would quickly abandon the superstitions cultivated under the cover of Judaism and accept Polish culture and the Western model of civilization. And in fact, it was at this time that an energetic grouping of Jewish integrationists—or in the terminology of the time, "Poles of the Mosaic faith"—appeared on the scene, displaying a strong sense of identification with the Polish language and nation and a powerful tendency toward modernization. But it soon became clear that these circles were fundamentally different from the "civil Christians" of whom the Polish reformers had dreamed, and that they in fact vehemently opposed the program of total abandonment of Jewish cultural distinctiveness. For the integrationists, linguistic and national assimilation did not mean resignation from the ideal of the renaissance of Jewish culture or from the battle against the desertion of those who were religiously indifferent. There could be no question here of the unconditional rejection of Jewishness and the acceptance of the "civilization" of Christian society, for the program of the integrationist camp consistently struggled against such tendencies. So it is not surprising that the first sign of the crisis in Polish-Jewish relations was the Polish press's accusations that the "progressive" Jewish circles were secretly cultivating separatism, succumbing to the anti-assimilationist tendencies of Orthodox circles, and betraying Polishness in the difficult period after the failed anti-tsarist uprising of 1863–64. These accusations soon became widespread, and it was the liberal journalists who had once engaged in the propagation of the Polish-Jewish rapprochement who most often articulated them.[73] The disappointment must have been greatest among those who most dearly cherished the ideal of assimilation.

From the point of view of the Polish ideologues, the modernized Jews did not in fact fulfill the hopes they had placed on them. Emancipation and its attendant integration did not lead to complete merger with the Polish nation even among the few Jews who proclaimed themselves progressive. And since progress and faithfulness to the inferior (in the reformers' opinion) Jewish "civilization" were clearly contradictory, integrationists maintaining Jewish identity must simply be dishonest. The tsarist policy of Russification, which could make assimilation to Polish culture unattractive, added to the verisimilitude of these accusations. The disappointed Polish reformers felt that the Jews approached Polish culture when it was to their advantage, but abandoned pro-Polish assimilation when they felt it was no longer in their interest.

But in the end who deceived whom? Did the course of events really demonstrate that the hopes placed in the reform and the modernization of the Jewish people were unfulfilled? Or was it that the Polish and Jewish reformers were talking about different things from the outset? An analysis of the goals of the Polish and Jewish reform proposals demonstrates that differences existed from the first pronouncements from the period of the Four-Year Sejm, and that the deepening misunderstandings were too often ignored by both sides. And even if the Jewish advocates of reform sometimes (too rarely and too weakly) expressed their reservations to the Polish reformers, the Polish side was not capable of conducting an authentic dialogue with representatives of Jewish society—mainly because of their condescending attitude toward them, but often also because of ordinary anti-Semitism. The two sides paid a high social price for these misconceptions, though ultimately it fell to later generations to settle the bill.

Notes

1. The main works on the subject of the Jewish question in the period of the Four-Year Sejm are Nathan M. Gelber, "Żydzi a zagadnienie reformy Żydów na Sejmie Czteroletnim," *Miesięcznik Żydowski* 1 (1931): 326–44, 429–40; Emanuel Ringelblum, "Projekty i próby przewarstwienia Żydów w epoce stanisławowskiej," *Sprawy Narodowościowe* (1934): 1–30, 181–224; Artur Eisenbach, *Emancypacja Żydów na ziemiach polskich 1785–1870 na tle europejskim* (Warsaw, 1989), published in English as *The Emancipation of the Jews in Poland, 1780–1870*, ed. Antony Polonsky, trans. Janina Dorosz (Oxford, 1991); Jerzy Michalski, "Sejmowe projekty reformy położenia ludności żydowskiej w Polsce w latach 1789–1792," in *Lud żydowski w narodzie polskim. Materiały z sesji naukowej w Warszawie*, ed. Jerzy Michalski (Warsaw, 1994), 20–44; Krystyna Zienkowska, "Citizens or Inhabitants? The Attempt to Reform the Status of the Polish Jews during the Four Years' Sejm," *Acta Poloniae Historica* 76 (1997): 31–52; Gershon D. Hundert, *Jews in Poland-Lithuania in the Eighteenth Century: A Genealogy of Modernity* (Berkeley, 2004), 211–31. The most important works on the subject of the debate and the reforms of the constitutional period of the Kingdom of Poland are M. L. Wishnitzer, "Proekty reformy evreiskogo byta v gertsogstve varshavskom i tsarstve polskom," *Perezhitoe* 1 (1909): 164–221; Nathan M. Gelber, "She'elat hayehudim bePolin beshenot 1815–1830," *Zion* 13–14 (1948–49): 106–43; Nathan M. Gelber, "Di Yidn-frage in Kongres-Poyln in di yorn 1815–1830," *Bleter far Geshikhte* 1/3–4 (1948): 41–105; Raphael Mahler, *Divre yeme Yisra'el: Dorot aharonim*, vol. 5 (Merhavia, 1970), 153–72 (see also Mahler, *A History of Modern Jewry, 1780–1815* [New York, 1971], 303–13). Eisenbach's, *Emancypacja Żydów* and Mahler's, *Divre yeme Yisra'el*, which treat both phases of the "Jewish debate," ignore their continuity, and the marked ideological coloring of both works limits their value.

Moreover, Eisenbach's work focuses too much on the legal aspects of emancipation, and Mahler discusses the reforms of the Four-Year Sejm only superficially.

2. The term "Christian" to indicate all non-Jewish participants in the debate seems inappropriate (though technically correct), since the basic line of the debate under discussion—despite claims to the contrary—defined Jews as a "nation," a "people," or an ethno-religious group. I use the term "Polish" to designate the non-Jewish participants in the debate without meaning to suggest that I consider the Jewish participants of the debate I describe as "non-Polish."

3. See for example Gelber, *She'elat*; 116; Mahler, *A History of Modern Jewry*, 304–6; Eisenbach, *Emancypacja Żydów*, 82–101.

4. See Tomasz Kizwalter, *Kryzys Oświecenia a początki konserwatyzmu polskiego* (Warsaw, 1987).

5. Those who ascribe to Jozefowicz anti-reform tendencies appear to be mistaken; they base themselves on stereotypes and on a superficial reading of his writings. See Mahler, *History of Modern Jewry*, 308; Eisenbach, *Emancypacja Żydów*, 101.

6. On Posner see for example Abraham Buchner, *Prawdziwy Judaizm czyli zbiór religijno-moralnych zasad Izraelitów, czerpany z klasycznych dzieł rabinów* (Warsaw, 1846), 160–67; "Polen. Warschau," *Der Orient* 4, no. 2 (1843); Nathan M. Gelber, *Ha-Yehudim vehamered ha-Polani: Zikhronotav shel Ya'akov halevi Levin miyeme hamered ha-Polani bishenat 1830–1831* (Jerusalem, 1953), 17–22; Adolf Różański, "Dzieje osad żydowskich we wsi Kuchary," *Biuletyn Żydowskiego Instytutu Historycznego* 9 , no. 1 (1858): 31–49.

7. His only biographer, Jacob Shatzky, in "Avraham Yakov Shtern (1768–1842)," *Joshua Starr Memorial Volume* (New York, 1953), 210, wrote that Stern was not "oyfgeklarte," but rather "frume."

8. The phrase comes from Johann Eisenmenger's *Endtecktes judenthum* (Frankfurt/Main, 1700). The classic example is Luigi Chiarini, *Théorie du Judaisme, appliquée a la Réforme des Israélites de Tous les Pays de l'Europe*, vols. 1–2 (Paris, 1830), modeled on Eisenmenger. However, it was not only those writers who were widely considered to belong to the anti-Semitic camp who made use of anti-Semitic literature. For example, Julian Ursyn Niemcewicz, *Lejbe i Sióra czyli Listy dwóch kochanków* (Warsaw, 1821), referred extensively to eighteenth-century German anti-Semitic literature.

9. See for example Tadeusz Czacki, *Rozprawa o Żydach i karaitach* (Vilna, 1807).

10. [Menahem Mendel Lefin,] "Essai d'un plan de réforme ayant pour objet d'éclairer la nation Juive en Pologne et de redresser par lá ses moeurs," in *Materiały do dziejów Sejmu Czteroletniego*, vol. 6, ed. Artur Eisenbach, Jerzy Michalski, Emanuel Rostworowski, and Janusz Wolański (Wrocław, 1969), 409–21 (hereafter cited as *MDSC*). See also Gelber, "Żydzi a zagadnienie reformy," 331–34; Gelber, "Mendel Lefin-Satanower vehaza'otav letikun orah hahayim shel Yehude Polin bifne haseym hagadol (1788–1792)," in *Sefer yovel likhvod harav dr Avraham Weis* (New York, 1964), 271–75; Mahler, *Divre yeme Yisra'el*, 4:73–75, 266–68; Nancy B. Sinkoff, "Strategy and Ruse in the Haskalah of Mendel Lefin of Satanow," in *New Perspectives on the Haskalah*, ed. Shmuel Feiner and David Sorkin (London and Portland, 2001), 97–101.

11. [Jacques Calmanson,] *Uwagi nad niniejszym stanem Żydów polskich i ich wydoskonaleniem* (Warsaw, 1797), 50. A shorter version appeared in French a year earlier under the title *Essai sur l'état actuel des Juifs de Pologne et leur perfectibilité* (Warsaw, 1796).

12. Mateusz Butrymowicz, "Sposób uformowania Żydów polskich w pożytecznych krajowi obywatelów," *MDSC*, 84–85; Butrymowicz, "Reforma Żydów," *MDSC*, 124–25.

13. Stanisław K. Potocki, *Żyd nie żyd? Odpowiedź na głos ludu izraelskiego* (Warsaw, 1818), 11–12. See also a similar opinion in Archiwum Główne Akt Dawnych (Central Archive of Historical Records in Warsaw; hereafter cited as AGAD), Centralne Władze Wyznaniowe (hereafter cited as CWW), record group 1448, p. 43; "Dodatek z Prowincji," *Rozmaitości* 13 (1820): 49.

14. Staszic's views on the Jewish question have not yet been analyzed in detail, and existing contributions have used fragments of his thought for the promotion of their own ideology. An attempt to characterize Staszic's views objectively can be found in Eisenbach, *Emancypacja Żydów*, index; see also Barbara Szacka, *Stanisław Staszic: Portret mieszczanina* (Warsaw, 1962), 147–49.

15. On Fleury's views and his influence on the "Jewish question" in France, see Arthur Hertzberg, *The French Enlightenment and the Jews: The Origins of Modern Anti-Semitism* (New York and Philadelphia, 1968), 41–43, 253–58, 279.

16. AGAD, CWW 1418, pp. 16–18.

17. It should be also noted that, despite Staszic's undoubtedly strong dislike of Jews, we may suppose that his anti-talmudic philippics were not always about the Talmud and the Jews. The harshness of his statements against the Jews may have fulfilled a compensatory function. A renegade priest who was known for his conflicts with the Catholic Church hierarchy, Staszic could not allow himself open criticism of the role of the Church in a state that was officially Catholic. (Even in the Kingdom of Poland, whose king, the tsar of Russia, professed Orthodoxy, Catholicism had a constitutionally guaranteed role as the state religion.) Judaism thus became an easy target for criticism, though it was neither the only nor even the primary target. The same was true in the writings of the enlightened men of France, where for various reasons it was not possible to direct that criticism against Catholicism. On this see Hertzberg, *French Enlightenment and the Jews*, 283–84. The influence of French literature on Staszic was very likely here.

18. Archiwum Państwowe w Lublinie (State Archives of Lublin), Akta miasta Lublina, record group 2158, p. 88.

19. This formula appeared among other places in the title of a pamphlet by Butrymowicz: "Sposób uformowania Żydów polskich w pożytecznych krajowi obywatelów," 78. See also Michał Czacki, "Refleksyje nad reformą Żydów," *MDSC*, 206; "Reforma Żydów: Projekt od deputacji do tego wyznaczonej," *MDSC*, 216. A declaration typical of the times of the Congress Kingdom is Walerian Łukasiński's *Uwagi pewnego oficera nad uznaną potrzebą urządzenia Żydów w naszym kraju i nad niektórymi pisemkami w tym przedmiocie teraz w druku wyszłemi* (Warsaw, 1917), 8; A. Smoczyński, "Krótki rys historyczny Żydów z dołączeniem uwag o ich cywilizacji," *Gazeta Wiejska* 48 (1818): 375.

20. See for example Piattoli's letter to Stanislaw Małachowski, 23 May 1792, in MDSC, 337. See also Zienkowska, *Citizens or Inhabitants?* 45–52.

21. Wincenty Krasiński and Gerard Witowski, both high-ranking state officials in the Congress Kingdom who were known for their animosity toward Jews, voiced such opinions. See [Wincenty Krasiński,] *Aperçu Sur les Juifs de Pologne par un officier General Polonois* (Warsaw, 1818); [Gerard Witowski,] *Sposób na Żydów czyli Środki niezawodne zrobienia z nich ludzi uczciwych i dobrych obywateli. Dziełko dedykowane posłom i deputowanym na Sejm 1818 r.* (Warsaw, 1818), 6.

22. AGAD, I Rada Stanu Królestwa Polskiego 436, s. 857.

23. Stanisław Staszic, "O przyczynach szkodliwości żydów i środkach usposobienia ich, aby się społeczeństwu użytecznemi stali," in his *Dzieła*, vol. 4 (Warsaw, 1816), 232 (first published in *Pamiętnik Warszawski* [1816], vol. 4). See also Staszic, *Ród ludzki* (Warsaw, 1959), 3:298–99.

24. See for example Hugo Kołłątaj, *Listy anonima i prawo polityczne narodu polskiego* (Warsaw, 1954), 2:328, 329; *O srzodkach aby reforma Żydów w Polsce mogła bydź skuteczną, przez Mowszę Jankielewicza* (Warsaw, 1819).

25. AGAD, CWW 1418, pp. 40–41. My emphasis.

26. See for example Witowski, *Sposób na Żydów*, 8; [Piotr Świtkowski,] "Uwagi względem reformy Żydów uprojektowanej przez jw. Butrymowicza," *MDSC*, 137.

27. Michael Stanislawski correctly indicated this in his *Tsar Nicholas I and the Jews: The Transformation of Jewish Society in Russia 1825–1855* (Philadelphia, 1983), 46.

28. See Eisenbach, *Emancypacja Żydów*, 181.

29. See AGAD, I Rada Stanu Królestwa Polskiego 436, pp. 860–61.

30. See for example "List przyjaciela Polaka," *MDSC*, 169–75; "Dwór Franka . . .," *MDSC*, 176–82; "Zwierciadło polskie dla publiczności," *MDSC*, 254–55; "Katechizm o Żydach i neofitach," *MDSC*, 466–80; [Ludwik Janowski,] *O Żydach i judaizmie, czyli Wykrycie zasad moralnych tudzież rozumowania Izraelitów* (Siedlce, 1820), 20–28; Krasiński, *Aperçu Sur les Juifs de Pologne*, 27–30; "O Żydach w Polszcze," *Rozmaitości* 20 (1818): 89–91.

31. See Janusz Tazbir, "Conspiracy Theories and the Reception of 'The Protocols of the Elders of Zion' in Poland," *Polin* 11 (1998): 171–82. Proposals to resolve the "Jewish question" through mass conversion had become unpopular already by the 1770s. See Jakub Goldberg, "The Changes in the Attitude of Polish Society Toward the Jews in the Eighteenth Century," in *From Shtetl to Socialism. Studies from Polin*, ed. Antony Polonsky (London and Washington, 1993), 56.

32. AGAD, CWW 1418, p. 35.

33. Two of the most important of these voices were [Józef Pawlikowski,] *Myśli polityczne dla Polski* (Warsaw, 1789), 101–15, and Łukasiński, *Uwagi pewnego oficera*. On Pawlikowski, see Goldberg, "Changes in the Attitude of Polish Society," 57. The phrase "remaking the Jews into Poles" was commonly used by many Polish reformers, most notably by Staszic, e.g., AGAD, CWW 1418, p. 15.

34. The exception was a pamphlet in French by Wincenty Krasiński, a Napoleonic general and the first president of the Senate of the Congress Kingdom, who in 1818 used the term "assimilation" in reference to the Jews, although it was—and this is important—in reference to the French Jews. See Krasiński, *Aperçu Sur les Juifs de Pologne*, 38.

35. Here we must rectify the opinion of Artur Eisenbach, who believed that the term "civilization" had appeared in the debate as early as the period of the Four-Year Sejm. See Eisenbach, *Emancypacja Żydów*, 104–5. On the evolution of concepts related to the reform of the Jews in the Russian empire, see John D. Klier, *Imperial Russia's Jewish Question, 1855–1881* (Cambridge, 1995), 66–83.

36. See Norbert Elias, *The Civilizing Process: Sociogenetic and Psychogenetic Investigations*, trans. Edmund Jephcott (Oxford, 2000), 5–52.

37. See for example Szymel Wolfowicz, "Więzień w Nieświeżu do Stanów Sejmujacych o potrzebie reformy Żydów," *MDSC*, 142: "the Jewish civility [cywilność], which is in essence *status in statu*." As an example of the multitudes of meanings of the term at the beginning of the nineteenth century see for example Samuel B. Linde, *Słownik języka polskiego*, vol. 1 (Lwów, 1854), 343.

38. See Elias, *Civilizing Process*.

39. A discussion of the changing conceptions of the term can be found in Jerzy Jedlicki, *Jakiej cywilizacji Polacy potrzebują: Studia z dziejów idei i wyobraźni XIX wieku* (Warsaw, 1988), 27–28, 34–35; Marian Henryk Serejski, "Początki i dzieje słów 'kultura' i 'cywilizacja' w Polsce," in Serejski, *Przeszłość a teraźniejszość. Szkice i studia historiograficzne* (Wrocław, 1965), 237–49.

40. See for example AGAD, CWW 1418, pp. 3, 5; Staszic, "O przyczynach szkodliwości żydów," 217, 231, 234, 236–37, 243. On Staszic's conception of civilizing see Serejski, "Początki i dzieje słów 'kultura' i 'cywilizacja,'" 240–41.

41. On the evolution of the concept of state and society in Polish discourse in this period see Andrzej Walicki, *Philosophy and Romantic Nationalism: The Case of Poland* (Notre Dame, 1994), 64–85; Jedlicki, *Jakiej cywilizacji Polacy potrzebują*, 26–27, 37.

42. AGAD, CWW 1418, p. 71.

43. The Jewish committee still awaits a critical discussion of its activities. From among older works, see Dawid Kandel, "Komitet Starozakonnych," *Kwartalnik poświęcony badaniu przeszłości Żydów w Polsce* 1, no. 2 (1912): 85–103; Eisenbach, *Emancypacja Żydów,* 193–96, 258–60.

44. On Chiarini see Arnold Ages, "Luigi Chiarini. A Case Study in Intellectual Anti-Semitism," *Judaica* 37, no. 2 (1981): 76–89.

45. See Calmanson, *Uwagi nad niniejszym stanem Żydów polskich*, 37–53.

46. "In the history of virtually all nations we see that the true and godly education and the civilizing that made the people happy occurred only after the priesthood itself took up the task of study and became more enlightened." See AGAD, CWW 1444, p. 14.

47. Abraham Buchner, *Katechizm religijno-moralny dla Izraelitów—Yesode hadat umusar haskel* (Warsaw, 1836).

48. A complete list of Jewish textbooks from the years 1817 to 1864 can be found in Shatzky, *Yidishe bildungs-politik in Poyln fun 1806 biz 1866* (New York, 1943), 224–28.

49. Typical book-checking actions, with the attendant investigations, took place for example in Będzin in 1842–43. AGAD, CWW 1481, pp. 236–418; See also reports from similar actions in AGAD, CWW 1463, pp. 262–96.

50. Shmuel Werses, "Hasifrut ha'ivrit be-Polin: Tekufot veziyune derekh," in *Kiyum veshever: Yehude Polin ledorotehem*, vol. 2, ed. Israel Bartal and Israel Gutman (Jerusalem, 2001), 163. On the readership of Haskalah papers in the Kingdom of Poland see, in the same volume, Mordecai Zalkin, "Hahaskalah ha-Yehudit be-Polin: Kavim lediyun," 408–9.

51. AGAD, I Rada Stanu Królestwa Polskiego, 285. A discussion of the basic elements of the committee's plan and the reasons for its failure are located in AGAD, Sekretariat Stanu Królestwa Polskiego 1999, f. 64–187.

52. AGAD, I Rada Stanu Królestwa Polskiego 285, pp. 18–19.

53. See for example Raphael Mahler, *Hasidism and the Jewish Enlightenment: Their Confrontation in Galicia and Poland in the First Half of the Nineteenth Century*, trans. E. Orenstein, A. Klein, and J. Machlowitz-Klein (Philadelphia, 1985), 175–88; Eisenbach, *Emancypacja Żydów,* 316–31. Views of this type were particularly strongly articulated in the works of lesser historians—for example, Dawid Kandel, "Żydzi w Królestwie Polskim po 1831 r.," *Biblioteka Warszawska* 70 (1910): 3:542–58; Yeshiya Warszawski, "Yidn in Kongres-Poyln (1815–1831)," *Historishe Shriftn fun YIVO* 2 (1937): 322–54.

54. A good example of this is the pamphlet by the Polish Franciscan Karol Surowiecki, *Głos ludu izraelskiego* (Warsaw, 1818), in which the author, under the

pseudonym Moses ben Abraham, criticizes the customs of the Christian part of Polish society. The pamphlet *O srzodkach aby reforma Żydów w Polsce mogła bydź skuteczna* is another example.

55. Nancy Sinkoff, "Benjamin Franklin in Jewish Eastern Europe: Cultural Appropriation in the Age of the Enlightenment," *Journal of the History of Ideas* 61, no. 1 (2000): 138; Nancy Sinkoff, *Out of the Shtetl: Making Jews Modern in the Polish Borderlands* (Providence, 2004).

56. Shatzky, "Avraham Yakov Shtern."

57. Niemcewicz, *Lejbe i Sióra*, 118–22 (I quote from an edition published in Cracow in 1931). See also Potocki, *Żyd nie żyd?* 31; Józef Wyszyński, *O reformie ludu Izraela* (n.p., 1818), 4.

58. See Michael A. Meyer, *The Origins of the Modern Jew: Jewish Identity and European Culture in Germany, 1749–1824* (Detroit, 1967), 11–28. An example from France (Mirabeau) can be found in Hertzberg, *French Enlightenment and the Jews*, 294.

59. See for example Hilary Nussbaum, *Historia Żydów od Mojżesza do epoki obecnej*, vol. 5 (Warsaw, 1890), 382; Jacob Katz, *Tradition and Crisis: Jewish Society at the End of the Middle Ages*, trans. B. D. Cooperman (New York, 1993), 226–27.

60. Such views appeared occasionally in the works of Antoni Eisenbaum (see [Antoni Eisenbaum,] "O Rabinach," *Rozmaitości* 10 [1822]: 40), Ezechiel Hoge (see AGAD, CWW 1410, pp. 4–5); the maskil from Kalisz, Dr. Schönfeld (see AGAD, Komisja Województwa Kaliskiego 702, pp. 5–6); the radical maskil from Częstochowa, Jakub Bursztyński (see AGAD, Komisja Województwa Kaliskiego 699, pp. 183–84); and above all the best-known critic of the Talmud, Abraham Buchner (see *Der Talmud in seiner Nichtigkeit* [Warsaw, 1848]).

61. On Stern's plans for the school, see Dawid Kandel, "Abraham Stern a Szkoła Rabinów w Warszawie," *Kwartalnik poświęcony badaniu przeszłości Żydów w Polsce* 1, no. 1 (1912): 120–25. On Tugendhold's involvement in making the school primarily an institution for training future rabbis, see Sabina Lewin, "Bethasefer lerabanim be-Varsha bashanim 1826–1863," *Gal-Ed* 11 (1989): 50–51.

62. Jakub Tugendhold, *Jerobaal czyli mowa o Żydach, napisana z powodu wyszłego bezimiennie pisemka pt. "Sposób na Żydów"* (Warsaw, 1818), 6.

63. See for example Jakub Tugendhold, "Odpowiedź na artykuł umieszczony w nrze 174 Kuryera Warszawskiego," *Kurier Warszawski* 131 (1821): 1887–88.

64. Izakowicz Cudek [Jakub Tugendhold], "Odpowiedź Mośkowi Jankielowi," *Rozmaitości* 4 (1822): 22.

65. Stanislawski pointed out the misunderstandings that arose between Russian bureaucrats and the local maskilim in his *Tsar Nicholas I and the Jews*, 54. Similar misunderstandings can serve as models for the relations between governments and maskilim throughout Eastern Europe in the first half of the nineteenth century. For more on this see my *Oświecenie żydowskie w Królestwie Polskim wobec chasydyzmu* (Warsaw, 2003), 82–86, translated into English as *Haskalah and Hasidism in the Kingdom of Poland: A History of Conflict* (Oxford and Portland, 2005), 73–77.

66. A telling example of this is Warsaw maskil Jakub Tugendhold's defense of Hasidism in the 1820s. See Marcin Wodziński, "Jakub Tugendhold and the First Maskilic Defence of Hasidism," *Gal Ed* 18 (2001): 13–41.

67. Characteristically, the only pamphlet openly criticizing the policy of the government of the Congress Kingdom toward the Jews appeared during the uprising of 1831, when censorship was repealed. See [Jan Glücksberg,] *Rzut oka na stan Izraelitów w Polsce, czyli Wykrycie błędnego z nimi postępowania, na aktach rządowych oparte* (Warsaw, 1831).

68. A good summation of the significance of these factors in Haskalah ideology can be found in Shmuel Feiner, "Towards a Historical Definition of the Haskalah," in *New Perspectives on the Haskalah*, ed. Shmuel Feiner and David Sorkin (London and Portland, 2001), 184–219. On the polemics with irreligious attitudes, see Feiner, "The Pseudo-Enlightenment and the Question of Jewish Modernisation," *Jewish Social Studies* 3, no. 1 (1996–97): 62–88.

69. It seems that Tugendhold disliked the term "civilization" and usually wrote instead of "reform" or "improvement"; Eisenbaum, on the other hand, used the term exceedingly readily and often. See for example Z. [Antoni Eisenbaum], "Zniesienie Kahałów. (Artykuł nadesłany)," *Rozmaitości* 3 (1822): 10; Z. [Antoni Eisenbaum], "O wychowaniu młodzieży żydowskiej," *Rozmaitości* 7–8 (1822): 27, 31.

70. Herszel Jozefowicz, "Myśli stosowne do sposobu uformowania Żydów polskich w pożytecznych krajowi obywatelów," *MDSC*, 100.

71. See for example AGAD, CWW 1411, p. 27 (an 1824 opinion by Staszic).

72. A good reconstruction of the events of the period of "Polish-Jewish brotherhood" is Artur Eisenbach, *Kwestia równouprawnienia Żydów w Królestwie Polskim* (Warsaw, 1972), 327–453; the best work on this subject is Magdalena Opalski and Israel Bartal, *Poles and Jews: A Failed Brotherhood* (Hanover, N.H., 1992). On the post-uprising sense of disappointment see also Israel Bartal, *Me-'uma' le-'leum': Yehude mizrah Eropa 1772–1881* (Jerusalem, 2002), 102–12.

73. On the shift of leading Positivists to anti-Jewish positions see Frank Golczewski, *Polnisch-jüdische Beziehungen 1881–1922. Eine Studie zur Geschuchte des Antisemitismus in Osteuropa* (Wiesbaden, 1981), 92–96; Alina Cała, *Asymilacja Żydów w Królestwie Polskim (1864–1897). Postawy—Konflikty— Stereotypy* (Warsaw, 1989), 255–67; Opalski and Bartal, *Poles and Jews*, 98–103; on the particularly telling evolution from philo-Semitism to "progressive anti-Semitism" see Theodore R. Weeks, "Polish 'Progressive Antisemitism,' 1905–1914," *East European Jewish Affairs* 25, no. 2 (1995): 49–68.

Part II
Mirrors of Popular Culture

Chapter 3
The Botched Kiss and the Beginnings of the Yiddish Stage

ALYSSA QUINT

Translation is like kissing the bride through a veil.
—*Haim Nahman Bialik*

Consider two remarkably similar moments in two of Avrom Goldfaden's (1840–1909) earliest comedies. In act 3 of his drama *Aunt Sosya* (1869), a young shtetl woman named Khantshe and her distant cousin, the city-dwelling medical student Zilberzayd, meet for the first time in a romantic rendezvous organized by Khantshe's sister Sosya.[1] It is not long before one senses Zilberzayd's distaste for Khantshe as he, likewise, grows ridiculous in her eyes. Still, the characters' brief exchange, slowed by misunderstanding and awkwardness, leads to Zilberzayd's unpredictable request for a kiss. Laughing, either nervously or flirtatiously—the text does not let on—Khantshe spells out the situation in terms she knows the young medical student will understand: "It seems to me we both suffer from the same disease: I need a groom and you need a bride" (70). "Pretend I am your groom," Zilberzayd offers in response. It is a cunningly ambiguous answer: does he mean to suggest that he wants to imagine them as bride and groom with the intention of marrying, or does it mean that imagination will bring her as close as she ever will be to becoming his bride? In the Enlightenment drama, pretense is either an indication of villainy, the camouflaging of inner evil (but we know Zilberzayd is not a villain), or it is applied to uncover a crime (though Khantshe has committed no crime). In short, neither the comedy nor the domestic drama provides for what happens next: responding to Zilberzayd's proposition, she murmurs, "In that case . . . ," after which the stage directions instruct: "*He wants to take her and give her a kiss*

when Ispanski enters the room. Khantshe feels ashamed and runs away" (70).
Before their lips are allowed to lock, they are interrupted.

In act 2 of *Bontsye the Wicklayer or the Grandmother and Her Granddaughter*
(written by 1875), also set in an unnamed shtetl, the aged, Yiddish-
speaking Bontsye is frustrated that she understands little of the German
books that her young granddaughter Odele studies with her tutor Ignats
and she asks Odele to translate a page for her.[2] Odele and Ignats agree
but deliberately mistranslate it: pretending to read the book aloud, the
tutor utters romantic words to Odele in German (which they both know
Bontsye would forbid if she understood), after which Odele fabricates a
"translation" she knows her pious grandmother would find acceptable.
This is how the scene plays out:

THE TUTOR [in German]: Show me no doubt; endow me with your trust,
      and I will make everything right.
BONTSYE: What does that mean in Yiddish?
ODELE: [in Yiddish] It means that there is no other way to be an
      honest Jew unless one follows the entirety of the 613 laws.
BONTSYE: Is that what it says? May you be blessed with a long life. Con-
      tinue reading. (17)

Relieved to know the pious content of her granddaughter's book, Bontsye moves to give her a kiss of approval but fumbles:

BONTSYE: Odele, let me give you a kiss. Now, you are worthy.
      In the same moment, the tutor runs between them and bends to say
      goodnight to Bontsye. Meaning to embrace Odele, Bontsye embraces
      the tutor and kisses him. (18)

Both moments are marked by what may be described as a botched
kiss. In each case, the kiss occurs between a cosmopolitan Jewish man
and a provincial shtetl woman. And in each case, the kiss is painfully
anti-climactic, releasing a vapor of shame into the drama's atmosphere
along with an intimation of sexual dysfunction that spells trouble, even
ruin, for the woman. The botched kiss starkly contrasts with the consum-
mating romantic kiss, a symbol of fecundity at the end of the Shakespearean comedy, the model more or less of the modern Yiddish drama
throughout the nineteenth century. Normally, visible evidence of love
and romance indicates that life will extend beyond the concluding
frame of a comedy through procreation and that the old, decaying society will be renewed. But Goldfaden's kisses are different; situated awkwardly midway through both dramas, they irrevocably disfigure the
comedic structure of his plays and figure as the kiss of death.

With rare exceptions, the written and published works of the modern Yiddish theater's first playwrights—such as Joseph Lateiner (1853–1935), Ish Ha-Levi Hurvitz (1844–1910), Joseph Judah Lerner (1849–1907), and his wife, Marie Lerner (née Miriam Rabinovitsh, 1860–1927), Nahum Meir Shaykevitsh (1849–1905) and, most egregiously, the father of the Yiddish theater, Avrom Goldfaden—have elicited little scholarly curiosity.[3] Goldfaden's works have been dismissed as hastily written adaptations of whatever was popular on the stage in his day.[4] Summing up the contempt of scholars and critical observers of the Yiddish theater alike, Leo Weiner remarked, "There is no merit whatsoever in [Goldfaden's] plays as their Jewish setting is merely such in name and as otherwise the plot is too trivial."[5] Actually, many of these plays merit a reconsideration by the historian of East European Jewish culture if not on strictly aesthetic grounds , then to fill out our understanding of the nineteenth-century Yiddish-language imagination. Indeed, if, as Dan Miron argues in *A Traveler Disguised*, the best modern Yiddish literature was distinguished by its "theatrical quality," what were the artistic properties of the contemporary Yiddish theater?[6] Or in other words, if Yiddish prose was dramatic, might drama have had its own character? Might *it* have been the genre par excellence of this language and culture? Moreover, if Weiner is correct that many of these plays were derivative in inspiration, they became richly distinctive in the end. Joel Berkowitz recently demonstrated that Yiddish translations and adaptations of Shakespeare's plays took on distinctive linguistic and cultural features that captured the concerns and habits of their Jewish target audience. Berkowitz's work should persuade scholars of Yiddish culture to reconsider all that has been dismissed as popular culture, shund, or adaptations. Translation cannot but function on many levels simultaneously. Notwithstanding Goldfaden's apparent reliance on borrowed plots and music, his operettas became the central canonical works of the Yiddish theater. A reading of Goldfaden's plays against earlier maskilic dramas that have long been accepted into the modern Yiddish literary canon suggests that the playwrights of the live Yiddish stage generated an oeuvre that pays homage to their forerunners, that engages contemporary concerns, and, in some ways, that boasts a comparatively richer artistic vision demonstrable in the printed matter of their operettas.[7]

The preoccupations with gender and language that animate Goldfaden's comedies are best articulated against his models, the small trove of bourgeois maskilic comedies penned throughout the nineteenth century intended to be read privately or aloud in the salon. Such a frame illuminates Goldfaden's *Aunt Sosya* (*Di mume sosye*) and *Bontsye the Wicklayer or the Grandmother and Her Granddaughter* (*Di bobe mit dem eynikl oder bontsye di kneytlegerin*, hereafter cited as *The Wicklayer*), two plays staged as operettas in the first years of the author's career in the theater (after 1876). Along with their shared poetics, both plays also center on aged, sexless Jewish matriarchs who cling fiercely to traditional ways even as all those around them defy tradition, with the moral backing of the play's community and author. Aunt Sosya acts ruthlessly to see her spinster sister marry a respectable man as she tries to stop her brother's marriage to a lower-class cousin she deems beneath the status of the family. Bontsye, less wealthy than Sosya and less sophisticated, acts similarly—and also to no avail—to see her granddaughter Odele betrothed to a learned Hasidic Jew. As failed comedies of a peculiar kind, structured by the poetics of the botched kiss, *Aunt Sosya* and *The Wicklayer* constitute the two poles of Goldfaden's comic world.

Goldfaden was groomed in a coterie of high-minded Russian Jewish reformers but adapted to the desires of the popular audiences who made his theater a commercial success.[8] The wedding he effected between salon and tavern helped him establish a commercially buoyant Yiddish theater that first gained traction in Jassy, Rumania, in the fall of 1876.[9] Goldfaden's life until this point followed a maskilic trajectory familiar to students of the Haskalah. He attended the prestigious Russian Jewish teacher's seminary in Zhitomir that cultivated a brand of Jewish creativity in Hebrew and, more marginally and belatedly, in Yiddish. Goldfaden first published Hebrew poetry but had long had a reputation as a Yiddish songwriter and went on to produce Yiddish songs and plays that established his reputation among the more nationally inclined Russian Jewish intelligentsia. He was a regular fixture in the highbrow Jewish salon culture in Russia and later in Rumania where he was invited to perform by Isaac Librescu, a modern and upper-middle-class Jew involved in community affairs. Librescu introduced him to the Yiddish entertainment scene in local coffeehouses, where he would see his first plays staged. According to his autobiography, his early comedies reflect the artistic compromises forced upon him by an audience he considered primitive.[10] In 1878 he returned to the Russian Empire, where his depiction of Jewish characters on the stage raised the ire of the Jewish intelligentsia but continued to attract mass audiences. Notwithstanding the many bureaucratic obstacles it bumped up against, the Yiddish theater enjoyed moments of remarkable success throughout Russia's Pale of Settlement and made significant inroads beyond it in St. Petersburg and Moscow before the government shut it down in 1883.[11] Goldfaden's historical dramas, staged as early as 1880 and depicting positive Jewish types, albeit in remote lands, made his early comedies, populated by laughable "negative Jewish types," a distant memory. Literary analyses of Goldfaden's oeuvre—such as they are—trace the development of Jewish performance (exposing the critics' anxieties about external artistic influences) and focus on continuities between Goldfaden and (a) the *purim-shpil* and (b) his Yiddish-writing maskilic predecessors.[12] While this essay is not invested in the proposition that the Yiddish theater was the product of an unadulterated Jewish or Yiddish creative impulse, it builds on the premise that Goldfaden wrote under the influence of his maskilic Yiddish-writing predecessors.

In fact, Goldfaden was an attentive student of maskilic Yiddish drama, and it was against its background that he established the idiosyncratic theatrical language that lent so much energy to his work. Maskilic comedy, for all its East European Jewish cultural flourishes, is, in narrative structure, patterned on Shakespearean comedy. Northrop Frye describes the Shakespearean comedy, or the "comic mode," thus: a young man desires a young woman, some force opposes him, but a plot twist enables the hero to "have his will." Underlying this simple pattern is a movement from one kind of society to another. At the end of the play the obstructing characters initially in charge of the play's society are recognized as usurpers and a new society crystallizes around the hero and heroine.[13] The usurpers are "preoccupied with trying to regulate the sexual drive, and so work counter to the wishes of the hero and the heroine."[14] In this fashion, the anonymously penned maskilic play *Hoodwinked World* (*Di genarte velt*, 1815) presents two villains, a hypocritical Hasidic tutor and a striving, smart-mouthed Jewish woman, who are foiled by the play's young heroes, the son and orphaned niece of a merchant. The young pair is betrothed by the play's final scene. Avraham Gottlober (1810–99), an ardent maskil and an instructor at the seminary Goldfaden attended, wrote a play named *The Veil, or Two Wedding Canopies in One Night: A Comedy in Three Acts* (*Der dektukh oder tsvey khupes in eyn nakht: A komedye in dray akten*)[15] that features a young couple that uses trickery to undermine the town's Hasidic establishment and marry against its wishes. The play parodies Hasidism and celebrates youth and love in a pastoral setting. The comedy insists on festive endings, no matter what plot twists are needed to get there.[16] Romance legitimized by marriage characterizes the comedy's happy ending that often features the young heroes' wedding canopy.

The value of female self-control that lies at the heart of maskilic drama and is exemplified by Shlomo Ettinger's (1805–56) *Serkele: The Anniversary of a Brother's Death* (*Serkele: Oder a yortsayt nokh a bruder*, 1839) reflects the strong influence of the French and German bourgeois theater.[17] In *Serkele* the devious title-character takes control of her brother Goodheart's household when he goes missing and is assumed dead, and thus the play depicts a world thrown into chaos when paternal authority vanishes. This is one of a number of bourgeois dramatic tropes that Ettinger successfully deploys. Goodheart reappears in the play's final act

to restore the good society. The other side of male authority in the bourgeois drama is the female who knows her place. According to Scott Bryson, the bourgeois playwrights' stage was "a disciplinary space where the
body is contained, constrained, retrained," a space where "bourgeois
values of thrift, peace, chastity and obedience and self-sacrifice" were
communicated.[18] The portrayal of the woman was central to communi-
cating this ethos, as Karen Kenkel writes in her study of Enlightenment
playwright and drama critic Gotthold Ephraim Lessing. In his review of
the theater of his time, Lessing "targets the proud, independent woman
as a key source of morally inappropriate pleasure."[19] Jewish Enlightenment drama also ends by silencing the talky Jewish woman and putting
her in her place. Goodheart, for instance, reduces Serkele to tears and
submission. Thus the solution to the Jewish pathology the maskilim
wanted so badly to correct is imagined in Ettinger's play: the Jewish
woman is feminized and tempered, absorbing all that is good from the
play's old Jewish society but rejecting the bad, and allowing the Jewish
man to recuperate his masculinity.[20]

As I show, Goldfaden's best comedies short-circuit romance and resist
the conventional happy ending: the females of the old guard cannot be
stifled, and the young heroes do not embody a youthful or modern version of the societies that produce them. Ultimately, his dramatic works
reject the maskilic fashioning of Yiddish into a language of Enlightenment instruction. In *Aunt Sosya,* for instance, Goldfaden's comedy turns
black in an ending that portrays his native Jewish culture and Yiddish
language as rotten, and yet, notwithstanding its deathly freight, as pre-
ternaturally resistant to death and deferring of it. *The Wicklayer* is *Aunt
Sosya*'s inverse: it presents a tragic ending in which traditional Jewish culture is equally doomed, but to the detriment of the drama's society.
Traces of the comic structure are legible behind the general arc of the
playwright's works, especially in the complexion of his characters and
the conflict that pits young lovers against an unyielding and more traditional member of the family. Alluding to a common social discourse—
the established motifs of the maskilic drama and, more generally, the
clichés of East European Jewish life—Goldfaden established solidarity
with his audience and invited them into a familiar world .[21] The mannish
matriarchs (and their submissive husbands) portrayed in these plays had
special appeal to popular audiences, though they touched a raw nerve
among his more assimilated peers.[22] But from cliché and convention,
Goldfaden built a dramatic world that departs meaningfully from the
familiar.

Goldfaden developed his own version of the comedy, what I call the
poetics of the botched kiss, because of the limitations the genre imposed
upon him, forcing him to maneuver in a kind of creative straitjacket.

Goldfaden felt, it seems, hemmed in by a disjuncture between the comic genre he inherited and his take on the East European Jewish experience. Each asserted what Roland Barthes calls its "powerful code" and "inflexible cultural structures" on his creative imagination.[23] In knitting together Yiddish and comedy while straining not to compromise the codes that set them apart, many of Goldfaden's comedies emerged twisted and unlike their predecessors. In the playwright's eyes, for instance, not only was romantic love, the telos of the conventional comedy, absent from traditional Judaism, but even the possibility of a Jewish (albeit new and modern) generation born of romance was culturally alien. Navigating his plot in order to avoid expected romantic moments, Goldfaden produces a vague sense of tragedy in *Aunt Sosya* that fully blooms in *The Wicklayer*. In Goldfaden's comedies, the pleasure principle is too feeble to vanquish the reality principle.

In part, Goldfaden's comedies were shaped by twin, albeit contradictory, anxieties: the tenacity of Jewish culture and its frailty—a paradoxical pairing personified in Goldfaden's rendering of the traditional Jewish woman. Miron describes a related tension that had accrued in the minds of Yiddish-writing maskilim vis-à-vis their native Ashkenazic culture in "Folklore and Antifolklore in the Yiddish Fiction of the Haskala":

One often senses that they themselves were aware of the collision between their ideology and other, less clearly defined attitudes. We see this most when they comment on the actual changes which the cultural behavior of Eastern European Jewry was undergoing before their very eyes; changes which they themselves propagated and celebrated. One realizes that this celebration almost always leaves a bitter aftertaste.[24]

Miron describes a sense of loss felt by those writers who encouraged the transformation of Eastern European Jewry in their work. Though it would become more prominent in the work of their literary descendants, this ambivalence was common among the first modern Yiddish-language authors—including those who wrote for the stage. This ambivalence accounts, at least in part, for the way Goldfaden fashioned his female characters, which betray the author's simultaneous feelings of nostalgia and loathing for the traditional Jewish woman—a character that best embodies what was most despised about the theater by its high-minded obvservers.

In any case, Goldfaden's comedy constitutes a counterpoint to the optimistic, bourgeois Jewish Enlightenment represented by plays such as Ettinger's. Goldfaden wrote *Aunt Sosya* in 1869, and it is as much a Yiddish Enlightenment comedy (funny, with clever twists, admirably complex construction, and entertaining song) as it is a commentary on the

Yiddish Enlightenment drama and a demonstration of the genre's exhaustion. A similar commentary arises in *The Wicklayer*, which Goldfaden worked on simultaneously with *Aunt Sosya* but completed only in the early 1870s. There modern western culture, represented by the archetypal German tutor and the expected display of romance, are so at odds with East European Jewish civilization, represented by Bontsye, his lover's grandmother, that the two cannot long be contained on the same stage. But it is Bontsye, the embodiment of Ashkenazic Jewry, who remains the audience's focus while the young lovers are pushed outside the drama's universe. *Aunt Sosya* never ends—or, rather, its ending suggests a grotesque incessancy of the Jewish woman; the play's last verbal exchange invokes its opening lines in Sosya's mordant curses. In *The Wicklayer*, a deathbed scene presents more finality than the conventional comedy can bear. While the first gestures toward the absurd, the second delivers tragedy. Hints of maskilic ambivalence about the price of Enlightenment—present in so much of nineteenth-century Yiddish literature—metamorphose into a decidedly theatrical rendition of traditional East European Jewish life. In the end, in all the comedy, tragedy, and absurdity, Goldfaden's stage becomes a field upon which a brand of maskilic cynicism mixes with post-bourgeois theatricality.

In both plays, Goldfaden's distinctive poetics recuperates and relishes what it presents as Yiddish's native character: a language and culture both of and wedded to the Jewish woman. It reverses the maskil's transformation of Yiddish into a language of restraint and sublimation, and, with it, his hope of reining in Jewish life. In *Aunt Sosya*, the matriarch Sosya is an untiring well of Yiddish profanation and material desire and, like her sister Khantshe-Genaydl (Khantshe), and even Bontsye, the pious matriarch of *The Wicklayer*, she cannot control her libidinal instincts. Through its women, Yiddish talks and talks and talks and is the very motor of Jewish life. To the extent that Sosya and Bontsye are Goldfaden's homage to Ettinger's *Serkele*, they very flatly reverse that protagonist's meaning. In Ettinger's drama, Goodheart puts his sister Serkele in her place and, by the end, she is a repentant and silent member of the drama's society. In contrast, Goldfaden's comedies reject the Enlightenment's provisional adoption of Yiddish to express the ultimate goal of a Western-Jewish symbiosis. In Goldfaden's world, one must choose either Enlightenment or Jewish culture. In the end, bourgeois propriety surrenders to the cantankerous Jewish woman; she becomes the motor of Goldfaden's stage where she simultaneously lives forever and dies completely. In Aunt Sosya's mouth Yiddish is anathema, in Bontsye's mouth it is sacred, and in both, it is the language of Ashkenazic extinction, relegated to the timeless universe of the stage.

Aunt Sosya

Romance never suffers more beneath Goldfaden's pen than in *Aunt Sosya;* accompanied by little adventure or daring on the part of the play's heroes, romance recedes beneath the accessories of Jewish marriage. Taking place almost entirely in the bourgeois household of Sosya and her husband, Dodye, the play's intricate plot unfolds in four acts, divided into two consecutive betrothals ("conditions" or *tnoyim* in Yiddish, referring to the mostly financial conditions that the families of the bride and groom are expected to meet). The first engagement follows the prescripts of the comedy; Acts I and II culminate in the betrothal of Dodye's poor and virtuous niece Khinke (a Cinderella type who works as a maid in Sosya's home) to Sosya's brother, the young and virtuous Moyshe. Acts III and IV progress shakily toward the evening on which the wedding of Moyshe and Khinke is to take place alongside the engagement of Sosya's aging sister Khantshe-Genaydl (Khantshe), a betrothal Sosya desperately wants. But again Sosya is foiled: Moyshe and Khinke are married by the beginning of act 4 according to everyone's expectations but, in the last moments of the drama, Khantshe's betrothal crumbles. The play's first acts perfunctorily unfurl an all-too-conventional comic plotline (in the romance of Moyshe and Khinke)— one that, remarkably, comments on its own conventionality—only to unfurl a second grotesque "romance," a funhouse mirror version of the first.

Sosya remains the axial figure of the play, not only as the chief obstacle to the virtuous pair, but also as the archetypal indomitable Jewish matriarch. Her marriage—and not romance—is Goldfaden's true subject of fascination in *Aunt Sosya.* The first scene introduces the reader to the toxic relationship of Sosya and Dodye:

DODYE (slowly): What do you want from me? Haven't I already told you to have things however you—
SOSYA: You should be six feet under! Maybe you haven't heard me, maybe you haven't understood . . .
DODYE: What did I—
Sosya (does not let him finish): Damn you!
DODYE: Let me speak—
SOSYA: Speak to your niece Khinke! Only Dodye, I swear to you that I'll see the earth cool over your grave . . . and that bitch will drive me into the ground—what have you placed on my head? What curse? That dissolute *shikse*! (34)

The play will slowly uncover the layers of meaning in these tense opening lines: Sosya's conviction that the presence of her beautiful niece

Khinke stands in the way of Khantshe finding a groom and her jealousy of her niece for claiming her husband's sympathy and her brother's heart. By the end of the drama, Goldfaden's text gives us no indication that Sosya has taken the path of self-searching remorse that we see, for instance, in the villainous title character of Ettinger's *Serkele*, nor is she ejected from the play's society like the villains of *Hoodwinked World*. Even with their resources pooled, the men who orbit the couple throughout the drama—Cousin Zilberzayd and Ispanski, a well-meaning family friend—fail to divest Sosya of all her authority. She is the ultimate phallic monster continually badgering her husband with inexhaustible reservoirs of spite. The play begins *in medias res*, opening onto an argument that we suspect its participants have rehearsed before, and ends *in medias res* as Sosya is about to tear into Dodye as she did in the opening lines. The Enlightenment drama, ordinarily crowned by youthful matrimonial bliss in a new society, becomes an unending dissection of Sosya and Dodye's marriage.

Impatient with the conventions of comedy, Goldfaden permits us little of the thrill and suspense of Moyshe and Khinke's romance: he constructs Sosya as an obstacle to their love but one, ironically, with little credible authority. In act 1, for instance, Moyshe confronts his sister Sosya, and explains that she poses no threat to his plan to marry Khinke:

MOYSHE: Sosya, you know me: if you go around angry, you'll make everything worse. . . . I can make a wedding without your blessing, even without your knowing it. What will your interference do to it? You'd end up the fool, you'd end up the ogre, and how everyone would enjoy seeing such a thing. (49)

In Moyshe, Goldfaden, in effect, deconstructs the typical Enlightenment play. The conventional obstacle is no obstacle at all. Moreover, in the beginning of the fourth and final act, Goldfaden shunts Moyshe and Khinke to the background when we are informed that "the young couple, fresh from the wedding canopy, are sitting far in the background (*gants vayt*) by a table and talking happily" (85). It is the last we hear of the happy couple. The marriage that typically marks resolution in the play's final frame occurs without fanfare, after which point it remains "*gants vayt*." The marriage is undramatic in no small measure because the engagement of Moyshe and Khinke that we witness in act 1 is almost as binding according to Jewish law as the marriage contract itself. True, the happy chatter of Moyshe and Khinke suggests that they are the healthy inheritors of the drama's future society. But they are all but forgotten by the comedy's end.

Attention to Khinke's story gives way to the growing dominance of Khantshe, who prepares for her engagement to a groom whom Yudke the matchmaker has desperately scared up at the last moment. Scenes that Goldfaden scattered throughout the drama have given us a glimpse of the groom, Faytl-Dovid: a happy-go-lucky clockmaker with a laughable Lithuanian accent who has recently taken up residence in the shtetl. Before the *tnoyim* are finalized with the shattering of a plate, Faytl-Dovid guiltily confesses that he has a family that he abandoned six years earlier, and though he thought his wife was long dead, he recently received a letter from her that is evidence to the contrary.[25] A moment later his *agunah* (grass widow) appears; reading the situation, she irritably assures everyone that Faytl-Dovid is married and curses him with promises of death and burial. The ending is one of dark comedy, with the rather cynical layering of a shrewish *agunah* (perhaps the only *agunah* depicted in maskilic literature without sympathy), a charlatan who sought to profit from a second marriage, a spinster in Khantshe, and an irate and barren wife in Sosya. However funny—and the scene was undoubtedly played for laughs on the stage—it is a pessimistic vision of Jewish life. In two successive "resolutions" of the marriage plot, Goldfaden has it both ways.

The presence and treatment of Sosya's sister Khantshe and Cousin Zilberzayd—the participants of the botched kiss—go furthest in rendering Goldfaden's comedy idiosyncratic. Both are patterned after recurring Jewish Enlightenment characters. Khantshe is reminiscent of the "foolish new generation," a maskilic type who is taken with modern sensibility, especially its material trappings, but is too dull-minded to appreciate the true value of Haskalah. She might remind the reader of Frederica in Ettinger's *Serkele*, Serkele's daughter who is romanced by a charlatan named Gabriel and is content to pretend to know German rather than learn to speak it properly. Zilberzayd is, even more, a prototype of Jewish Enlightenment drama: the enlightened Jewish medical student who falls in love and marries the society's unmarried maiden, often (as Khantshe is) a cousin with whom he grew up or from whom he has been unnaturally separated.[26] Thus Khantshe and Zilberzayd seem destined for a shared wedding canopy and a long life together. Such a marriage would mirror the first marriage of the play, between Moyshe and Khinke, and invoke the weddings of past maskilic dramas. But soon after he arrives, Zilberzayd beats a hurried retreat. He is far from charmed by shtetl values and, unlike the worldly, German-speaking students in previous Yiddish dramas, he does not find his romantic equal and does not inherit the drama's society. Still, his brief appearance in Sosya's home and the botched kiss they share allow the odd couple to crystallize into a dark counterpoint to Moyshe and Khinke, charging the drama with unexpected meaning.

Zilberzayd's motivation for kissing Khantshe touches on what really drives the action of this comedy, and it is quite contrary to the archetypal hero's quest to marry a pure-hearted maiden: the text repeatedly suggests that Sosya's sister has a soiled reputation. This is substantiated by Sosya's desperate but fruitless attempts at finding her a husband. Although Khantshe never appears in the first two acts, we understand that she is marrying disturbingly late in life (age twenty-six) and that, even with the promise of a generous dowry, Sosya's marriage broker, Yudke, cannot find her a match. When Sosya casually asks a visiting rabbi about a prospective groom, we find out that Yudke has been scraping the bottom of the barrel: "He is a pauper, although he is full of himself," the rabbi responds candidly. "He has already been a groom a few times, this bride doesn't please him. . . . At one moment he is singing her praises and at the next moment she is dirt" (56). Sosya and Yudke's conversation about Khantshe's marriage possibilities is, moreover, strangely elliptical. Conveying a compliment about Sosya's niece Khinke by one of her suitors (in itself enough to infuriate Sosya), Yudke, in the same breath, relays the suggestion (made by a prospective groom) that Khantshe behaves indecently:

YUDKE: "While [Khinke] occupies herself with the affairs of the house," so he says, don't take this the wrong way, "at the same time, another girl runs around with young people and dances around in the streets," and he says, "when there's smoke there's fire." I took him to task and defended your sister . . . but he laced into me, told me to shut up, and said that he knows secrets. (56)

Buttonholed by Sosya, Yudke brings up Khantshe's indiscreet gallivanting, her cavorting with young men—in code, "danc[ing] around in the street." Instead of the playing out of a natural erotic impulse according to the comic modality, Khantshe's erotic impulses are disturbingly prolific and require stifling. And in the end, the comedy refuses her marriage. Finally, at a certain point in their meeting, Zilberzayd becomes convinced that he may have his way with her. When Ispanski interrupts them and botches their kiss, Zilberzayd is embarrassed but does not run off. The wise Ispanski's reassurance, "Don't worry, don't worry, there is no danger," implies that he is not guilty because the experienced Khantshe is "too far gone" to be violated. Feeling more comfortable or picking up on Ispanski's scorn for Khantshe, Zilberzayd berates Khantshe's crass manner; "she is an animal," he says, and disdainfully mentions her loquacity, disowning his own part in the kiss. In turn, Ispanski seems to understand that she initiated sexual contact and comments nonchalantly, "What could you have expected from an unmarried woman who spends her time in a tavern and has no dealings with suitable men." "*Zi is shoyn fartig,*" Zilberzayd says coldly to Ispanski, meaning, "She is done for" or, perhaps more suggestive, "She is fully ripened."

Goldfaden portrays Khantshe as an extension of Sosya and implicates Sosya in her unchecked sexual appetite. Despite the required show of umbrage she mustered at the insinuations the marriage broker awkwardly conveyed about Khantshe, the text slyly reveals that Sosya is painfully aware of her sister's overactive sexual curiosity—and it is precisely because of this awareness that it dawns on her to match Khantshe with Zilberzayd. Sosya has tried doggedly to stifle her sister's sexuality. As Khantshe carelessly mentions to Zilberzayd, Sosya is always trying to hide her boots—with their deep cavernous shape, themselves symbols of female sexuality—so she cannot go "walking" (an act that carries indecorous connotations). Apparently the opposite of Khantshe, Sosya, though bound in traditional matrimony, shows no proof that she has consummated her marriage to Dodye, or at least has no children to show for it. In her ambition to craft a future in her own image, she, alas, must rely on her wayward sister, and Zilberzayd seems her last hope.

Her choice of Zilberzayd as a groom for Khantshe represents a change in the strategy with which Sosya attempts to defy societal and comic convention. Rather than stifling Khantshe's boundless sexuality, Sosya decides that she will employ it to appeal to a more cosmopolitan and presumably more lax gentleman—the slicker, or more "*Zilberzayd*" (literally, silver-silk), the better. When Sosya and Zilberzayd speak briefly before his rendezvous with her sister, Sosya is herself loose-tongued, which could only be deliberate. When Zilberzayd asks to see the sister whom Sosya claims to be so beautiful, Sosya replies, "What, you think you need permission to see her, does she not go out into the world?" Actually, the assumption that Zilberzayd cannot see the unmarried Khantshe without a chaperone is the only respectable one to make in the context of the shtetl. Finally, a brief stage direction reveals that Sosya spies on the couple, "watching through the crack in the door" after she, quite provocatively, leaves them alone in her parlor. She watches silently as clues to Khantshe's sexual appetite drop from her sister's mouth and does not object to Zilberzayd's brazen sexual advance. The barren Sosya, incapable of tenderness toward her husband, obtains vicarious sexual fulfillment through her sister. Instead of a chaperone ensuring chastity, she is a voyeur encouraging sexual indiscretion.

Khantshe and Sosya represent a female element of the shtetl that has

grown grotesquely unwholesome. As Zilberzayd elaborates on his initial
disgust with shtetl women:

I mean [they are] ugly in character. There exist women who are not beautiful
but are still charming . . . and there are also many that are beautiful, healthy on
the outside but there is only a piece of wood there, a piece of meat with eyes,
how does one put it, like those mannequins that are in the window of the wig-
makers, they flash with black eyes but there is nothing else to them. (64)

Zilberzayd finds a metaphor for the shtetl's women of "ugly character"
in a shop window, and it will aptly come to describe his romantic inter-
locutor. Khantshe displays a fully ripened enchantment with luxurious
clothes and gifts, and she haphazardly and frequently links her desire
for these items with inappropriate relationships and to the possibility of
marriage. The only noteworthy feature of the virtuous Moyshe and
Khinke's wedding is his refusal to accept a dowry from her—to link their
love with material exchange. In contrast, neither Khantshe nor Sosya
can speak of her potential engagement without speaking of money—
either the traditional dowry and payment of the marriage broker when
Sosya pursues conventional means in finding a husband for her sister,
or the crude discussion of the money foreign men ("officers" and "the
Greek man") would pay for Khantshe if they do not, she puts it, "steal
her away" like an object. In such passages, Goldfaden refers obliquely
to the white slavery traders rumored to prey on shtetl girls.[27] Here, the
stage becomes a brothel, itself a stand-in for the crass commercialism of
the Yiddish theater. In *Aunt Sosya*, however, the playwright suggests that
Khantshe shrewdly invites such activity. When Zilberzayd does not
understand, "How does one steal a person?" Khantshe responds, "What
kind of question is that?" "How does one steal a coat or a samovar or a
horse?" (67–68), she offers by explanation. Khantshe and Sosya's
speech pollutes romance and marriage with casual talk of money, indi-
cating the incursion of a corrupting modernity into the shtetl as it
indicts the shtetl's native tradition of marriage brokerage.

Finally, the rotten state of the drama's society accrues in its language.
Khantshe's loose talk and Sosya's curse-laden speech show Yiddish to be
irretrievably degraded. Yiddish devours sensible talk and mangles meaning. Sosya swallows the speech of her husband with her interruptions
just as Khantshe translates Zilberzayd's high-minded Russian question
regarding "*Tsivilizatsye*" (civilization) into Yiddish-language talk of "*tsi-
bilis*" (onions), how much of them she fries and puts into her *kashe un
varnishkes* (kasha and bowtie noodles, a traditional Jewish dish). Alongside Yudke, the parasitical marriage broker who runs evasive verbal circles around Sosya when he is not helping himself to large portions of
Sosya's food and drink, the women own the Yiddish language; it enables

their rotten behavior and their linguistic abuses. In a discussion with Ispanski after this rendezvous, Zilberzayd complains about Khantshe's logorrhea: "Even though I asked her nothing, she recounted to me everything under her tongue and under her lung." Already linked to Sosya's curses, Zilberzayd associates Yiddish with Khantshe's crass verbiage, her readiness to reveal all that in turn touches on her sexual looseness. In *Aunt Sosya*, Yiddish is the language of rampant desire, both material and sexual, and of crude consumption.

Yiddish is also *Aunt Sosya's* unresolved linguistic tension: for Yiddish both is the language of death and resists death. From its first scene to its last, Yiddish is reduced to profanity in Sosya's mouth, frequently articulating visions of her death and burial, however sardonic. But it is also resists death. Consider the scene of Moyshe and Khinke's nuptials in which it becomes clear that Moyshe duped his sister and successfully entered into a lawful engagement to Khinke. By Sosya's side is her equally cantankerous mother ("Muter") who seemingly has no other role in the drama but to heighten the cacophony of Sosya's already vituperative language. According to the text, Sosya reacts ("What you liar? . . . Mother, I am going to stab myself, mother, I am going to kill myself, that liar, that phony . . .") simultaneously with her mother. She hurls invectives at her son for his betrayal ("That scoundrel! That wicked man!" [58]). Without a father in the scene, and without children, Sosya and her mother, alongside Khantshe, become a self-generating female society in which Yiddish and all it represents resist male authority—a far cry from Goodheart—and grotesquely resist death. The play ends with a scene in which Sosya launches into a stream of curses against Dodye: she gets the last word, her speech a sign of her life and of her death.

That shtetl life has become unsustainable—mostly due to the debased nature of its women—is not the worst of the bad report that *Aunt Sosya* offers; rather it is that the play's heroes (Moyshe and Khinke) and the new society they will spawn are literally unknowable in terms of the Yiddish play. In previous Jewish Enlightenment plays, readers can guess what lies beyond the play's last scene. In *The Hoodwinked World*, for instance, the hero's bedroom symbolically represents his worldview: a violin hangs on his wall, a chessboard lies on his desk, and secular and holy books, "*bikher*" and "*sforim*," stand side-by-side on his bookshelf. In Gottlober's *The Veil, or Two Wedding Canopies*, the protagonists exchange clever Yiddish rhymes and light-hearted Talmud-like arguments; they rebel against the corrupt Hasidic establishment that tries to thwart their love, but their actions are infused with a vital form of Judaism. Even *Serkele*, which idealizes the young German-speaking couple, endorses the wedding of two very different couples—including the marriage of the heroine's cousin to Shmuelke, a Yiddish-speaking tavern keeper with dis-

tasteful attributes who nonetheless can benefit the conservative bourgeois society the comedy valorizes. Traditional Jews inherit the drama's
society alongside its westernized Jews. In *Aunt Sosya*, the young couple
never expresses a clear set of values. The last scene of the drama treats
Jewish marriage farcically, taking the reader from Khantshe's ruined
engagement to the rift between Dodye and Sosya, who claims the last
cursed word of the play. Khinke and Moyshe, for all their virtues, do not
point toward a Jewish future. Their one gesture as a couple is to reject
the Jewish marriage's reliance on a dowry. However much we hate to
admit it, Sosya's cursing of Khinke—that she is a *shikse*—has a faint ring
of truth by the end. In *Aunt Sosya*, Goldfaden cannot muster a redeem-
able Jewish trait.

The Wicklayer

Following the logic of Goldfaden's dramatic universe, *The Wicklayer* is his
conciliatory response to history. *The Wicklayer* is less complex than *Aunt
Sosya*: in place of a cast of twelve, *The Wicklayer* is written for a cast of
four, and instead of the bourgeois setting of *Aunt Sosya,* it takes place in
the modest home of a wicklayer, a character reminiscent of the matriar-
chal figures whom Yiddish entertainers parodied on tavern stages in Goldfaden's era. The devout Jewish woman who controls her family with
threats and guilt was a mainstay of the folksinger's trunk of characters,
perhaps even more of a cliché than the character of Aunt Sosya.[28] The
play opens as Bontsye, a devout Hasid of the Saruga Rebbe and a layer
of wicks, finalizes a match for Odele, the granddaughter in her care.
When Odele finds out she is to be married to a descendant of the rebbe,
she and her German tutor, Ignats, plot to escape and marry. In the last
act, Bontsye lies dying, abandoned by her granddaughter and foiled in
her dream to see the Land of Israel. Act 1 starts with a conventional
Enlightenment worldview with its moral weight behind the young
Odele, but it quickly gives way to a complicating commentary on the
expressive potential of a Jewish Enlightenment comedy.

   Schematically presented, the Hasidic grandmother steeped in arcane
eschatological beliefs is pitted opposite the witty and educated granddaughter Odele. Bontsye tells Odele the grisly details of a dream she had
the night before in which an angel took her on a tour of hell, where she
witnessed *"daytshn"* (modern Jews) being skinned alive and dismembered because they allowed their Jewish observance to lapse. Her
debauched vision of hell lingers on a description of a man and woman
who sneak around together though they are not husband and wife, and
so, in their afterlife, they are made to boil in pots of their own blood.
Odele deciphers the wicklayer's dream matter-of-factly: the angel is Bon-

tsye and the *"daytshn"* are the chickens that she skinned, dismembered, and tossed into a seething pot to make her blood-red Passover borsht. In classic Enlightenment language she pleads with her grandmother to open her eyes to the world around her. Likewise, when Odele discovers that she is being married off to an unknown Hasidic groom, she accuses her grandmother of wanting this match so "you can have it good in the world-to-come, a *likhtikn gan-eden,* while, in this world, I must suffer a hell." Odele antagonistically guts Bontsye's worldview of its potency, transforming her reference to a literal hell into empty metaphor. It isn't long before Odele and Ignats plot their escape together under the nose of Bontsye, who remains deaf to the true substance of their German exchanges. At the end of act 2, Bontsye discovers that Odele is missing. *The Wicklayer*'s conventional maskilic plot is capped by the *khupe* (wedding canopy) of Odele and Ignats, but only as it is conjured by the failing consciousness of Bontsye, whose expiration constitutes the play's final moment. Beginning as a schematic maskilic comedy, *The Wicklayer* barely provides a happy ending.

The Wicklayer's misshapenness begins when Ignats and Bontsye share the botched kiss described in the first pages of this essay. The German tutor laughs it off, but Bontsye is shaken, spitting, *"Tfu! Tfu!* Woe is me, what have I done? *Tfu, tfu!"* as if to ward off a persistent evil spirit. When Tuvye the *shadkhen* (marriage broker) enters the home and announces the successful *shidukh* (match) of Odele, Bontsye can only complain and confess to him about the botched kiss. Knowing Bontsye's devoutness, Tuvye dismisses it as "nothing" ("a *kleynikayt*") (21). As Bontsye intuits, however, the kiss is anything but nothing. It lends form to the danger inherent in the traditional Jew's attraction to rationalist Enlightenment values, her granddaughter's enthusiasm for cosmopolitan interests, as well as her own restrained curiosity about Odele's books. Goldfaden winks at his audience when the "translation" Odele concocts is an axiom of Jewish observance that foreshadows the ineluctable tragedy the drama will trace: "It means that there is no other way to be an honest Jew unless one follows the entirety of the 613 laws." Bontsye's world must be inherited in a way that is "all or nothing." The botched kiss forces on Bontsye the realization that even the slight concession she made to modernity, permitting Odele to learn German ("These days you must," she says by way of explanation to Tuvye), has undone all that Yiddish embodies. Languages are not empty vessels but are embedded in culture; translation is a cruel ruse. The botched kiss is Bontsye's and Yiddish's kiss of death.

For all its pretense to the comic mode, *The Wicklayer* is a tragedy. In the final scene, Bontsye lies solitary, on her deathbed with, tellingly, a volume of Yiddish stories as her only company. In the end, the playwright adopts the tragic perspective of Bontsye instead of the predictably happy ending of the Europeanized Odele and Ignats. Bontsye prays for forgiveness for not permitting Odele to marry the man she loves and beseeches God to reunite her with her granddaughter before she falls asleep. The scene continues thus:

ANGEL: Because you sinned in this world, you are not worthy to see the Land of Israel in life, nor are you worthy to see your granddaughter. Only, in the hour before your death you will dream: in your first dream you will see the Land of Israel and in the second you will see Odele and her husband. (38)

In the depths of the stage a wall opens and the following scene materializes: the grave of Rabbi Meir Ba'al Ha-Nes (Meir the Miracle Worker), upon which rests a faint fire and "*eretz yisroel yidn*," Jews who reside in the Land of Israel and sing Lamentations softly, "Remember God, what we had, We have no king, we have no prophet, we have no priest. . . . Renew us as in days of old" (38). When this image is replaced by one of Ignats and Odele, Bontsye cries out, "Odele," and falls dead. Like Moyshe and Khinke, the married couple is "*gants vayt*," barred from the foreground of the stage. The final scene delivers tragedy's autumnal mood.[29]

Although death comes for Yiddish, Goldfaden moves beyond his stultifying portrayal of Yiddish in *Aunt Sosya*. From the beginning of *The Wicklayer* Yiddish is a vehicle of holiness. When we first meet Bontsye she is at the side of Tuvye, saying the Yiddish-language *Havdole* blessing reserved for women (that concludes the Sabbath). Her sacred literature, the *Tsenurena* we see her read and the *tkhines* she recites, are not Hebrew but Yiddish. When Tuvye leaves to see the rebbe she calls out: "Journey with good health and the right foot, the Supreme One should endow your trip with luck and success" (5). When Tuvye wishes her "a good week," Bontsye responds: "A good week to you, to us all, and to all of Israel" (4). Unlike *Aunt Sosya*, which begins with a glut of curses, *The Wicklayer* ushers us into Bontsye's world with a surfeit of blessings. Although Goldfaden integrates German speech into his text, Yiddish recuperates its dominance by act 3 and remains the language of the drama's universe. Recall Ettinger's *Serkele* in which its heroes Markus, Hinde, and Goodheart speak German; in its society, Yiddish has its place but German is a superior language of a superior culture. In *The Wicklayer*, the stage cannot contain the granddaughter's German books alongside the grandmother's *Tsenurena*, and so each retreats to her own room—each to one side of the stage—as the divide between them widens.

Bontsye represents an amplified expression of Yiddish that includes a cultural system embodied in two Jewish practices—wicklaying and the belief in Meir Ba'al Ha-Nes—that figure prominently in the play. According to Chava Weissler, laying wicks was a practice associated with Jewish women who followed the ritual of *"keyver-mestn"* (measuring the circumference of a loved one's grave with candlewick while reciting *tkhines*, women's prayers).[30] Families would then make candles from the wicks and burn them on Yom Kippur. Making candles in memory of dead relatives, called "laying wicks," was a specialized task performed by an older woman known for her piety. With the dead "beholden" to the living for receiving their prayers, they must reciprocate the favor by interceding on behalf of their living relatives while God judges them during the "Days of Awe" leading to Yom Kippur. Also on the wane by the time Goldfaden wrote this play was the Meir Ba'al Ha-Nes *pushke* or charity box that had previously been universal in Jewish homes throughout Eastern Europe. Women were most closely associated with the boxes because of the tradition of putting money in it before baking bread on Friday. The sympathetic references to Meir Ba'al Ha-Nes in the play are particularly remarkable since the charity boxes with his name on them became the target of maskilic censure.[31] Both practices tie Bontsye to the Land of Israel. As Weissler notes, by measuring graves, the wicklayer and the living relatives she represented "hoped to rouse the souls of those in that cemetery to communicate with other souls, and so on and so forth, all the way back to the patriarchs and matriarchs buried in the Land of Israel to pray for the living."[32] The proceeds of the boxes were used for the *Halukkah*, the money dispersed among Jews living in the Land of Israel or to buy candles to burn at the reputed tomb of Meir. After Odele abandons her grandmother for her lover, Bontsye puts money into the *pushke* (three times eighteen coins, eighteen being the value ascribed to the letters of the word *chai*, or life in Hebrew) and calls upon the miracle-working powers of Rabbi Meir to reunite her with her granddaughter. Bontsye's practices bind her to the earth, to those dead and beneath it, and to the Holy Land.

Bontsye's death scene plays out against the backdrop of a particularly diasporic image of the Land of Israel, as a focus of Ashkenazic prayer and as an intermediate space between the living and the dead, a no-man's-land between this world and the days of the Messiah. Deprived of the journey to the Holy Land she had hoped to take after Odele's wedding, Bontsye is granted a glimpse of it before her death, inviting a comparison between Bontsye and Moses in Deuteronomy. The kiss of death she received in act 2 from Ignats might come into focus, albeit as a crude (even parodic?) rendition of the storied kiss of death that the rabbis believed withdrew Moses' soul and ended his life.[33] But another kiss figures more prominently, at the end of the previous act: after Bontsye has read aloud to us from her *Tsenurena*, she closes it and piously kisses its cover before setting it down beside her bed where it will remain throughout the last act. Like Sosya, she cannot cheat death. But the figure of the wicklayer transcends time and space, collapsing the distance between herself and Israel, between the living and the dead.

Conclusion

Modern Yiddish theater grew like dandelions, in fits and starts, trailing an extended genealogy of various dramatic and musical influences; it evolved at an accelerated pace in the late 1870s, with an increasing number of performances of greater sophistication. As the "father of the Yiddish theater" Goldfaden lent Yiddish performance momentum and a repertoire. But notwithstanding Goldfaden's importance during the theater's early years, the mythology of "Goldfaden the father of the Yiddish theater" does not tell us about the idiosyncratic development of modern Yiddish theater. It tells us even less about the culture in which it was embedded and that its writers and actors sought to represent. One strand of the theater's beginnings lies in the transforming ideological complexion of Yiddish drama. The poetics of the botched kiss, the exhaustion of maskilic comedy, lead Goldfaden from the salon to the tavern, from the discipline of the text to the hazards of performance and from the silenced woman to the woman whose rage or piety forcefully claims the end, dramatic rules be damned. With these shifts, Goldfaden moves from the refined culture of the parlor to the raucousness of the tavern, coffeehouse, and beer garden. These venues had long been the home of Yiddish performance, but Goldfaden did not surrender the apparatus of the Enlightenment comedy as he crossed the threshold.

By way of the botched kiss, the two plays comment on the decline of the bourgeois Jewish drama and the cultural irrelevance of the salon culture that sustained it. I have attempted to argue that Goldfaden's early appetite for the tavern is traceable to his first plays, themselves a product of his encounter with maskilic drama. Apropos such a creative trajectory on the part of Goldfaden, the circumstances of his encounter with Ettinger's *Serkele* are particularly interesting. According to a brief memoir penned by the Hebrew writer Avraham Paperna, fellow student of Goldfaden at the Zhitomir seminary, a young Goldfaden contributed to a private staging of the drama, a performance that was seen as provocative by members of the seminary and the Jewish intelligentsia in Zhitomir. Would that Paperna had offered us more details of what I sense to be a turning point in Goldfaden's evolution as a purveyor of Jewish popular culture.[34] For not only did Goldfaden take a hand in organizing the staging, he also performed as the female lead, the villainous and loud-mouthed Serkele. At least in ethos, Goldfaden's transvestite inter-pretation of Ettinger's *Serkele* shifts the drama from the salon, where the dramas are read aloud with text in hand according to bourgeois pre-scription, to the tavern, where performance erases the original text. Ettinger, for instance, never indicates Serkele may be played by a man, and most likely doubted that it would ever be performed at all. Goldfa-den's wayward cross-dressing performance, its irreverence and its depar-ture from the text, might have been ample preparation for his creative departure from his Yiddish-writing predecessors. His cross-dressing introduced the refinement of Ettinger's salon curiosity to the subversive-ness of the tavern—and all was contained in the belly of the Jewish woman.

Notes

1. "Di mume Sosya," *Di yidene: Farsheydene gedikhte un teater* (Odessa, 1872), 34–92. Quoted as parenthetical references. All translations mine unless other-wise noted.

2. I quote from the earliest version of the play that was simply titled *Di bobe mit dem eynikl* (Odessa, 1879). A later version containing significant changes is titled *Di bobe mit dem eynikl oder Bontsye di kneytlekhlegerin: Melodrama in drei aktn mit gezang* (New York, 1893). For the complete performance history of both these plays, see Zalmen Zylbercweig, *Leksikon fun yidish teater* (New York, 1931–70), vol. 1. Also quoted as parenthetical references.

3. These are only a number of the most productive playwrights of the Yiddish theater's first period. Although Hurvitz's plays were rarely published, many of his rival Lateiner's work were published. Hurvitz and Lateiner, both from Europe who later wrote for the most successful (rival) theater companies in New York City, are considered the greatest *shund* (lowbrow) producers in the Yiddish theater. Joseph Lerner's adaptations of world operas and original plays were published as was *Di agune* of Marie Lerner. All these works demand scholarly attention to better assess the role of the theater in Yiddish cultural life at the end of the nineteenth and beginning of the twentieth centuries. For bibliographical information on each of these playwrights, consult Zylbercweig, *Leksikon fun yidishn teater*, 6 vols.

4. In 1926, writers, scholars, and critics marked the founding of the Yiddish theater by reassessing Goldfaden's legacy on the pages of various Yiddish jour-nals. Little enthusiasm was expressed for his dramatic oeuvre. The words of liter-ary critic Shmuel Niger summarizes their thoughts: "Avraham Goldfaden . . . occupies an important place in the history of the Yiddish theatre. . . . He has not, as far as we know, written even one dramatic work that has real literary-artistic value—even his best texts make sense only when the floodlights of the stage falls upon them." Niger was an admirer of Goldfaden's poetry and describes Goldfaden as the first to express an unfettered nationalist impulse in his poetry. "Di lider fun avrom goldfadn: Tsu goldfadns yuvilium," *Tsukunkft* 3 (1926): 150. To Yiddish critic Y. Schipper, Goldfaden was a "transitional figure" whose work reflected the primitive performance of Yiddish tavern entertainers.

See "Der uftu fun avrom goldfadn," *Literarishe bleter* 95 (1926): 133–34. See the entire issue of *Literarishe bleter* 95 (1926) for similar opinions on Goldfaden. Soviet scholars A. Bilov and V. Veletnitski sought to reclaim Goldfaden's plays—especially his comedies—and argued for their significance for the development of Jewish theater, the sources of Goldfaden's works being the Enlightenment closet dramas and the *purim-shpil*. See A. Bilov and V. Veletnitski, "Di kvaln fun goldfadns teatrale shafn," in *A goldfadn: Geklibene dramatishe verk* (Kiev, 1940).

5. Quoted from *The History of Yiddish Literature in the Nineteenth Century* (New York, 1899), 237. Weiner did single out *Aunt Sosya* as constituting a good drama.

6. "The theatricality of Yiddish led to the development of certain narrative techniques and structures, the exclusion of others, the employment of certain stylistic devices, certain literary achievements, as well as many demonstrable limitations. It pervaded the whole matrix of artistic consciousness in which Yiddish fiction was formed." *A Traveler Disguised: The Origins of Modern Yiddish Literature* (New York, 1973), 94.

7. See Berkowitz's *Shakespeare on the American Yiddish Stage* (Iowa City, 2002). Critics might have drawn their conclusions on the basis of performances, which were often very different from texts. Consider the remarks of the Yiddish actor Jacob Adler about the older Yiddish actor Sigmund Mogulesco. "Mogulesco learned his trade in the early theatre of Goldfaden. He saw no reason to stick to a text." Lulla Adler Rosenfeld, *The Yiddish Theatre and Jacob P. Adler* (New York, 1988), 103–4.

8. I supply a historical treatment of nineteenth-century Yiddish literature and the theater—particularly the question of their relative audiences—in " 'Yiddish Literature for the Masses?' A Reconsideration of Who Read What in Jewish Eastern Europe," *AJS Review* 29 (2005): 61–90.

9. For a comprehensive and accessible history of the Yiddish theater, see Nahma Sandrow, *Vagabond Stars: A World History of Yiddish Theatre* (Syracuse: Syracuse University Press, 1996). For recent scholarship on the Yiddish theater including some essays on Goldfaden, see Joel Berkowitz, ed., *Yiddish Theatre: New Approaches* (Oxford and Portland, 2003). A concise description of the state of the field and general discussion of Yiddish theater is offered in Joel Berkowitz and Jeremy Dauber's introduction to *Landmark Yiddish Plays* (Albany, 2006), 1–71.

10. "Fun shmendrik biz ben ami," *Oysgeklibene shriftn*, ed. Shmuel Rozhanski (Buenos Aires, 1907), 22.

11. It is ironic that 1883, the year in which the tsar outlawed the Yiddish theater, coincides with the liberalizing of the Russian-language theater. For more on the prohibition, see John Klier, "Exit, Pursued by a Bear: The Ban on Yiddish Theater in Imperial Russia," in *Yiddish Theatre: New Approaches*, 159–74. I believe Klier underestimates the stifling effect the law had (as it was meant to have) on the Yiddish theater in late Imperial Russia. Still, it is an important and richly informative chapter.

12. The recurring quotations of the *purim-shpil*, references to it, and *purim-shpils* crafted into modern historical operettas deserve more attention, although in general I am not sure that these (perhaps with the exception of the latter) amount to literary influence. On the resonance of the *purim-shpil* and its perceived association with the modern Yiddish theater, see Michael Steinlauf's important article, "Fear of Purim: Y. L. Peretz and the Canon of Yiddish Theatre," *Jewish Social Studies* 1 (1995): 44–65.

13. Northrop Frye, *Anatomy of Criticism: Four Essays* (Princeton: Princeton University Press, 1957), 163. Frye's discussion of the comedy's elements or what he

calls the comic modality is still widely relied upon by scholars and has yet to be surpassed in eloquence or precision. For more on the principles of the comedy, see Paul Lauter, ed., *Theories of Comedy*, (Garden City, N.Y., 1964), and Zvi Jagendorf, *The Happy End of Comedy* (Newark, Del., 1984).

14. Northrop Frye, *A Natural Perspective: The Development of Shakespearean Comedy and Romance* (New York, 1965), 74.

15. Included in A. Fridkin and V. Reisen, eds., *A. b. gotlobers yidishe verk* (1876; Vilna, 1927).

16. Frye, *Natural Perspective*, 75–76.

17. See *Ale ksovim fun shlomo etinger* (New York, 1925). For a recent analysis of the play, see my article "The Currency of Yiddish: Ettinger's *Serkele* and the Reinvention of Shylock," *Prooftexts* 24 (2004): 99–115.

18. Scott S. Bryson, *The Chastised Stage: Bourgeois Drama and the Exercise of Power* (Stanford, 1991), 23, 35.

19. "Monstrous Women, Sublime Pleasure, and the Perils of Reception in Lessing's Aesthetics," *PMLA*, no. 3 (May 2001): 546.

20. For a comprehensive list of lesser-known maskilic drama published in the 1860s and 1870s, see my "'Yiddish Literature for the Masses?'" 69n.27.

21. See Ruth Amossy and Elisheva Rosen, *Les Discours du cliché* (Paris, 1982).

22. One reader of the Russian-Jewish newspaper *Russkii evrei* wrote: "In [Goldfaden's] humor there is not one note of the elevated love of one's people that one must possess through and through before punishing a people for its flaws. Everyone agrees that the situations in Goldfaden's comedies are not the product of Jewish life. Where in this life, for instance, did Goldfaden find the belief in witchcraft that he depicts in *The Sorceress* or the husband-bashing (*Mener-freseray*) he depicts in *Aunt Sosya* or *Brayndele the Cossack?*"

23. Roland Barthes, "Structural Analysis of Narratives," in *Image—Music—Text*, trans. Stephen Heath (New York, 1970), 123.

24. Dan Miron, *The Image of the Shtetl and Other Studies of Modern Jewish Literary Imagination* (Syracuse, 2000), 65.

25. For a recent study of the practice of Jewish men abandoning their wives to marry again (without divorcing), see Chae Ran Freeze, *Jewish Marriage and Divorce in Imperial Russia* (Hanover, N.H., 2002).

26. See Dan Miron's important discussion of the figure of the Jewish doctor in nineteenth-century Jewish fiction in *Le Médecin Imaginaire: Studies in Classical Jewish Fiction* (Tel Aviv, 1995).

27. See Edward J. Bristow, *Prostitution and Prejudice: The Jewish Fight Against White Slavery, 1870–1939* (New York, 1983). Also see Joel Berkowitz, "The Brothel as Symbolic Space in Yiddish Drama," in *Sholem Asch Reconsidered*, ed. Nanette Stahl (New Haven, 2004), 35–50.

28. See for instance Mikhl Gordon, *Di bord un dertsu nokh andere sheyne yidishe lider, ale fun a groysen hosid* (Zhitomir, 1868).

29. Frye, *Anatomy of Criticism*, 36.

30. Chava Weissler, *Voices of the Matriarchs: Listening to the Prayers of Early Modern Jewish Women* (Boston, 1998).

31. Some maskilim argued the charity box's association with Hasidism and complained that it was yet another way for the rebbe to extract money from his adherents, but the practice of collecting charity in the name of Meir Ba'al Ha-Nes predated Hasidism and was popular beyond the Hasidic community. The Talmud never mentions that Rabbi Meir was a miracle worker, but the practice evolved to make collections in the home in the name of Meir Ba'al Ha-Nes. See

Nancy Sinkoff on Joseph Perl's polemic against the charity boxes as a Hasidic *minhag* in *Out of the Shtetl: Making Jews Modern in the Polish Borderlands* (Providence, 2004), 246–47.

32. Weissler, *Voices of the Matriarchs*, 139.

33. Based on their interpretation of the words that describe Moses having died "by the mouth of the Lord." See Michael Fishbane, *The Kiss of Death: Spiritual and Mystical Death in Judaism* (Seattle, 1994), 19.

34. A. Paperna, "Di ershte yidishe drame un der ershter yiddisher spektakl," in *Pinkeys,* ed. Shmuel Niger (Vilna, 1913).

Chapter 4

The Polish Popular Novel and Jewish Modernization at the End of the Nineteenth and Beginning of the Twentieth Centuries

EUGENIA PROKOP-JANIEC

The "Jewish Novel"

In 1892, the Warsaw assimilatory weekly *Izraelita* published a short piece by the chief editor of the magazine, Nahum Sokołów, discussing the problem of the "Jewish novel."[1] Critics of the time applied the term "Jewish novel" to works that referred to Jewish life, but Sokołów's article disputed the use of the term in this sense. In his opinion, a "Jewish novel" could and should refer only to works that show the Jewish world from an interior perspective, guaranteeing that it would render a true image, not one falsified from lack of knowledge or deliberate bias. "The inner Jewish life as if covered by a magical mist; its charms, spells, superstitions and beliefs formed of the Jews' own pain and hardship, are incomprehensible to the general public," he wrote. "They could only be sensed and rendered by those who spent their childhood in this atmosphere, who grew up there, who began to understand the world and to live there, who know the nature and the customs of the people, understand their speech, legends, sayings and proverbs—yet those are not writers."[2] Convinced that such a believable and authentic image could be offered only by literature created by Jews in Polish or in Jewish languages, he ended the text with praise for folk stories by I. L. Peretz and a call for translations of Yiddish literature.

This short text by Sokołów deserves attention for several reasons. First, Sokołów joined a group of authors who were describing and analyzing the origins of Jewish literatures in European languages and provided the agenda for such literature. Second, he drew his readers' attention to the ways in which literary images of the Jewish world depended on the perspective they adopted, internal or external. The problem thus lay in the point of view adopted by the narration, which was also understood as a cultural category[3]—that is, as related to the cultural origins and the cultural experience of the narrator, which became apparent in the ways he described the world.

Sokołów was motivated to make this argument by the novel *Zięciowie domu Kohn et Cie* (Sons-in-law of the House Kohn and Company) by Count Wincenty Łoś, a now forgotten but at the time quite popular author of short stories about the world of the nobility and upper-class romances. The piece was part of a cycle of novels called *Świat i finanse* (High society and financiers), set among wealthy and emancipated Jews who were rising in high society and mixing with the Polish aristocracy and nobility. The series, comprising the novels *Zięciowie domu Kohn et Cie* (1892), *Ze Starżów pani Appelstein* (Mrs. Appelstein, née Starża, 1896), and *Drugie życie pani Appelstein* (Mrs. Appelstein's second life, 1904), was about mixed marriages. The topic had appeared in Polish literature several decades earlier, yet it reached its peak in the 1890s; Łoś was among many authors who made it their *specialité de la maison*. The theme had already become conventionalized, occurring both in historical romance and adventure stories (for example, the novel *Wychrzta* [A baptised Jew] by Michał Synoradzki [1904], set in the seventeenth century), as well as novels with an anti-Jewish tendency (such as *Szachraje* [The duffers, 1899] and *Nawrócony* [A Convert, 1901] by Artur Gruszecki). The broad spectrum of uses of this theme reflects on the one hand, the characteristic nineteenth-century literary tendency to clothe Polish-Jewish relations in historical costume,[4] and on the other hand, the ideology that saw literature on Jewish topics as a polemical tool. Mixed marriages were also discussed in the journalism: in 1911, in the brochure *O sprzecznościach sprawy żydowskiej* (On the contradictions of the Jewish case), the well-known poet Antoni Lange described them as one of the most important ways to achieve integration of the two groups.

Novels by Łoś, like works by other authors of popular romances—for example, Marian Gawalewicz's *Filistry* (Philistines, 1888) and *Mechesy* (Baptised Jews, 1892), Antoni Miecznik's *Cztery dni* (Four days, 1903), or Kazimierz Tetmajer's *Panna Mery* (Miss Mary, 1902)—linked the plot, with its romantic twists and turns, to observations about ongoing social changes. These texts combined traditional generic patterns and new forms.[5] On the one hand, they contained traces of the sentimental tendency to argue for "the Jews' equal rights to emotions,"[6] the traditions of Enlightenment, and Positivist prose on Jewish topics that called for Jewish assimilation and reforming Jewish culture. On the other hand, they betrayed the visible impact of the naturalist environmental novel that studied and described the life of different social groups. With the combination of these two conventions, the Jewish novel of the turn of the twentieth century was converted into a sort of popular environmental novel—a genre belonging to the most characteristic forms of Polish popular literature of the period.

Although targeted at a specific audience and conveying separate literary conventions, the popular environmental novel demonstrates that popular literature took over and adapted elements of highbrow literature.[7] It was of vital importance that popular fiction play a key function of the modern novel: analysis and interpretation of contemporary modernizing society. So one of the characteristic features of the popular novel was the use of contemporary themes and the introduction of real conditions, phenomena, or events. Because of this, it could draw close to the journalistic novel that reacted quickly to topical events, or to novels that offered literarily transformed versions of contemporary scandal (*Cztery dni* by Antoni Miecznik was seen as such a novel).

The popular Jewish novel of the turn of the century was a varied phenomenon, representing different ideological tendencies and using different plot conventions. There were romances using the model of ideological novels of purpose and devoted to resolving the problem of assimilation; there were anti-Jewish novels; and along with works with sensationalist plots, there were melodramatic works where the love story was mingled with ideology. In addition, Jewish themes occurred in popular short stories and novels about the nobility (such as *Zrośli z ziemią* [Rooted in the land, 1901] by Kazimierz Laskowski and *Przy naszych dworach* [At our courts, 1895] by Wincenty Łoś).

The authors of popular Jewish novels were interesting in themselves: along with descendants of aristocratic families (when publishing upper-class romances, Wincenty Łoś did not hesitate to place the title of Count next to his name) and the impoverished nobility (Klemens Junosza Szaniawski), they included journalists (Antoni Miecznik, Michał Synoradzki), actors, theater entrepreneurs (Marian Gawalewicz), professional writers of a new type who devoted their literary production to satisfying the needs of a broad public (Artur Gruszecki), and authors of highbrow literature who admitted they dealt with popular literature for material reasons (Kazimierz Tetmajer). From the 1890s, this group also included writers of Jewish origins (Aniela Kallas [actually Aniela Korngutówna], *Nasz żydowski światek: Z pamiętników przyjaciółki* [Our small Jewish world: From a friend's diaries, 1893]).

This is the popular novel I analyze in this essay. Until now, the Jewish themes in Polish popular literature have rarely been analyzed, even though due to its broad impact, popular literature is a significant tool for building a national "imagined community" and negotiating its identity and borders. By examining it, I hope to partially reconstruct the image of Polish-Jewish relations characteristic at the turn of the twentieth century in works designated for a broad and non-elite public.

Popular Literature and Social Problems

The fact that the popular novel of the turn of the century filled the traditional functions of highbrow literature was visible inter alia in the ways it continued models of social prose and the Positivist novel of purpose, with its ideological tendentiousness and persuasiveness. In the case of the Jewish popular novel, the continuation mainly took the form of references to traditional views of the Jewish question. Although assimilation and emancipation were no longer the ideological postulates or social projects proposed by authors, the echoes of the pro-emancipation and pro-assimilation slogans of several decades earlier were still audible.

Images of the increasing acculturation of Jews who adopted Polish customs and lifestyles, took new names, or went through religious conversion—that is, images of blurring cultural boundaries—were used broadly in popular romances. This type of novel differs in many aspects from works with protagonists of other nationalities, such as Germans or Russians. In Jewish novels by Łoś or Gawalewicz, there are no motifs of intergroup antagonism. In the social imagination Jews are strangers, yet they are internal ones, part stranger and part guest, seen as one group within Polish society, unlike Germans, who are perceived as external, as strangers-enemies.[8] Also, the division into positive and negative characters does not follow national boundaries. Even in novels with clear anti-Jewish tendencies, such as *Szachraje* by Artur Gruszecki, there are noble Jewish idealists who were modeled on the chief protagonist of *Meir Ezofowicz* (Meir Esofovich) by Eliza Orzeszkowa, a novel that described a Jewish assimilation program and appealed for integration. The Jewish novel was fundamentally topical and thus could claim to offer readers more than entertainment: a record of changing social reality, the recognition of new phenomena, and comments on current events.

Romantic plots combined with social criticism appeared in very popular novels by Łoś. In *Ze Starżów pani Appelstein* and *Drugie życie pani Appelstein*, the melodramatic story of a beautiful and unfortunate heroine, the wife of a Jewish banker, suffering from the ingratitude of her family and excluded from snobbish salons, was commented on by the narrator, who considered it to be a story of the birth of a democratic "new world, a cosmopolitan world, that would value condition no more than property, talent, race and beauty."[9] The novel *Zięciowie domu Kohn et Cie*, criticized in *Izraelita*, begins with a description of social relations in Warsaw, where Polish salons were seemingly attacked by wealthy, assimilating, and emancipating Jews. In the opinion of one of the protagonists, everything showed that soon "there will be no family in Poland which will not have a cousin with stein or berg in their name."[10] Therefore, intergroup differences would be blurred or would be radically shifted. Significantly, the plot was set in Warsaw, itself presented as the center of the changes brought by urbanization and as a city quickly adopting the style of great European capitals. When in one novel the plot is set in Lvov, this underlines the modernity of Warsaw and contrasts its democratic character with the conservatism of the provinces that persist in maintaining old notions of caste. Characteristically, Jewish novels by Gawalewicz, Miecznik, Tetmajer, and Gruszecki are also set in Warsaw.

Moving from the sphere of ideological projects to the sphere of contemporary social problems, Jewish acculturation and assimilation ceased to be the domain of ideological discourse alone and began to be treated in other discourses, such as the language of personal experience. In popular novels, this was expressed inter alia by weakening the clear bias of the novels, with the clear, dominating voice of the omniscient narrator replaced with the voices of protagonists representing various ideological options, views, and assessments. As a consequence of such measures, texts incorporated various positions, which were, however, usually framed in the ordering perspective of the narrator, and subjective commentaries were juxtaposed with distanced, seemingly objective descriptions of the phenomena. Novels by Łoś or Gawalewicz therefore offered conservative and liberal views, the voices of aristocrats and members of the intelligentsia, as well as assimilated and anti-Jewish characters. In particular the presence of the last two requires attention. These worldviews were frequently juxtaposed, and novels by Gawalewicz, for example, featured recurring scenes of discussions between journalists writing for the anti-Jewish press and assimilated Jews or Poles entering the wealthy class. The popular novel thus attempted to speak on behalf of the Jews and represent their position in a form imagined and interpreted by Poles.

By discussing the Jewish world and experience in this manner, the popular novel used a narrative strategy from Enlightenment prose on the Jewish issue. The strategy consisted in speaking on behalf of the Jews, in the illusion of allowing the Jewish world itself to speak. This convention can be seen in the sentimental Enlightenment epistolary novel *Lejbe i Sióra, czyli Listy dwóch kochanków* (Leib and Sarah or Letters of two lovers, 1821) by Julian Ursyn Niemcewicz, where the criticism of traditional Jewish culture was expressed by the author in the form of letters written by Jewish protagonists and presented in the guise of criticism from inside the Jewish community. Niemcewicz was the first writer who widely used the convention of Jewish protagonists speaking in their own voice.

One of the heroes, Abraham, a supporter of the Haskalah, writes to the protagonist of the novel, young Leibe:

The elements of contemporary Judaism are hatred and obstinate prejudice; as long as this mordant darkness dwells in our hearts there can be neither improvement nor any approach to other nations in the world and therefore no goodness for us can be expected. We are trying in vain to treat with curative ointments what has been affected by a deadly gangrene. It has to be cut out first and only then can remedial balms be sought. I know that rabbis, the elders of the kahals and fraternities find great personal benefits in their stubborn renunciation of national laws even in their political aspects; but I also know how much a great deal of our people lose because of that.[11]

The shifts in perspectives and the tendency to present assessments of the situation in the internal voices of the characters is striking in turn-of-the-century popular novels dealing with Jewish immigration from Russia (*Litwackie mrowie* [The Litvaks' lot, 1911] by Artur Gruszecki, and *Litwaki* [The Litvaks, 1911] by Kazimierz Laskowski). The conflict between Poles and Jews is transformed there into a clash within the Jewish community, an internal struggle between Polish and Russian Jews, representing various cultural options, loyalty types, and political alliances. A similar situation appears in anti-Jewish novels, where ideological commentary occurs through self-discrediting monologues and dialogues by Jewish protagonists (as for example in Miecznik's novel).

When popular romances are compared with stories from the turn of the century written by assimilated Jews such as Aniela Kallas, we see that the romance authors speaking on behalf of Jews were genuinely attempting to come close to the social experience of Jews. The popular novel registers a range of approaches to acculturation and assimilation, from opportunistic and material ones to thoroughly ideological ones. In the assimilated protagonists' analyses of their own new situation and changing social status, they utter both fatalistic phrases about the flaw of an origin that can neither be erased nor forgotten and accusing commentaries about social discrimination. Regardless of their adoption of Polish culture and their personal merits and efforts, from the perspective of Polish society assimilated Jews still remain Jews. Being a Jew is considered by the world they are attempting to enter to be a fatal flaw. This attitude of the protagonists is often supported by the omniscient narrator. In the novel by Łoś, this occurs in the episode of the suicide of a boy who inherits the title of a duke from his father, yet who cannot bear to be reminded of the "shame" of his mother's Jewish origin.[12] Gawalewicz's prose includes a duel sparked by the dishonor of a public reminder to the Polish and Jewish protagonists of their relations with the Jewish world.

Therefore, even the pro-assimilation bias and the criticism of caste privileges and beliefs about "good birth" in the ideology of the popular novel could not erase a hierarchy of values where whatever was Polish was higher, and whatever was Jewish was lower. This hierarchy was also visible in the figure of the Jewish hero portrayed as a parvenu, or the depiction of assimilated Jews who conceal their relations with the non-assimilated part of the family, break off social contacts with them (*Mech-esy* by Gawalewicz), or avoid marriage with other assimilated Jews because they are Jews (*Cztery dni* by Miecznik, *Panna Mery* by Tetmajer). In the short story *Duch czasu* (The spirit of time, 1898) by Aniela Kallas, love and democratic views cannot exempt the heroine from the obligatory conversion, considered by everyone—including herself—a necessary element of a socially accepted scenario for a Polish-Jewish couple. Emancipation and integration must, therefore, occur on the terms defined by the dominant group and—regardless of the universal and democratic ideals postulated in the assimilation projects—they confirm the values and ideals of this group.[13] The cultural and religious segregation in these novels seem to apply only to social relations, whereas commercial relations are not subject to it, which conforms with the traditional pre-modern model of Polish-Jewish relations restricted to the economic strata.

Inter-Group Relations: Open and Hidden Boundaries

In the synthesis *Polska literatura współczesna* (Polish contemporary literature, 1911–12), published in the early twentieth century, the well-known critic Antoni Potocki described the democratization processes reflected by literature as the expansion of a modern nation, to which further groups are incorporated, groups that formerly had not participated in it with equal rights. Indeed, the social criticism of the popular contemporary novel of the turn of the century, set among the intelligentsia, financial tycoons, or aristocracy, reflected and realized the impression of changing group boundaries. It did not, however, record only their expansion but also their maintenance and their redrawing in new locations. Such mechanisms were analyzed, for example, in novels set among the aristocracy, where attention is drawn to stories of intrigue, social boycott, scandals, affronts, ostracism, caste superstitions, or racial prejudices. Novels introducing such motifs are partially transformed into studies of the changing nature of social distance and the character of inter-group relations: the possibilities for strangers to live near one another, become friends, even get married.

Group scenes, especially, usually focus on Polish-Jewish relations. Descriptions of salon society, the shareholders of a company, the participants in a religious ceremony, or a family meeting often stress the lack of bonds, divisions, and boundaries between Polish and Jewish circles. Novels with an anti-Jewish bias (such as *Cztery dni* by Antoni Miecznik) stress the sharp antagonisms, finally justifying them as racial conflict. Due to the presentation of both groups as isolated and not integrated, novels (such as those by Łoś and Gawalewicz) introduce the separate figure of the go-between: a person known in the salons, a mediator and informer, who devotes his time (and frequently also makes his living in this way) to participating in conflicts of interests and struggles over status and prestige.

The phenomenon of assimilation without integration is often analyzed by the Jewish protagonists. Assimilated figures consider themselves to be people deprived of a defined social place: they are already outside the group they originated from, but also outside the community they hoped to join. Thus the protagonist of Łoś's novel *Ze Starżów pani Appelstein* speaks of his sense of belonging to the Polish world, but also about his exclusion from it, or at most the conditional acceptance he (or rather his wealth) can enjoy. In a speech he addresses to Poles, he uses phrases such as "you" or "your world," which express distance and a lack of belonging.

The trap prepared for the assimilated Jews[14] also consists in the fact that although the open boundaries between communities, marked by religion, language, and custom, were blurred, hidden boundaries remained untouched.[15] And the protagonists learn about that only when it turns out that adopting a new language, culture, and even religion does not mean integration. Regardless of the blurring of the differences, and indeed as a result of it, the boundaries remain—persistently maintained or hastily organized anew. The assimilated protagonist of Łoś's novel comments on his situation in the following way: "You shouldn't have socially merged with the Appelsteins. You should have set clearly a demarcation line. . . . Perhaps they would have created their own world had they known that they could not merge with yours. But they didn't know that."[16] Boundaries are therefore shifted and concealed, yet they are not weakened or removed.

Thus the ending of *Mechesy* by Marian Gawalewicz becomes symbolic: separation both from the Polish and the Jewish world is presented as a condition of both the marriage and the family happiness of the Polish-Jewish couple. The protagonists can only act as partners to each other by locating themselves outside the social space of being Polish or Jewish, by choosing a type of refuge in a neutral zone established by themselves. By doing so they conform to the opinion (explicit in novels by Łoś or Miecznik) that a merger between the Polish and Jewish worlds is impossible.

An indirect confirmation of the permanent and irremovable boundaries between the communities lies in the figures of protagonists of the Polish-Jewish romances. Those who blur and cross boundaries, in particular the Jewish protagonists (this is also true in the anti-Jewish novels), are presented as unique, different from the group they originate from, or in an open ideological conflict with their environment or family. In Łoś's novels, this difference also takes on a "racial" character: the narrator of *Ze Starżów pani Appelstein* stresses the non-Jewish appearance of the protagonist who wishes to enter the Polish world. His uniqueness becomes increasingly important through the contrast with the character of his brother, presented as a model Jew and someone who would never want to leave the boundaries of the Jewish community. In turn, Gawalewicz (*Mechesy*) stresses the difference in character and ideals that alienates the protagonist from his family and environment. This uniqueness also appears in the Polish protagonists. The Polish partner of the Jewish hero of *Mechesy* is an unconventional girl who is treated by her community as "wild" and "original." In Łoś's *Drugie życie pani Appelstein,* the Polish count who is in love with a girl from a Polish-Jewish family is completely outside of the lifestyle and thinking of his sphere: he is a traveler, a sailor, a cosmopolitan free of social superstitions and worship of the familiar.

The Differences

The blurring of social and cultural differences motivates a psychological mechanism whereby people search for differences in order to distinguish between groups that have become similar to one another. The differences that construct the map of social space are always selected arbitrarily, yet are presented as things that cannot be questioned or removed, that is, as features that have the status of natural differences.[17] Such an obsessive focus on small differences both establishes boundaries and builds identity.

In Jewish novels, both the narrator and the protagonists too frequently think about differences. These are differences in physical appearance and cultural differences: nuances in use of the Polish language or the traces of former customs in everyday life (in *Nawrócony* by Gruszecki, the assimilated protagonist would, for example, wash his hands before his meal, "according to the eastern habit").[18] What is also characteristic here is the tendency to divide up roles: if the characteristic racial differences are performed and witnessed by the protagonists, the differences revealed by elements of the background such as the interiors are described by the narrator.

At the level of rhetoric, cultural difference is a chiasmatic figure,[19] one built on parallelism, comparison, or juxtaposition. These devices appear most frequently in the presentation of the interiors of rooms or houses. Łoś (*Zięciowie domu Kohn et Cie*) juxtaposes descriptions of aristocratic and plutocratic salons. Gawalewicz (*Mechesy*) describes a manor decorated by a wealthy Jewish financier, and then redecorated by his daughter-in-law, a Pole. A nobleman's manor house remodeled by its Jewish owner is designed to dazzle with opulence:

Inside the entire furnishing was changed and only in a few rooms the old-fashioned furniture was left to recall the antiques of the long-ago residence and its former owners. From walls covered with costly wallpapers and old tapestries in freshly gilded frames looked the faces of forefathers blackened with age, as if fetched out of darkness. . . . They felt somehow awkward in these new surroundings, luxurious and glittering, as if furnished for show, catching the eye with a pomp that was out of harmony with the character of the rural manor house.[20]

The Polish daughter-in-law, on the other hand, "got rid of the excessive luxury with which her would-be father-in-law wanted to boast. . . . The place looked more and more modest, but also more dignified; velvets, satins, and gilding on expensive furniture and walls no longer caught the eye; there was no more gross and evident desire to impress with wealth and comfort out of place in a rural manor house."[21] When attention is drawn to differences, Polish interiors are transformed into a texts speaking of national history and tradition, while Jewish ones prove cosmopolitan and speak of ostentatious new wealth. The salons of the Jewish parvenus are not decorated, but even though they are stuffed with precious items, they do not protect and store treasures; rather, they expose and exhibit the markers of ties with the noble past, such as armor, a coat of arms, or ancestors' portraits.

Having entered into the Polish world, the Jews become new people without a history or tradition, and their own past must be erased and forgotten. The behavior of the acculturating protagonists is described as role-playing: having married a count, a banker's daughter in Miecznik's novel attempts to master her pose as a countess. Comparisons of this sort construct the difference between the natural and the acquired, the spontaneous and the non-spontaneous or artificial. Strangers are revealed as newcomers and parvenus; their behavior and environment are, in turn, revealed as improper, excessive, artificial, and stylized. The new people cannot distinguish between the high and the low, the valuable and the fashionable, the foreign and the innate: in *Filistry* by Gawalewicz, in a plutocratic salon, Chopin's music must give way to a performance by a medium who reads people's minds.

The lines of social boundaries are often drawn along contrasts in physical appearance. The opposition between "oriental types" and Polish looks is a constant key to social categorization for Łoś's protagonists.

Among the observations of salon society, every now and then the narrator makes comments such as, "While dancing he frequently noticed faces that were beautiful, yet too oriental in appearance."[22] "Race! Race!" is how Gawalewicz's protagonist in *Mechesy* describes the situation. Racial difference is also discussed at length in the protagonist's monologues in Gruszecki's *Nawrócony*.

The phrase "foreign blood" or racial fatalism appear, and descriptions of characters framed within a typical racial scheme[23] following common stereotypes occur not only in these novels. Racial rhetoric is one of the most characteristic features of the popular Jewish novel of the turn of the century. According to the well-known formula of Tzvetan Todorov, an increased interest in racial issues is closely related to the blurring of differences in social life, and race becomes a metaphor for a final, undeniable difference. As a result, race acquires all the weight that can no longer be attributed to social causes.[24]

Some authors of the turn of the century use the term race according to the nineteenth-century convention, as a synonym for nation. Simultaneously, new categories related to race appear: Semitic and Aryan. Usually these do not, however, adopt the form of Aryan Manichaeism that contrasts everything Aryan with everything Semitic and considers the Aryan and Semitic "races" to be antithetical.[25] Writers such as Łoś or Gawalewicz only to some extent associate the Semitic with the oriental, which still has the positive connotations characteristic of romantic prose. In their novels, beautiful Jewish girls charm with their oriental appearance, while noble assimilated protagonists are granted "oriental looks,"[26] and they all have "the hot blood of exiles from Palestine."[27]

Even those authors, however, treat race in the naturalistic way developed by the anti-Jewish novel. One of the most disturbing racist scenes can be found in Gawalewicz's novel: a child of a mixed couple is scrutinized "in the racial aspect" by the servants and assessed using a broad repertoire of common racial stereotypes and prejudices:

"Well, a boy is a boy," the younger servant was saying to the cook with a scornful smile, as if frowning with disgust, "but he is so Jewish that he couldn't be more so."
"And has Miss Agnes noticed how protruding his ears are? . . . It's the first time I have seen such big ears in a small child."
"And he is as surly as a poodle."[28]

A similar situation appears in works by other authors (e.g., Łoś or Gruszecki): common people (servants or peasants) form a court judging assimilated Jews or their children. In all scenes of this type, the authors reproduce discriminating anti-Jewish discourse—without any visible hesitation or attempts to censor the relevant range of insults. The popular novel appeals to common thinking and uses its categories. These novels do so explicitly with clear references to popular authority, or—to paraphrase the well-known formula by Michael Billig, who calls the expressions of nationalism in everyday life "banal nationalism"—banal racism, and with the introduction of common protagonists who hold such views, together with the quotation of their contemptuous or hostile comments.

The range of motifs shared by the anti-Jewish novel and the popular novel of manners is much broader. The protagonists' characteristics include, for example, the trace of a strong element of anti-Jewish stereotypes: unfamiliarity with nature. The rural estate of a plutocratic family is called *Brylantówka* (a diamond manor), and the very ostentatious reference to wealth testifies to the characters' lack of connection to the countryside and lack of knowledge of traditional Polish toponymy (*Filistry*). Another example of this kind was the motif of instinctive racial repugnance. In the journalistic novel by Gawalewicz (*Mechesy*), such a motif is seen when a mother rejects her "Jewish" child, who evokes a vivid and uncontrollable dislike just by his "Semitic" looks.

Interpreting episodes of this type, Sander Gilman notices that the conviction that racial features were intensified in the children of mixed couples was common in the late nineteenth century.[29] This conviction is apparent in novels by Gawalewicz, Łoś, and Miecznik, where children from mixed couples are usually stigmatized by an otherness that is further intensified by the contrast of their physical appearance with that of their parents. For example, in Łoś's *Drugie życie pani Appelstein,* the mother is called a "prototype of national Polish beauty,"[30] while her daughter is referred to as a "little Jewess" and described as an oriental type, her strangeness associated with an erotic charm. The exclusion of mixed-race children from the Polish world is most radical in Miecznik's novel *Cztery dni,* where the father, an aristocrat, considers himself the last of the family and denies the right of his son from a mixed marriage to continue the family traditions.

The power of racial stereotypes is, in fact, largely expanded in the popular novel: they are used not only by Polish protagonists, but also by assimilated circles. This is so because in its most radical forms assimilation is expressed by internalizing the negative image of one's own group that is present in the dominant culture. In Łoś's novels, such motifs include the dream of a wealthy Jewish banker about a grandson with "golden-fair hair, a pointed nose, and a broad lip made for a heavy, bushy moustache."[31]

Anti-Semitism

In novels by Łoś, Gawalewicz, and Miecznik, the social prestige and the social standing of assimilating protagonists, the open and hidden boundaries between the Polish and the Jewish worlds, and the blurring differences or newly imposed differences between them are directly related to the problem of growing anti-Semitic prejudices and phobias. "I am an anti-Semite,"[32] some protagonists declare openly. Sensitive to topical problems, the popular novel registers the shift at the turn of the century from a universalistic approach and assimilatory rhetoric toward segregation and separatism. In many novels, these two rhetorics merge.

Such separatist tendencies were openly expressed by the anti-Semitic novel that focused on the strangeness of the Jews and aimed at presenting it as irremovable and innate. (Extended analyses of the nature of Jewish strangeness appear in Miecznik's *Cztery dni* and Gruszecki's *Nawróceny*.) At the turn of the century, the anti-Semitic novel was basically a modern novel, where social criticism focused on acculturation and emancipation. It is worth recalling here the opinion of the writer Piotr Jaxa Bykowski, author of stories about former noblemen who often introduced traditional Jewish types: "Israel . . . of today, the trendy people, with carriages, bankers, tailcoats—that is all this *sheine moreine* [wealthy Jews], it is already the prey of Jan Jeleński."[33] Anti-Semitism is directly related here to modernity and to emancipation and acculturation. As a matter of fact, anti-Jewish tendencies appear much less frequently in historical novels such as Michał Synoradzki's *Wychrzta*, set in the seventeenth century, where the Jewish protagonist attempts to become part of the Polish society with felony and crime, for which he is punished with death.

Anti-Semitism, as a new phenomenon, is interpreted and assessed in varied ways. Sometimes it is treated as an example of aristocratic phobias, a defensive reaction of the old world, a new strategy in the struggle for status and power. This is so in novels by Łoś, where the "anti-Semitic party," or—as the author puts it—the "anti-Semitic gang," is recruited from people belonging to "historic families." It is, in fact, a sort of anti-Semitic clique, a group formed to protect the traditional elite positions threatened by upstarts. It originates in an aristocratic salon, where social intrigues are engineered, and the leader of the action aimed at boycotting the Jews might be a countess who wishes to find a daughter-in-law among the plutocrats in order to save her family from bankruptcy with the dowry. Anti-Semitic tactics are used by this society only instrumentally and cynically as an effective tool in the struggle for their own interests.

Along with interpretations of this type, there are, however, other representations of anti-Semitism as an ideological phenomenon, relating it to the formation of contemporary political fractions and the impact of the press. In particular the latter seems characteristic. In Gawalewicz's novels, the editorial office of anti-Jewish journals is described ("Ojcowizna" [The patrimony] in *Filistry*, and "Strażnica" [The watch-tower] in *Mechesy*), as well as the circle of journalists from such journals, and the discussions between representatives of this circle and the assimilated protagonists set the terms of one of the principal ideological debates in the novels. Yet another interpretation appears in novels that relate the growth of anti-Semitism to the immigration of "foreign" Jews from Russia or to the birth of Zionism (*Litwackie mrowie* and *Cztery dni*).

To sum up, the popular novel dealt with the symptoms of acculturation and emancipation among the intelligentsia, the wealthy, and the bourgeoisie, in the cities and provinces.[34] Accounting for current events, it recorded the beginnings of modern, ideologically motivated anti-Semitism, the birth of Zionism, and conflicts raised by the immigration of Jews from Russia. Its specialty was the rendition of types of Polish-Jewish relationships that were undergoing diversification parallel to the modernization process. Those were no longer the limited relationships between country or shtetl Jews and the gentry, but the relationships between Jewish financiers or bourgeois and Polish aristocrats or between assimilating or assimilated intelligentsia and the Polish environment. By registering the phenomenon of bridging group boundaries, aiming at their redefinition and their reestablishment in altered conditions, the popular novel thus records one of the most characteristic phenomena of modernity: a desire to create an order that excludes strangers.[35] By linking universalist and separatist rhetoric, it introduces (and reconstructs) a modern tension between the general and the particular. Therefore, its depiction of contemporary tendencies is as sharp and penetrating as in the literature of the elites.

Notes

1. S-w. [N. Sokołów], "Czym jest i czym powinna być tzw. *powieść żydowska*," *Izraelita*, no. 18 (1892).
2. Ibid.
3. About point of view as an anthropological category cf. M. Czermińska, "Punkt widzenia jako kategoria narracyjna i antropologiczna w prozie niefikcjonalnej," *Teksty Drugie* 2003, no. 2–3.
4. An example of this type of tendency might be *Mirtala* by Eliza Orzeszkowa or numerous historical novels on Casimir the Great and Esterka. Cf. C. Shmeruk, *The Esterke Story in Yiddish and Polish Literature: A Case Study in the Mutual Relations of Two Cultural Traditions* (Jerusalem, 1985).
5. For a discussion of works that combine the patterns associated with different genres, see M. Głowiński, "Trzy poetyki *Niecierpliwych*," in *Porządek, chaos, znaczenie. Szkice o powieści współczesnej* (Warsaw, 1968), 211–21.
6. The tendency of "the Jews' equal rights to emotions" in the prose of the nineteenth century was written about by Wacław Borowy, "Z dziejów uczuciowego równouprawnienia Żydów," in *Kamienne rękawiczki* (Warsaw, 1932).

7. The adoption of the means of high literature by popular literature of the turn of the century was analyzed in detail by Jacek Kolbuszewski, "Oswajanie modernizmu. O poetyce powieści popularnych lat 1896–1905," in *W kręgu historii i teorii literatury. Księga pamiątkowa ku czci Jana Trzynadlowskiego*, ed. B. Zakrzewski and A. Bazan (Wrocław, 1976).

8. This is the classification used by G. Simmel, "Obcy" in, Simmel, *Socjologia*, trans. M. Łukasiewicz (Warsaw, 1986). See also W. T. Bartoszewski, "Poles and Jews as the *Other*," *Polin* 4 (1989).

9. W. Łoś, *Ze Starżów pani Appelstein* (Warsaw, 1897), 1:59.

10. W. Łoś, *Zięciowie domu Kohn et Cie* (Warsaw, 1895), 1:5.

11. J. U. Niemcewicz, *Lejbe i Sióra, czyli Listy dwóch kochanków* (Kraków, 1931), 112.

12. W. Łoś, *Drugie życie pani Appelstein* (Warsaw, 1904), 48. "But it just happened in Bonn at the university that young Kroński, whom his pals accused of being born of a mother whose maiden name was Cohn, killed himself."

13. This is the assessment of the assimilation project by Z. Bauman, *Wieloznaczność nowoczesna, nowoczesność wieloznaczna*, trans. J. Bauman (Warsaw, 1995).

14. The assimilation project as a trap is discussed in ibid.

15. The notion of open and hidden boundaries comes from sociology. Cf. E. Nowicka, S. Łodziński, *U progu otwartego świata. Poczucie polskości i nastawienia Polaków wobec cudzoziemców w latach 1988 –1998* (Kraków, 2001).

16. Łoś, *Ze Starżów pani Appelstein*, 1:36–37.

17. Z. Bauman, *Etyka ponowoczesna*, trans. J. Bauman, J. Tokarska-Bakir (Warsaw, 1996).

18. A. Gruszecki, *Nawrócony* (Warsaw, 1901).

19. Cf. H. Bhabha, "DissemiNation: Time, Narrative, and the Margins of Modern Nation," in *Nation and Narration*, ed. H. Bhabha (London, 1990).

20. M. Gawalewicz, *Mechesy* (Lwów, 1925), 1:290–91.

21. Ibid., 2:360.

22. Łoś, *Zięciowie domu Kohn et Cie*, 2:41.

23. The scheme is reconstructed in his works by Sander Gilman.

24. Cf. T. Todorov, "'Race,' Writing, and Culture," in *"Race," Writing, and Difference*, ed. H. L. Gates (Chicago and London, 1986).

25. About racial manicheism, see L. Poliakov, *The Aryan Myth: A History of Racist and Nationalist Ideas in Europe*, trans. E. Howard (Edinburgh, 1974), 101, 272–77.

26. Such descriptions in romantic prose are discussed in more detail in my article "Tematy żydowskie wobec orientalizmu," in *Problematyka żydowska w romantyzmie polskim*, ed. A. Fabianowski and M. Makaruk (Warsaw, 2005).

27. Łoś, *Drugie życie pani Appelstein*, 1:70.

28. Gawalewicz, *Mechesy*, 1:326.

29. S. Gilman, "The Jewish Nose: Are the Jews White? Or, The History of the Nose Job," in *Encountering the Other(s): Studies in Literature, History, and Culture*, ed. G. Brinkler-Gabler (New York, 1995).

30. Łoś, *Drugie życie pani Appelstein*, 1:15.

31. Łoś, *Ze Starżów pani Appelstein*, 1:15.

32. Łoś, *Drugie życie Pani Appelstein*, 1:31.

33. P. Jaxa Bykowski, *Faktor hetmański. Powieść zeszłowieczna* (Warsaw, 1881), 3. Jan Jeleński was a propagator of anti-Semitic views and editor-in-chief of an anti-Semitic periodical, *Rola*.

34. A synthetic view of the assimilation of the Jews in Polish literature is presented in H. Markiewicz, "Asymilacja Żydów jako temat literatury polskiej," in *Literatura i historia* (Kraków, 1994).

35. Z. Bauman, "Sen o czystości," in *Ponowoczesność jako źródło cierpień* (Warsaw, 2000), 25.

Chapter 5

Cul-de-Sac: The "Inner Life of Jews" on the Fin-de-Siècle Polish Stage

Michael C. Steinlauf

This chapter uses the vicissitudes of Polish popular theater in the late nineteenth and early twentieth centuries as a portal through which to explore Polish-Jewish relations at a key moment in the history of both peoples. The phenomenon of Polish-language theater aimed at a Jewish popular audience emerged as Poles and Jews encountered each other amid mass audiences in new urban settings. It was a product of the cultural interplay stimulated by urban life. But unlike in Western Europe and the United States, the potential of a unitary mass culture was undermined by growing currents of national cultural strife to which Polish-Jewish theater ultimately succumbed.

Theater was of particular importance for both Poles and Jews in the half century before World War I. Russian retribution for the 1863 uprising included an assault on Polish language and culture. With schools and cultural institutions closed, it was only on the stage that the Polish language could still publicly resound. A comparable situation prevailed in Prussian Poland amidst the so-called *Kulturkampf* against Polish culture. In Austrian Galicia, where political and cultural freedom prevailed, the neo-Romantic movement known as Młoda Polska (Young Poland) flourished, with its celebrated dramatist Stanisław Wyspiański (1869–1907). While throughout Europe during these decades, star-struck audiences swooned in fashionable "theatromania," in Poland such passions were intensified by powerful national symbolism; Polish theater became a "national pantheon of virtue" and "field of national battle."[1]

But also during this period, as masses of small-town Jews moved into the largest Polish cities, Jews became increasingly evident in Polish theater audiences. Already by mid-century the Warsaw Jewish plutocracy had become fixtures in the front rows of the State Theaters (Teatry Rządowe), while in the upper balcony (the so-called *paradyż*), Yiddish-speaking Jews in traditional dress were a common sight.[2] Such Jews also attended the popular garden theaters that multiplied in the 1870s.[3] "Jews" in various incarnations were also ever-present on the stage. Most common was the singing and dancing little Jew (*żydek*), grimacing and babbling a broken Polish-Jewish jargon, a kind of Polish Black Sambo. Increasingly common was the figure of the Jewish assimilator, attempting to trade his newly acquired fortune for a pretty Polish wife and a noble title.[4] A new figure was Józio Grojseszyk (Big Chic), the popular hero of Feliks Schober's *Podróż po Warszawie* (A journey through Warsaw) and several sequels, a high-spirited wheeler-dealer who knew all the ins and outs of the Warsaw demimonde. Józio was the avatar of a new urban world in which national distinctions seemed to blur in the simple search for pleasure.[5]

None of these figures or the plays in which they appeared were directed specifically at a Jewish audience. Indeed, a mass Jewish theater audience did not emerge until the rise of Yiddish theater several years later. In the early 1880s, the Yiddish plays of Avrom Goldfaden, the "father of Yiddish theater," were first staged in Warsaw; in 1886 Goldfaden himself oversaw Warsaw productions of his popular historical operettas *Bar Kokhba* and *Shulamis*. Goldfaden's plays created a large and enthusiastic theater audience. But in the years immediately following and until the 1905 Revolution, tsarist authorities made it difficult to stage Yiddish works; during this period, many Yiddish actors and directors abandoned the Russian Empire for London and New York.[6] In the absence of a Yiddish theater, Polish versions of Goldfaden's plays were mounted. A cabaret couplet attributed to Polish actors attests to the popularity of these productions: "*Jak by nie Sulamita/To by dawno z nami było kwita*" (If not for Shulamis/ We'd have been finished long ago).[7]

As masses of Poles and Jews began to encounter each other in new urban environments, their traditional relationships began to change. On one hand, an emerging popular culture, comparable in this respect to its counterparts in Western cities, brought Jews recently arrived from small towns and Poles from peasant villages into regular contact as they searched for inexpensive entertainment. A new popular audience in Warsaw sought out summer diversions such as garden theaters, traveling zoos, marionette theaters, military bands, gas balloons, and fireworks.[8] But in Eastern Europe there was a powerful countervailing process as well: the emergence of new forms of national consciousness, inevitably political, which aimed to reconfigure identity and therefore reconstruct social barriers on a new foundation.

For Poles, the last years of the nineteenth century saw the founding of two modern political parties espousing two different national aspirations: the Polish Socialist Party (PPS) and the National Democratic Party

(Endecja). The PPS inherited the approach of the Polish Positivists of the 1870s and 1880s: those Jews who identified as Poles, presumably increasingly numerous, were to be welcomed into the struggle for an independent Poland. Frequently cited were the works of the Positivist writer Eliza Orzeszkowa, in whose most celebrated novel *Meir Ezofowicz*, first published in 1878, an enlightened Jewish hero enamored of Polish culture takes on the backward and corrupt Jewish establishment.[9] More ominous for Jews was the ideology of the Endecja, whose "integral nationalism" identified "Polishness" with Polish ethnic stock and Roman Catholicism. Pointing to the lack of a native Polish middle class as a national weakness and espousing the slogan "national egoism," the National Democrats, amidst European repercussions of the Dreyfus Affair, began to regard Jews as an alien element whose influence had to be combatted and whose economic functions taken over by ethnic Poles.

The turn of the century also witnessed the founding of the first Jewish political parties. Despite a multitude of ideological differences, Jewish political activity as such heralded a new Jewish consciousness that expressed itself in demands for civil and national rights and a new Jewish culture in Yiddish and Hebrew. In Poland, assimilationism was put on the defensive; by World War I, even as increasing numbers of Jews learned Polish, it had become largely irrelevant as an ideology. In relation to Poles, Jewish activists were prepared to offer, but also expected to receive, cooperation in the struggle against tsarism. But if such solidarity was scorned, the increasingly prevalent Jewish response was combative. In 1912, the Yiddish writer and culture hero Y. L. Peretz declared to Poles: "If you don't want our cooperation, that's your business. You will *push us out*, and we will defend ourselves: defend ourselves with all the strength of our racial stubbornness."[10] Such a stance began to emerge as well in Jewish responses to Polish culture, especially where images of Jews themselves were concerned. In 1903 in Warsaw, the future Yiddish folklorist and political leader Noyekh Prilutski (Pryłucki, 1882–1941) was arrested for organizing a demonstration protesting the performance of an anti-Semitic Polish play.[11]

The first studies of Jewish folklore also began to appear at the fin-de-siècle. Polish interest in *ludoznawstwo*, the study of peasant folklore and ethnography, had begun earlier[12] and for some Poles at least stimulated a corresponding interest in the folkways of the Jewish *lud*, whose "inner life" had first been revealed in Orzeszkowa's *Meir Ezofowicz* and Klemens Junosza's Polish translations of modern Yiddish literature.[13] But in the 1880s, systematic knowledge of Jewish folklore did not yet exist. The Polish-speaking Jewish intelligentsia, its only possible source, were either incapable or unwilling to initiate such study, and it was not until the very last years of the nineteenth century, and, indeed, primarily at the initiative of Polish ethnographers, that the first such studies were under-taken.[14]

The representation of folklore was particularly suited to the stage. In Kraków, Wyspiański's symbolist spectacles were steeped in folklore, while the following "recipe" for the "folk plays" that flooded the garden theaters appeared in the contemporary Polish press: "Take a woman drunkard and a peasant with bad instincts, add to this a scoundrelous Jewish tavern keeper, mix together with the kindly oldest patriarch in the village, baste with a sauce of pseudo-poetic bucolic idyll, sprinkle everything with spells, prayer, wonders, and you will have a folk play."[15] Criticism of such plays sparked efforts to create a didactic "folk theater" that would "educate and elevate" Polish artisans and factory workers, particularly about the importance of sobriety. The result was the government-sponsored Teatr Ludowy, established in Warsaw in 1899.[16]

There were parallel calls for the creation of a Polish-language "folk theater" for Jews.[17] Encouraged by such voices, by the success of Goldfaden's plays on garden theater stages, and the languishing condition of Yiddish theater, garden theater impresarios began to search for a way to attract the mass audiences that had made *Sulamita* such a lucrative enterprise. The major obstacle to such an endeavor was a complete lack of suitable plays,[18] reflecting pervasive Polish ignorance of Jewish folkways. It is ironic yet hardly uncharacteristic of the vicissitudes of Polish-Jewish cultural relations that when Lucjan Dobrzański, who had brought *Shulamis* to the Polish stage, finally commissioned a new "Jewish play" for his garden theater, the playwright was a Pole sympathetic to Jews, but with little experience of traditional Jewish life or contact with the new Jewish ethnographers. The play was *Małka Szwarcenkopf*, its author Gabriela Zapolska.

Zapolska (Maria Gabriela Stefania Piotrowska, 1857–1921), novelist, journalist, playwright, actress, and theater director, was an anomalous figure in turn-of-the-century Polish literature.[19] Influenced by Polish Positivism, more so by French naturalism, relatively oblivious to fashionable neo-Romantic currents, and habitually encircled by violent controversy and scandalous gossip, Zapolska declared lifelong war on bourgeois society and identified with its victims: peasants, artisans, servants, workers, and especially women. Many of her early works are built around the figure of a noble-spirited woman struggling against scoundrelous manipulating males; later in her career, savage parodies of domestic hypocrisy predominate; sensational subjects such as infanticide and venereal disease are common in her work. Zapolska sought to appeal to a popular audience: "I like to write for the masses and to have masses at my disposition," she declared in an interview. "I like melodrama and aspire to refine it."[20] As an actress, she was acclaimed for her role as Ibsen's Nora, yet she never realized her dream of performing in the State Theaters and instead spent years touring with provincial troupes and performing in Warsaw garden theaters, finally, however, achieving recognition on the "respectable" Kraków and Lwów stages. Zapolska's insider's knowledge of the theater world was rare among Polish dramatists; her plays— "not books, but scenarios"—were no sooner written than staged, often directed by or starring Zapolska herself.[21]

In 1895, upon her return from several years in Paris and finding the State Theaters still closed to her, Zapolska began to perform at Dobrzański's Wodewil "garden," supplying him as well with a stage adaptation of one of her novels, which played with little success. In 1897 Dobrzański decided to operate on a grander scale and rented two theaters, including the large Eldorado, whose regular public by now consisted "primarily of *kapote*-wearing Jewry"[22] attending Yiddish and Polish plays. But after staging a series of flops, he realized, in the words of the theater historian Zbigniew Raszewski, that "only some sensational novelty could save him." Moreover, "it was no secret what kind of repertoire could save the Eldorado. Unfortunately, discovering a drama that would tempt an audience from Nalewki or Muranów [Warsaw Jewish neighborhoods] did not come easily."[23] Finally, in May 1897, Dobrzański commissioned Zapolska to write an appropriate play. "Possessing all the riddles and secrets of the theater public's taste," and lacking prejudice ("to the contrary, the anti-Semitism coming into fashion at that time . . . could only provoke her to a public assertion of her views"), Zapolska was "really the only dramatist working with the 'gardens' who could fill the severe gap in their repertoire."[24] Scarcely a month later the play was finished and opened at the Eldorado, with an all-Polish cast, on 10 July 1897.

Małka Szwarcenkopf was a "stupefying success."[25] Already during the first days of the production, "thousands of Jews daily mob[bed] the box office,"[26] while on Długa Street scalpers hawked contraband tickets.[27] During the first several weeks, the audience never numbered fewer than a thousand.[28] Poles were amazed by the size and character of this audience. One critic wondered at "the army of *kapote*-wearing Jews whose crowds frequent the Eldorado. Their naive though often coarse cries, their raptures when they see a characteristic scene of their life are the best recommendation that the play was written from carefully gathered documents of life. And these *kapote*-wearers listen to a play written in Polish and understand perfectly."[29] At one performance, an attempted protest by Orthodox Jews was deafened by applause,[30] while a contemporary cartoon depicts a crowd of Jews explaining to the janitor of Zapolska's building that they "would like to see at least her maid."[31] According to an anonymous verse: "Jews are laughing in delight,/ At every other moment./ When someone pipes up louder,/ 'Shtil!' they yell at once."[32] When Zapolska herself appeared in the title role on 14 August, she was deluged with flowers and gifts.[33] Even governing circles noticed; for the first time in the history of the garden theaters, a production was attended by an official Russian representative.[34] By the end of the summer, Dobrzański had staged *Małka* in three different theaters,[35] pocketed a fortune, and attained another first: the extension of the garden theater season to permit further performances of the play.[36] From Warsaw, *Małka* went to Łódź, Lwów, Poznań, Lublin, and Kraków.[37] In the latter city, a bastion of high Polish culture, the play was performed by some of the greatest stars of the Polish theater;[38] the reception after the premiere was held at the Jewish-owned Hotel Metropol, and invitations were printed in Polish and Yiddish.[39] *Małka* became the most popular play in the history of the garden theaters[40] and continued to be staged for years to come; until World War II it was produced in Poland more than twenty-five times[41] and was staged as well in Czech, German, Russian, and Yiddish.[42]

Małka Szwarcenkopf,[43] like Orzeszkowa's *Meir Ezofowicz* and Karl Gutzkow's *Uriel Acosta*,[44] its influential predecessors in Polish literature and theater, respectively, is about the doomed struggle of the one against the many, individual light against collective darkness. The play is enacted by a heroine cut from Zapolska's characteristic mold. Małka, whose father sells matches in front of the Eldorado, has had the good fortune to be sent abroad for her education by a wealthy aunt. When Małka's aunt dies, however, and her fortune is squandered by her wastrel heir, Małka has no choice but to return to the "ghetto." There she falls in love with Jakub Lewi, an "enlightened" young lawyer's assistant, to whom she laments: "I was rescued from a stinking cellar of superstitions and allowed to breathe with a full breast, until suddenly . . . I was thrust into the darkness which I had left."[45] But when Jakub informs Małka that his parents have betrothed him to a wealthy young woman, Małka consents to her father's plans for her marriage to the simpleton Jojne Firułkes. She becomes a shopkeeper and devotes herself to her husband: "If only I could rouse that snail-like soul to life and strike some sparks of noble instinct."[46] Jakub returns, however, and asks for Małka's hand if she will but divorce Jojne. Before her assembled family, Małka announces her desire for a divorce because "every human being has the right to want to live and be happy." Moreover, "no document, no marriage contract permits you to imprison the soul of a woman who apprehends life differently from you and needs something else from life."[47] Furious with rage, her father locks her in his room and commences, along with Małka's father-in-law, to haggle with Jakub over financial arrangements. Only Jojne, transformed by Małka's power, refuses to bargain: "I won't sell her," he declares to Jakub, "but I'll give her to you."[48] Just as, unknown to her, an agreement is reached, Małka poisons herself.

What was there in this melodrama that appealed so mightily to Jewish as well as Polish audiences? Polish critics, regardless of their assessment of the play's dramatic virtues, unanimously pointed to its sensational novelty. *Małka Szwarcenkopf*, like Orzeszkowa's *Meir Ezofowicz* and Junosza's Yiddish translations, was treated as a cultural breakthrough that seemed to offer Poles an authentic glimpse of an exotic world located so near and yet so far from Polish reality. In a characteristic formulation, a contemporary critic declared: "Madame Zapolska, for the first time in theater, with great dramatic power and profound knowledge of the environment, was able to draw aside a corner of the mysterious curtain beyond which hides that 'terra incognita' which is the Jewish community, and first brought it onto the stage with an intention other than mockery."[49] The notion of the Jewish world as a dark continent that required exploration remained rooted in Polish perceptions of Jews until World War II.[50] Zapolska, according to reviewers, had breached the darkness particularly with her "genre scenes" (*sceny rodzajowe* or *obyczajowe*), the "greatest ornament of the play," in which the author had drawn from the "treasure-house of [Jewish] custom."[51] Therein, it was assumed, lay the secret of the play's appeal to Jewish audiences as well.

But Zapolska's ethnography was problematic. For example, the scene of Małka's engagement, presided over amid "Jewish" dances and songs by a *marshelik* (wedding jester or *badkhn*) speaking and singing in "Yiddish," inspired widespread acclaim. But this scene, even in the printed version of the play,[52] bears little resemblance to any known Jewish ceremony. It is filled with errors of ritual (e.g., a group of young girls dance around Małka and present her with flowers) and language (the engagement contract itself [*tnoyim*] is called *tuchim*) and is written in a stylized Polish-Yiddish jargon, with which, indeed, the play as a whole is filled. Moreover, in the original stage version of the play, in which Zapolska left the jester's actual lines to the discretion of the stage director and the actor playing the role, a "certain deception" occurred, according to the Polish-Jewish journalist and ethnographer Henryk Lew: "The [theater] direction turned to one of the local 'marsheliks' for the Hebrew text to the engagement act; the clever 'marshelik,' convinced that in the theater they wanted to mock the engagement ceremony, in place of the real text gave a parody consisting of curses and cheap jokes."[53]

In contrast to previous Polish writers of "Jewish plays" but like Orzeszkowa in *Meir Ezofowicz*, Zapolska indeed made efforts to assure the "authenticity" of her work: "The couplets and *tuchim* [*sic*] were written by an authentic *marshelik*," she stated in a letter to a Polish newspaper, "[and] my engagement scene I wrote from the information of two peddlers of used goods."[54] Jewish audiences may have sensed Zapolska's good intentions, but their laughter, well noted by Polish critics, was doubtless not that of delight. Ironic and indicative of the cultural abyss that continued to separate Poles and Jews is the Polish interpretation of this Jewish mirth, as well as the very writing of a "Jewish play" which, with the best of intentions, could only parody actual Jewish customs.

Beyond ethnography itself, however flawed, were the uses to which it was put. As reviewers for the Polish-language *Izraelita* pointed out, *Małka* had broken with the "commonplace and threadbare caricatures,"[55] the staples of garden theater fare, and "without racial-denominational hatred, without a prior desire to present Jews in a negative or positive light, Madame Zapolska peered into the Jewish community, and with a photographic device, flickering to be sure, captured an entire succession of characters."[56] Unlike Wyspiański, for whom folklore elaborated a mysterious national mythology, Zapolska used her "ethnography" to capture "unvarnished" social reality on the stage. However far from the aspirations of Młoda Polska, naturalism was hardly exhausted elsewhere in Polish theater nor further abroad. Gorky's *The Lower Depths*, which premiered in Stanislavsky's Moscow Art Theater in 1902, created a huge stir with its brutal representation of lost souls crammed into a Russian rooming house. And in New York beginning in the 1890s, the Yiddish melodramas of Jacob Gordin were hailed as a historic breakthrough in depicting the actual life of the Jewish masses.

Zapolska's work was cut from similar cloth. Her Jewish world, dark, to be sure, was not, however, as unremittingly bleak as Gorky's. There is a kind of dignity in some of her figures, as, for example, the market vendor Jenta, whose folk wisdom guides Małka through the mores of her new environment, and who laments dealing in stolen goods in order to feed her sick mother and four children.[57] There are assimilated Jews as well, but here Zapolska makes them the object of ridicule, and from a Jewish perspective: an elegant cardsharp with the unlikely name Kolumna Wiedeński (Viennese Column) is unmasked by Jenta as her long-lost brother-in-law Mowsze in a slapstick scene,[58] while Jakub Lewi proudly announces to several decadent assimilators that he wouldn't change his name for anything in the world.[59] Furthermore, in focusing on the custom of arranged marriages as the instrument of Małka's destruction, Zapolska chose a theme hardly foreign to Jewish audiences, but placed it in a modern context. Arranged marriages (as well as *hadorim* [traditional elementary schools], the object of her concern in *Jojne Firułkes*, the sequel to *Małka*) had been regularly attacked by Jewish and Polish reformers since the beginning of the nineteenth century and were constantly parodied in Yiddish literature and theater. Indeed, Jojne Firułkes bears more than a passing resemblance to Goldfaden's famous

Kuni Leml, the stuttering yeshiva student whose name became synonymous with what a Jewish girl least wanted in a husband. What was new, however, was situating such a character not in a folklorized shtetl but in the "realistic" urban environment of contemporary Warsaw.

Finally, and perhaps most significant, there is Małka herself. There is nothing particularly Jewish about her; she is, rather, a conventional Zapolska heroine, ensnared this time in Jewish "darkness." Yet precisely because of her "universality," for many young turn-of-the-century Warsaw Jews, whose lives had begun to be rent by profound intergenerational and domestic conflicts, Małka's simple declaration that "every human being has the right to want to live and be happy" probably struck a responsive chord. In *Małka Szwarcenkopf*, therefore, Warsaw Jews gained something even Goldfaden had not been able to give them: the first, however flawed, theatrical reflection, several years before the production of comparable Yiddish plays,[60] of themselves, and of the domestic tensions within modern urban Jewish society. Simultaneously, and against the backdrop of rising national tensions, Zapolska's play presented for the first time, for those Poles who chose to see what was similar rather than what was alien, everyday Jews who were human despite their customs. *Małka Szwarcenkopf* taught Poles, in the words of a contemporary critic, "to love the human being in the Jew, and as such [bore] a wonderful element of harmony and understanding."[61]

"If such a *Małka Szwarcenkopf*," declared an article in *Izraelita*, "which, it is true, betrays sparks of talent, acuteness of observation in several parts, which, however, cannot be considered an accomplished work of realistic art, if such a *Małka* met with such a warm reception, what will happen if Madame Zapolska or another with her talent, with complete concentration, gravity and scrupulousness, describes the inner life of Jews!"[62] The enormous success of *Małka Szwarcenkopf* inspired a new development in Polish theater: the production of a succession of "Jewish ethnographic [*ludoznawcze*]" plays on garden theater stages.[63]

These plays, of extremely varying quality and "tendency," none of which remotely approached *Małka Szwarcenkopf*'s popularity nor, with one exception, rivaled it as a work of "realistic art," were, however, a "trend" that was widely noted. The premiere of *Jojne Firułkes*, Zapolska's sequel to *Małka*, led one critic, exaggerating only slightly, to remark: "The Wodewil Theater has devoted nine-tenths of its repertoire during this summer season to Jews. The success of *Małka Szwarcenkopf* last year prompted Mr. Dobrzański to stage the ostensible sequel, [which], let us hope, for the following year will beget Laja [Jojne's sweetheart] with children whom they will raise to be heroes of a new Jewish tragedy."[64] Two years later, a review of Wilhelm Feldman's *Cudotwórca* (The miracle worker) begins: "When several years ago, Zapolska for the first time presented *Małka Szwarcenkopf* to the theater public, no one expected that the play would be the beginning of a small 'current' in our literature, the first of a whole series of works based on Jewish themes."[65] And in a note on the premiere of *Cudotwórca*, the Polish Jewish critic Alfred Lor, having referred to the presence in the theater of his colleagues from *Izraelita*, testifies to the interest of the Yiddish literary world as well: "Looming out of the distance, the dark profiles of Y. L. Peretz and . . . Dr. Eliashev [the young Yiddish literary critic Bal-Makhshoves]."[66]

In Zapolska's *Jojne Firułkes*,[67] her sequel to *Małka Szwarcenkopf*, Małka's bumbling, simple-minded husband, literally haunted by his martyred beloved, is transformed into an apostle of "enlightened" education, productive labor, and brotherly love ("an ethic," a Polish reviewer declared, "no longer having anything in common with the habits, customs and beliefs current in Jewish society")[68] for his benighted co-religionists. When Jojne happens upon his father attempting to burn down his store in order to collect insurance money, old Firułkes, stricken by apoplexy, hurls an oath of *chajrem* (*kherem*, excommunication) at his son with his dying breath. Workers at the matzah factory where Jojne is employed learn of the curse, and Jojne is beaten and expelled. A homeless wanderer, Jojne finally arrives at the cemetery where Małka is buried, and there, amidst the other-wordly figures of the old cemetery caretaker and his beautiful young daughter, finds his refuge.

Like *Małka Szwarcenkopf*, *Jojne Firułkes* was widely praised in the Polish press for its realistic re-creation of Jewish customs and "atmosphere." And indeed, Lucjan Dobrzański, who purchased this "Jewish play" as well from Zapolska, this time for the unheard of sum of three thousand rubles,[69] made extraordinary efforts at "authenticity." He brought the famous Ludwik Solski from Kraków to direct and star in the production, and, as Zapolska herself wrote, "gave him carte blanche for expenses, so that decorations were made in the State Theater [and] an entire *kheyder* along with *belfers* [assistant teachers] was engaged."[70] Such efforts were in vain, however. Neither a *kheyder* where Jewish children don't know the Hebrew alphabet, nor a "Purim ball" featuring a can-can, nor a child's funeral at which the grieving mother reckons up burial costs, nor the use of a *kherem* (employed, and rarely, only by religious authorities) by a father to curse his son—none of this bears any resemblance to anything Jewish and, as the Polish-Jewish journalist Henryk Lew correctly noted, "in fact, stands in contradiction to the Jewish spirit."[71]

Nor is there anything authentic or even sympathetic in the characters who populate this play. Humorless, driven by brutish hypocrisy and a desire for material gain already excessive in *Małka Szwarcenkopf* but here taken to tastelessness, they are largely interchangeable ciphers who, as Lew remarks, "were [they] dressed, instead of in *kapoty*, in *czi czun cza*, then we would have a Chinese melodrama, which naturally would have as much connection to Chinese life as [the play has] now to Jewish life."[72] *Jojne Firułkes*, moreover, fails dramatically as well. *Małka Szwarcenkopf*, unabashed melodrama, possessed plot development, dramatic tension, and a heroine with whom audiences could identify. In *Jojne Firułkes*, Zapolska, still aiming at a popular audience yet apparently aspiring to a "higher artistic level" as well, turned the simple Jojne into a moralizing symbol clothed in fashionable poetic haze and led him through a series of unmotivated martyrdoms to an absurd neo-Romantic denouement.[73]

Jojne Firułkes premiered at Dobrzański's Wodewil garden theater (the earlier part of the summer having featured a revival of *Małka Szwarcenkopf*)[74] on 23 July 1898, but closed after only nineteen performances.[75] Despite the considerable efforts of Zapolska and her collaborators to attract a Jewish audience, Jews "came reluctantly."[76] Zapolska herself, describing the Kraków production, wrote: "It was apparent that Jews were insulted. . . . Orthodox Jews *walk out of the theater* while the intelligentsia feels deeply offended. . . . At the second performance there was even hissing."[77] Although Zapolska attributed this reaction to changes introduced into the play by actors without her knowledge, it should be evident from the preceding that Jews were responding to the play as a whole.[78]

At the same time, a number of Polish reviewers began to sound a new note. Although *Małka Szwarcenkopf* had not gone without some criticism for its use of "żargon" on the Polish stage, with *Jojne* such objections multiplied and began to provoke further questions.[79] "Madame Zapolska will have to answer to serious charges," declared one Polish reviewer, "for the corruption of the Polish language on the stage. In what language and for whom is this work written?"[80] Another reviewer concluded that a work "not at all written in Polish" cannot be considered as belonging to Polish literature.[81]

Although such comments in themselves were as much a function of contemporary Polish nervousness about the integrity of Polish culture in the face of continuing Russification as of antipathy to Jews, there were also other, openly anti-Semitic responses which attacked the very presentation of Jewish subject matter on the Polish stage. "What concern can all this be to us?" polemicized the reviewer for a Warsaw tabloid:

That the *kheyders* are cramped, stuffy, and unhealthy for Jewish children is a matter for [the Hebrew periodical] *Ha-zefirah* and *Izraelita* to demand changes about, not the Polish stage; that there is ignorance and baseness among Jews, for that there are their own moralizers; but why present all this to us on the stage? If, on the other hand, Madame Zapolska wanted to show us that even a Jew can sometimes be noble, then it seems to us that she hasn't convinced anyone. Exceptions may and must occur everywhere, since there are even, it appears, gypsies who don't steal horses! Let us leave this kind of subject to Jewish authors, and this kind of theatrical masterpiece . . . to jargon theaters; it is a waste using Polish actors to sermonize to . . . Jews![82]

And another critic asked why "Jews, alone among themselves, for themselves alone, as a separate world, their blind fanatical ignorance among themselves," should concern Poles any more than the life of Hottentots or Zulus, and also concluded that such plays were "good for Jewish theater, but not for the national stage."[83] For the time being, such views were still in the minority and the reviewer for the mainstream Warsaw daily *Gazeta Warszawska* could respond to them by arguing: "We don't think that it compromises the Polish stage for a work of theater to propagate humanitarian and progressive ideas and exhort people to brotherly love; we believe, in fact, that it is its responsibility, as it is the responsibility of all right-thinking people to aid in this task."[84]

Some six weeks after the premiere of *Jojne Firułkes* at the Wodewil, Dobrzański opened another *"ludoznawcze"* play at his theater that brought Jew-baiting directly onto the stage. This was a work by the professional anti-Semite Teodor Jeske-Choiński entitled *Sara Weisblut.*[85] The play, named after a secondary character from an unstaged version of *Małka Szwarcenkopf,* and described by a Polish reviewer as a "monument to lack of talent and sense,"[86] centers around the efforts of its assimilated hero, freshly returned from African safaris, to reform small-town Jewish life. "We—work?" reply his co-religionists. "What are we, gentiles [*goye*], that we should work? We are a big, gigantic, enormous pike [*a grojser ogromner wielki szczupak*] which needs to swallow all these little fish. Come into partnership with us, and we'll swallow together." When the hero refuses, his neighbors respond by burning down his property. Pursued to the cemetery by a mob of what he has come to realize are "loathsome, blood-eating beasts," he shoots in self-defense but strikes and kills his beloved Paris-educated Sara Weisblut.[87]

A work of an entirely different sort, indeed, the first informed Polish-language play about Jewish life, was Wilhelm Feldman's *Sądy Boże* (God's judgments), which, starring the Jewish actor Julian Oskar, premiered at the Odeon garden theater in July 1899.[88] Feldman (1868–1919), born into a traditional Galician Jewish family, at an early age embraced both Polish culture and the mission of reforming Jewish society.[89] A talented writer, Feldman devoted himself primarily to Jewish matters in both essays and fiction until about the turn of the century. Thereafter he turned increasingly to Polish cultural affairs and gained renown as a political activist, literary critic, and the first historian of Młoda Polska. In his early fiction, Feldman examined the dilemma of Jews in the process of breaking away from traditional Jewish society, as well as the ambigu-

ous and often desolate situation of the already assimilated. The Polish
Jewish critic Ignacy Suesser credits him with "the truth of life in all its
nakedness, deeply felt and sharply seen," rather than either "sweet and
narcotic idealized scenes" or "nerve-shattering images of baseness and
corruption."[90] In his essays for *Izraelita* and the Lwów Jewish weekly *Ojczyzna* (Fatherland), Feldman advanced a typical assimilationist program
including demands for the abolition of *khadorim* and the eradication of
Yiddish.[91] He also advocated the creation of a Polish-language "folk theater" for Jews.[92] *Sądy Boże* was apparently Feldman's attempt to put into
practice this part of his cultural program, but in a manner far from ten-
dentiously assimilationist.

The play, set in a small Galician town, is about the fate of Manes, a
ruthless self-made rich man, who attempts to defraud the venerable
scholar Jochaja of his life savings. Manes claims that Jochaja entrusted
him with only eight hundred rubles when the latter traveled to the Holy
Land; Jochaja insists that the sum was eight thousand rubles, but cannot
produce the receipt. In desperation, Jochaja challenges Manes to swear
an oath in synagogue to the truth of his claim. When Manes, who has
labored all his life to achieve a social status that is now suddenly threatened, goes through with the ceremony, Jochaja, aghast at the blasphemy
to which he has brought Manes, falls dead. The townspeople now turn
against Manes, as does his own conscience. In the final act, while a stone
is erected on Jochaja's grave, a ruined Manes, babbling and child-like, is
led away from the cemetery by his family.

Sądy Boże was characterized by the Polish-Jewish critic Alfred Lor as
"the first attempt at a purely Jewish play"[93] on the Polish stage. Not only
is it, like *Małka Szwarcenkopf*, set exclusively among Jews, but it unfolds in
a closed realm little threatened by external change. For the first time,
"enlightenment" is not the issue. Indeed, amidst a gallery of well-drawn
traditional Jewish figures, the only assimilated characters (and the only
ones directed to speak in "pure Polish"), Manes's son Józef and the latter's fiancée Rózia, are the most compromised. When, in the play's climactic scene, Józef appears with the lost receipt, Rózia, concerned about
her future father-in-law's finances, convinces him to give it to Manes,
who destroys it and continues with his false oath. At the play's end, Józef
and Rózia, whose marriage will forever be tainted by their ugly secret,
are as crippled morally as Manes is psychologically.

If *Sądy Boże* has a specifically Jewish "moral," it is to point to the power
of Jewish religious ritual: the oath in synagogue, a celebration of Succos,
the dedication of Jochaja's gravestone.[94] Such scenes, romanticized to be
sure, but reflecting Feldman's knowledge of Jewish folkways, determine
the play's tone and structure and were doubtless its major attraction for
both Jewish and Polish audiences. Spectacular depictions of Jewish ritual

would be widespread in Yiddish theater when it reemerged in Poland after 1905. What *Sądy Boże*, in comparison with *Małka Szwarcenkopf*, chiefly lacked were positive heroes, and this Feldman set out to remedy in his next and last "Polish-Jewish" play, *Cudotwórca* (The miracle worker).

Staged by Dobrzański at his Wodewil theater in July 1900, *Cudotwórca* is set among Galician Hasidim.[95] While the play has several well-drawn minor characters (especially the half-assimilated Kayle-Chane, who calls herself "Szarlota-Żaneta" and dreams of "tyjatr" and "cybilizacja" [mispronunciations of "theater" and "civilization"]), this Jewish world is suffused with meanness and hypocrisy on the whole. The play is centered around two rather uninspiring and stereotypical "Jewish heroes." Feldman's heroine, the Kraków-educated Perla, contrasting Hasidic "dirt, stagnation, poverty, despair" with the "tidiness, work, prosperity, intelligence, great ideas"[96] among assimilated Jews, struggles against the decree of the fanatical "miracle worker" requiring her to marry the humble yeshiva student Gabryel. But Gabryel falls in love with Perla, reads the works of Orzeszkowa under her influence, and in the final scene suddenly transforms himself into a champion of "enlightenment" who excoriates the Hasidic "false prophet" from the synagogue pulpit. Menaced by a mob of Hasidim, Gabryel and Perla resolve to flee together in order to "further seek truth" and to "work . . . struggle . . . suffer!"[97]

Cudotwórca was denounced in the pages of *Izraelita* by Alfred Lor, who bewailed its "threadbare platitudes" as unworthy of "the creator of *Sądy Boże*."[98] Gabryel, Lor declares, is yet another in the increasingly enfeebled line of fictional Jewish reformers, beginning with Gutzkow's Uriel Acosta and Orzeszkowa's Meir Ezofowicz and ending with Jojne Firułkes and the hero of Jeske-Choiński's deplorable play, who "everywhere stand up . . . against rabbis, community councils, miracle workers, repeating the banal slogans of a quarter of a century ago, everywhere lecture the people from a pulpit and walk on high heels made of cheap cardboard, everywhere are false and unnatural."[99] In *Cudotwórca*, it seems, Feldman's assimilationism impoverished his imagination. He could not envision any arena worthy of Jewish heroism other than the already antiquated and schematicized struggle of "light" against "darkness." Lor, neverthless, ends his review with a positive assessment of Feldman's potential. He is a writer who "thanks to his knowledge of the milieu, the powers and nature of his talent, possesses all the requirements for creating true Jewish theater art [*sztuka żydowska*]. May it happen soon!"[100]

Yet for Feldman it was not to happen; *Cudotwórca* was his last "Jewish play."[101] Discussing these works, the Polish theater historian Zygmunt

Greń writes: "Feldman, in the last years of the century, during the most aggressive advance of modernist literature, with which he himself was in the fullest sympathy, returned in his 'hasidic' dramas to the ideas and ideology of the Positivists, to an issue which they had not ultimately resolved."[102] Feldman's positive hero, in other words, like Zapolska's, was old-fashioned. Aiming at a new mass audience, both writers returned to Orzeszkowa's stories of exemplary Jewish enlightenment and the "realistic" conventions of Positivist fiction. But whereas Orzeszkowa's writings epitomized the views on the "Jewish question" of an influential sector of the contemporary intelligentsia, by the turn of the century leading ideologues and their followers, both Polish and Jewish, were shifting to nationalist programs rather distant from the Positivist moralizing of *Cudotwórca*. For Feldman, the first Jew to write Polish-language plays intended for a Jewish audience, the disjunction between the demands of ideology and art was apparently too great. He could find no way of reconciling his concerns about the "Jewish question" with his devotion to Polish modernist culture, and the latter alone, finally, determined the course of his subsequent career. When, in 1920, Hasidism burst onto the stage with S. An-sky's *The Dybbuk*, it was a reconfigured Hasidism in the service both of modernist art and Jewish national renewal.[103]

Cudotwórca, Feldman's last initiative in the realm of "Jewish theater art," provided the occasion for Alfred Lor to initiate a series of articles in *Izraelita* entirely devoted to the subject.[104] In addition to reviewing and commenting on current productions (lamenting, for example, the "tasteless couplets, Jewish can-cans, and other . . . *majufesy*" which garden theater impresarios customarily introduced into all "Jewish plays"),[105] Lor approaches the phenomenon of "Jewish theater" as a whole. He critically summarizes the history of "Jewish plays" and characters on the Polish stage, describes the Jewish and the Polish theater audiences for such productions,[106] and, finally, predicts the development of "a new category of Jewish [theater] art," diversified, like its Polish counterpart, along genre and class lines. Such theater would include "works about the life of the Jewish masses, to employ a technical term, *in crudo*," as well as works presenting an "objective and comprehensive" picture of the Jewish intelligentsia.[107] But, having sketched a program for a future "Polish-Jewish theater,"[108] Lor concludes by expressing doubts about the entire project, placing them in the mouth of his "friend," Dr. E., a passionate part-time Zionist, "Cyprist," and card player: "You forget, that because of the fathomless racial difference, Aryan society will not be able to feel and understand real Jewish art. So all the work will be in vain, and for Jews it's already better to write in Yiddish or to introduce Hebrew onto the stage."[109]

These words proved remarkably prescient. During the 1905 Revolution and after, official barriers to the staging of Yiddish theater as well as the publication of Yiddish newspapers were lifted. In Warsaw, numerous Yiddish companies began to perform and daily newspapers printed reviews and schedules. A mass Jewish culture surged into being nearly overnight, with newspapers and theaters as its cornerstones. "Jewish folk theater" became a reality, though not with the goals nor in the language that Wilhelm Feldman had proposed. The garden theaters and the official Teatr Ludowy closed their doors; the loss of their Jewish audiences was probably a major factor in their disappearance. Over the following decades, a canonized Yiddish theater, some of it, like *The Dybbuk*, modernist in impulse, developed as well, but most Jewish theater in Poland until World War II remained popular in character. Significant numbers of Jews also followed Feldman's path into high Polish literature and theater, where, like Feldman, their links to Jewish concerns were minimal.[110]

A Polish-language culture intended for Jews developed most extensively in the realm of journalism, secondarily in literature.[111] As tensions grew between Poles and Jews in interwar Poland, theater, the locus of powerful national aspirations on the part of both peoples, largely resisted hyphenation. The primary exception, the career of Mark Arnshteyn (Andrzej Marek, ca. 1879–1943), proved the rule. His Polish productions of Yiddish "classics" in the 1920s provoked bitter accusations from the Jewish side that Arnshteyn was encouraging assimilation; he soon abandoned the enterprise.[112] Large numbers of Jews achieved full command of the Polish language, and Poles and Jews came into contact with each other in myriad ways, including in Polish theater audiences. In addition to attending Yiddish theater, Jews often constituted, it seems, a majority of the audience for Polish theater.[113] Nevertheless, most of cultural life as a whole and theater in particular developed along two tracks, and Poles were generally unaware of the Jewish culture flourishing in their midst. A "Chinese wall," it was commonly said, separated the two peoples.

At the turn of the century, it had seemed possible that within a new urban environment a common culture might develop, along the western model, in which national distinctions would blur, and that theater might "propagate humanitarian and progressive ideas and exhort people to brotherly love."[114] But the very processes that brought people together in the big cities also divided them in new ways in Eastern Europe. The initiatives of Zapolska and Feldman, even as they offered Polish Jews a reflection of their own lives often before the comparable representations of Yiddish theater, proved to have little future.

Notes

This chapter is based on a chapter of my forthcoming book, *Hazards of the Borderlands: Mark Arnshteyn and Polish-Jewish Theater.*

1. "Pantheon cnoty narodowy" (national pantheon of virtue): J. Kościelski, "Prolog na otwarcie Teatru Polskiego w Poznaniu," *"Proscenium"*— *Teatr Polski 1875–1965* (Poznań, 1965), 54, as cited in Stanisław Marczak-Oborski, *Teatr w Polsce 1918–1939: Wielkie ośrodki* (Warsaw, 1984), 7. The poem hailed the opening of a new Polish theater in Poznań in 1875. "Pole narodowej bitwy" (field of national battle): Artur Oppman [Or-ot], "Pierwszy wieczór," in his *Wiersze wybrane* (Warsaw, 1958), 135, as cited in Marczak-Oborski, *Teatr w Polsce 1918–1939*, 8. The poem was dedicated to the opening performance of Arnold Szyfman's Teatr Polski in Warsaw in 1913. See also Michael C. Steinlauf, "Jews and Polish Theater in Nineteenth-Century Warsaw," *Polish Review* (New York) 32 (1987): 442–43.

2. The State Theaters, which were operated by the Russian government, were an important source of income. By mid-century there were two theaters, Wielki and Rozmaitości; by the end of the century there were seven. After the 1863 uprising, with one exception, their directors were Russian.

3. See Steinlauf, "Jews and Polish Theater," 444–52.

4. See Michael C. Steinlauf, "Mr. Geldhab and Sambo in Peyes: Images of the Jew on the Polish Stage, 1863–1905," *Polin* 4 (1989): 98–128.

5. See Michael C. Steinlauf, "Józio Grojseszyk: A Jewish City Slicker on the Warsaw Popular Stage," forthcoming in a work tentatively entitled *Jewish Theatre*, edited by Edna Nahshon.

6. On the theater ban, see John Klier, " 'Exit, Pursued by a Bear': Russian Administrators and the Ban on Yiddish Theatre in Imperial Russia," in *Yiddish Theatre: New Approaches*, ed. Joel Berkowitz (Oxford, 2003), 159–74.

7. Zalmen Zilbertsvayg [Zylbercwaig], "Goldfaden af der poylisher bine," in *Teatr mozayik* (New York, 1941), 231; on Goldfaden in Polish see also Jacob Shatzky, "Goldfaden in Varshe," *Yivo bleter* (New York) 15 (1940): 265–80.

8. Albert F. McLean Jr., in his *American Vaudeville as Ritual* (Lexington, Ky., 1965), calls this audience the New Folk.

9. On Orzeszkowa and her influential "Jewish" fiction, see Gabriella Safran, *Rewriting the Jew: Assimilation Narratives in the Russian Empire* (Stanford, 2000), 63–107.

10. "Di frage," *Haynt*, 1912; reprinted in Y. L. Peretz, *Ale verk*, vol. 9 (New York, 1947), 273. The words emphasized by Peretz were common Endecja rhetoric. His racial rhetoric suggests a stance that is the counterpart of his Polish antagonists. Poles, of course, could not read Yiddish. But Peretz doubtless felt that their inability to decipher words addressed to them in the leading Jewish daily was their problem and not his. His words were also intended to influence Jewish voters during an important electoral campaign.

11. *Leksikon fun der nayer yidisher literatur*, vol. 7 (New York, 1968), col. 217.

12. Oskar Kolberg (1814–90) had pioneered in the field of Polish ethnography as early as the 1840s, but it was not until the 1880s and particularly in Warsaw when interest in peasant life began to assume political significance, that *ludoznawstwo* came into its own. In 1885, Jan Popławski founded the weekly *Głos*, whose platform called for the incorporation of the peasant into Polish national life (Popławski later moved from populism to the Endecja as one of its founding

ideologues). In 1887, *Wisła* (Vistula), the first Polish journal exclusively devoted to folklore and ethnography, began to appear in Warsaw under the editorship (from 1888) of Jan Karłowicz (1836–1903).

13. Junosza [Szaniawski] published translations of two works by Mendele Moykher Sforim [Sh. Y. Abramovitsh]: *Donkiszot żydowski. Szkic z literatury żargonowej* (an adaptation of *Masoes Binyomin hashlishi*, Warsaw, 1885); *Szkapa* (an adaptation of *Di klyatshe*, Warsaw, 1886).

14. In 1890, Aleksander Świętochowski, the dean of Polish Positivists, published an appeal in *Wisła* for information on Jewish provincial life, but relatively little came of his as well as Jan Karłowicz's initiatives for a number of years. It was not until 1897, when a small group of Jewish ethnographers came together under Karłowicz's direction and *Wisła* initiated a regular section entitled "Ludoznawstwo żydowskie," that material on Jewish folkways began to appear somewhat regularly. Several members of the Jewish *Wisła* group deserve special notice. Alfred Lor and Henryk Lew (F. H. Lewestam, d. ca. 1918, husband of the harpsichordist Wanda Landowska) were also theater reviewers for *Izraelita* and devoted particular attention to Purim and *purim-shpil*. Another early *Wisła* collaborator, Regina Lilientalowa (1877–1924), went on to dedicate her life to Jewish ethnography. About 1900 and partly as a result of contacts with these first Jewish ethnographers (Henryk Lew was one of his earliest translators), Y. L. Peretz became fascinated with Yiddish folksongs and folklore, and soon inspired a circle of young Yiddish-speaking intelligentsia to begin collecting material. See Mark Kiel, "Vox Populi, Vox Dei: The Centrality of Peretz in Jewish Folkloristics," *Polin* 7 (1992): 88–120.

15. *Tygodnik Illustrowany*, 9 July 1881, cited from Witold Filler, *Melpomena i piwo* (Warsaw, 1960), 147.

16. Maria Wosiek, *Historia teatrów ludowych; polskie zespoły zawodowe, 1898–1914* (Wrocław, 1975).

17. On Wilhelm Feldman's 1891 appeal for such a theater, see below. For a similar proposal several years later, see Hael [Henryk Lew], "O potrzebie teatru ludowego," *Izraelita*, no. 39, 1 October 1897.

18. In 1889, Orzeszkowa's *Meir Ezofowicz* was reworked for the garden theaters, but was apparently never staged. See Zbigniew Raszewski, "Zapolska— pisarka teatralna," in Gabriela Zapolska, *Dramaty*, vol. 1 (Wrocław, 1960), lvii–lviii.

19. For a reliable summary of her career, see Jadwiga Czachowska, "Gabriela Zapolska," in *Literatura polska w okresie realizmu i naturalizmu* (Warsaw, 1971), 179–224; the article includes an extensive bibliography and excerpts from Zapolska's work. For a brief and and severe evaluation in English, see Czesław Miłosz, *The History of Polish Literature* (Berkeley, 1983), 359.

20. Szary, "U Gabrieli Zapolskiej," *Kraj* (St. Petersburg), no. 36, 21 September 1900 ("Dział Ilustrowany").

21. Raszewski, "Zapolska—pisarka teatralna," xiii.

22. "Kapotowe żydowstwo"; see "Echa warszawskie," *Przegląd Tygodniowy*, no. 29, 17 July 1897.

23. Raszewski, "Zapolska—pisarka teatralna," lx.

24. A. Nowaczyński, "Dramat polski XIX w., studium impresjonistyczne," *Ateneum* (Warsaw), 3 (1900): 22; Raszewski, "Zapolska—pisarka teatralna," lxi.

25. Raszewski, "Zapolska—pisarka teatralna," lxx.

26. Kirkor [W. Korycki], "Nieco zimnej wody! (Uwagi z powodu 'Małki Szwarcenkopf' p. Gabryeli Zapolskiej)," *Niwa* (Warsaw), no. 31, 31 July 1897.

27. *Kolce* (Warsaw, 1897), no. 31, cited in Raszewski, "Zapolska—pisarka teatralna," cxvii, n. 108.

28. Jadwiga Czachowska, *Gabriela Zapolska: Monografia bio-bibliograficzna* (Kraków, 1966), 173.

29. Jan Błeszyński, "Z literatury dramatycznej. 'Małka Szwarcenkopf,'" *Kurier niedzielny* (1897), no. 30, pp. 354–56, as cited in Czachowska, *Gabriela Zapolska: monografia bio-bibliograficzna*, 173–74.

30. L. Szczepański, *Życie* (Kraków, 1897), no. 5, cited in Raszewski, "Zapolska—pisarka teatralna," lxviii. Both sides probably wore *kapotes.*

31. *Mucha* (Warsaw, 1897), no. 34; the cartoon is reprinted on p. lxix of Raszewski's study.

32. "Żydki śmieją się z radości,/ Wciąz, co parę chwil./ Gdy odezwie się kto głośniej,/ Zaraz wrzeszczą 'still!'" *Kolce* (1897), no. 29, as cited in Raszewski, "Zapolska—pisarka teatralna," cxvii, n. 107.

33. *Kurjer Warszawski* (1897), no. 224; *Echo muzyczne, teatralne i artystycane* (1897), no. 35, cited in Raszewski, "Zapolska—pisarka teatralna," cxviii, n. 110. For a review of Zapolska's performance, see Bogusławski's review in *Gazeta Polska*, no. 185, 16 August 1897.

34. On 15 July 1897, Prince Obolenski, acting governor general of Warsaw, viewed the play from a special loge; see Witold Filler, *Melpomena i piwo* (Warsaw 1960), 220.

35. As late as the summer of 1901, *Małka*'s popularity warranted its production in three different Warsaw theaters; see M. Ar. [Mark Arnshteyn], "Odglosy. Z teatru," *Izraelita*, no. 22, 7 June 1901.

36. Filler, *Melpomena i piwo*, 221.

37. On these and subsequent productions, see Czachowska, *Gabriela Zapolska: monografia bio-bibliograficzna*, 176–81.

38. The key role of the *marshelik* was played by the celebrated actor and director Ludwik Solski (1855–1954); on his subsequent collaboration with Zapolska, see below.

39. Raszewski, "Zapolska—pisarka teatralna," pp. lxxiv–lxxv. In response to an anti-Semitic attack on *Małka* in the Kraków paper *Głos Narodu*, at the next performance of the play Zapolska placed dog muzzles in the seats of the paper's theater critics and further responded with her novella *Antysemitnik*, published in 1897–98.

40. Raszewski, "Zapolska—pisarka teatralna," lxxiii, lxxxviii.

41. The last revival in Warsaw was directed by Mark Arnshteyn in 1928, but as late as 1938, *Małka* was staged in Łódź, where it inspired controversy; see ibid., cxx, n. 134.

42. A Yiddish version, translated by Leon Gotlib and directed by Zigmund Faynman, played at the Windsor Theater in New York in 1903; see Zalmen Zilbertsvayg, *Leksikon fun yidishn teater*, v. 1 (New York, 1931), col. 257. A Yiddish version also played in Warsaw in November 1917; see Czachowska, *Gabriela Zapolska*, 181.

43. *Małka Szwarcenkopf. Sztuka w 5 aktach* was first published as the third volume of the first edition of Zapolska's collected plays: *Teatr Gabrieli Zapolskiej*, 8 vols. (Warsaw, 1903). I have used a critical edition of the play published in *Dzieła wybrane*, vol. 13 (Kraków, 1958), 245–371.

44. *Uriel Acosta*, based on historical accounts of a seventeenth-century Jewish heretic, presents an "enlightened" hero destroyed between allegiance to his family and the "torch of reason." First published in 1847, the play was reprinted

in German nine times during Gutzkow's lifetime and translated into English, French, Italian, Swedish, Hungarian, Czech, Polish, Russian, Yiddish, and Hebrew. The Polish version premiered in Warsaw in 1888.

45. Act 2, scene 8, p. 293.

46. Act 4, scene 4, p. 343.

47. Act 4, scene 8, p. 352.

48. Act 5, scene 6, p. 369.

49. "Echa warszawskie" in *Przegląd Tygodniowy*; there were numerous similar statements.

50. When the Polish literary journal *Wiadomości Literackie* decided in the 1930s to devote space to an examination of contemporary Jewish life, it published a series of articles of the travelogue genre entitled "Dark Continent—Warsaw." See Wanda Melcer, "Czarny ląd—Warszawa," 1934, nos. 14, 22, 40; 1935, nos. 4, 15, 36. Reflecting in the 1920s on such "expeditions," comparable, he suggests, to Amundsen's to the North Pole, the editor of the Polish Jewish newspaper *Nasz Przegląd* concluded: "How does one get to Nalewki? . . . . It's only we Jews who think it's so easy: one gets into [trolley] number seventeen—and buys a ticket for fifteen groszy." See Pierrot [Jakób Appenszlak], "Między wierszami. Jak się jedzie na Nalewki?," 26 May 1925.

51. *Wędrowiec* (Warsaw), no. 29, 17 July 1897.

52. Act 3, scene 8, pp. 321–29.

53. H. L., "Z teatru," *Izraelita*, no. 28, 16 July 1897. Examining the numerous errors in the play, Lew terms the third act "a collection of ethnological inconsistencies."

54. "Jeszcze w sprawie 'Małki Szwarcenkopf,'" *Kurier Codzienny* (1897), no. 266, as cited in *Listy Gabrieli Zapolskiej*, vol. 1, ed. Stefania Linowska (Warsaw, 1970), 488. On Orzeszkowa's efforts to acquaint herself with Jewish culture, see Safran, *Rewriting the Jew*, 77–78.

55. "Odgłosy. Jeszcze o 'Małce Szwarcenkopf,'" no. 29, 23 July 1897.

56. Lew, "Z teatru."

57. Act 2, scene 8, p. 298. This character was singled out for praise by most reviewers.

58. Act 2, scene 5, pp. 287–88.

59. Act 1, scene 5, p. 260.

60. "Realistic" plays by Jacob Gordin, Sholem Aleichem, and Dovid Pinski were not performed in Warsaw until 1905–6.

61. W. Baranowski, "Teatr polski," *Kurjer litewski* (Vilna), no. 292, 10 January 1907.

62. "Odgłosy. Jeszcze o 'Małce Szwarcenkopf.'"

63. The canonized Polish theater also reflected this trend, albeit in its own way. See, for example, the *Izraelita* review of *Rothnerówna* by Stanisław Graybaer and Maryan Prażmowski (Henryk Kohn, "Z teatru," no. 1, 5 January 1900); the play was about marriages between upper-class Christians and *mechesy* (Jewish converts).

64. Józefat Nowiński, "Teatry warszawskie," *Głos*, no. 39, 12 September 1898.

65. Gabryel Kempner, "Ze scen letnich," *Przegląd Tygodniowy*, no. 29, 21 July 1900.

66. Alf. L., "Odgłosy. Po premierze w Wodewilu," *Izraelita*, no. 27, 13 July 1900. Lor continues: "All these gentlemen with prophetic visages await whichever [of them] will begin the criticism of the play, contenting themselves for the time being with a short, fitful 'hm, hm. . . .'" Neither Peretz nor Bal-Makh-

shoves, however, at the time both contributors to the influential new Yiddish periodical *Der yud*, chose to consign their impressions about this Polish-Jewish play to writing.

67. The play was first published in the same year in two different versions: *Jojne Firułkes. Sztuka w 5 aktach* in the fourth volume of the first edition of Zapolska's collected plays: *Teatr Gabrieli Zapolskiej*, 8 vols. (Warsaw, 1903); and *Jojne Firułkes. Sztuka w 5 aktach z tańcami i śpiewami na tle stosunków żydowskich* (Kraków, 1903). I have used a critical edition of the play published in *Dzieła wybrane*, vol. 14 (Kraków, 1958), 5–133.

68. Kazimierz Puffke, "Z teatru," *Słowo* (Warsaw), no. 167, 26 July 1898.

69. Bruno Las, *Kolce* (1898), no. 31, as cited in Raszewski, "Zapolska—pisarka teatralna," cxx, n. 141.

70. Letter to Ludwik Szczepański, 19 July 1898, in *Listy Gabrieli Zapolskiej*, 1:503. In his memoirs Solski recalls how he and Zapolska, at the latter's suggestion, wandered through the streets and basement apartments of Jewish Kraków (Kazimierz) as part of her research for the writing of *Jojne* ("Zapolska jako aktorka," *Ilustrowany Kurier Polski*, 1947, no. 24, as cited in Raszewski, "Zapolska—pisarka teatralna," lxxvi). Prior to the premiere of *Jojne* in Kraków, last minute changes in "yiddishisms" in the script were made on the advice of a Jewish street vendor and her barber husband (see Zapolska's letter to Ludwik Szczepański [21 January 1899] in *Listy Gabrieli Zapolskiej*, 1:578–79).

71. "Z teatru," *Izraelita*, 29 July 1898. For a similar opinion, see the review of the Lwów performance in the Zionist weekly *Przyszłość*, no. 16, 5 June 1899.

72. Lew, "Z teatru." The only possible exception is Awrumel, a humane and hence persecuted *belfer* who writes Hebrew and Yiddish verse and accompanies Jojne on some of his wanderings.

73. In contemporary reviews, Jojne was often compared, generally to his detriment, to Uriel Acosta and Meir Ezofowicz. And Henryk Lew's long essay, "Meir Ezofowicz i Jojne Firułkes" (*Izraelita*, nos. 32–34, 19 August–2 September 1898), concludes: "*Meir Ezofowicz* is a masterpiece of its kind with great literary and social value; *Jojne Firułkes* is only a pretentious melodrama with songs, dances, and couplets."

74. At the same time, the Odeon began its season with Ignacy Grabowski's *Weksel płatny* (A payable note), an "old-style" Jewish comedy; see Hael [Henryk Lew], "Ze scen ogródkowych," *Izraelita*, no. 22, 10 June 1898. After discussing Grabowski's play, Lew concludes that it is no longer enough merely to exhibit a Jew in a *kapote* to be assured of popularity, for "now the public demands real and consistent characters on the stage, in a word, demands that actors be actors, and not clowns and buffoons."

75. Raszewski, "Zapolska—pisarka teatralna," lxxxii. It was subsequently performed in Lublin, Kraków, Lwów, and Łódź in 1898–1900, and revived in Kraków in 1904 and 1906; for details, see Czachowska, *Gabriela Zapolska*, 204–7.

76. Raszewski, "Zapolska—pisarka teatralna," lxxxii.

77. Letters to Ludwik Szczepański (22 and ca. 26 January 1899) in *Listy Gabrieli Zapolskiej*, 1:580–81; emphasis in the original. Zapolska, who was ill, did not attend either the Warsaw or Kraków productions; her description is based on the reports of acquaintances.

78. "Today Jews, both lower-class and educated, came to visit me," wrote Zapolska. They complained about a parody of a prayer, numerous vulgarities, and "thousands of details which terribly disturbed them and insulted their religious feelings." Zapolska, probably supported by the diplomacy of her Jewish

visitors, was able to blame all this on the actors who "murdered *Jojne* for me in Warsaw and in Kraków," and concludes with the vow typical of a theatrical *grande dame*: "Never again will I permit a play to be staged without me!" (Letter to Ludwik Szczepański [ca. 26 January 1899]).

79. A review by Roman Poliński ("Teatr," *Iris* [Lwów], June 1899) provides a rare description of actual stage language: "Hasidic Jews express themselves always in *żargon* [that is, stylized Polish-Yiddish], . . . while Jojne . . . and other more 'liberated' characters speak a nearly entirely pure Polish—although certainly with an appropriate accent." Henryk Lew ("Z teatru") mentions the absurdity of Jojne's father speaking from the grave in "Nalewki dialect" and concludes: "The play presents, after all, the inner life of Jews, speaking Yiddish to each other; what was required, therefore, was either dialogues in Yiddish or in a Polish translation."

80. "Protest przeciwko każeniu języka na scenie," *Niwa* (1898), no. 3, as cited in Raszewski, "Zapolska—pisarka teatralna," lxxxi. And it is indeed a "corrupted" Polish, and not Yiddish, that is here the immediate issue, though not perhaps the political agenda. Bearing in mind Lew's comment in the previous note, one could reply that this was a work written neither in Polish nor Yiddish, but in the imagined dialects of a new Polish-Jewish borderland.

81. Józefat Nowiński, "Teatry warszawskie," *Głos*, 12 September 1898.

82. Włodzimierz Trąmpczyński in *Dziennik dla Wszystkich* (1898), no. 167, as cited in Henryk Lew, "Nasi krytycy o 'Firułkesie,'" *Izraelita*, no. 30, 5 August 1898.

83. Dr. Eug. B. [Eugeniusz Barwiński], "Teatr," *Dodatek do "Gazety Narodowej"* (Lwów), no. 141, 21 May 1899.

84. B., "Teatry letnie," no. 183, 14 July 1897.

85. *Sara Weisblut. Sztuka współczesna w 5 aktach* premiered on 8 September 1898 in Warsaw and on 17 February 1900 in Łódź. Only an earlier unstaged version of the play was ever published: *Na straconym posterunku* (At a lost outpost). *Dramat współczesny w 5 aktach* (Warsaw, 1891). For the stage version, I have relied on the following reviews: Józefat Nowiński, "Teatry warszawskie," *Głos*, 12 September 1898; Cor. [Kazimierz Sterling], "Z teatru," *Izraelita*, no. 36, 16 September 1898; H. Lew, "Jeszcze o 'Sarze Weisblut,'" *Izraelita*, no. 38–39, 30 September –14 October 1898. Jeske-Choiński (1854–1920) was the author of a large number of works including *Syjonizm w oświetleniu antysemity* (Zionism illuminated by an anti-Semite, Warsaw, 1904); *Poznaj Żyda!* (Know the Jew!), Warsaw, 1912, 1913, and 1919; and "Legenda o mordzie rytualnym" (The legend of ritual murder), *Przegląd Katolicki*, 1914; as well as an historically useful compendium on Polish Jewish converts to Christianity (*Neoficy polscy. Materiały historyczne*, Warsaw, 1905).

86. Nowiński, "Teatry warszawskie."

87. Citations according to Lew, "Jeszcze o 'Sarze Weisblut,'" *Izraelita*, 30 September 1898. In the printed version of the play, though probably not in the stage version, Sara gratefully accepts baptism with her dying breath.

88. It was subsequently staged in Łódź the same year and in Lwów the following year. Feldman first published the play under a pseudonym and a different title in *Izraelita* (F. Kreczowski, *Wina i Kara* [Guilt and punishment], nos. 1–19, 6 January – 19 May 1899), and then in book form under his own name as *Sądy Boże. Dramat w 4-ch aktach z życia żydowskiego* (Warsaw, 1899). On Oskar, see Steinlauf, "Jews and Polish Theater in Nineteenth Century Warsaw," 456.

89. On Feldman, see the article by Ezra Mendelsohn: "Jewish Assimilation

in Lwów: The Case of Wilhelm Feldman," *Slavic Review* 28 (1969): 577–90. But Mendelsohn oversimplifies in characterizing Feldman's "Jewish" plays, stories, and novels as "more interesting as propaganda than as literature, [though] impressive for their powerful condemnation of life in the Jewish town" (583–84). Certainly *Sądy Boże* (a work with which Mendelsohn is apparently unfamiliar) and, judging from contemporary criticism, perhaps others of his works as well, transcend this characterization and merit reexamination.

90. "Z piśmiennictwa" (review of Feldman's novel, *Żydziak. Szkic psychologiczno-społeczny* [Lwów, 1889]), *Izraelita*, no. 12, 22 March 1889; see also Suesser's review of Feldman's collection of stories, *Nowelle i obrazki* (Kraków, 1889): "Z piśmiennictwa," *Izraelita*, no. 23, 14 June 1889.

91. See Mendelsohn, "Jewish Assimilation in Lwów," 583.

92. "Let us therefore bring the matter to the question of a [Polish] folk theater [*teatr ludowy*] and its popularization among the Jews of Poland" (*O żargonie żydowskim. Studium publicystyczne* [Lwów, 1891], 65, as cited in Raszewski, "Zapolska—pisarka teatralna," lvii); Feldman's essay was first serialized in *Ojczyzna* (1890), nos. 19–24.

93. "Z teatru," *Izraelita*, no. 28, 20 July 1900.

94. This is suggested as well in a contemporary review: Hieronim Cohn, "Z teatru," *Izraelita*, no. 26, 7 July 1899.

95. The play was also produced the same year in Kraków and published the following year in Warsaw and Lwów as *Cudotwórca. Sztuka w 4 aktach.* It was translated into German by Samuel Meisels as *Das Gottesgericht. Drama aus dem galizischjüdischen Leben in 4 Acten* (Vienna, 1902).

96. Act 2, scene 1.

97. Act 4, scene 7.

98. "Z teatru," no. 28, 20 July 1900.

99. Ibid.

100. Ibid. *Sztuka* means "play" as well as "art"; the term *sztuka żydowska* may therefore also refer to an individual work, in which case it may be translated as "Jewish play."

101. In the years immediately following, Feldman published several plays (*Czyste ręce* [Clean hands], 1901; *Cień* [Shade], 1903; *Życie* [Life], 1903), but none of these dealt with Jewish matters.

102. *Rok 1900. Szkice o dramacie zapomnianym* (Kraków, 1969), 279. Like Mendelsohn, however, Greń, who discusses Feldman's "forgotten" dramas on pp. 274–90 of his study, assumes that both *Sądy Boże* and *Cudotwórca* are equally tendentious.

103. See Michael C. Steinlauf, "'Fardibekt': An-sky's Polish Legacy," in *The Worlds of S. An-sky: A Russian Jewish Intellectual at the Turn of the Century*, ed. Gabriella Safran and Steven Zipperstein (Stanford, 2006), 232–51.

104. "Z teatru," nos. 28, 29, 36, 44; 20 July, 27 July, 14 September, 16 November 1900, respectively.

105. "Z teatru," 27 July 1900 (review of *Cudotwórca*). *Majufes* was a Jewish dance performed on the Polish stage; on this word and the history of its meanings, see Chone Shmeruk, "*Mayufes*: A Window on Polish-Jewish Relations," *Polin* 10 (1997): 273–86. Lor laces his remarks with the barbed humor characteristic of contemporary feuilletonists. For the benefit of beginning Polish-Jewish dramatists, for example, he provides some possible plot outlines, including *Dwa światy* (Two worlds), whose cast consists, on one hand, of pathetic ruined aristocrats and victims of a Jewish conspiracy, and, on the other, characters such as

"Szmul Perelman, courtyard peddler and ritual murderer, Berek Wygodny, house-painter and well-poisoner, . . . Wigdor Pędziwiatr, carpenter and member of the debauched organization 'All. Isr.' [Alliance Universelle Israelite], [and] Chana Rosenwetter, market vendor and reckless feminist"; a historical drama entitled *Paznokieć Drejfusa* (Dreyfus's fingernail); a play set in the future, entitled *Strajk szabesgojów w Syonie* (The strike of the *shabes-goyim* in Zion); and a contemporary tragicomedy entitled *Solidarność żydowska* (Jewish solidarity), in whose climactic scene "the symbol of Jewry, in the figure of a grey, emaciated wanderer in torn clothing, loudly crying for a crust of bread, is dying of hunger while being tugged from all sides by a variety of dwarves symbolizing assimilation, Zionism, nationalism, radicalism, progress, backwardness, Hasidism, and countless other currents great and small, who, instead of feeding the starving man, show him some faded banners with futile but thunderous slogans" ("Z teatru," 16 November 1900).

106. His comments on Polish audiences emphasize their attraction to the "great, mysterious sphinx called the Jewish masses" ("Z teatru," 14 September 1900).

107. Ibid.

108. In a note, Lor mentions that his article is only a sketch for a larger study which apparently, however, was never published.

109. Ibid.

110. See Marcie Shore, *Caviar and Ashes: A Warsaw Generation's Life and Death in Marxism, 1918–1968* (New Haven, 2006).

111. See Michael C. Steinlauf, "The Polish Jewish Daily Press," in *From Shtetl to Socialism: Studies from Polin*, ed. Antony Polonsky (London, 1993), 332–58, reprinted from *Polin: A Journal of Polish-Jewish Studies*, 2 (1987): 219–45; and Eugenia Prokop, *Polish Jewish Literature in the Interwar Years* (Syracuse, 2002).

112. See Michael C. Steinlauf, "Mark Arnshteyn and Polish-Jewish Theater," in *The Jews of Poland Between Two World Wars*, ed. Yisrael Gutman et al. (Hanover, N.H., 1989), 399–411. Another Polish-Jewish theatrical borderland, still remaining to be studied, are the Jewish skits, jokes, and sketches known as *szmoncesy*, which were popular in interwar Polish literary cabarets.

113. Steinlauf, "Jews and Polish Theater in Nineteenth Century Warsaw," 458.

114. See n. 84.

Part III
Politics and Aesthetics

Yosef Haim Brenner, the "Half-Intelligentsia," and Russian-Jewish Politics, 1898–1908

Jonathan Frankel

Among modern Hebrew writers, Yosef Haim Brenner was ranked high from the moment that his early works of fiction were published in the Russian empire during the first years of the twentieth century. His subsequent entry into the fields of Hebrew-language journalism and literary criticism gradually added to his reputation: a writer and thinker who, in his own small sub-world, could not be ignored. And his death—he was killed while still a relatively young man during the Arab riots in Jaffa in 1921—provided him with a unique place in the collective memory of the *yishuv* (the Jewish community in Mandatory Palestine). The sense of the tragic that pervades almost everything he wrote was then, as it were, sealed forever: retroactively sacrilized by his violent end in the looming conflict between Jews and Arabs in the land claimed by both peoples.

It is in no way surprising, therefore, that Brenner's life and writings have been the object of sustained attention ever since his murder. In this respect, pride of place has to go to Yitzhak Bakon, whose two-volume biography and other studies of Brenner in his early years represents a work of meticulous research and an invaluable source for all subsequent scholarship.[1] To gain a true impression of the canonic status enjoyed by Brenner, though, it is enough to mention that the list of those who have published significant articles or books about him includes among many others, Alexander Siskind Rabinovich (AzaR), Yaakov Fichman, Dov Sadan, Baruch Kurzweil, Dan Miron, Natan Zach, Gershon Shaked, Menachem Brinker, and Hamutal Bar-Yosef.[2]

However, in this scholarly output the emphasis has for the most part been placed on the literary aspects of Brenner's life and letters (Yitzhak Bakon being a partial exception). Here, by contrast, an attempt will be made to reexamine Brenner's ideological positions and party commitments within the context of the politics reigning on the "Jewish street" during what can loosely be called the period of the 1905 revolution. A study of this kind warrants a full-length monograph, while all that is attempted in this article is to try to distinguish in broad outline the atypical from the typical and representative in his thinking. Such an approach will, it can be hoped, carry discussion of Brenner as both observer, commentator, and activist somewhat further into areas mapped out by Bakon.

For a wide variety of reasons, Brenner did not lay down a clearly delineated ideological trail during the decade that preceded his emigration to Palestine in 1909. Among the factors at work here was his sheer absence from the Russian-Jewish heartlands. Brenner's attention in this period remained steadily focused on developments within the Pale of Settlement and Congress Poland, but he was not physically present in that region for most of the time involved. From November 1901 to January 1904, as a recruit in the tsarist army, he was stationed deep inside Russia, in the town of Orel. Following his flight from the army and his subsequent escape from the tsarist police, he ended up by April 1904 in London, where he remained until his move to Lemberg (Lvov/Lwow/Lviv) in 1908. As he himself sometimes explicitly stated, he was reluctant to take an unambiguous stand on issues which he could not evaluate at first hand.[3]

More significant than geography in this respect was psychology. Brenner at times clearly felt that he was duty-bound to commit himself, his energy, and his pen to a given political ideology or party, but such commitments clashed with his pronouncedly individualistic and skeptical temperament. His natural inclination was, on the contrary, to fall back on his role as a critical, independent, complex—and hence unpredictable—observer of Russian-Jewish politics.

This meant that he was more at home writing fiction and literary criticism than political journalism. As a novelist and short-story writer, he did not have to align himself unreservedly with any clear-cut ideological credo. Indeed, by the time that he—then twenty years old—came to write his first novel in 1901, *Bahoref* (In the winter) he was already developing his characteristically dialogic form of narrative. This literary device permitted him to present contradictory viewpoints without his necessarily having to declare a clear-cut stand of his own.

He explicitly shunned the thought that his creative impulse might be directed toward crudely propagandistic ends. The following dialogue from his second full-length novel *Misaviv lanekudah* (Circling the point) touches the issue of party-mindedness in the writer. Asked by Hava Blumin, a young Jewish but Russified revolutionary about the contents of a short story he had written, Yaakov Abramzon, a writer and the main protagonist of the novel, replies:

"What's the story about? . . . It isn't about anything. Our modern [Hebrew] literature is still in search of a theme. That's to say, the story's about a young Jewish
woman. No! a woman who was born Jewish, but was working alongside Russians,
[revolutionaries] in the 70s. And then after the pogroms . . . of the 80s."

"Became a Zionist?" interrupted Blumin contemptuously, and as though cha-
grined. "I knew it, I knew it . . ."

Abramzon was mortified: "No, the young narrator is really gifted, and has a
good grasp of things. He would never commit a sin like that. . . . That woman
did not become a Zionist. . . . There is no tendentiousness in this small story. It's
simple; it deals with her feelings. But to tell the truth, real life has not provided
us with the material needed to describe such feelings. To their shame, or to our
shame, and it's tragic, those young women and young men did not have *those*
kinds of feelings. . . . But what's described here isn't the way it really was, but
how it ought to have been."[4]

As is so often the case with Brenner's fiction, the reader is left with no
choice but to peel off layers of (apparently contradictory) meaning in
order to reach the author's probable intent. Thus, at one—the most intimate—level, we are simply made witness here to the contortions of a
young man notoriously awkward in such encounters with the opposite
sex, trying desperately to impress a beautiful and intelligent young
woman who happens to belong to a different cultural and political
milieu. To some extent Abramzon here is clearly modeled on Brenner
himself (just as Hava Blumin had a real-life equivalent, Haya Volfson),
although the degree of overlap between fact and fiction, here as frequently elsewhere, cannot be fully ascertained.

And then again, at another level entirely, what does Abramzon mean
when he states his goal, or that of his fictional author, to be the description not of "what was, but of what ought to have been"? On the face of
it, this seems to be an affirmation of that very tendentiousness which he
had repudiated so vehemently a mere moment before. But in all proba-
bility he is, rather, making a declaration of faith in literature not as a
mere reflection of reality, but rather as the essence distilled from life at
a given time and place—and hence as the most authentic expression of
the national existence. Or as Menachem Brinker puts it:

Brenner not only had the natural desire of a novelist to provide his readers with
a narrative that would be of interest and holding; [he was also moved by the
belief] that his works of fiction would give voice to the pressing issues of concern
to his generation. In this respect, he was clearly heir to the tradition characteristic of both the literatures—the Hebrew and the Russian—on which for the most
part he had been reared. . . . In the former, the Hebrew tradition, the writer—
especially one known to speak for the younger generation—was [widely]
regarded as somebody of great moral stature, as a sharp-eyed observer of Jewish
life, as a guide to the perplexed.[5]

Brinker argues convincingly that Brenner's transition from the literature of direct social protest characteristic of his early short stories to the

less overtly engagé form of his subsequent fiction is largely to be explained by the replacement in his eyes of Dmitrii Pisarev by Vissarion Belinsky as a dominant critical authority.[6] In the wake of Schelling, Belinsky maintained that a writer (and he, of course, saw supreme examples in *Evgenii Onegin* and *Dead Souls*) could exert great influence by, to quote Francis Randall, "grasping his nation's condition and making its reading public realize it, thereby pushing, moving, transforming and shaping that nation anew."[7]

Randall remarks perceptively that here was a viewpoint which involved Belinsky in the "simultaneous championing of two contrasting literary ideals: the social purpose of literature and the autonomy of art."[8] This is an insight no less applicable to Brenner as writer and critic. Of Brenner's fiction, it can be said that he chose to paint on a very small canvass. But even that would be misleading, because, apart from describing in some detail the features and general appearance of his characters, he shunned the visual dimension of things. Historians of the period cannot turn to Brenner for the vivid descriptions of the public space—the meetings, the strikes, the *birzhe*, the angry confrontations in the synagogues and *boteimidroshim*, the outbursts of violence in the name of class war on the Jewish street, the self-defense groups out on patrol, the demonstrations—that he can find in the contemporary novellas and novels of Ansky, Kabak, Sholem Aleichem, Weissenberg, and Spektor.[9]

As against that, though, Brenner does permit the reader to eavesdrop, to overhear the intense conversations conducted by his characters: dialogues (as in the above passage), monologues, or at times many-sided exchanges. Coming together in small rooms, often in the midst of the long Russian winter, the protagonists interact in persistently claustrophobic settings. And these confined spaces can be seen as symbolizing Brenner's conception of the Jewish people in Eastern Europe and in their emigrations: a people enclosed and self-enclosed in a metaphorical ghetto, dark and airless.

What Brenner chose to forfeit in breadth, he compensated for in depth. Nobody else surely recorded with such intensity, with such obsessive concentration, the search of the *polu-intelligentsiia*, (the half-intelligentsia)—that section of the radicalized youth who had some formal Jewish education, but otherwise were autodidacts, denied access to the *gimnaziia* and the university, uprooted and penurious—for some meaning to life in general and to Jewish life in particular. And within the half-intelligentsia his focus was primarily on his own specific and minute milieu: the ex-yeshiva students, with their first-class knowledge of Hebrew, of Aramaic, of rabbinic texts and of Yiddish, their mother tongue, but with only a late-acquired and patchy grasp of Russian (or Polish) and of the corpus of secular learning provided to their peers in the modern institutions of learning.[10] Although, included among the characters in his fiction were *gimnazisty, eksterny,* and members of the artisan (working-class) intelligentsiia, center stage was normally reserved for the *polu-intelligentsiia,* very often none other than some fictional version of Brenner himself, his friends, and his circle of acquaintances.

Furthermore, he not only wrote about that which he knew firsthand and intimately, he also insisted, with his decision to publish almost exclusively in Hebrew, on addressing himself to that same small circle of his own kind. Most Russian Jews could not cope with the language, and of those who could, the majority were traditional, Orthodox, and unwilling to read the work of the rebels, the *apikorsim.*

However, even though Brenner thus prided himself on his individuality and, indeed, on his eccentricity, he followed a path of intellectual—and political—development that was in many ways typical of that taken by significant sections of the Russian-Jewish intelligentsia. Or, to put it more specifically, he too, like so many of his generation, found himself pushed and pulled between the ideologies and parties that from the turn of the century combined socialism and Jewish nationalism in ever-changing permutations.

Brenner's teenage years were marked by the same fearful encounters with forbidden Haskalah literature; the same hesitations and concealments; the same punishments meted out by the rabbinical authorities; and the same peripatetic and poverty-stricken wanderings that were the lot of so many of his contemporaries in the world of the yeshiva, the *bes medresh,* and the *kloyz* in the 1890s. But more is known about the details of his inner life—the twists and turns that punctuated his painful transition from childhood to young manhood—than perhaps about those of anybody else in his generation and milieu. His penchant for writing, be it letters, poetry, articles, or fiction, emerged extremely early; and while much of that teenage output has been lost, what remains enables us to follow closely the way in which he chose to describe the gradual alienation, experienced by himself and (or) by others in his peer group,[11] from the moral authority of the established order.

In *Bahoref,* the father of the boy about to leave his hometown for the first time, on his way to a yeshiva, is warned by a friend that the result could be disastrous:

"You know, . . . I myself read *Hamelits* . . . but the truth has to be told: terrible breakaways [*shkotsim*] have come out of Volozhin."
"Not my Yirmiya," answered my father, confidently, almost in anger.[12]

But in the novel, just as in the life, the attraction of the banned books and *bikhlekh* read in secret, anything that came to hand—Mapu, Shomer, Smolenskin—proved irresistible. More subversive still, in the Pochep yeshiva, Brenner (together with the young Uri Nisan Gnessin, the son of the yeshiva's head, a highly venerated rabbinic scholar) went from reading to writing. The clandestine journal they brought out for the benefit of a few friends was (at least according to the fictionalized account in *Bahoref*) made up of "various disputes between the Torah and the Haskalah, the poor and the rich, the yeshivot and the sons of the well-to-do [*bnei baalei habatim*], faith and criticism [*hakirah*], Hasidim and Mitnagdim, nationalists and assimilationists. These latter two terms we picked up wholesale from the newspapers without our having any clear idea of what they meant."[13]

The flight from the yeshivot and all that they represented took on epidemic proportions in the quarter of a century that preceded the First World War. But from Brenner, as from Feierberg and Berdyczewski, we can learn just how tortured a process was often involved.[14]

Pulling the Talmud students back to the entrenched way of life were powerful forces. Many (and Brenner was surely among them) were strongly drawn to the ideal of the rabbi as ascetic, as the embodiment of a pure spirituality—be it in the image (as he put it in his short story, *Mizvah*) of

those great souls who subject themselves to every form of asceticism, shut away day and night as they dedicate themselves to destroying the husks [*kelipot*], . . . or [in that of] those holy men who, concealing their true identity, work away at the simplest, most menial labor by day, only to have Elijah the Prophet and our Sages revealed to them at night.[15]

But there were also far more mundane pressures. Was not a brilliant student of the Talmud all but guaranteed a large dowry and security in his future life? ("Famous merchants," Yirmiya is told by his infuriated father in *Bahoref*, "well-known doctors, leading lawyers, wealthy and powerful men—men, not idle beggars like you—all chase after a dowry: of course, a dowry suited to their standing, ten thousand rubles, twenty, fifty, a hundred thousand, but a dowry.")[16]

As against that, though, there was the corrosive loss of faith. In a remarkable passage in one of his earliest short stories, "Briyah aluvah" (A miserable being), Brenner describes a young man who dedicates himself unreservedly to a totally spiritual life, only in the end to be left without answers to "the most profound questions." He was as willing as anybody to play his part in retrieving the holy sparks, the *nitsotsot*, from the *kelipot* and raising them up to the *Ein-Sof*—but "if the whole point is a return to the source, then what is the creation of the world all about?"[17]

In this story, the disillusioned enthusiast is forced to divorce his (wealthy) wife, denounced as mad, driven from his hometown and left to wander friendless from pillar to post. Brenner, the young subversive, also at times found himself declared "mad,"[18] but losing belief in a God-centered world and in the binding power of the rabbinic texts, he turned for salvation to all the other books that he could lay his hands on, whether fact or fiction, history or philosophy, in Hebrew, Yiddish, or Russian (which he began to learn laboriously from his mid-teens). "All that I want," says Yirmiya at one point in *Bahoref*, "is to be somebody whole, to know about the world, about life, about mankind and about myself."[19]

To read whatever he wanted, to write, endlessly, to learn a trade (for a time Brenner worked at becoming a scribe) all this provided compensation for what he had chosen to forfeit. Or in Yirmiya's words:

I truly rejoiced in the religious shackles lifted from my soul, in the liberty that was now mine, in the yoke thrown off. To behave with complete freedom, no longer to believe in nonsense—for me that provided a positive and satisfying faith. The emptiness that this negation produced had still not revealed itself in all its terror.[20]

Another window onto forbidden territory was opened by politics. While still embedded in the old order, Brenner identified himself with *Hibat Zion* (the Palestinophile organization founded in 1884) and, after 1897, with the Zionist movement. (Yirmiya's father was horrified to find him in possession of Ahad Ha'am's famous collection of articles *Al parashat drakhim* [At the crossroads]).[21] And once he had broken away entirely from the traditional way of life, casting off the *kapote*, the long black coat that he had continued to wear into his late teens, he moved into the orbit of the Jewish revolutionary and Marxist party, the Bund.

Relatively little is known about Brenner's period of working for the Bund, but what evidence there is suggests that it extended from late 1899 until his recruitment into the army two years later. During this time he served briefly as an editor of the party's clandestine journal in Homel, *Der kampf*, even recruiting to the journal—and to the party—one of its most famous future leaders, Borekh Mordkhe Virgily Cohen (also a *polu-intelligent*).[22] A short piece in *Der kampf* has been clearly identified as penned by Brenner. Entitled "No, and a Thousand Times No," it took the form of an agitational speech by a revolutionary worker to his fellow workers. (The uncomplicated and single-minded tenor of the piece made itself felt in the opening sentences: "No brothers; I say no! Things have to be different, different! We have to understand once and for all that we are not animals, that we are human beings, people with souls, people who with all their heart . . . have to want to be free, to be rid of their bridle, and of their yoke. We must not forget that everything produced is made by us, with our work and our sweat.")[23] During the course of 1901, Brenner was for much of the time in Belostok which then housed the Bundist central committee as well as its main journal, *Di arbeter shtime*, and there are good grounds for the assumption that he was heavily involved in the Yiddish-language publishing activities of the party.

In his biography, Yitzhak Bakon describes Brenner's ideological evolution in the years 1899–1901 as moving "from Ahad Ha'amism to Bundism."[24] According to this scheme of things, one political credo (strictly nationalist) was displaced by the other (revolutionary Marxism on the "Jewish street"). But, arguably, the configuration of politics at that particular time was less cut-and-dried than Bakon suggests. True, since the First Zionist Congress of 1897, Ahad Ha'am himself had been putting forward a biting critique of Theodor Herzl, his style of leadership, his concept of nationalism, and his political strategies. But the Democratic Faction (led by Leo Motzkin and Chaim Weizmann), which supported many of Ahad Ha'am's ideas, did not form itself until 1901 and even then sought to reach an accommodation with Herzl, not to displace him.

The situation in the Bund was equally inchoate. Only at its Fourth Congress, held in Belostok in 1901, did it first adopt in principle the idea of Jewish national—Diaspora—autonomy, but nonetheless the organization (still at the time a subsection of the Russian Social Democratic Labor Party) refrained from including that idea in its official program, for fear, it was stated, of clouding the class-consciousness of the Jewish proletariat. Not until late in 1905 did cultural national autonomy take its place among the formal demands put forward by the Bund as part of its so-called minimal program. The fact is that "Bundism," as it would later become—a synthesis of revolutionary Marxism, internationalism, Diaspora autonomism, and Yiddishism—was then still in its early stages of crystallization, and many of its leaders strongly opposed the national turn advocated, inter alia, by Vladimir Kossovsky, John Mill, and Mark Liber. It was presumably to dispel any suspicion of a nationalist deviation that the Fourth Congress adopted a resolution which for the first time specifically excluded all Zionists from the ranks of the Bund.[25]

The existing evidence strongly suggests that the young Brenner (he did not reach the age of twenty until 1901) was very much part of this broader phenomenon of ideological ferment. He personally found it impossible to confine himself within a neatly defined set of political beliefs, even though he saw that a clear party line and strict party discipline had much logic on their side. In the following obviously although not explicitly autobiographical fragment, Brenner in 1912 looked back to those days and to the tensions inherent in his position. He referred to a committed Hebrew writer whose first creative output predated 1900 . . . ; that is the period of the Bund in its heyday, when a spirit of nothing less than holiness reigned among its members of whom he too was one.[26] . . . He was then involved in producing proclamations [for the party] in Yiddish and stories drawn from the life of the poverty-stricken masses in Hebrew. His writing in Hebrew caused him to feel embarrassment and to develop a "guilty conscience" vis-à-vis his fellow party members.[27]

Be that as it might, Brenner continued to write and publish in Hebrew even in this—his Bundist—period. Indeed, the short stories with their strong note of social protest that Brenner mentioned in his reminiscence of 1912 were collected and published as a book, *Baemek akhor* (In the valley of trouble), in Warsaw in 1901. Similarly, it was at this same time that he was writing his first novel (also, of course, in Hebrew), *Bahoref.*

The original manuscript of this work, held in the Kotik publishing house in Belostok, was destroyed by fire in 1902 when Brenner was already serving as a recruit in the army, but he found the strength to rewrite it during that same year. It was brought out in installments during 1903 by *Hashiloah*, the Hebrew monthly founded by Ahad Ha'am and edited at that time by Joseph Klausner.

Reflected in the novel was that same indeterminacy, that same inner conflict, which Brenner briefly described in his retrospective comment of 1912. The duality, as has often been noted, was even proclaimed in the names given to two of the key protagonists: Feierman, the would-be but highly skeptical Zionist, and Haimovich, the committed revolutionary Marxist. Both names overlapped that of the novelist: the former being more or less synonymous with Brenner; and the latter enveloping his middle name.[28]

Even as he gropes for some firm faith, Feierman is plagued by doubt. At one time, he decides that he is to be a disciple of Lev Tolstoy, to become a simple artisan and to identify himself with mankind as a whole:

It would happen that I found myself strongly drawn to the spirit of "universalism"; to a vantage point, as it were, high above all the concerns of nations, languages and states, and then I would see nothing but the drama of ordinary men—and no longer that of a particular people caught up in its own specific situation.[29]

But such moments of escape did not last and Feierman would return to his

thoughts about "the sons who have deserted their father's table"; about the great and strange historical tragedy of an ancient people that has been dying for two thousand years; that burns but is not consumed; . . . about its fine young men rotting away in cellars or deserting it for other worlds and forgetting its very existence; about the contempt and the poverty that the entire world heaps onto this bent over but proud people; about its awakening to life and its chance for salvation, for redemption; about its literature and its thinking which are so explosive and yet so utterly ethereal. . . . But, of course, random thoughts could not lead me to . . . Zionism in the usual and obvious sense. Whatever I undertook in the way of Zionist work at the time was limited and eccentric partly because I lack the attributes of a social activist, partly because of my inclination to keep apart, to observe from the side, to analyze, and partly because my ideas about the Jews and Jewry were so extremely skeptical.[30]

While Feierman thus emerges as the embodiment of ineffectuality, condemned to flounder between competing faiths (and, very much in character, to fail in his advances to the woman who attracts him desperately), Haimovich stands psychologically at the opposite pole or, as Feierman, the narrator in the novel, puts it:

For Haimovich everything is crystal clear. The two terms—the "bourgeoisie" and the "proletariat"—consume him completely. All the issues of life are subsumed for him under the single question of labor and property; or, to be more exact, for him there is simply no other issue in life at all. . . . I, unfortunately, cannot explain everything to myself in this way. True, there have been moments in my life when I too became totally caught up by this universal question and, dragged along by the Haimoviches, saw in it and in its solution the be-all and end-all: the fight for justice, for a powerful ideal, for putting the world aright [*tikun 'olam*]. . . . But alongside the enthusiast in me there was also the critic and the analyst—and they filled me with heretical doubts, revealing to me much that was Quixotic, confused, populistic, ugly, ridiculous, superficial [in the outlook of the Haimovitches].[31]

In *Bahoref*, Brenner creates a balance between these two friends; and he allows Haimovich to put the case against Feierman's tentative Zionism with devastating cogency:

Zionism! I'm not even talking about its being utopian, although it is a sheer utopia, especially given the political situation in Europe and Asia. . . . And apart from your Zionism being reactionary, totally reactionary, a real regression, and generally a joke . . . who are the Zionists? A few yeshiva students and a few members of the bourgeoisie [*baalei batim*]! . . . All right, let's grant, as you say, that Zionism doesn't require us to go to synagogue every day and bow down to the rabbi and to the high-and-mighty—nor to beat a retreat to Asia; and let's assume that Zionism doesn't necessarily have to stand in the way of other essential undertakings. . . . Let's even grant that there could be a miracle and that reality changes, then I ask you: how would this bourgeois idea do anything to improve the situation of our proletariat? . . . You yourself have told me about the situation of the colonists in the "Holy Land" working under the control of Rothschild. And you are still bemoaning the [need to recruit] "our young forces." . . . Zionism will never win over to its side those young people who are dedicated to ideals.[32]

For all the unsparing criticism and ironic tone that Feierman adopts toward Haimovich, he nonetheless envies him his unwavering sense of certitude and political commitment. At one point in the novel, for example, he notes the contrast between attempts to organize some singing among his non-affiliated and philosophically skeptical friends with similar efforts among the revolutionaries, the party members. In the former setting, "everybody would begin to sing on his own, hardly breaking the silence, songs about the emotions and about despair, and soon enough the voices would grow weaker until they died out altogether." And then they turned to drinking. But at Haimovich's, "when they try to sing, it works out well. There they sing in unison 'On the Banks of the Volga' and songs about the prowess of Stenka Razin and so on."[33]

In the novel's climactic scene Feierman finds himself enraged by a self-satisfied and socially established young man, Borsiv, who dismisses the fact that Haimovich has recently become a factory worker as nothing more than a gesture designed "to show off his originality . . . to show that he is not one to follow the beaten path. . . . I'm sure that his factory work won't last long."[34] Mortified for his friend and for himself—Borsiv is having success with the woman whom he secretly loves—Feierman spits in Borsiv's face. (And we soon learn that Haimovich has, indeed, left the factory.)

The Brenner who escaped from Russia in mid-1904 turned out to be far more decisive in terms of political advocacy than he had been up until 1901. And this was the case not only in his journalism but also in his works of fiction. In broad terms, the ideological positions that he adopted over the next four years followed mainstream developments within the radical wing of the Russian Zionist movement. But within that context, his voice sounded its own distinctive note. Much that Brenner wrote was bitingly critical of major trends within his own camp.

Whether in the army or whether in London, Brenner (as already noted) had to observe from outside the succession of events that exerted a dramatic impact on the life and politics in the Pale of Settlement and Congress Poland during the period 1903–1907: the Kishinev pogrom of 1903; the Uganda crisis at the Sixth Zionist Congress in that same year; Herzl's death in 1904 and the territorialist schism following the Seventh Zionist Congress in 1905; the unfolding revolution across Russia; the large-scale participation of the Jewish youth in that revolution; the October Manifesto and the October pogroms; the elections to the First and Second Dumas in 1906–7; and the final defeat of the revolution with the electoral law of 3 June 1907. Nonetheless, he closely followed the rapidly evolving situation and made his viewpoint known whenever the opportunity arose.

Until the pogroms of October 1905, Brenner was committed to the faction within the Zionist movement, usually known as the Zionei Zion, which demanded unwavering loyalty to Palestine/Eretz Yisrael as the only possible national homeland for the Jewish people and so rejected outright the search for any more accessible region. From late 1904, and throughout most of 1905, Brenner was a key figure, together with Kalman Marmor, in organizing what was—in ideological terms—an affiliate of the Zionei Zion faction: the Poale Zion movement in England.[35] And the line of thought that he then advocated was broadly consistent with the position taken at the time by the Poale Zion in Minsk, led by Yitzhak Berger, and also by Ber Borokhov in his articles of 1905 in the journal *Evreiskaia zhizn'*.[36]

What he and those like-minded had aimed at, Brenner wrote retrospectively from late in the year, was

not Zionism as philanthropy; not Zionism on some plot of land anywhere under the sun to be reserved for emigrants; not some dubious corner set aside for a meager group of the poor from Eastern Europe . . . but rather—a grand hope—the rebirth of the Jewish nation: the return of the Jews to their own land. Not a state . . . but a free community [*yishuv hofshi*]—that, [so we argued], is what we need if the Jewish people is to be revived, and that is what can be achieved by such a revival; not Ugandism for those tumbling out of Russia, but Zionism for the Jews of the entire world; no, not the Ingathering of the Exiles, as that term is usually understood, for that is beyond anything feasible, . . . but [Zionism] as a way to forestall the threat of extinction now facing our people.[37]

As was the case with Borokhov and Menachem Mendel Ussishkin, the leader of the Zionei Zion in that period, so Brenner advocated a strongly voluntarist strategy. Without an avant-garde drawn from within the youth, Zionism was doomed to fail:

To return to Zion, . . . to restore national determination and courage to the Jewish nation, to repair the past, to overcome our fractured history—that can only be undertaken by the best among our youngsters, those who are most at one with themselves, have the greatest sense for the aesthetic, and are the most sensitive.[38]

With this focus on the formation of a nationalist elite and on settlement in Eretz Yisrael, Brenner might logically have opted to oppose the participation of the Jewish youth in the Russian revolution. That, at least until 1904 or perhaps even later, was the position advocated by the influential Poale Zion group in Minsk. But Brenner thought otherwise; and in this respect his views simply reflected the major trend on the left-wing of the Russian Zionist movement.

That the Jewish people in the tsarist empire had to organize self-defense units against pogroms was considered axiomatic across a broad political spectrum, ranging from Ahad Ha'am at one pole to the Bund at the other. And only a small, albeit not inevitable, step was required for an armed underground designed for defense to join the revolutionary offensive against that autocratic regime held responsible (whether wholly or partially) for the pogroms.

In a letter written to a friend from his army base in Orel in April 1903, Brenner had commented laconically on the recent pogrom. "And so there is news out there in the world: Kishinev! If we just stand and yell day and night, we won't achieve much. All our cursing will gradually evaporate away."[39] The implicit message was clear: actions, not words were what was needed. And this was the view which Brenner put forward forcefully once he was able to express himself free from the tsarist authorities.

Thus, to recall what was probably the most extreme example, mention can be made of the tiny booklet, entitled *Hu amar lah* ("He told her") which Brenner brought out in London in the summer of 1905, following the recent pogrom in Zhitomir. Any profit to be made from its sales was "to be dedicated to the Jewish self-defense in Russia."[40] In tone and message, it was reminiscent of Bialik's extraordinarily influential poem of two years earlier, "In the City of Slaughter."[41] Penned as a monologue by a seventeen-year-old Jewish youth whose father, a peddler, had been brutally murdered by the local peasants, it was nothing less than a desperate call to arms not just to defend the Jews but also—and even more—to take revenge against the Ukrainian *pogromshchiki* who were visualized as heirs to Khmelnytsky, Mazepa, and the perpetrators of 1881–82. (Or, in the words of the lad: "Is this going to help? No? But a nation's whole being rests on its mourning, on its vengeance and on its honor.")[42]

In depicting the pogroms as the result of myths and mindsets rooted deep in the collective consciousness of the majority nationality, Brenner anticipated by half a year Dubnov's bitter analysis in his series of articles published in the wake of the October events: "Lessons from the Terrible Days."[43] And, paradoxically, he, too, like Dubnov, held the view that, despite all its apparent illogicality there could be no denying the revolutionary imperative. Even though it was doubtful, he wrote in the spring of 1905, whether the revolution would end in victory—the army, after all, had so far not switched sides[44]—there could be no neutrality in the fight for liberty: "There is no other way. We have to be among the first, in the advanced guard. We have nothing to lose. Worse than it is now it cannot be."[45] And at the end of the year, despite everything that had occurred in between, he could still write: "In truth, as human beings, do the people of Russia in all their variety have any choice but to fight against the absolutist regime? . . . Whether they are citizens or denied citizenship do they have any option other than to break this monster that devours everything, enslaves everybody and bans whatever it can lay its hands on?''[46]

In his biography, Yitzhak Bakon writes that during this, Brenner's first year in London, he became an active, even a leading member not only of Poale Zion, but also of the émigré branch in the West of the Party of Socialist Revolutionaries (the SRs).[47] But this assumption is highly questionable. Brenner, as Bakon describes, was indeed recruited by the famous revolutionary veteran, Nikolai Chaikovsky, to translate material extracted from the SR periodical, *Revoliutsionnaia Rossiia*, for reproduction in the Yiddish journal, *Kampf un kempfer*. Under the joint editorship of Brenner and S. A. An-sky, this journal was printed initially in London.[48] It has to be remembered, however, that at the time, Brenner was searching desperately for ways in which to earn some minimal income in order to keep body and soul together—and he, indeed, received payment for his work from the SRs.[49]

Doubtless, he found it far more appealing to use his skills as Yiddish translator and editor on behalf of the Socialist Revolutionaries than on behalf of the Social Democrats for whom he also worked for a time out of sheer financial necessity. After all, he shared the voluntarist and ethically based beliefs advocated by most of the SR ideologists as well as their consequent scorn for the laws of scientific determinism characteristically advocated by the Russian Marxists.[50]

Nevertheless, it is hard to envisage Brenner, if provided the luxury of free choice, as an active member of the Party of Socialist Revolutionaries. That party, after all, saw itself as heir to the narodnik tradition and as the primary champion of the peasantry (albeit in alliance with the revolutionary proletariat and intelligentsia). For his part, though, Brenner, time and again, whether in his belletristic or in his journalistic writings, made it crystal clear that he saw a yawning gulf dividing the Jewish from the Russian and Ukrainian peoples.

It was not just that, with a few notable exceptions, the Jews were depicted by Brenner as hopelessly puny when compared with their sturdily built, much taller neighbors. Rather, he emphasized the extreme divergence in their outlook, habits, and modes of behavior, with both sides drawn in less than flattering colors. Thus, for example, in the novella, broadly based on his army experience, *Shana ahat* (A single year), the Jewish soldiers are for the most part over-individualistic, unreliable and devious, while their Russian and Ukrainian counterparts tend to be hopelessly stolid, unthinking, eager to drink themselves into the ground, and routinely hostile to the Jews with whom they are living side by side.[51] Even those Russian *intelligenty* who on occasion made an appearance in Brenner's fiction (Grigorii Nikolaevich Petrov in *Misaviv lanekuda*, or Shakhtarov in *Min hameizar* [From the narrows], for example), although revolutionaries cannot overcome their built-in contempt for Jews.[52]

The SRs are rarely mentioned in Brenner's writings. (Petrov and Shakhtarov are both Marxists.) But in the novella *Mialef 'ad mem* (From A. to M.), which was first published in 1906 and which drew on his experience in 1904 as a prisoner, brought by étape from Orel to Bobruisk, a young couple, both SRs, are assigned a brief but significant part. They are described as highly refined—he wears a pince-nez, and she, for example, cannot decide whether to address one of the more easy-going soldiers on guard in the polite plural form, *vy*, in accord with her "humanity," or by the contemptuous singular, *ty*, as would be correct vis-à-vis an armed representative of the regime. "Such are the difficult situations that plague the life of a *baryshnia* [a young lady], particularly that of a *baryshnia* who . . . with her partner, likewise an *intelligent*, is on her way to 'distant parts.'"

This couple were SRs and they busied themselves making propaganda among the tailors [fellow prisoners] from Mozyr who were Bundists. They set out to prove what great hopes had to be placed in the [Russian] village. He argued with vast confidence and she intervening, sighed quietly and on an even note: "Oh, our Russian peasant" [*A nash russkii muzhik*].

Given the sharply ironic nature of this vignette, Brenner did not have to spell out his belief that this same *muzhik* was a potential pogromshchik, and that the place of the Jewish revolutionaries (at least one of the SR couple is a Jew) was in their own national movements and in their own self-defense units.[53]

Nonetheless, however focused Brenner had become by 1905 on the danger of anti-Jewish violence, the October pogroms of that year still exerted a shattering effect on him (and that was the case even before he heard that Haya Volfson had been killed in the course of a pogrom in Melitpol). For all his long-held conviction that the Jewish people were forever precariously situated on the brink of disaster, he clearly had not anticipated the extent of the anti-Jewish violence that, far more deadly than in 1881–82, now swept across more than six hundred cities, towns, and shtetls in the tsarist empire.

From the series of articles published late in 1905 and early 1906, primarily in the Hebrew-language journal which he had recently founded in London, *Hame'orer*, it emerged that Brenner had totally reversed long-held and fundamental ideological positions. Judeophobia could no longer be treated as an issue of secondary importance compared to the imperative of reconstructing the internal coherence, pride, and national self-consciousness of the Jewish people. Or as he put it in his piece entitled *Mikhtavim lerusiyah* ("Letters to Russia"):

Nothing can heal the wounds inflicted on the mass of the Jewish people by the Russian nation. . . . And there is no strategy to save ourselves in the short run. . . . We are not being slaughtered for our faith, murdered for our faults, stabbed for our virtues, nor being burnt as martyrs. We are forever the victim because we are hated, and we are hated because all men are wolves to each other—they hate and are hated—but while each wolf pack possesses its own separate forest, we do not; we are exiles and aliens.

> Let us put an end to that. . . . Let us find an empty country and prepare it for our children and our children's children. . . . A country [*erez*]! Any country that can be had, any country that we can begin to build up as our home soon; a country not for today—it is too late for that—but for the morrow, for the generations to come, for the orphans of Nemirov in twenty, fifty, a hundred years.[54]

However abrupt this volte-face—Brenner now found himself in the camp not of Ussishkin but of Israel Zangwill—it was by no means surprising. The surge toward the territorialist ideology carried all before it in the Poale Zion movement during the period of the revolution and the pogroms. Of the four revolutionary socialist parties that emerged from that hitherto ill-defined movement, three became fully committed to territorialism: the Socialist Zionist Labor Party (the SSRP); the Jewish Territorialist Labor Party—Poale Zion; and the Socialist Jewish Labor Party (the SERP). Even Nahman Syrkin, who relied heavily in his way of thinking on romantic, historically rooted, and mythological factors, now became a vociferous territorialist. The only party to remain loyal to Palestine was that led by Ber Borochov: The Jewish Socialist-Democratic Labor Party—Poale Zion.

In the face of the mass politics, the pogroms, the unprecedented waves of Jewish emigration and the persistent opposition of the Ottoman regime to Jewish settlement in Palestine, it was only natural that the idea of an alternative country could now win such support. The use of Yiddish, in the press as in literature, and the popularity of Yiddishism, likewise benefited directly from the rapidly changing realities of the time. Brenner, as a committed Hebrew writer, could not be entirely neutral in the so-called "language war," but he did now declare that the war should be set aside. "Even though," he wrote, characteristically,

> the future of Yiddish is clouded in doubt and the new generation is not being educated in it, the rock-solid fact remains—and it cannot be ignored—that despite all this, Yiddish is the spoken language of the majority of our nation. And only obtuse people can underestimate its validity or deny its popular and political significance.[55]

Nonetheless, even though Brenner's political thinking during his London years thus evolved along lines broadly characteristic of the Zionist left, in one respect his voice emerged as highly distinctive. Nobody else at the time wrote so persistently and angrily in condemnation of the move toward Marxist determinism that was then sweeping all before it among the radicalized youth on "the Jewish street."

Together with the revolution, its quasi-messianic expectations and its calls for sacrifice, had come the fast-growing belief in politics as a science. To apply the correct laws of critical analysis; to discover the direction of the prevailing socioeconomic currents in the given historical period; and to navigate the Jewish proletariat—and, ultimately, the Jewish people—along the route of least resistance came to be seen as the basic task of the political party. The Bund, of course, had always insisted on its Marxist orthodoxy and on its doctrine as in full accord with the capitalist and industrial development of the Russian empire.

But now the revolutionary ideologues of the younger generation emerging from the Zionist movement, whether Jacob Lestchinsky and Moyshe Litvakov of the SSRP, for example, or Ber Borochov of the Palestine-oriented Poale Zion, claimed for their respective parties a still greater scientific authority. While Bundist doctrine was focused narrowly on developments within the Russian empire, they argued, were not their theories more in line with Marxist doctrine in that they emphasized the importance of the worldwide economy, of intercontinental migration, of interethnic competition within the working class, and of European colonization overseas as a necessary consequence of capitalist crisis? Given these fundamental factors, was not the creation of a Jewish, and, ultimately socialist, state a necessity whether in Palestine (*pace* Borochov) or in some other more suitable territory (according to the SSRP)? Could there be any doubt that not consciousness (*soznatel'nost*) but self-propelling social and economic forces (*stikhiinost*) would determine the future? And, if so, was not the conduct of class warfare in the here and now the overriding duty of the party (be it territorialist or oriented toward Palestine)?

Brenner's scornful opposition to this entire trend of thought was constantly repeated in his works of fiction and in his journalism alike. This was an opposition that stemmed logically from his particular psychological frame of reference. Of key importance in this context was, surely, his unyielding commitment to the cause of Hebrew literature. In *Misaviv lanekudah*, we are told that Yaakov Abramzon already in his teenage years "was aware of the powerful impulse awakening within him. . . . He knew that 'he would become a Hebrew writer' . . . a writer amidst the Jewish people. Could there be any other happiness in the world? Could there be anything greater or more admirable than that?"[56]

While, of course, Abramzon cannot simply be identified with the novelist who created him, everything suggests that these were, at times, indeed Brenner's feelings at the parallel stage of his life. And while the mood of exaltation rarely returned, the underlying sentiment always would. As already noted in the discussion of Brenner and his work for the Bund, loyalty to Hebrew when combined with loyalty to mass politics represented an all-but-untenable stance.

During the years of revolution, Yiddish—freed at last from governmental restrictions—rapidly won a dominant and unprecedented status in the Russian Jewish world. The Hebrew journals *Hazefirah* and *Hashiloah* had to close down; and the sale of nonreligious books in that language went into decline, threatening the survival of *Achiasaf,* a publishing house.

In the face of this crisis, Brenner's reaction was not to switch to writing in Russian or Yiddish (although, as already noted, he did at times publish in Yiddish, sometimes out of ideological conviction, at other times as a source of livelihood),[57] but rather to insist that devotion to a lost cause, however quixotic, was not without honor nor, indeed, without purpose. Writing in *Hame'orer* in January 1906, he responded bitterly to the Yiddishist triumphalism then so prevalent:

"What," they ask . . . , "is a language from the past doing in the life of the present?" . . . And it is true: there is no need for a dead language. . . . But what is to be done if it is in that dead language that we possess a literature which is three thousand years old and is not dead? And what is to be done if by sweeping that dead language out of our lives, we destroy with our own hands the spiritual achievement of all the generations past?[58]

Time and again, Brenner returned to the thought that the renaissance of Hebrew as a modern and national language was on the verge of extinction and that defiance, be it as heroic, be it as a last stand, was the only acceptable response. "We shall remain on the ramparts to the last"[59] was how he concluded his January article. Or again (in the summer of 1906): "Let us sing of sorrow and death—and disappear!"[60] And (later in that same year): "Despair, too, is part of life and poets have need of it."[61]

The stronger the support on the Jewish left for the idea that ideology had to serve as a reflection of "life," the more space Brenner devoted to his caustic comments on Marxist determinism. True, in his *Misaviv lanekudah* of 1904, the signs of irritation were still mild. Even though the novel was no longer marked by the dualism (with Zionism and revolutionary Marxism held in balance) that had characterized *Bahoref,* his negative depiction of the dogmatists remained relatively good humored. Thus, Abramzon has only half an ear for the one acquaintance (Haverstein) who as " 'an orthodox Marxist' expounds with a voice full of confidence his unswerving ideas about 'the mighty hand of the historical process' "; or for an other (Burlak, "the eternal ekstern"), who pontificates about "the Jewish question in relation to 'the movement' and proves on the authority of Karl Kautsky and others— . . . with a kind of gleeful satisfaction—that the Jews lack all the attributes required according to the experts to be considered a nation and that the only solution is 'categorically' to merge into the majority nationality."[62] And the same mildly ironic tone is maintained in the passage where Abramzon's Marxist friends explain his unfashionable ideas by pigeonholing him as, objectively, a representative of "the Jewish petty bourgeoisie which, due to the economic conditions, is in decline and losing the ground from under its feet, and hence sinks into fantasies and builds castles in the air."[63]

However, by 1905 the tenor of Brenner's critique was changing radically. He was ready to grant that the Bund had created an impressive revolutionary machine and displayed genuine courage in the face of the pogroms,

but what has all this to do with their scientific priesthood? Or with their organizing themselves to rebel against "the oppressive regime of the Jewish bourgeoisie"? All right, let them have their Marx! But to see in them heroes of the Jewish people? . . . And that . . . when [among other things] the faithful are running their own fund-raising drives [for self-defense] separate from everybody else?[64]

His greatest irritation, though, was directed at the SSRP. True, from late in 1905, he shared the party's basic goals: territorialism, socialism (in some form), and participation in the revolution. But he rebelled against its reliance on "history to drive the Jewish proletariat in Russia to the realization of territorialism."[65] He regarded its attempts to compete with the Bund, and even to outflank it from the left, as unrealistic and hence pathetic—especially as its members generally shared all the faults familiar from the Bund (their original home in many cases, according to Brenner):

Nothing is missing: the same "scientific" theories; the same contempt for anything that smacks of the spiritual; the same tendency to pin labels on all human emotions; the same insistence on forcing life in all its variety into straitjackets. So, obviously, one cannot talk to them in terms of the national ethos which for them is simply non-existent. . . . In general, they reject any idea of the nation as a single whole, and they have no time at all for the history that has formed it. Their only concern is with the historical development of the contemporary Jewish condition—only today, with no reference heaven forbid, to the past.[66]

Or, in the words of Yohanan (like Brenner, a Hebrew writer and, at the time, a territorialist) in Brenner's play Mi'ever legevulin (Beyond the limits) published early in 1907:

It's . . . simple; anybody who has some little familiarity with human nature and who torments himself with questions that cannot be answered won't find contentment in a set ideology that focuses on the development of property relations and on the historical process as expounded by the dialectics of scientific socialism.[67]

In his novella *Mialef ad mem,* the members of the Poale Zion in prison found themselves always on the defensive:

All that [they] . . . sought to do with all their might was to demonstrate, to prove, to their opponents that they, Poale Zion—despite being Poale Zion—are . . . not reactionary, not bourgeois! At the same time, for all that, deep down in their hearts they harbored a sense of guilt and of inferiority in the face of the socialists pure and simple whose Marxist position did not shake with every wind. . . .

[If] the true Marxists concentrated their attention on the conditions of life, then they had to do likewise. But in life do we not see that some nations dominate and others are dominated! . . . At that moment, though, the rot of doubt would set in, warning them that the theory of Marx—may his soul rest in peace—dealt with nothing else but class-warfare . . . and if so, they were in danger of developing a "non-proletarian ideology." And a "non-proletarian ideology" filled them with deadly fear. Only one accusation could, perhaps, be worse, downright libelous: Eretz Yisrael![68]

And Brenner sounded a similar note in his description of a meeting in the East End of London, held early in 1905, at which the speaker on behalf of Poale Zion assured his audience that they had no reason "to be afraid of him, as a Zionist . . . for he carries on the fight against bourgeois Zionism . . . even more vigorously than the socialist socialists. . . . His Zionism is only a means, with socialism as the end."[69]

Throughout his years in Russia, England, and Austria-Hungary, Brenner declared that his one hope lay in the possible emergence of what he called "young forces"—forces of rejuvenation—from within the Jewish people. He did not spell out exactly what he meant by that term, but it is clear enough that he was thinking primarily of potential recruits from within his own social sub-group: the youth who, before breaking away from the old world, had gone through some or all the stages of the traditional Jewish education: the *heder,* certainly, but preferably also as the case might be, the *bes medrash,* the *kloyz,* or the yeshiva. This was the "half-intelligentsia."

Much less apparent was what role he expected this group to play in concrete terms. At times, he appeared to have in mind primarily identification, whether as writers or as readers, with the (almost lost) cause of Hebrew literature. If, as he not infrequently declared in despair, "there is no Jewish nation across the world: the Galut has defeated us at last,"[70] their literary achievement—the actual translated into the aesthetic—was the most to be hoped for. Or, as he formulated it with reference to his journal, *Hame'orer*: "The national language, Hebrew, and nationalism itself are not so important in themselves . . . but rather only in so far as they give fitting and significant expression to our inner being, to the individual soul of each and every one of us: the two or three people in a given city, the tiny remnant scattered across the various states [of the world]."[71]

More generally, though, he clearly was thinking of the part to be played by the youth (literate in Hebrew) in the attempt to reimbue the Jewish people with a strong sense of self in the present and with pride in its past. However bleak an eye Brenner cast on the small-town Jewish libraries and the would-be national schools in his fiction, he still undoubtedly regarded them as of indispensable importance in the over-all scheme of things. And only the *polu-intelligenty* were fully equipped to further that cause effectively.

Beyond all that, of course, was the political arena. It was clear enough what Brenner was against. He had no time for the complex ideological theories, for the doctrinally monolithic parties, and for the noisy compe-tition for money and prestige between the rival organizations. Surely, an alternative of some kind could be provided by that small number among the youth that was both loyal to the nation but also "free from all spiri-tual servitude and narrow party discipline."[72]

How exactly Brenner expected so marginal a group to assert political leadership on "the Jewish street" was unclear, but he undoubtedly held to the view that there was no viable alternative. "Let us put aside theo-ries," he wrote in 1906, "[and] if anything can be saved let us try to do it."[73] Unable to find any major force in the world of Russian Jewish poli-tics that could advance the national cause as he understood it, Brenner (influenced inter alia by Nietzsche and Mikhailovsky) thus fell back on extreme forms of voluntarism and avant-garde thinking.[74]

However, during the course of 1908 when he was already in Lemberg, Brenner's belief—hitherto almost devoid of concrete meaning—that "the young forces" would somehow take on a leadership role abruptly gained real focus. In that year, the Hapo'el Hatsair (young worker) Party, established in Palestine by a few dozen young immigrants from the Russian empire, began to bring out its Hebrew-language journal under that same name.

The party had been created in 1905, but at that time and over the next year or two, it does not appear to have caught Brenner's attention. Its foundation, after all, had coincided with his move toward territorial-ism. With the failure of Israel Zangwill and the Jewish Territorial Organi-zation (ITO) to locate any region of that world suited to their goal, however, Brenner like many others, including Nahman Syrkin, began to drift back toward the idea of Palestine as the only conceivable (albeit, in their eyes, still highly unrealistic) option. From 1907 onward his letters contained frequent references to the possibility that he himself might opt to go to that country ("not as a Zionist, but as somebody with a longing for the sun. . . . I want to work there as an agricultural laborer?").[75] Other options raised in his correspondence at the time included moving to New York, returning to London, staying longer in Lemberg, or moving to some small Galician town where he would work undisturbed as a typesetter.

Within this context, the appearance of the new journal, *Hapo'el Hatsair*, could only be perceived by Brenner as something of a deus ex machina. Here was an organized group drawn from among those "young forces," "new Jews,"[76] on which—in the abstract—Brenner had always counted. The Hapo'el Hatsair party was situated in Palestine; championed Hebrew as the language to be adopted by the *yishuv*, saw itself as integrally involved in the project of national regeneration along roughly the lines advocated by Ahad Ha'am and other ideologues of the Hibat Zion movement; and had a membership drawn from young men and women who had dedicated themselves as agricultural workers to the cause of "productivization."

In an article of 1908, Brenner attacked the official monthly of the World Zionist Organization (the newly founded *Ha'olam*) for ignoring the existence of the party and its broader significance:

Everything that you could possibly want is discussed there [in *Ha'olam*] . . . but nowhere in it is to be found the slightest hint of what is absolutely crucial and without which there is no hope for Zionism—the immigration of young pioneers to Eretz Yisrael. In Palestine today there is a small group of true Zionists, of real workers (at least, in so far as one can judge by what they say in print, in their truly appealing journal, *Hapo'el Hatsair*). And this group is calling for young idealists in the Galut to come and join them.[77]

And in another article of 1908, responding to somebody who had accused him of being a Yiddishist—and hence in contrast to himself not a true nationalist or Zionist—Brenner wrote: "A Zionist? I am not sure. I am under the impression that he has never considered—and will never consider—the possibility that he himself might go to Palestine in order to make a contribution of his own to developing the Yishuv."[78]

Not long afterward, Brenner departed Lemberg for Jaffa. He would spend the next, and last, twelve years of his life in Palestine. He himself, after all, belonged to that same younger generation within the half intelligentsia that formed the core of what would become known as the Second Aliya. And in 1909, he was still only twenty-eight years old. However, the eye with which he was to observe life in the *yishuv* would remain as mordant as ever, and his pen as caustic.

Conclusion

Even when Brenner's literary and formalistic writings are subjected to close scrutiny, significant difficulties remain in trying to trace the development of his political credo, allegiances, and activity in the European period of his life. Was he ever truly committed to a party and, if so, to which party or parties? How far did his thinking reflect the ideological trends of the time, and how far, on the contrary, were they idiosyncratic?

Scholarly opinion regarding these issues is sharply divided. On the one hand, there is the leading authority on the young Brenner, Yitzhak Bakon, whose research has uncovered a veritable treasure trove of detailed knowledge about his early life and writings. Basing himself on the fact—in part, his own discoveries—that Brenner was ready to put his skills, variously as a translator, editor, and writer of agitational materials at the disposal of many different groups, Bakon depicts him as something of a political chameleon, emerging in rapid succession first as a disciple of Ahad Ha'am's version of Hebrew-based nationalism and then as an activist member of the Bund. Once in London, in 1904, he at first played a leading role as a member both of the Poale Zion Party and simultaneously—as Bakon describes it—of the émigré branch of the Party of Socialist Revolutionaries; only then, disillusioned with these organizations, to go on late in 1905 to join a branch of the Yiddish-speaking anarchist movement, while at the same time agitating vigorously on behalf of territorialism.

At the opposite extreme is an alternative reading of Brenner's politics. To see him as a fully committed and activist member of any specific party or advocate of any predetermined ideology is, according to this view, to misunderstand the essential nature of the man. He was too much of an individualist, too skeptical, and too pessimistic to identify with any form of group thinking. The dialogic and, often, polyphonic character of Brenner's fiction has thus to be seen as not only a literary device but, rather, as reflecting the temperament of a lonely figure unwilling to be tied down by doctrinal formulae.

Or as Menachem Brinker has put it, Brenner saw himself

together with the national literature itself as above any type of narrow party-mindedness. Seeing the life of the nation in dualistic terms, as combining a long-drawn-out process of mortal decline with some few signs of a new vitality that might or might not lead somewhere, the critical observer could be led to a temporary identification with one or other of the various parties on the "Jewish street." . . . [However], frequently enough he did so not because of, but despite the party programs. . . .

His [Brenner's] commitment to the role of writer and critic stood higher with him than any other obligation; and translated into the duty to observe reality with an unsparing and even merciless truthfulness. Guided by this sense of self, he became as it were his own party—a party which he shared with all those writers and critics whom he respected: "the writers' party." . . . Brenner never participated in the hopes that were built into the programs of those parties which he joined.[79]

When set, then, against these conflicting viewpoints, what conclusions can be drawn from the discussion developed in this article? First, certainly, there can be no denying Menachem Brinker's thesis that Brenner's devotion to his role as a writer in the Hebrew language, giving voice to his own generation and to his own kind, carried overwhelming weight in his psyche. But from this fact it does not necessarily follow that his political commitments and party attachments were always tentative and tangential.

On the contrary, we have argued here that in his Homel and Belostok years (from approximately late in 1899 until late in 1901) he combined loyalty to the Hebrew-based cultural nationalism of Ahad Ha'am with active membership in the Bundist underground—an unusual combination of allegiances, to be sure, but not impossible at that inchoate stage of Russian Jewish politics. Once in London in 1904–5, his active, even leading role in the Poale Zion movement, and specifically in its pro-Palestine wing, has likewise to be seen as the expression of a well-elaborated belief at the time (in contrast to his work for SR and anarchist publications that he would hardly have undertaken if he had not desperately needed paid employment).

As with his Bundism, so now with Poale Zion, Brenner was swimming with the tide—both movements were very much on the upswing when he joined them. The same was true when, in the wake of the calamitous pogroms of October 1905, he abandoned his loyalty to Eretz Yisrael and became an impassioned champion of the territorialist cause.

But the difference now was that, despite this ideological turn so characteristic of that moment, he found himself unable to identify with any given party within the socialist wing of the territorialist movement—or, indeed, with the revolutionary Left on "the Jewish street" generally. Pouring scorn, often in prophetic style, on the then-dominant hold of Marxist determinism, of "scientific" socialism and class-war doctrine, he advocated—however much out of fashion—both national unity in the face of the pogroms and of the territorialist imperative, and also the formation of an avant-garde to advance the settlement of a Jewish homeland somewhere in the world.

With the collapse of the Russian revolution in 1907, Brenner, already cut off from his would-be allies, thus ended up all but totally isolated ideologically and organizationally. His decision of late 1908 to go to Palestine and to join forces with the Hapo'el Hatzair Party—oriented, as it was, toward youth, Hebrew, and labor—has therefore to be seen as a desperate attempt to re-anchor himself in the world of Jewish politics.

Notes

The preparatory work on this article was undertaken during the academic year 2002–3 when I was most fortunate to be appointed a fellow first at the Center for Advanced Judaic Studies at the University of Pennsylvania and then at the Institute for Advanced Studies at the Hebrew University of Jerusalem. I wish to thank both institutions; the colleagues who organized the research groups (David Ruderman and Ben Nathans in Philadelphia, and Israel Bartal and Hamutal Bar-Yosef in Jerusalem); and Menachem Brinker, who read over the piece and whose advice I took on many points, although, of course, I am alone responsible for the final version.

1. Yitzhak Bakon, *Brener haz'air: Hayav vizirotav shel Brener 'ad lehofa'at "hame'orer" belondon*, 2 vols. (Tel Aviv, 1975); and his *Brener belondon: Tekufat "hame'orer" (1905–1907)* (Tel Aviv, 1990). On Brenner's life and political development up until 1908, see also Y. Ya'ari-Poleskin, *Mihayei Yosef Hayim Brener* (Tel Aviv, 1922), 1–97; M. B. Hillel-HaCohen, "Yosef Hayim Brener," *Hashiloah* 39 (1921), particularly 356–60; H. Zeitlin, "Y. H. Brener: 'Arakhim vezikhronot," *Hatekufah* (1922): 617–45; and, a brief elegiac overview, A. Z. Rabinovich, *Yosef Hayim Brener: Hayav utkhunato haishit vehasifrutit* (Jaffa, 1922).

2. On Brenner as writer and literary critic, see for example M. Brinker, *'Ad hasimtah hateveriyanit: Maamar al sipur umahshavah bizirat Brener* (Tel Aviv, 1990); Yosef Even, *Omanut hasipur shel Y. H. Brener* (Jerusalem, 1977); Ada Zemach, *Tenu'ah banekudah: Brener vesipurav* (Tel Aviv, 1984); and Hamutal Bar-Yosef, *Mag'aim shel dekadens: Bialik, Berdichevski, Brener* (Jerusalem, 1997). Articles by Fichman, Sadan, Kurzweil, Miron, Zach, Shaked, and many others have been collected in Y. Bakon, ed., *Yosef Hayim Brener: Mivhar maamarim 'al yezirato hasipurit* (Tel Aviv, 1972). See too Ariel Hirschfeld, "Hasemel bizirato shel Y. H. Brener" (Ph.D. dissertation, Hebrew University of Jerusalem, 1950).

3. Yosef Hayim Brener, "Rishmei sha'ah," *Ketavim* (Tel Aviv) 3 (1985): 58; first published in *Hazofeh*, no. 680 (4/17 April 1905). (E.g.: "We, the wandering exiles, only hear echoes resounding from the events, and we do not see the picture as it is.")

4. "Misaviv lanekudah," *Ketavim* (Tel Aviv) 1 (1978): 471–72; first published in *Hashiloah* 14 (1904): 410–11. In that text, this dialogue is broken up by the following authorial comment:

The Zionism of Abramzon, as of the story's narrator and of all their kind, did not stem only from the Jewish problem, [from persecution and exclusion]. Even if the Jewish people were at long last to find itself fully accepted in the lands of the dispersion, even then—or rather only then—would they feel the true necessity of Zionism. True, the optimists are wrong, or so it seems, to sense firm ground under their feet. Abramzon, and those who share his views, see things differently from the optimists, but actually high hopes would do nothing to raise their depressed spirits. For them, for Abramzon and those like-minded, there can be nothing more terrible than the idea that the Jews would not be redeemed, that their days would not be renewed, that they would not gain their rights—or alternatively, that winning their rights they would simply melt away among the host nations, disappearing without a trace.

5. Brinker, 'Ad hasimtah hateveryanit, 20.

6. Ibid., 17–20.

7. Francis B. Randall, *Vissarion Belinskii* (Newtonville, 1987), 39.

8. Ibid., p. 50.

9. See, e.g., S. An-sky, "V novom rusle (povest)," *Novye veianiia: Pervyi evreiskii sbornik* (Moscow, 1907), 88–286; for the shorter Yiddish version, see "In shtrom: Ertselung fur der yidisher revolutsionerer bavegung," *Der fraynd* (3/16 January 1907 and in later installments); A. A. Kabak, *Daniel Shafranov* (Warsaw, 1912); Sholem Aleichem, "Der mabl," *Di varhayt*, no. 437 (30 March 1907 and in later installments); Y. M. Weissenberg, "A shtetl" (supplement to *Der veg*, apparently attached to the issue of 14/27 January 1907); M. Spektor, "Avrom Zilbertsvayg," *Der fraynd*, no. 6 (8/21 January 1907 and in later installments). On the response to the 1905 revolution in the Yiddish-language literature, see the excellent book by Mikhail Krutikov, *Yiddish Fiction and the Crisis of Modernity* (Stanford, 2000). (Cf. my "Youth in Revolt: An-sky's 'In shtrom' and the Instant Fictionalization of 1905," in *The Worlds of S. An-sky: A Russian-Jewish Intellectual at the Turn of the Century*, ed. Gabriella Safran and Steven J. Zipperstein (Stanford, 2006), 137–63.

10. For a useful glimpse into the milieu of the "half intelligentsia," see for example A. Litvak (C. Y. Helfand), *Vos geven: Etyudn un zikhroynes* (Warsaw, 1926), and A. Lesin (Valt), *Zikhronot vehavayot* (Tel Aviv, 1943); this latter volume, a selection of articles translated from the original Yiddish, was edited and introduced by Berl Katznelson, himself a *polu-intelligent*. (It is Litvak's use of the term "half-intelligentsiia" that is accepted here.)

11. Of particular importance for our knowledge of Brenner in his teens are his letters of 1897–98 to Uri Nisan Gnessin: *Igerot Y. H. Brener*, ed. M. Poznansky (Tel Aviv, 1941), 4–41.

12. "Bahoref," *Ketavim* 1:137, first published in *Hashiloah* 11 (1903): 313.

13. "Bahoref," *Ketavim* 1:144; *Hashiloah* 11 (1903): 410. The name of the fictional journal described in *Bahoref* was *Hamaor hakatan* (The small light), while in the Pochep yeshiva, the real-life journal was called *Haperah* (The flower); another of its journals was *Hakof* (The monkey) (cf. Bakon, *Brener haz'air*, 1:23–25).

14. See for example M. Z. Feierberg, "Lean?" *Hashiloah* 5 (1899) and M. Y. Berdyczewski, *Mibait umihutz: Temunot veziyurim* (Petrokov, 1899). Ada Zemach notes that the process of rebellion by the yeshiva youth against the traditional world had found frequent expression in Hebrew literature long before Brenner described it in his first novel. But she argues that *Bahoref* is nonetheless "the first modern novel within the most innovative Hebrew prose." What distinguishes its anti-hero from earlier fictional models was his realization of "the terrible truth that the life he was living was no life at all. 'That he had no present and no future,' 'only one thing remained: the past.'" *Tenu'ah banekudah*, 98–99.

15. "Mizvah (zikaron)," *Ketavim* 1:38; first published in the collection of Brenner's short stories, *Mi'emek akhor: Ziyurim ureshimot* (Warsaw, 1900), 28.

16. *Ketavim* 1:223; *Hashiloah* 12 (1903): 333.

17. "Beriyah 'aluvah (reshimah)," *Ketavim* 1:86; *Mi'emek akhor*, 73. (In the collected works, this story is entitled "Nedudim" [Wanderings].)

18. Brenner to U. N. Gnessin, winter 1897–98, *Igerot Y. H. Brener*, 20–21 ("All

the lads in the *kloyz* regarded me as mad. . . . All he does is write day and night. . . . And he gets his free meals. . . . For what? He hardly studies. . . . Have you ever seen anybody as mad?'').

19. *Ketavim* 1:165; *Hashiloah* 11 (1903): 518.

20. "Bahoref," *Ketavim* 1:156; *Hashiloah* 11 (1903): 518.

21. "Bahoref," *Ketavim* 1:150; *Hashiloah* 11 (1903): 414.

22. Mordkhe Cohen (Virgily was a pseudonym), unlike Brenner, came from a prosperous family, but he too received his formal education in the *heder* and yeshiva. On Brenner's role in bringing him into the Bund, see M. Gintsburg, "An ovent mit Virgilin," in *B. Kohen-Virgili: Zamlbukh tsu zayn biografiye un kharakteristik* (Vilna, 1938), 54–66. For his biography in outline, see "Hoyptdates fun B. Kohen's lebn," *B. Kohen- Virgili*, 10–17. (Even though the facts are not directly relevant to the theme of this essay, it might be of interest to note here that Virgily-Cohen was the nephew of a prominent Hebrew writer and Hovev-Zion, Mordechai Ben-Hillel Ha-Cohen; the father of Arkadius Kahan, a professor at the University of Chicago who specialized in the economic history of Russia and Russian Jewry; and the uncle of Yitzhak Rabin, twice prime minister of Israel.)

23. "Neyn un toyzent mal neyn (ertseylung un erklerung fun a balmelokhe)," in Brenner, *Haketavim hayidiim: Di yidishe shriftn,* ed. Y. Bakon (Beersheva, 1985), 57; first published in *Der kampf,* no. 3 (March 1901).

24. Bakon, *Brener haz'air,* 1:58–91.

25. For lengthy extracts translated into English from the resolutions adapted by the Bund at its Fourth Congress, see P. Mendes-Flohr and J. Reinharz, eds., *The Jew in the Modern World: A Documentary History* (New York, 1995), 420–21; for the full text, see "Der ferter kongres fun algemaynem yidishn arbeter bund in rusland un poyln," *Der yidisher arbeter,* no. 12 (1901): 99–100.

26. A very similar comment appears in Brenner's novella of 1907, *Min hameizar* (From the narrows), where it is said of Avraham Menuhim, the story's heroic protagonist, that "for years he was a loyal member of the Bund in Lithuania—at the time when that organization was imbued with the holy spirit!" *Ketavim* 2:1047; *Ha'olam,* no. 3 (20 January/2 February 1909), 7.

27. "Rishmei sifrut," *Ketavim* 3:749; first published in *Heahdut,* no. 19 (28 Shevat 5672/16 February 1912), 9. (Of Brenner's period in Homel, Hillel Zeitlin, who was then a very close friend, later recalled: "At the time when we first met he was an active Zionist [*ziyoni 'askan*]; and a few months later an active Bundist [*bundai 'askan*] but between us we never talked about either Zionism or Bundism" (Zeitlin, "Yosef Hayim Brener," *Hatekufah* [1922], 626). What did concern them were philosophical issues (Nietzsche, Schopenhauer, Tolstoy), on the one hand, and the Jewish question and its possible solutions, on the other.

28. For a discussion of Feierman and Haimovich as two sides of a "split personality," see Bakon, *Brener haz'air* 2:333–37.

29. *Ketavim* 1:176; *Hashiloah* 12 (1903): 18. According to Hillel Zeitlin, their group in Homel (with Brenner to the fore) briefly toyed with the idea in early 1901 that, in accordance with Tolstoy's principles, they should found an agricultural cooperative somewhere in America (Hillel Zeitlin, "Y. H. Brener: 'Arakhim vezikhronot," *Hatekufah* [1922], 633–37).

30. *Ketavim* 1:176; *Hashiloah* 12 (1903): 18.

31. *Ketavim* 1:178–79; *Hashiloah* 12 (1903): 19.

32. *Ketavim* 1:177–78; *Hashiloah* 12 (1903): 19.

33. *Ketavim* 1:200; *Hashiloah* 12 (1903): 123.

34. *Ketavim* 1:253; *Hashiloah* 12 (1903):394.

35. On Brenner and the Poale Zion movement in London, see the memoirs—not entirely accurate, as Yitzhak Bakon has persuasively demonstrated—of Kalman Marmor, who was the leading figure in the group (earlier known as Maaravi). Brenner was provided with lodging space by Marmor in his Whitechapel flat for a few months; and, inter alia, he helped Marmor edit the group's monthly, *Der yidisher frayheyt* (K. Marmar/Marmor, *Mayn lebensgeshikhte*, vol. 2 [New York, 1959], 707–20; cf. Bakon, *Brener haz'air*, 1:174–83). Brenner's allegiance to the Zionei Zion in this period (from 1904 until October 1905) found clear expression in his short sketch, "Nekhe-ruah: 'Alon," which—written in ironic tones—was given the form of a monologue spoken by a supporter of the Uganda project (*Ketavim* 1:699–701; *Hame'orer*, no. 2 [February 1906]: 14–16 [signed Lo-'aloni]).

36. On the Poale Zion movement in Minsk, see for example M. Zinger [Singer], *Bereishit hatenu'ah hasozialistit: Perakim udmuyot* (Haifa, 1957). Borochov's two major articles written in support of the ideology of the Zionei Zion as led by M. M. Ussishkin were "K voprosam teorii sionizma" and "K voprosu o Sione i territorii."

37. "Mikhtav arokh shalah li," *Ketavim* 3:76 (first published in London as a separate pamphlet in late 1905). (The reference to a "free community" as opposed to a state should presumably be seen as evidence of anarchist influence; for an extensive discussion of this theme, see note 57 below.)

38. "Mikhtav arokh shalah li," 3:77. (The emphasis on the aesthetic sense as a necessary characteristic of the would-be political elite echoes, it would appear, Nietzschean ideas; on Nietzsche's influence on Brenner, see Brinker, *'Ad hasimtah hateveriyanit*, 139–49.)

39. Brenner to Z. Enokhi (27 April 1903) in *Igerot Y. H. Brener*, 104.

40. "Hu amar lah: Daf mekut'a mikuntres katan," *Ketavim* 1:596.

41. Bialik's poem, like Brenner's *Hu amar lah*, was understood as a bitter condemnation of Jewish passivity in the face of violence. The poem was first published under a different name in order to satisfy the censorship: "Masa Nemirov (A tale of Nemirov), *Hazeman: Measef lesifrut ulemad'a*, no. 3 (July-September 1904), 3–15.

42. "Hu amar lah," *Ketavim* 1:600–601.

43. The article, "Uroki strashnykh dnei" (Lessons from the terrible days), was published in installments in *Voskhod* (*Nedel'naia khronika*) nos. 47–48 (1 December 1905), 1–10, and nos. 49–50 (16 December), 1–5. The article has been published in part in English: see S. Dubnov, *Nationalism and History: Essays on Old and New Judaism*, ed. and with an introduction by K. S. Pinson (Philadelphia, 1958), 200–214.

44. "Rishmei sha'ah," *Ketavim* 3:62; *Hazofeh*, no. 680 (4/17 April 1905), 2. (E.g., "We hear promises and then we hear those promises being reversed, time and again. And won't the time come when the soldiers, well-trained and well-armed, emerge as one—and together with them all the police, the judges and the guards: all the rats and the fleas who, crawling, sneering, waiting, are hidden away in the sink holes of the revolution and in the cracks of the gendarmerie.")

45. "Rishmei sha'ah," *Ketavim* 3:63.

46. "Mikhtavim lerusiyah," *Ketavim* 3:100–101; *Hame'orer*, no. 1 (January 1906): 8 (there signed Bar Yohai).

47. Bakon, *Brener haz'air*, 2:183–197.

48. On the cover page of *Kampf un kempfer*, it is stated that the journal was published by the Party of Socialist Revolutionaries and edited by Z. Sinani and

Yohanan Hakanai (pseudonyms of An-sky and Brenner, respectively). It appears to have been made up entirely of translations.

49. Terms of payment for the work of translation are mentioned in specific sums (twenty-five rubles for sixteen printed pages) in a letter from Chaikovsky to Brenner (23 October 1905); see Bakon, *Brener haz'air*, 1:193.

50. Bakon emphasizes the fact that Brenner's flight from the army was facilitated by a group of SRs in Orel and that among them was Haya Volfson. But Bundists were responsible for his rescue from the étape in Bobruisk; and there does not appear to be enough evidence to associate Brenner with membership in either party at this stage of his life (early 1904). On his double escape, see ibid., 110–20.

51. "Shanah ahat," *Ketavim* 2:881–1018 (and particularly 968–79, where there is a detailed description of the Jewish soldiers in the brigade); *Hashiloah* 19 (1908), particularly 411–17.

52. For example, "Petrov . . . knew that the god of the Jews, as Marx himself had stated, was money, money, money, and that they had no god." ("Misaviv lanekudah," *Ketavim* 1:526; *Hashiloah* 14 [1904]: 508). As for Shakhtarov, who tried to stab Avraham Menuhin to death, he is described in the act as a "drunken beast . . . [whose] screaming made him sound like a wild pig" ("Min hameizar," *Ketavim* 2:1089; *Ha'olam*, no. 15 [21 April/4 May 1909], 6).

53. "Mialef 'ad mem," *Ketavim* 1:667–68; *Hame'orer*, no. 6 (June 1906), 6. Writing in 1906 (admittedly somewhat later than the time of Brenner's supposed membership in the Party of Socialist Revolutionaries), he referred scornfully to those Jewish socialists—Bundists and Poale Zion—"who, turning apostate have renounced everything and are fighting under the flag of the SD or SR as though they were actually Russians" ("Bibliografiyah," *Ketavim* 3:121; *Hame'orer*, no. 5 [June 1906]: 32 [signed H. B. Zalel]).

54. "Mikhtavim lerusiyah," *Ketavim* 3:101–2; *Hame'orer*, no. 1 (January 1906): 8–9. (The reference to Nemirov, a town in Ukraine, carried a double resonance: its Jewish population was massacred by the Cossacks under Khmelnytsky's command in 1648; and its name had become a codeword for the Kishinev pogrom of 1903—which left many homeless orphans—since the publication of Bialik's "Masa Nemirov" [cf. n. 36 above].) Haya Volfson's murder undoubtedly accentuated Brenner's reaction to the October pogroms still further. (See, in particular, the piece dedicated to her memory, although she is not mentioned by name: "Hu siper le'azmo," *Ketavim* 1:713–24; first published in New York in 1906 in a booklet entitled *Lo klum*; see *Ketavim* 1:ix, n).

55. "Min hasifrut ha'ivrit: Sihot," *Ketavim* 3:187. This article was apparently first published in the Polish-language journal brought out in Lwow: *Moriah: Miesiecznik mlodiezy zydowskiej*; the Hebrew original was only published much later (see *Ketavim* 3:192).

56. *Ketavim* 1:439; *Hashiloah* 14 (1904): 309.

57. Yitzhak Bakon has argued convincingly that Brenner gradually shed his reluctance to write in the Yiddish press and began to publish thoughtful articles there on such figures as N. Mikhailovsky and Y. L. Peretz. It is almost certainly overstated, however, to conclude (as Bakon does) that Brenner's employment in the production of the anarchist journal *Di fraye arbeter velt* involved his identification with the anarchist ideology and politics as generally understood at the time. In the Russian Jewish world, anarchism was associated primarily with both radical internationalism (or "cosmopolitanism") and also a theatrical anti-clericalism (Yom Kippur balls, for example)—a combination totally alien to Brenner, even though a strongly libertarian strand can be discerned in his thought.

In the sketch ("A kleyner felieton") that he published in the *Di fraye arbeter velt* in December 1905, Brenner exploited the dialogic form to put forward his own credo, pitching a naive and near-hysterical youngster, a territorialist, against the mature editor of an anarchist periodical (*Di fraye arbeter velt*, no less!). But with an ironic twist, all the strong lines were given to the wild young man who, fiercely rejecting the class analysis that blamed the pogroms all but exclusively on the tsarist autocracy and the "counterrevolution," argues that "a radical solution to the Jewish question is to be found only in a territory, a country of our own." For his part, the editor brushes aside the idea that he publish this viewpoint: "People would start saying that *Di fraye arbeter velt* has become a Zionist paper!" "That's shameful!" responds the youngster. "It's bad enough that the program of the Social Democrats does not permit them to see with open eyes just how black the world is. . . . [But] those who speak in the name of real freedom should value the truth in life above all else and the suffering of a people should be placed above the fear of what this small *kloyz* or that clique might say."

The smallest possible print was used to publish Brenner's piece on the last page of the journal which, in general, followed a line typical of mainstream anarchism. (Y. Abramzon [Brenner], "A kleyner felieton," *Di fraye arbeter velt* [8 December 1905], 8; also in Brenner, *Hakatavim hayidiim*; *Di yidishe shriftn* [ed. Y. Bakon] [Beersheva, 1985], 194–201. Cf. Bakon, *Brener haz'air*, 1:221–37.

58. "Dapim (mipinkaso shel sofer 'ivri)," *Ketavim* 3:104, *Hame'orer*, no. 1 (January 1906): 12 (signed H. B. Zalel).

59. Ibid., 3:109; *Hame'orer*, no. 1 (January 1906): 14.

60. "Pinkas katan," *Ketavim* 3:133; *Hame'orer*, nos. 7–8 (July-August 1906): 72 (signed Bar Yohai).

61. "Mikhtavei sofer," *Ketavim* 3:140; *Hame'orer*, no. 9 (September 1906): 36 (signed H. B. Zalel).

62. "Misaviv lanekudah," *Ketavim* 1:461; *Hashiloah* 14 (1904): 321–22.

63. *Ketavim* 1:486; *Hashiloah* 14 (1904): 419.

64. "Mikhtavim lerusiyah," *Ketavim* 3:100; *Hame'orer*, no. 1 (January 1906): 7.

65. "Mikhtav arokh shalah li," *Ketavim*. 3:80.

66. Ibid., pp. 78–79.

67. "Mi'ever legevulin," *Ketavim* 1:778; *Hame'orer*, no. 2 (February 1907): 83.

68. *Ketavim* 1:681–82; *Hame'orer*, nos. 7–8 (July-August 1906): 19.

69. "Ma'asim," *Ketavim* 3:28; *Hazeman*, no. 57 (14/27 March 1905): 1. Of the four parties that emerged from the amorphous Poale Zion movement during the revolutionary period, only the Jewish Territorialist Labor Party: Poale Zion was spared the full brunt of Brenner's scorn. He approved of the fact that this party, a territorialist and revolutionary reincarnation of the Minsk Poale Zion, invested less effort than the others in trying to prove its class-war credentials. Reviewing its journal, *Dos naye lebn*, in 1906, Brenner wrote that despite its modish rhetoric regarding " 'the proletariat and the broad Jewish masses,' they understand the *true* situation of the Jewish petty bourgeoisie very well . . . ; and they do not see their territorialism as a mere means to their social goals. Their territorialism is all of a piece, out in the open, broad and national. They understand that unless this idea is realized, we will be utterly and totally lost" ("Bibliografiyah," *Ketavim* 3:23; *Hame'orer*, no. 5 [June 1906]: 33 [signed H. B. Zalel]).

70. "Pinkas Katan," *Ketavim* 3:125; *Hame'orer*, nos. 7–8 (July-August 1906): 68.

71. "El hahotmim vehakorim," *Ketavim* 3:145; *Hame'orer*, no. 11 (November 1906): back cover.

72. "La 'mitkaven letovah,' " *Ketavim* 3:151; *Hame'orer*, no. 1 (January 1907): back cover.

73. "Mikhtavim lerusiyah," *Ketavim* 3:102; *Hame'orer,* no.1 (January 1906): 9.

74. In this context, it is understandable that Brenner and Radler-Feldman decided to find space in *Hame'orer* for Thomas Carlyle's ideas on heroes and heroism. (See, in particular, Brenner's comment, "He'arah," *Ketavim.* 3:151–153; *Hame'orer,* no. 2 [February 1907]: 88.)

75. Brenner to Y. Klausner (25 March 1907) in *Igerot Y. H. Brenner,* 360. (In a letter written in Yiddish of 20 July 1907 to Yehoshua Radler-Feldman [Rav Binyamin], Brenner remarked that "I am no longer going to Palestine; I am hostile to the chosen people [*'am hanivhar*] and to the corpse-like would-be Erets-yisroel"; *Igerot Y. H. Brenner,* 381.)

76. For Brenner's use of the term "the new Jews" see for example "Mikhtavei sofer," *Ketavim* 3:140; *Hame'orer,* no. 9 (September 1906): 36. ("We hear the cry constantly: give strength to the new Jews! But what qualities do we expect these new Jews to have? Where have they come from? Where *can* they come from? And whither are they headed?")

77. "Dapim mipinkas sifruti," *Ketavim* 3:184; *Hed hazeman,* no. 64 (15/28 March 1908), 2. (In the newspaper, the article is entitled "Mitokh hapinkas.")

78. "Mitokh hapinkas," *Ketavim* 3:232; *Hed hazeman,* no. 121 (4/17 March 1908), 1. (In the collected works, the numbering of the sections in this series of articles is incorrect; the passage quoted here is actually from section 5, while what is given as section 5 in the *Ketavim* was no. 6 in the paper, no. 122 [5/14 March 1908]).

79. Brinker, *'Ad hasimtah hateveriyanit,* 208–9.

Chapter 7

Recreating Jewish Identity in Haim Nahman Bialik's Poems: The Russian Context

Hamutal Bar-Yosef

In his book *Haim Nahman Bialik and the Poetry of His Life* (1950), Yosef Klausner (1874–1958), who after Ahad Ha'am was the most influential Hebrew thinker and literary critic, wrote:

Haim Nahman Bialik was an extraordinary phenomenon in literature. Usually a poet who is of real talent finds at the beginning, together with admirers among his contemporaries, great *opponents* who attack his poetic works, denying his talent, and only after a long war he becomes respected by everyone. *Bialik has no opponents.* . . . In this respect he resembles Rabbi *Yehuda Halevi.* Like him Bialik dove into the Jewish nation's soul and raised precious pearls from it. Therefore, whoever possesses even one spark of the nation's soul cannot refrain from kneeling before this great national talent, before the real Jewish poet who is more than a mere artist.[1]

It was Klausner who in his enthusiastic criticism of Bialik's first collection of poetry (1902) crowned the young artist with the title "poet of the Jewish national revival."[2] Not distinguishing between biography and the lyrical, Klausner claimed that Bialik was a "poet prophet," the inheritor of the biblical prophets who formulated a unique Jewish identity.[3] Although later Klausner rightly found the poet Shaul Chernikhovsky (1875–1943) to be more worthy of the title "Poet of National Renaissance" than Bialik,[4] it was Bialik who remained the exemplary National Poet for many of his Jewish and non-Jewish readers and critics.[5]

The hallmark of this identity was, according to Klausner, neither a developed intellect nor an aesthetic sensitivity, which are the criteria of great literature in the Western tradition, but an intensity of moral emotions.[6] In Bialik's poems, even in his love poems, Klausner found this characteristic Jewish quality. Bialik's poetry was a reflection of Jewish identity.

Following Klausner, Bialik's poetry was understood by many of his contemporary and later readers as both national and prophetic. Bialik's own attitude toward this image was ambivalent: his early poems show an effort to become a National Poet, following Semyon Frug (1860–1916) and the poetry of *Hibat Tsiyon* (Lovers of Zion). A few years later he succeeded in transforming his deepest personal experiences into a symbol of Jewish psychological and moral identity. After his acquaintance with Russian Symbolism (beginning circa 1902),[7] Bialik dedicated many of his poems to the conflict between the poet's commitment to his national mission and his wish to be a purely personal poet, free from his national identity.[8] These poems show that in spite of the poet's longings for purely individual existence and personal literary creation, such a role was alien to him: he was unable to disconnect himself from his deep involvement and identification with the nation's fate. The difference between the Jewish people and other nations—Bialik had in mind European Christians—was a constant theme throughout Bialik's poetry and thought. Bialik's canonical place in Zionist culture, ritual, and school curriculae[9] made his poetry a source of influence on modern Jewish spiritual and moral identity, especially for the reader of Hebrew literature.

Against this background, examination of the changing Jewish identities that appear in his poetry and tracing their sources provide not only greater understanding of Bialik's work but also a map of the options that Bialik proposed to his readers. The aim of this article is to show that these options were sometimes innovative and that some of them were inspired by Russian literature and thought.

Unlike the German maskilim, who were interested mostly in the philosophical aspect of Judaism, and unlike the Russian maskilim, who were interested mostly in the social aspect of Jewish life, Bialik's concept of Judaism embraces both the Jewish spirit and contemporary Jewish life. While the literature of the Haskalah sought to create a European literature in Hebrew, written by and for the European Jew according to German and Russian models, Bialik belonged to the post-Haskalah generation who—following Ahad Ha'am's idea of "imitation through competition"[10]—wished to strengthen the unique national character of Hebrew culture.

The extent to which Hebrew literature should be a part of European culture was a major point of discord in Bialik's time, with the writers David Frishman and Micha Yosef Berdychevsky fighting against Ahad Ha'am's position.[11] In fact, Hebrew literature at the turn of the twentieth century, including Bialik's poetry, was, on the one hand, aspiring to find its place within the ranks of world literature and, on the other, greatly influenced by the context of Russian literature and culture.[12] The search for the revival of Jewish roots, which in practice meant the selection and activation of traditional Jewish elements, was guided by contemporary

West European and Russian ideas. Thus for example the European fashion of mysticism and literary Symbolism, which was very strong in tsarist Russia at the end of the nineteenth century, helped inspire Hebrew writers such as Y. L. Peretz and M. Y. Berdychevsky to revive the Hasidic story in a modern literary style.

Even the meaning of the title "poet prophet" as it was used in Hebrew literature in Bialik's time had Russian roots. In the context of late nineteenth-century Russian literature, the poet-prophet was *not* a poet who foresees the future or writes about contemporary national problems and aspirations, but a "national poet" or "poet of the people" (*narodnyi poet*) who expresses the depths and the uniqueness of the nation's soul and aspirations. His personal identity should be completely absorbed by the national inner experience, making him the best formulator of the national essence, even when he writes personal poems. In comparison to the poet laureate in Western literatures, in Russia during the mid- and late nineteenth century the ultimate poet was not just an outstanding artist but the voice of the national moral spirit.[13]

A Living Nation?

Jewish national identity was created in Europe in the context of Romanticism. Against this background the idea of "a living nation" was a main criterion of national existence. Activity, vitality, and creativity were the signs of the nation's life. Beginning in the late eighteenth century Hebrew writers were rewriting biblical and post-biblical sources where they could find proof of Jewish heroic activity: poems and stories about the period of Jewish political independence, kingdoms, and wars contributed to the idea that the Jewish people were and could still be "alive." H. Weseley's "Poems of Glory" (1789–1829), considered the first modern Hebrew literary work, is an epos on the heroic life of Moses. The theme of Exodus often appeared in nineteenth-century Hebrew poetry as well as in the "national" Russian Jewish poetry of Semyon Frug.

Bialik published only three poems that rewrite the Bible, all of which deal with the Exodus from Egypt: "On the Head of Har'El" (Al rosh har'el, 1893), "The Last Dead of the Desert" (Meitei midbar ha-aharonim, 1894), and the long poem "The Dead of the Desert" (Meitei midbar, 1902).[14] In these poems the desert has a symbolic meaning: the impossibility of life.[15] In all of them, immobility appears as a mysterious Jewish power. In "On the Head of Har'El" Moses is pictured as standing motionless on the mountain spreading his hands and holding the Tablets of the Covenant, while two giant enemies are trying in vain to attack him. It is implied that Moses' immobility is a manifestation of his victorious greatness. In "The Last Dead of the Desert" the people of Israel, while entering the Holy Land under the leadership of Joshua, look back with longing for Moses, their spiritual leader. Instead of going further they are "standing still," their eyes searching for the dead Moses, "their great loyal shepherd." Their refusal to move characterizes their loyalty to their past and their preference for the spiritual rather than the political love of Zion. In "The Dead of the Desert" the Jewish people are symbolically depicted as giants who are frozen like stones in an eternal sleep. They are attacked by wild beasts, but no beast can touch them because of their mysterious power. Again immobility serves as the paradoxical secret of their power to ward off attacks by their beastly enemies and to continue their eternal, beautiful still life. In this long poem the giants attempt to arise and change their situation, but the attempt is ephemeral: their eternal power lies in their immobility, while their revolution is a futile attempt to change the natural order of the world.

Bialik's first attempt to write a national poem was his unpublished "In the Tent of Sacred Study" (Be-ohel ha-torah), written in August 1890 at the age of seventeen, while he was still studying in the Volozhin yeshiva.[16] The title of the poem hints at the biblical characterization of Jacob as "a dweller in tents" (Genesis 25:27), in contrast to Esau who was a hunter and a warrior. The poem describes a yeshiva student at night, studying the Talmud, "silent as a stone," not in the customary movements and loud reading of Talmud study. The poem ends with the lines: "Here is your power for God/ Yaakov son of grandfather Israel," namely, Jewish powers are spiritually very active, although externally immobile.

This does not mean that Bialik was against Zionist activity. On the contrary, in many of his poems he mocks and chides the laziness of his contemporaries' attitude toward the Zionist project. His encouragement of activity is, however, accompanied with advice to do things not in a revolutionary way, but little by little. "Who is mocking at trifles? Fie upon the mockers!" he wrote in "A Blessing for the People" (Birkat am 1894). He was skeptical of dramatic political moves, and especially of the idea of revolution, which filled the air in his time.[17] As is well known, Bialik was a disciple of Ahad Ha'am's "Spiritual Zionism," which based the Jewish renaissance on moral and spiritual rather than political grounds. Poems that describe Jewish vitality as paradoxically immobile can be understood as supporting Ahad Ha'am's ideas. It is noteworthy, however, that Ahad Ha'am never spoke in praise of immobility. On the contrary, he argued that in order to activate history, an extreme power (of the "prophet") should be initiated, so that its conflict with reality (the contrasting extreme) will produce a synthesis, practical ("priestly") results.

Bialik chose an image that recalls Tolstoy's *War and Peace* (1869), where the Russian victory over Napoleon's well-equipped army is achieved by the sleeping General Kutuzov, the personification of a mysterious Russian superiority over other nations. In the long poem "The Dead of the Desert" (1902), the people of Israel are frozen in an eternal sleep, the secret of their survival. For both Tolstoy and Bialik, sleep is a symbol of a nation's tendency to solve its historical problems by patience, not by aggression or revolution. It also expresses their belief in the mysterious, magical powers of their nations. The image of the Sleeping Beauty, a popular motif in Russian folklore, appears in Bialik's uncanonical long poem "On My Ancestors' Grave" (Al kever avot, 1891, sent to a friend in a letter and not published during Bialik's life)[18] and in his long poem "The Lake" (Ha-breikha, 1904). In "On My Ancestors' Grave" the people of Israel are compared to a sleeping princess who was buried and seems dead but in fact is just sleeping and will come back to life. In "The Lake" Bialik compares the lake to a sleeping sacred princess surrounded by knightly guards, one of whom is the poet himself, her chosen one. In this poem the lake is the source of sacredness and creative vitality. It is clearly influenced by Vladimir Solov'ev's poems "[Lake] Saima" (1894) and "At Saima in Winter" (1894), where the sacred spirit of the world is found in the woman-like sleeping lake.[19] Like his predecessors in Hebrew literature and thought, Bialik constructed the image of a living nation. However, he paradoxically found a hidden Jewish vitality in the Jewish refusal to change, in loyalty to the Jewish past, an idea characteristic of Russian anti-Western ideologies.

A People of Which Book?

The Bible was the foundational text of modern Jewish identity during the Haskalah period. In contrast, the Talmud was considered to be the product of a legalistic, emotionless mind. Such an attitude toward the Talmud was characteristic of Christian Romantic thought during the nineteenth century and was absorbed by German maskilim. Therefore, they made great efforts to revive the Bible's language and to base modern Jewish identity on it, while shunning the Talmud and its commentaries. Similar ideas were reformulated at the turn of the twentieth century by Berdychevsky (1865–1921), whose thinking was close to Nietzsche's. Bialik rejected the maskilic and neo-romantic tendency to base modern Jewish identity on the Bible or even on pre-biblical Jewish culture, while dismissing the Jewish culture created in the Diaspora with the Talmud at its core. His innovative attitude also had innovative stylistic results: not the Bible but post-biblical sources serve as the main intertexts of Bialik's poems. Even his few biblical poems are based on post-biblical sources.

Already in "In the Torah's Tent" (Be-ohel ha-torah) Bialik defined the *differentia specifica* of the Jewish people in contrast to non-Jewish nations: dedication to studying the Talmud. The poem describes a young student sitting at his Talmud book at midnight in the house of study, carried away by his almost ecstatic experience that makes him indifferent to the needs of his body and to the outer world. Here, as in many of Bialik's other poems, Talmud study is the vital seed from which the Jewish spirit has ever grown. It is interesting that while in his "To Legend" (El ha-agada, 1892) Bialik glorifies the talmudic legend as a source of creative inspiration for the Jewish soul, both in "In the Torah's Tent" and in the long poem "The Yeshiva Student" (Ha-matmid, 1894) it is the talmudic legalistic text that inspires the yeshiva students.

Bialik refuted the accepted Romantic idea that the study of the Talmud was a dry intellectual activity; he discovered and showed the Talmud's spiritual vitality and its power to inspire the Jewish soul with enthusiasm and ecstasy, even when the text is legalistic. He explained this view in his essay "Law and Legend" (Halakha ve-agada, 1915). There Bialik argues that talmudic laws should be understood symbolically. He shows the noble principles of moral philosophy hidden behind the dry, practical, detailed laws of the Talmud. He also speaks of the great vitality of spirit invested in talmudic discussions.

Thus Bialik turned the search for a modern Jewish identity from the Bible—a text which represented the dream of another Jewish life—to the talmudic and Jewish mystical literature—texts studied in innumerable prayer houses, part of traditional cultural life in the shtetl.

The *beit midrash*, where the Talmud and its commentaries were the main object of study, appears in Bialik's early poems as a symbol of Jewish roots. This is where Jewish identity is forged. In "If You Want to Know," he glorifies the *beit midrash* as the fountain of Jewish spiritual powers and says that here he received intellectual, emotional, and moral sustenance for his whole life. In "Alone," the *beit midrash* is the last shelter of the *shekhina*, a symbol Bialik uses for the Jewish spirit. When Bialik speaks of national revival, he describes the resurrection of the *beit midrash*, not the Temple in Jerusalem. The *beit midrash*, not the synagogue, which was the place of religious ritual, is for him the central symbol of Jewish spiritual identity. For Bialik, not the performance of the religious ritual and law (including the prayers!), but the enthusiastic study of Jewish texts kept Judaism alive in the Diaspora and protected its innermost identity.

As mentioned, in the 1890s Bialik wrote only two poems in which he engaged the story of the Exodus, and one more in 1902 where he already used post-biblical materials. Bialik was the first Hebrew poet who turned to Jewish mysticism both as an intertextual source and as a characteristic of Jewish identity. Thus, in "Midnight Prayer" (Tikkun hatsot,

1898) he describes the shtetl as a terrible place of darkness, where the only light seen is from a lonely window behind which a Jew says the *tik-kun hatsot* (a midnight prayer in memory of the destruction of the Temple). Jewish mystical ritual represents here the only remnant of Jewish spiritual life. Bialik's move from the Bible to post-biblical texts created an additional option for modern Jewish identity, which does not reject the post-biblical and the Diasporic Jewish spiritual existence as a source for modern Jewish revival.

Bialik's "rehabilitation" of the Talmud and of Jewish mysticism had a basis in contemporary post-Romantic Russian culture. It took place in a historical-cultural context that, although often called "neo-Romantic," in fact grew out of a sense of disappointment with the optimism of the populist movement[20] and the subsequent turn to political and existential pessimism, mysticism, and the study of esoteric texts. This turn was taken by the "early Symbolist" writers (sometimes also called "the Decadents"), especially by Dmitrii Merezhkovsky, Fedor Sologub, and Nikolai Minskii (Vilenkin). Interest in esoteric traditions and cults flourished in Russia toward the end of the nineteenth century.[21]

Again, Vladimir Solov'ev's influential personality and ideas should be mentioned. Solov'ev began his academic career by showing the bankruptcy of Positivism. A former student of the Moscow theological academy, he turned to Spinoza, Hellenistic Gnosticism, and Jewish Kabbalah in order to formulate his vision of Russian and universal redemption. In 1896 he published an article refuting attacks on the Talmud and defending the moral beauty implicit in talmudic laws.[22] As a result, in 1910 parts of the Mishnah and the Tosefta were translated into Russian by the orientalist Nehemiah Pereferkovich. In 1896 Solov'ev wrote an introduction and footnotes to David Ginzburg's article on Kabbalah, which he (Solov'ev) brought to publication in *Voprosy filosofii i psikhologii*.[23] Solov'ev's interest in Kabbalah[24] was part of a general interest in mysticism in Russia and other European countries (especially Germany) toward the end of the nineteenth century.[25] This background could have been a source of inspiration for Jewish writers and intellectuals—including Bialik—who turned to post-biblical Jewish texts for the redefinition of modern Judaism.

A Suffering Victim?

During the nineteenth century Jewish literature dealt either with the glorious Jewish past or with its mournful present, in that same chronological order: during the first half of that century it dealt mainly with biblical history, while contemporary Jewish suffering was a dominant theme during the second half. The Jewish nation as suffering woman—a widespread *topos* in both Jewish and non-Jewish cultures—symbolized its mournful fate in the Diaspora, as for example in the Hebrew poetry of *Hibat Tsiyon* during the 1880s and 1890s. This was the situation in non-Hebrew Jewish literature as well: Semyon Frug's Russian poems constantly invoke Jewish suffering.[26] Mendele Mokher Sforim bravely revealed Jewish suffering from anti-Semitism in tsarist Russia in his Yiddish novel *The Nag* (Die Kliache, 1873).[27] A vast Jewish literature and folklore in Hebrew, Yiddish, and Russian mourned the sufferings of the Cantonists (Jewish children drafted into the Russian army for twenty-five years during the years 1827–55).[28] The identity of the suffering nation had a special apologetic appeal in the context of Russian culture, where suffering was highly valued as a sign of moral purity and even of sacredness.[29] Idealization of suffering as a characteristic of Christian-Russian roots was a dominant theme in Dostoevsky's writings, idolized by the Symbolist poets at the turn of the twentieth century. Russian poetry during the 1880s tended to lachrymose sentimentalism, and the Hebrew poetry of *Hibat Tsiyon*, which flourished during the same period, adopted this tendency. In this poetry the suffering of the Jewish people, often allegorized as a suffering woman, became a focus of Jewish identity, replacing the model of the enlightened new Jew.

In his earliest published poems, Bialik continued this tradition, sometimes changing the feminine image of the nation into the image of an old man or a semi-autobiographical lyrical "I." In "To the bird " (El ha-tsipor1891), "Back from the Distance" (Mi-shoot ba-merkhakim, 1892), "In the Field (Ba-sadeh, 1894), "A Small Letter She Wrote" (Mikhtav katan li katava, 1894), and "To Legend" (El ha-agada, 1894), the poet complained about the misfortunes of the Jewish people in Russia, implying the need for a radical change in the Jewish situation. In these poems the image of the Jewish nation—with which the poet identified his fictional self—was that of a suffering, oppressed, choked, despised, tortured human being. The rhetoric here is much more energetic and full of revolt than the melancholic tone of Bialik's predecessors, but the idea is the same: to be a Jew means to belong to a suffering nation, victim of unjust persecutions. The strongest image of the Jewish people as a victim—here without any hope of change—is to be found in Bialik's "On the Slaughter"(Al ha-shehita, 1903), written a short time after the Kishinev pogrom.

Side by side with such works, the young Bialik also wrote poems about the special powers of Judaism, enabling the Jews to survive in spite of their external sufferings, and even to be superior to other nations. This idea can be traced in "Jewish Poetry" (Shirat Yisrael, 1894), "To Legend" (El ha-agada, 1894), "On the Threshold of the *Beit Midrash*" (Al saf beit ha-midrash, 1894), and especially in the long poem "The Dead of the Desert." According to these poems the Jewish people possess mysterious eternal powers. In contrast to other nations, whose powers are measured by victories in wars, Jewish power is spiritual and moral. Judaism and/or the Jewish people are contrasted with other nations and are found to have a superior power, which enables them to survive in the face of existential challenges.

In "Jewish Poetry" Bialik makes clear his distinction between the powers of other nations, whose mission is war, and the Jewish nation, whose mission is spiritual: "God did not call me to fanfares of war./ Even its smell frightens me./ I quiver when I hear the trumpet aloud / Violin or sword—give me a violin."[30] This poem is perhaps an echo of two others, both entitled "The Dagger," one by Pushkin (1821), the second by Lermontov (1838). Both poets mythologize the dagger and praise its power. In Lermontov's poem the dagger—the poet's best friend—embodies the ancient, primitive values of freedom, the right for vengeance, love, and loyalty.[31]

In "On the Threshold of the *Beit Midrash*" the poet stresses the difference between the aggressive, lion-like Nietzschean utopia spreading among contemporary non-Jewish peoples and even among Jewish intellectuals[32] and the Jewish mission of justice, truth, and spiritual purity. Unlike the pessimistic tone of the above-mentioned early works, this poem ends with a vision of the resurrection of "the tent of Shem," namely, the renaissance of the unique Jewish spirit and culture. Here the present Jewish suffering is part of its sacred mission to all the nations—a biblical messianic idea (Isaiah 2:2–4) deeply rooted in Russian thought.[33] In this context the Russian people had a "prophetic" mission—to redeem itself and Western Europe from sin and evil by its suffering. The Russian idea of the people-prophet was adopted by Ahad Ha'am and by Bialik. In Bialik's poem the "prophetic" role of Judaism is different from the original biblical meaning: in the Bible the Temple in Jerusalem will be a center of knowledge and wisdom for the nations, while in Bialik's poem the Jews, doomed to be eternal wanderers, will purify the nations of their sins. This view of the national prophetic role shows the clear influence of the Russian model.

In Russia, beginning with Gogol and culminating in Dostoevsky and Solov'ev, this image of the poet was tightly connected with the idea of the messianic role of the nation, the poet being an incarnation of the pure and authentic national spirit. Russian literary tradition attributed to the National Poet the title of "a poet prophet." This role was first attributed by Gogol and Belinsky to Pushkin, especially to his poem "The Prophet" (1826),[34] where Pushkin metaphorically describes the poet (himself?) as a biblical prophet (in the Romantic vein), who abandons all earthly interests and dedicates himself to the sacred mission, fighting against social mediocrity.[35] In this famous poem Pushkin, writing in the first person, describes God's revelation to him according to the description in Isaiah 6: like Isaiah, Pushkin's prophet sees a "six-winged Seraph" who (unlike the biblical text) tears out his tongue and puts in its place a snake's tongue. The Seraph also puts a burning coal instead of the prophet's heart (in the biblical text one of the Seraphs touches Isaiah's lips with a burning coal). This poem, well known to Russian readers, created a Russian model of the Prophet.

Following Ahad Ha'am, in his early poems Bialik chooses Moses as the model of the prophet, while later he refers to Isaiah as a prophetic model. He cites Isaiah in his prophetic poems "Surely the People Is Grass" (Akhen hatsir ha-am, 1897) and "The Word" (Davar 1904). He also uses images from Isaiah 6 in his "I Have Not Gained My Light" (Lo zakhiti ba-or min ha-hefker 1902) and in his long poem "The Scroll of Fire" (Megilat ha-esh, 1905). Of course, Bialik knew the book of Isaiah before he knew Pushkin, but his choice of Isaiah could be motivated by the Russian model, which was already widely known among Hebrew readers as well.

In his 1881 eulogy of Pushkin, Dostoevsky immortalized his predecessor as both a "National Poet" and a "Poet Prophet." He established these titles as essential for the true Russian writer, whom he described as a national Messiah. Dostoevsky's understanding of "prophet" was more nationalistic than Pushkin's. These ideas became a commonplace in Russia toward the turn of the twentieth century. The great poet was expected to dedicate his life to the mission of ensuring the moral purity and the authenticity of the nation's soul against alien cultural powers that threaten its existence. The title "Prophet" seemed to be a matter of Jewish reclaiming of Jewish sources, but in the modern Hebrew context its meaning was significantly inflected by the Russian setting. Sacred, not humiliating, suffering was part of the Russian image of the poet-prophet and the nation-prophet. The image of the suffering prophet who is a voluntary victim on the altar of his people bears Christian traces, which were absorbed in the Russian literary tradition. The Russian poet-prophet is traditionally a poet of the people who attacks the ruling powers. Only in this sense he is "in the desert," an outsider from society. In contrast, the Jewish biblical prophet is living among his people, with whom he is in constant tension. His wrath is directed against the people's sins no less than against the ruler.

In his prophetic poems Bialik combined the two traditions. Sometimes, as in his "I Have Not Gained My Light," the poet-prophet sacrifices himself on the altar of his readers, endowing them with his sacred light: "And when my heart bursts/ under the hammer of my troubles,/ a spark will fly to my eye,/ and from my eye—to my rhyme// And from my rhyme it flies to your hearts/ disappears in your fire which I set/ and it is I with my flesh and blood/ that will pay for the fire."[36] More often, however, the poet-prophet's listeners—contemporary Jewry—are pictured as a lazy, corrupt, decadent, hollow, demonic band. Thus, in "On Your Desolate Heart" (Al levavkhem she-shamem, 1902), modern Jews are symbolically described as a band of jesters and vain idlers incessantly throwing wild parties in a ruined temple. Their joy will soon be driven away by the "beadle of ruined temples"—despair—and on the Jewish heart, which used to be a sacred altar, bored cats will sit and meow.

In Bialik's "prophetic" poems—"Surely the People Is Grass," "On Your Desolate Heart," "The Word," When the Days Go By (Ve-haya ki ya'arkhu ha-yamim, 1929), and "In the City of Slaughter (Be-ir ha-harega, 1903)—Jews appear as petty, sly merchants, cowards, and beggars, even in their greatest suffering. Bialik's severe criticism of contemporary Jewish life is part of his general anti-sentimental, sometimes anti-Romantic, approach to reality.

A Jewish Revival?

The Romantic idea of national revival guided the *haskalah* throughout the nineteenth century. It was based on belief in the emotional and moral vitality, even moral superiority, of the Jewish people. The emergence of Hebrew literature was considered a manifestation of such a revival and a proof of the nation's living spirit. The Hebrew writer was expected to serve this goal by reflecting living Jewish reality.

Toward the end of the nineteenth century, however, the Romantic belief in national revival was endangered by the Decadent movement in European literature and thought.[37] Decadent historical thought was deterministic and pessimistic: races, nations, and cultures, like organic entities, have a limited lifespan; when they become old and overloaded with culture they begin to decay, disintegrate and die. During the second half of the nineteenth century the idea of Decadence extended to include psychological phenomena as well. It implied the supposition that modern, urban human beings suffer from *genetic degeneration:* just as all living beings do, societies and nations go through childhood, youth, adulthood, and old age; they must get old and die. Modern society is in the last stage of its existence. The symptoms of modern decadence are physical, emotional, and moral alike. Modern anti-Semitism was partly based on the idea that modern Jews were on the list of decadent races. Russian literature and culture absorbed the ideas of Decadence during the 1890s.

Pessimistic fin-de-siècle moods and ideas penetrated modern Jewish culture together with the Jewish "decadent" identity.[38] The belief in the moral superiority of the Jews over gentiles was shaken. In his cycle of stories *From My Small Town* (Me'iri haktana, 1899), Berdychevsky depicted shtetl life as absorbed with decadence, and in his novels *Two Camps* (Mahanayim, 1899) and *Nonsense* (Orva parakh, 1900) the main heroes are decadent Jews. The decadent image of the Jewish people was exposed in Max Nordau's Zionist writings and in Otto Weininger's *Sex and Character* (1903).

Bialik was a Zionist. Beginning with his first published poem, "To the Bird" (1891), he expressed the longing of the Diaspora Jew to live safely and proudly in his motherland. The ending of "In the Field" (Basadeh, 1894) is a warm blessing to the Zionist pioneers in Eretz Israel. In "A Blessing for the People" (Birkat am) and "To the Volunteers" (Lamit-nadvim ba-am, 1900), Bialik enthusiastically called his brethren to aid the Zionist project. However, in poems written between 1896 and 1906 the image of contemporary Jewish life might raise the question: can such a people revive itself? Contemporary Judaism is sometimes viewed by Bialik as the embodiment of Decadence. In "Upon my return" (Bitshu-vati 1896), a Jewish youth returning to his home finds only degenera-tion. Everything is hollow, mechanical, monotonous, evil, and lazy. In this poem Judaism is not a loving home, but a dangerous, destructive death trap. In "On Your Desolate Heart" contemporary Jewry is a dese-crated temple where a band of semi-demons is still wildly feasting, but they will soon be driven out and nothing will remain but complete deca-dence (symbolized by the meowing, impotent cat). In "The Word" the prophet sees his people as a band of "villains" who have no other inter-est but their hedonistic pleasures, utterly indifferent to the remnants of their nation's sacred mission (indifference being the characteristic deca-dent mood). The desert is the symbolic image of Judaism in several poems. Thus, in the long poem "The Scroll of Fire" and in "Call the Serpents" (Kir'u lanehashim, 1906) the Jewish spirit wanders in a self-made desert where nothing can grow, leading to annihilation. In "On This Cape of Death" (Al kef yam mavet zeh, 1906) Judaism is an island that once had a castle, a navy of battle ships, and a lighthouse, but now this island is completely dead. How could the national poet produce such pessimistic pictures of the Jewish situation? These pessimistic depic-tions of the Jewish condition were usually interpreted as warnings by the "poet-prophet" aimed at awakening the national energies. However, it is also possible to read these poems as reflecting the decadent image of the Jewish people popular in Bialik's time.

Even in the long poem "In the City of Slaughter," a response to the terrible Kishinev pogrom, Jewish behavior is depicted as morally cor-rupt. In this long poem Bialik did not mention Jewish self-defense and other facts that could have made the picture of the Jewish mentality less dark. Captivated by Decadence, he conferred decadence upon Jews even when they were victims of cruel anti-Semitism. The decadent mood of inner death—indifference, cynicism, depression, the death wish—appears as a personal experience in Bialik's "A Graveyard" (Beit olam, 1901) and in "Stars Sprout and Die" (Kokhavim metsitsim vekhavim 1901). Characteristic of Bialik's poetry is the complete harmony between personal and national experiences, including the decadent mood and Jewish decadence. Thus Bialik gave literary expression to the ideas of Jewish Decadent identity, an idea that Brenner, Gnessin, Y. Stienberg, D. Vogel, A. Reuveni, D. Kimhi, and others continued to develop in their writings.

The Jewish Spirit—Justice or Love?

In his poem "To Ahad Ha'am" (1903) Bialik wrote: "Accept our blessing, Teacher, our loyal blessing/ For all that we have learned and will learn from you."[39] Bialik was a loyal follower of Ahad Ha'am's "Spiritual Zionism." Ahad Ha'am formulated new definitions of Judaism, especially vis-à-vis Christianity, not on the basis of religion, but on what he considered to be the unique Jewish moral attitude. In his essays "The Quality of Justice and the Quality of Mercy" (1891), "Moses" (1904), and "At the Crossroads" (1910), Ahad Ha'am argued that Jewish ethics is based on justice, which is a higher moral value than mercy and altruism, the declared moral bases of Christianity.

Echoes of this view can be heard in Bialik's early poem "On the Threshold of the *Beit Midrash*" (1894). Speaking of what the Jew receives in the *beit midrash*, the poet mentions "productive thought, vivid intellect." Further the Jewish voice says: "I have not taught my hand to hit with my fist,/ nor was I exhausted by alcohol and whoredom;/ I was born to sing the song of God in the world,/ my spoils are of justice,—my loot is of judgment."

Later, however, Bialik redefined his understanding of the Jewish spirit. Instead of justice he saw merciful, motherly, chaste love. The first signs of this turn are to be found in "Daughter of Israel" (Bat Yisrael, 1903), which begins as an ode to love. The speaker makes great efforts to convince his listener that love is a spotless, sublime idea, then suddenly he turns to tell him about his own mother, saying that she taught him to bear love in the deepest part of his heart. He says that from her he inherited his conception of love as reflected in the quiet, modest, sacred light of Shabbat candles. Here Bialik distinguishes Jewish love from all others. He also erases the difference between the Jewish mother, Jewish love, and his own Jewish self. In contrast to "The Hungry Eyes" (Ha-einayim ha-re'evot, 1897?), where love was a threat to the poet's moral purity, in

"Where Are You? (Ayekh? 1904) the beloved woman and the Talmud are equated in the poet's soul: love becomes sacred. The feminine image of Judaism appears in "The Scroll of Fire" as Morning Star, a Divine woman of mercy and love, the opposite of the vengeful, destructive God. She appears in heaven after God in his fury has destroyed both the earthly and heavenly Temples. In contrast, she toils to save and preserve the remnants of Jewish sacredness. The poet-prophet, who is the hero of this Symbolist long poem, follows her. Here Bialik rejects severe justice, revenge and revolution (symbolized by God and by the boy with the angry eyelashes) as well as contemporary Christian ecumenical ideas that attracted many Jewish intellectuals and writers of his time (symbolized by the group of naked girls). Instead he chooses the light of the Morning Star, the feminine symbol of quiet, modest, and responsible love, as the real light of Judaism.

This choice, which is a far cry from Ahad Ha'am's view of Judaism, seems to be a result of Bialik's acquaintance with Russian Symbolist poetry[40] and with members of the *golgoftsy* (Golgotha) group in Odessa, followers of Solov'ev.[41] Sophia, an ancient Gnostic symbol of all-unifying love, is a main pillar of Solov'ev's mystical and ecumenical teaching.[42] In Bialik's poems of 1904–5 ("Where Are You?" "Come Out," "Take Me under Your Wing," "The Lake," "The Scroll of Fire") we find a divine feminine image that resembles Solov'ev's Sophia, sometimes as a symbol of the Jewish spirit (especially in "The Scroll of Fire").[43] In these poems love or the beloved is depicted, as in Solov'ev's poems on Sophia,[44] as a divine feminine being, hiding in a secret abode, who is expected to bring redemption to the man-poet. The woman here is sometimes a Shekhina and sometimes a queen or a princess whose dedicated knight is the man-poet.

Interesting for us is the dialogue between Bialik and Solov'evian ideas in "The Scroll of Fire," whose main theme is the true way of redemption versus the false one. This long symbolist poem raises the central question: Can love be redemptive? Bialik rejects the Solov'evian idea of redemption through love, as well as the Russian Symbolist idea of apocalyptic redemption achieved in catastrophe and evil. Three seemingly parallel feminine figures appear in the long poem's plot: the first is *Ayelet ha-shahar* (the female morning star, or Aurora, literally the doe of dawn, a term with rich kabbalistic overtones); second is the beloved girl (who appears naked to the hero wandering in the desert); third is the collective image of naked girls. All three possess clear sophiological traits: they seem to be merciful, pure, and motherly. But while the protective and responsible *Ayelet ha-shahar* takes care of the sacred fire, the girls are sleepwalking, hands spread, with constant smiles fixed on their faces. They look as if they were suspended on the spider-web-like rays of the moon. Called *alamot* (virgins), which carries Christian connotations, they symbolize the illusion of false redemption. The resemblance between them and *Ayelet ha-shahar* is specious: only she represents the Jewish spirit, while they symbolize the neo-Christian ideas of redemption through love and through total unity rejected by Bialik.

"The Scroll of Fire" tells about personal and public destruction as a result of blindly following false visions of redemption, inspired by the new Solov'evian Christian ecumenism, to which Bialik himself was formerly attracted. The poet uncovers the cruel, inevitable split between the fire of sexual passion and the moral claim of dedication to a mission. According to Bialik, such dedication, which is the real poet's way, demands uncompromising moral purity and readiness for a life of loneliness. While rejecting Solov'evian theosophy, Bialik adopts his feminine symbolism, albeit Judaizing it by the use of kabbalistic terms. To be sure, Solovyov's idea of Sophia itself was partly influenced by Kabbalah, which he read in his youth in Latin translation. In his Hebrew poems Bialik gave the Solov'evian Sophia a Jewish face. However, the contemporary Jewish reader could have had the impression that the woman in Bialik's poems had the face of the Madonna, the face of Alexander Blok's *prekrasnaia dama* (wonderful lady).[45] Bialik's concept of Judaism as a nation of love and mercy, although influenced by current moods in Russian literature, did not express his sympathy toward Christianity but his opposition to extreme Jewish revolutionary and nationalist trends, which were gaining popularity in Odessa at the beginning of the twentieth century.

Bialik's view of Judaism as a tradition of love and mercy, which opposes aggression and bloodshed, became stronger during the Russian Revolutions of 1905 and 1917.[46] How then does this view of Judaism as a tradition of love and mercy reconcile with Bialik's call to arms in the poem "You Must Have Long Hated Us" (Ein zot ki rabat tsrarunu, 1899?; first published 1903) and with his critique of Jewish passivity in "The City of Slaughter" (1903)? In "You Must Have Long Hated Us" Bialik suggests that anti-Semitic hatred and cruelty transformed the Jewish people into hateful beasts, and that they should now fight for their life. The early twentieth-century literary critic Yeruham Fishl Lachover argued that this uncharacteristic work was written under the influence of Tchernikhovsky's poems of revenge in his *Dreams and Melodies* (Hezionot u-manginot, 1899), while the literary critic Dan Miron doubts that the poem was written in 1899 and suggests that it was written, like "On the Slaughter," in 1903,[47] under the shock of the Kishinev pogrom. In "On the Slaughter," however, Bialik rejects human revenge and envisions a natural revenge that will take place by itself. Bialik was criticized for his disregard of Jewish self-defense in Kishinev in "The City of Slaughter," which according to the usual interpretation expresses Bialik's criticism of Jewish passivity. It is time to notice that in this poem Bialik criticizes not Jewish passivity, but Jewish disgrace and shame. He criticizes Jews who accept this state of shame and do not show any dignity. The poem does not suggest military activity as a solution. In fact, it ends with total despair.

The image of the nation as a sacred woman was shared by Hebrew writers who followed Bialik, such as Abraham Shlonsky, Uri Zvi Greenberg, and Nathan Alterman. However, they did not view Judaism as a loving, merciful mother. Alterman, who in his *The Joy of the Poor* (1941) followed Bialik's "The Scroll of Fire" by writing a Symbolist long poem about the fate of Judaism, contrasted the traditional image of the suffering woman with a new image of a vital, wild, fighting woman, thus presenting the difference between Judaism in the Diaspora and in its Zionist metamorphosis.

In summary, Bialik's poetry is a rich source for the understanding of modern Jewish identities that were being created in Jewish literature and thought at the turn of the nineteenth and the beginning of the twentieth centuries. Bialik's poems illuminate a series of views on contemporary Judaism and the Jewish spirit. His views of the Jewish spirit and contemporary Jewish life are innovative, sometimes revealing the dark side of his worldview. However, his concept of Judaism was not idiosyncratic: it was inspired by Hebrew, Yiddish, and Jewish-Russian literary traditions as well as by contemporary Russian literature.

Notes

1. Y. Klausner, *Haim Nahman Bialik ve-shirat hayav* (H. N. Bialik and the poetry of his life) (Dvir: Tel Aviv, 1951), 29. Emphasis in the original.

2. In his essay "Sifruteinu" (Our literature), *Ha-shiloah* 10 (1902): 534–52.

3. Klausner later titled the same essay "Poetry and Prophecy," its main argument being that Bialik was the inheritor of the biblical prophets. The essay begins with the question "What is the difference between a prophet and a poet?" and continues with a long discussion of the difference between European poetry and "prophecy." See *Haim Nahman Bialik ve-shirat hayav*, 30–36.

4. In his "Shaul Chernikhovsky," *Ha-shiloah* 25 (1912): 263–75, 367–76, 458–74.

5. D. Frishman tried in vain to turn these tables in his "Mikhtavim al dvar hasifrut" (Letters about literature), letter 13, *Ha-olam* 1, no. 25 (26 June 1907): 310–12. For Russian readers the "national" image of Bialik was supplied by Vl. Zhabotinsky's translations, first published in 1911 and in four additional editions in the following three years. His selection of poems and introduction was guided by this view of Bialik. Reviews of Bialik's poems in Russian also emphasized the national theme, sometimes (as in the case of Gershenzon) seeing it as an artistic limitation.

6. Like Ahad Ha'am, Klausner based Jewish identity not on religious but on moral criteria. However, for Ahad Ha'am "objective justice" was the highest

moral value, while Klausner says here that moral emotions and "pathos" are the sign of Jewish ethics.

7. It is not clear which Russian Symbolist poets were known to Bialik. On his contacts with Russian Symbolist poets, see Greta Slobin, "Heroic Poetry and Revolutionary Prophecy: Russian Symbolists Translate the Hebrew Poets," *Judaism* 51, no. 4 (2002): 408–18. On the influence of Russian Symbolist poetry on Bialik, see Esther Nathan, *Haderekh le-metei midbar* (The road to "The dead of the desert": The influence of Russian poetry on H. N. Bialik's long poem) (Tel Aviv, 1993), 120–86; H. Bar-Yosef, "Sophiology and the Concept of Femininity in Russian Symbolism and in Modern Hebrew Poetry," *Journal of Modern Jewish Studies* 2, no. 1 (2003): 59–78. On Bialik and the poetics of Russian Symbolism see my "Al Andrei Biely, ha-symbolizm ha-russi u-Bialik" (On Andrei Biely, Russian symbolism, and Bialik), *Mikarov* (Winter 2002): 38–57.

8. "Davar" (The word, 1904), "Habreikha" (The lake, 1905), "Megilat ha-esh" (The scroll of fire, 1905), "Lifnei aron ha-sfarim" (In front of the books, 1910), "Khozeh lech brach" (Prophet, run away, 1910). Dan Miron et al., eds., *Haim Nahman Bialik: Shirim* (Tel Aviv, 1983–2000), vol. 2 (1899–1934), 197–98, 205–10, 222–34, 282–84, 288, respectively.

9. Bialik's poems are taught in Israel from kindergarten through high school. He is the only obligatory modern Hebrew poet for matriculation exams.

10. In his essay "Hikui ve-hitbolelut" (Imitation and assimilation) Ahad Ha'am recommended imitation through competition with non-Jewish cultures as a formula for a successful modern Jewish revival.

11. On the differences of views between Ahad Ha'am and Frishman, see Iris Parush, *National Ideology and Literary Canon* (Hebrew) (Jerusalem, 1992), 50–119. On Berdychevski's criticism of Ahad Ha'am, see Gershon Shaked, *Hebrew Narrative Fiction 1880–1970* (Tel Aviv, 1977), 1:166–68.

12. According to Slobin, "Heroic Poetry and Revolutionary Prophecy: Russian Translate the Hebrew Poets," *Judaism* 51, no. 4 (2002): 408–18, Hebrew literature, especially Bialik, influenced Russian poetry in the 1910s. On the Russian influence on modern Hebrew literature, see D. Segal, "Russian and Hebrew Literature in Cross Mirrors," in *Jews and Jewish Life in Russia and the Soviet Union*, ed. Y. Ro'i (Ilford, 1995), 237–47. Segal denies Hebrew influence on Russian literature in the twentieth century. See also my "Reflections on Hebrew Literature in the Russian Context," *Prooftexts* 16 (1996): 127–49; Rina Lapidus, *Between Snow and Desert Heat: Russian Influences on Hebrew Literature 1870–1970* (Cincinnati, 2003); Zoya Kopelman, "Nokhehuto shel Mikhail Lermontov ba-shira ha-ivrit me-emtsa ha-me'ah ha-19 ad yameinu" (M. Lermontov's presence in Hebrew literature from the mid-nineteenth century to our time) (Ph.D. dissertation, Hebrew University, 2003).

13. The title *narodny* poet, meaning both a national poet and a poet of the people, was first conferred on Pushkin by Gogol in his essay "A Few Words about Pushkin" (1834). It was later attributed to I. Nekrasov, F. Dostoevskii, Vl. Solov'ev, Blok, A. Belyi, A. Akhmatova, N. Gumilev, Vl. Maiakovskii, V. Khlebnikov, and other Russian poets. Before Bialik, Semyon Frug won the title of *meshorer leumi* (national poet). See R. Breinin's introduction to *Shirei Frug* (Frug's poems), trans. Kaplan, 2 vols. (Warsaw, 1898), 1:iii.

14. Among his unpublished poems there are three more, "Hava and the Snake," "The Queen of Sheba," and "Jacob and Esau." Miron et al., *Haim Nahman Bialik*, vol. 1 (1890–1898), 102–4, 107–18, 172–78. Bialik also wrote "legends" using biblical materials.

15. This symbolic meaning had a rich tradition in Russian poetry, continued by Frug. On "desert" as a symbol of desolation, depression, and inner death see my *Maga'im shel decadence* (Trends of decadence): *Bialik, Berdychevski, Brenner* (Jerusalem, 1997), 93–94.

16. Miron et al., *Haim Nahman Bialik*, 1:97–98.

17. On Bialik's attitude toward the idea of revolution, see my "'Lanu ha-yehudim hashkafa akheret': Khayei Bialik bizman ha-mahapeikhot be-russia ve-yakhaso le-ra'ayn ha-mahapeicha" ("We Jews have another view": Bialik's life during the Russian revolutions and his attitude toward the idea of revolution), in *Mi-Vilna l-Irushalayim: Mekhkarim be-toldoteihem u-ve-tarbutam shel Yehudei mizrakh Eiropa mugashim li-professor Shmuel Verses* (From Vilnius to Jerusalem: Researches in the history and culture of East European Jews, offered to Professor Shmuel Verses), ed. D. Asaf et al. (Jerusalem, 2002), 427–48.

18. Miron et al., *Haim Nahman Bialik*, 2:165–70.

19. On the influence of Solov'ev's poetry on Bialik's "The Lake," see my "Sophiology and the Concept of Femininity in Russian Symbolism and Modern Hebrew Poetry," 67.

20. The main Russian Populist thinkers were A. Herzen, V. Belinsky, N. Chernyshevsky, P. Lavrov, and N. Mikhailovsky. Populism in Russian literature, although not Romantic in its focus on social reforms, was close to Western European Romanticism in its emphasis on love, nature, and national authenticity. See Richard Wortman, *The Crisis of Russian Populism* (Cambridge, 1967). On de-Romantization in early Zionist literature and thought, see my "De-Romanticized Zionism in Modern Hebrew Literature," *Modern Judaism* 16 (1996): 67–79.

21. Elena Blavatskaia (1831–91) contributed a great deal to this fashion, which she popularized in many Western countries. See her *The Secret Doctrine: The Synthesis of Science, Religion and Philosophy* (Adyar, Madras, India, 1962).

22. In his essay "Halakha ve-aggada" (Law and legend, 1916), Bialik follows Vladimir Solov'ev's "The Talmud and Recent Polemical Literature about It in Austria and Germany" (1886), where Solov'ev refutes anti-Semitic views of the Talmud. He enthusiastically cites a series of talmudic laws and sayings, arguing that they prove the nobility of Jewish moral views. See Solov'ev, "Talmud i noveishaia polemicheskaia literatura o nem v Avstrii i Germanii" (The Talmud and the newest polemic literature about it in Austria and Germany), *Sobranie sochinenii* (collected works in 12 vols.) (St. Petersburg, 1901; reprint, Brussels, 1966), 6:3–32.

23. David Gintsburg, "Kabbala, misticheskaia filosofiia evreev," *Voprosy filosofii i psikhologii* no. 3 (1896): 277–300. Solovyov's introduction is on 277–79.

24. Judith Deutsch Kornblatt, "Solovyov's Androgynous Sophia and the Jewish Kabbala," *Slavic Review* 50, no. 3 (1991): 487–96; "Russian Religious Thought and the Jewish Kabbala," in *The Occult in Russian and Soviet Culture*, ed. Bernice Glatzer Rosenthal (Ithaca, 1997), 75–95. See also the entry "Solovyov, Vladimir Sergeevich" written by Naftali Prat (unsigned), in *Kratkaia Evreiskaia Entsiklopediia* (Jerusalem, 1996), 8:418–21.

25. D. Mendeleev, *Materialy dlia suzhdenia o spiritizme* (Materials to judge spiritism) (St. Petersburg, 1976); D. N. Tsertelev, *Mediumizm i granitsy vozmozhnogo* (St. Petersburg, 1885); P. I. Rozenbach, *Sovremennyi mistitsizm: kriticheskii ocherk* (Contemporary mysticism: A critical note) (St. Petersburg, 1891), 6–7. See also V. V. Kravchenko, *Mistitsizm v russkoi filosofskoi mysli xix-nachala xx vekov* (Moscow, 1997); Bernice Glatzer Rosenthal and Martha Bochachevsky-Chomiakov, eds., *A Revolution of the Spirit: Crisis of Values in Russia, 1890–1924* (New York, 1990).

26. Examples are his famous "Legenda o chashe" (A legend on the glass), "I dlinnyi riad vekov" (And a series of centuries), "Klevetnikam Izrailia" (To the defamers of Israel). S. G. Frug, *Stikhi i proza* (Poems and prose) (Jerusalem, 1976), 33–34, 69–70, 107.

27. On this novel's difficulties with the Russian censor, see V. Kelner, "Glazami Tsenzora" (From the censor's point of view), *Ocherki po istorii russkoevreiskogo knizhnogo dela vo vtoroi polovine xix – nachale xx v* (Notes on the history of Russian-Jewish publications during the second half of the nineteenth and the beginning of the twentieth centuries) (St. Petersburg, 2003), 120–25.

28. On the cantonists, see E. Ofek, "Kantonists: Jewish Children as Soldiers in Tsar Nicholas's army," *Modern Judaism* 13 (1993): 277–308; O. Litvak, *The Literary Response to Conscription: Individuality and Authority in the Russian-Jewish Enlightenment* (Ann Arbor, 2000).

29. On the moral status of suffering in Russian culture, see D. Rancour-Laferriere, *The Slave Soul of Russia: Moral Masochism and the Cult of Suffering* (New York, 1995). On the Russian cult of martyrdom and its literary reflection, see M. Ziolkowski, *Hagiography and Modern Russian Literature* (Princeton, 1988).

30. My literal translation. Miron et al., *Haim Nahman Bialik*, 1:247.

31. Both poets treat the dagger as created by non-Russian peoples. Pushkin writes that the dagger was created by Hephaistos, the Greek god, while Lermontov says that the dagger was forged by a "thoughtful Georgian" and "a free Cherkes." On Lermontov's influence on Bialik, see Kopel'man, *Nochekhuto shel Mikhail Lermontov*.

32. On the reception of Nietzsche in Russia at the turn of the twentieth century, see B. Glazer-Rosenthal, ed., *Nietzsche in Russia* (Princeton, 1986). On the Jewish reception of Nietzsche, see Y. Golomb, *Nietzsche ba-tarbut ha-ivrit* (Nietzsche in Hebrew culture) (Jerusalem, 2002).

33. See P. J. S. Duncan, *Russian Messianism: Third Rome, Revolution, Communism, and After* (London and New York, 2000), 6–47.

34. A. S. Pushkin, *Polnoe sobranie sochinenii* (Complete works), ed. D. Bonch-Bruevich, 17 vols. (Moscow, 1937–59; reprint, Moscow, 1994–97), 3/1:30–31. The title "prorok" was added between April and August 1827; ibid., 3/2:1130.

35. On Pushkin as poet-prophet, see N. Gogol, "Neskol'ko slov o Pushkine" (1832, rev. 1834), in *Polnoe sobranie sochinenii*, ed. N. L. Meshcheriakov et al., 14 vols. (Moscow and Leningrad, 1937–52), 8:50–55; V. G. Belinsky, "Literaturnye mechtaniia (Elegiia v proze)" (1834), in *Polnoe sobranie sochinenii* (complete works), 13 vols. (Moscow, 1953–59), 1:48. On the poet-prophet in Russian literature, see B. M. Gasparov, *Poeticheskii iazyk Pushkina kak fakt russkogo literaturnogo iazyka* (Poetic language as a fact in Russian literary language) (St. Petersburg, 1999), 231–55; P. Davidson, "The Moral Dimension of the Prophetic Ideal: Pushkin and His Readers," *Slavic Review* 61, no. 3 (Fall 2002): 490–518; P. Davidson, "The Validation of the Writer's Prophetic Status in the Russian Literary Tradition: From Pushkin and Iazykov through Gogol to Dostoevsky," *Russian Review* 62, no. 4 (October 2003): 508–36. On the poet-prophet in Hebrew literature, see R. Shoham, *Poetry and Prophecy: The Image of the Poet as a "Prophet," a Hero and an Artist* (Leiden, 2003).

36. My literal translation of "Lo zachiti ba'or min ha-hefker," from Miron et al., 2:145.

37. On Decadence in Russian literature and thought, see R. Poggioli, *The Poets of Russia 1830–1890* (Cambridge, Mass., 1960), 89–115; E. Bristol, "Idealism and Decadence in Russian Symbolist Poetry," *Slavic Review* 39, no. 2 (June

1980): 269–80; E. Clowes, "Literary Decadence: Sologub, Schopenhauer and the Anxiety of Individualism," *American Contributions to the Tenth International Congress of Slavists* (The Hague, 1988), 111–21.

38. On Decadent ideas in Hebrew periodicals and thought, see H. Bar-Yosef, *Decadent Trends*, 13–41.

39. "Le-Ahad Ha'am," in Miron et al., 2:149.

40. Yaacov Fichman writes that after coming back from Warsaw to Odessa in spring 1904 they were strolling along the shore talking about Russian Symbolist poetry. Y. Fichman, *Sofrim be-khayeihem* (Writers' lives) (Jerusalem, 1942), 58.

41. See my "Stikhi Bialika v perevodakh Aleksandra Gorskogo," *Vestnik evreikogo universiteta v Moskve* 7, no. 25 (2002): 295–334.

42. On Solov'ev's theosophical idea of Sophia, see Samuel Cioran, *Vladimir Solov'ev and the Knighthood of the Divine Sophia* (Waterloo, Ont., 1977). On Sophiology in Russian literature, see Avril Pyman, *A History of Russian Symbolism* (Cambridge, 1994), 226–42.

43. See my article "Sophiology and the Concept of Femininity in Russian Symbolism and in Modern Hebrew Poetry," *Journal of Modern Jewish Studies* 2, no. 1 (2003): 59–78.

44. See, for example, Solov'ev's poems "Vsia v lazuri" (All in azure), "U tsaritsy moei" (My empress has), "Saima" (Lake Saima), "Na Saime zimoi" (At Lake Saima in winter), and "Tri Svidania" (Three meetings), in Vladimir Solovyov, *Stikhotvoreniia, Proza, Pis'ma, Vospominaniia sovremennikov* (Moscow, 1990), 22, 23, 91, 96, 118.

45. M. Ginzburg wrote: "The deification of woman is alien to Judaism. Lilith—the empress of sin and seduction—yes, but the cult of 'The Beautiful Lady' is unknown to Jews." "H. N. Bialik" (Russian), *Novyi Voskhod* (June 1910): 32.

46. See my article "Bialik and the Russian Revolutions," *Jews in Eastern Europe* 1, no. 29 (Spring 1996): 5–31.

47. D. Miron's introduction to "Ein zot ki rabat tsrartunu," in Miron et al., 2:44.

Chapter 8

Not *The Dybbuk* but *Don Quixote*: Translation, Deparochialization, and Nationalism in Jewish Culture, 1917–1919

KENNETH B. MOSS

Writing in the weeks before the February Revolution in the Moscow newspaper *Ha-am*, the Zionist-Hebraist publicist A. Litai called for the creation of an organized, publicly funded program to translate "the famous works of the great figures of the nations of the world" into Hebrew.[1] There was nothing remarkable about Litai's interest in the translation of canonical foreign literary works per se. A concern for this sort of translation (as distinct from intentional adaptation, imitation, and other forms of literary importation) was by 1917 a normal feature of both the Hebrew and Yiddish literary spheres in Russia and beyond. In Russia's Hebrew literary sphere, the inauguration of a world literature series by the Hebrew writer Ben-Avigdor's Tushiyah publishing house in 1896 marked a shift from intermittent, idiosyncratic manifestations of interest in literary translation throughout the nineteenth century on the part of figures like Micha Yosef Lebensohn or the missionary/translator Y. Zalkinson to more sustained and normative attention.[2] By 1911, there was a Hebrew publishing venture, Turgeman, devoted solely to translating the shared European canon of children's literature (Twain, Jules Verne, Mayne Reid, *1001 Nights*).[3] Belated but parallel developments marked the individuating Yiddish literary sphere, where by 1913, the Yiddishist journal *Di Yidishe Velt* carried translations of Greek and Babylonian epic.[4]

But if Litai's interest in literary translation was not especially noteworthy, his proposal was striking for other reasons. Remarkable, first, was his vision of a grand program of encompassing literary translation run by a public body standing above the market and the idiosyncrasies of writers and publishers. Even more notable were the motivations underpinning it: in a rhetoric of cultural crisis usually reserved for more pressing matters than literary translation, Litai insisted that the very perpetuation of modern Hebrew culture and even "our national language" itself now depended on such an immediate, massive translation effort. Most remarkable of all was the extraordinary resonance and amplification these ideas—arrived at quite independently and simultaneously by other cultural actors—would enjoy in the Hebrew and Yiddish cultural spheres in the two explosive years to come.

Litai wrote at a critical juncture in the history of the Jewish nationalist intelligentsia's endeavor to create a new kind of Jewish culture. Since the turn of the century, growing numbers of young Russian Jews, locked in a dialectical relationship with the metropolitan Russian culture to which many of their peers were acculturating ever more fully, had come to share a vision of a modern Jewish 'high culture' in an (idealized) European mold. This putative culture was humanist, historicist, essentially secular, shot through with Romantic conceptions of language and nationhood, and predicated above all on the ideal of Art as the highest end of human individual and collective expression. Its adherents hoped that it would overcome traditional Jewish culture, displace market-driven Yiddish popular culture, compete with metropolitan Russian, Polish, and German cultures on their own terms, and reconstitute both a putative Jewish nation and the Jewish individual in the process. Though such dramatic achievements remained far out of reach—and though this cultural vision itself was increasingly sundered by tensions over language, political affiliation, and definitions of Jewish culture itself—there did emerge a distinct and substantial Jewish cultural sphere by 1914. By January 1917, when Litai called for his grand translation project, the situation seemed on the surface quite different: the war and wartime censorship had brutally snuffed out the key journals, publishing houses, and cultural organizations of this cultural endeavor.[5] Yet the vision that had driven this institution-building remained a deeply internalized commitment for a substantial part of the East European Jewish intelligentsia. It drove Litai's pen at a moment when it seemed that the institutions of the cultural sphere were shattered for good, and it proved ready to reemerge full-blown under the right circumstances: the unprecedented freedoms of expression and institution-building offered by the Revolution of February 1917 opened the way for numerous Jewish intellectuals, activists, and artists to throw themselves once again into the task of creating the new culture.[6]

This return to cultural activity after two years of desperate silence drew added impetus from such post-February factors as the apparent triumph of secular nationalism in Jewish political life and the challenges of national revolution across Eastern Europe; the promise of cultural autonomy and state support for Jewish culture, especially in Ukraine; the perception that for good or for ill, the war had finally destroyed traditional Jewish society; the spontaneous burgeoning of new aesthetic trends in the arts at the hands of a host of newcomers to the Jewish cultural sphere; and, with the Bolshevik coup in October, the promise or specter of a more encompassing revolution, cultural as well as sociopolitical. But although 1917 is often treated as point of fracture in Jewish cultural history, it is important to understand that these developments actually did *not* usher in a radical new beginning for the Jewish national cultural project, even on the Yiddishist left. Rather, they provoked an urgent cultural stocktaking and reassertion: across hardening divisions of political ideology, linguistic commitment, and cultural aspirations, the culturally engaged Jewish intelligentsia almost unanimously (if separately) seized this moment to reassert, expand, and realize cultural agendas long in the making. This consolidating sensibility derived impetus not only from the new opportunities but also from a widespread conviction that the future of this culture could only be secured by organized endeavor. Thus, in April 1917, Hebraist activists in Moscow called on Hebraists to obey "the commandment of this great hour" and "turn our spiritual energy to the work of national creation"; a year later, his Yiddishist opponents echoed the same mix of enthusiasm and urgency: "But in this time when it is possible for spiritual culture to develop freely, one begins to feel the need to unify our powers, to organize cultural work, . . . to bind together all initiatives."[7]

One of the most striking manifestations of this process of consolidation was the intensification of prewar efforts to shape the new Jewish aesthetic culture by incorporating sources outside its definitional boundaries. Most famously, some Jewish cultural producers like Haim Nahman Bialik and Sh. An-sky renewed prewar efforts to recuperate indigenous Jewish sources, whether pre-modern Hebrew texts or East European Jewish "folk culture," so that they might serve as the cornerstone of a new, secular-national yet "authentic" Jewish culture.[8] Wrested from their traditional moorings and reworked in accordance with secular nationalist and Romantic aesthetic values, these products of traditional Jewish creativity would provide a defining aesthetic and even ethical framework for modern Jewish culture. In recent years, these efforts to recuperate indigenous Jewish sources (which yielded, among other things, the most impressive flowering of Jewish plastic art in modern times in the work of figures like El Lissitzky and Iosif Tchaikov)[9] have begun to receive the scholarly attention they warrant.[10] They have also come to define our understanding of modern Jewish culture as a whole: this negotiation between the modern self and pre-modern Jewish expression has come to seem *the* paradigmatic move of modern Jewish culture, with Hebraists recuperating classical Hebrew sources and Yiddishists doing much the same with Jewish folklore.

Yet an examination of Jewish cultural activity as a whole in the 1917–19 period, rather than through the particular lens of such indigenizing strategies, yields a surprising finding: these continued efforts to recuperate pre-modern indigenous Jewish sources as the fundaments of the new Jewish culture were paralleled by, ideologically *overshadowed* by, and even vigorously denigrated in favor of a third, largely unexamined strategy of culture-building, namely, systematic, massive, immediate, and non-adaptive[11] literary translation of a posited unitary, universal canon of Western literature into Hebrew or Yiddish. When Litai echoed and amplified this argument the following year in the newly restored Hebraist journal *Ha-shiloah*,[12] he was no longer a lone voice but one of a choir of intellectuals who shared his sense that a grand project of translation was perhaps the most pressing need of the cultural moment. This was, moreover, a remarkably strange choir: its members traversed the full range of political, linguistic, and cultural commitment, from uncompromising integral Zionist-Hebraists like Litai or *Ha-shiloah*'s editor Yosef Klausner to the Hebraist pro-Communist Eliezer Shteynman, from the Hebraist aesthete David Frishman to the revolutionary and radical Yiddishist Moyshe Litvakov.

This discourse on the centrality of translation intersected, moreover, with an increasingly predominant discourse in the Jewish cultural sphere that, far from valorizing traditional indigenous sources, declared them a secondary value or even an obstacle to the attainment of a compelling modern Jewish culture. Some of the proponents of translation wedded their plans to full-fledged attacks on strategies of recuperation, asserting that what Jewish culture needed was not the indigenous but precisely the alien. Others hewed a more compromising line, but the linkage between the discourse on translation and the outpouring of attacks on "parochialism" in Jewish culture by an ideologically varied cohort of cultural figures dramatizes the importance of rethinking what "Jewish culture" had come to mean by 1917 through the lens of translation.

These emphatic calls for placing organized translation at the center of Jewish cultural life found more concrete institutional expression in a new breed of Hebrew and Yiddish publishing houses that emerged in 1917–18. The Hebraist Stybel and Omanut publishing houses and the Yiddishist Kiever-Farlag, Folks-Farlag, and Kultur-Lige Farlag (and numerous other small Yiddishist publishing ventures) understood themselves less as businesses than as shapers of Jewish culture as a whole in accordance with coherent overarching visions. Eclipsing veteran cultural publishers like Bialik's Moriah or the Yiddishist Kletskin Farlag, these new publishing ventures sought, as Stybel's chief editor Frishman put it, to "build the Pithom and Ramses of a whole literature,"[13] or, in the words of Nokhem Shtif of the Folks-Farlag, to "be *the* cultural institution to build our literary cultural work and chart a path." [14] Significantly, almost all of these major publishing houses (and many smaller ones) made large-scale literary translation a defining feature of their programs. Thus, by 1918, Litai was no longer calling for action, but commenting on a massive translation program by the Stybel press, merely one of the most remarkable instances of an astonishing outpouring of translations and discourse about translation that convulsed Hebraist and Yiddishist cultural life at this juncture.[15]

This chapter examines the rhetoric and practice of translation in the post-February Jewish cultural sphere as a means to investigate several larger issues central to the history of the Jewish cultural project in Eastern Europe. It focuses on the key Jewish cultural circles of Moscow, Kiev, and Odessa, during the brief but critical period following February 1917 but prior to the decisive penetration of Bolshevik and Yevsektsiia power into Jewish cultural life from within and without, roughly late 1918 in Moscow and European Russia and mid-1919 in Ukraine and the borderlands. In other words, this chapter treats the Jewish cultural sphere at the juncture when its participants felt both free and compelled to clarify and reassert their longstanding cultural project but were not yet seduced or forced to dramatically recast their visions by the new revolutionary reality.[16] Moving between conceptions of translation and other discourses and practices concerned with "Europeanizing" Jewish literary culture, it seeks to explain why a wide swath of the Jewish nationalist intelligentsia, Hebraists and Yiddishists both,[17] had come by 1917 to see wholesale incorporation of an imagined encompassing, unitary canon of Western literature, more than or even instead of the reincorporation of indigenous Jewish sources, as a key to the creation of a satisfactory modern Jewish secular culture. It argues that the driving force of this sensibility was a paradoxical form of Jewish cultural nationalism, found among both Hebraists and Yiddishists and across the political spectrum, which sought (in some respects out of necessity) to remake Jewish culture as a branch of a posited multilingual "universal" (European) culture; it thus builds on the efforts of Benjamin Harshav, Yaacov Shavit, and Seth Wolitz, among others, to redefine our concepts of Jewish culture, Yiddishism and Hebraism, and Jewish nationalism by examining how they operated in league with rather than against "universal" culture for contemporaries.[18] At the same time, this chapter investigates how the dynamics of high culture itself and the sociological realities of Diaspora existence operated to reshape Jewish cultural nationalism.

Translation and the Future of Jewish Culture

Litai was, as noted, one of an array of intellectuals, critics, writers, and activists who separately articulated an explicit conception of what we might call programmatic translation in the 1917–19 period. If Litai was the most rhetorically urgent of these, it was Moyshe Litvakov, the leading Yiddishist theorist of his day, who offered the most ramified expression of this stance in a 1919 essay in the Kiev Yiddishist cultural journal *Bikher-velt* entitled "The System of Translations."[19] Litvakov argued that Yiddish literature had reached a stage of stagnation and decline beyond which it could move only by means of a massive, systematic program of translation from the "world poetry of all generations, peoples, and languages," especially the "living waters" of contemporary European literature.[20] Such a project required planning, adherence to principles dictated by a larger vision of what Yiddish literature truly needed to become—namely, a self-sufficient, all-encompassing art-literature—and the leadership of the literary and intellectual elite. Litvakov emphasized both the critical significance of this undertaking and the model for it through an invocation of the early-nineteenth-century German literary sphere and to a lesser extent the nineteenth-century Russian literary sphere as exemplary instances in which literary elites had undertaken ramified programs of translation "as a type of national-cultural function on behalf of the vital interests of the national literature."

As a literary critic and theorist, Litvakov was an aggressive proponent of the most avant-garde literary streams of the day and an impatient, demanding critic of anything he deemed old-fashioned or epigonic. He was also, by mid-1919, a committed supporter of the Bolshevik Revolution; by the time the second half of this article was published in August 1919, he held a position in the Yiddish cultural institutions of the newly installed Bolshevik government in Kiev (the first half, published in January 1919, was written before the Bolshevik takeover). Yet neither of these commitments found much echo in Litvakov's translation program:

These must be translated: works which have had the most significant influence on the formation and development of our literary feelings, thoughts, and ways of speaking, whose images, symbols, figures, and expressions have made their way into our everyday lives [*tog-shteyger*]. Works which have called forth particular literary-social streams and become a jumping-off point for a new development. Works in which the eternal beauty of the artistic word is crystallized. The major epic works of the various peoples and lands. Works of writers who characterize or embody a significant epoch or interesting strata of society. Above all, works which represent boundary markers in the development of literary forms, genres, and tendencies.[21]

Indeed, Litvakov summarily dismissed any notion that this program of translation should suit itself to any immediate political needs or even the needs of Yiddish readers ("the masses") themselves; simultaneously, he just as explicitly asserted that translation should *not* be organized to further any particular literary movement or aesthetic: "There are phases in the history of a national literature when neither this or that individual translator-devotee nor the public but rather [the literature] itself requires translation for its growth and development."[22]

Not everyone made the same surprising double move; one reviewer for the same journal welcomed a Yiddish translation of Byron's *Heaven and Earth* in part because Byron's art was supposedly "a direct means of struggle . . . with that world which the great Revolution has just outlived."[23] But the leading proponents of translation shared Litvakov's general views on both counts. Eliezer Shteynman—aggressively pro-Bolshevik though deeply Zionist, and committed to a vague but heartfelt program of revolution in Hebrew literature itself—numbered among the Stybel press's chief merits precisely the fact that it had no limiting aesthetic or political agenda: in the pages of the Hebrew anthology *Erets*, which yoked together Bolshevik sympathies, Zionism, and a call for "youth" revolution in Hebrew literature, Shteynman praised the Stybel press's massive translation program for bringing "everything, everything to us: from the first fruits of realism, from the flowers of Romanticism, and from the grapes of modernism."[24] Litai propounded a slightly more focused agenda, opining that the Stybel press should translate fewer Decadent works and more Romantic ones in view of their salutary impact on Jewish consciousness. But he also welcomed the grandly encompassing effort to bring "the literature of the world" into Hebrew all at once—and the absence of a political line in Stybel's *Ha-tekufah.*[25]

The primary purpose of the envisioned global translation was less to reshape a general reading public (though these champions of translation certainly hoped that readers might benefit) than to reshape Hebrew or Yiddish literature themselves. One means by which translation would accomplish this feat was by catalyzing the development of a *neutral* literary language free of Jewish clichés. Litvakov made the avoidance of unwarranted Judaization in translation an explicit principle. The Yiddishist critic Nokhem Oyslender devoted close attention in his review of a Yiddish *Hiawatha* to the question of whether the translator had managed to avoid giving the "wigwam . . . the smell of the Jewish study house."[26] By the same token, successful non-Judaized translation was deemed the ultimate test and symbol of the maturation of a literary language, and contemporaries responded to translations of the era as though they were referenda on the possibilities and achievements of Hebrew or Yiddish literature in their entirety. Yosef Klausner laid out clearly what was at stake in his jubilant comments on H. Taviov's translation of Wilde's *Picture of Dorian Gray* for the Stybel press. *Dorian Gray* was, in Klausner's view, not only a distinctly difficult "modern" work—a challenge for the translator under any circumstances—but also a "story which has no connection to Israel [Jewish matters]." Taviov's translation, which Klausner deemed possibly "the *first complete* Hebrew translation" of a work with no such Jewish connection, thus demonstrated that Hebrew had become a living language "sufficient to all the needs of feeling and thought and description of the modern person."[27] For Moyshe Kulbak, Max Weinreich's 1913 translation of book nine of Homer's *Iliad* was similar proof that Yiddish was a mature literary language, presumably because of the common assumption that the Homeric tradition was the very antithesis of classical Jewish literary expression.[28] The 1917 announcement that the great Hebrew poet and translator Shaul Tshernikhovsky would translate the same text into Hebrew generated great excitement in the Hebraist literary community, further suggesting how widespread this sensibility was.[29]

These two *Iliad* translations themselves enacted a translation poetics in deep accord with this sensibility. Both translators endeavored to hew to the complex dactylic hexameter of the original insofar as the respective poetic structures of ancient Greek, Hebrew, and Yiddish allowed it: "*Kokhoh hifkidu ha-Troyim shoymrehem; akh benei ho-Akhaim/retet akhozom vofakhad, ho-akhim li-eymoh u-mnusoh*"; "*Ot azoy hobn di Troyer gevakht: un a gvaldike eyme/hot di Akheer bafaln, gevorfn in ayzikn yeyish.*"[30] As Aminadav Dikman notes in his assessment of Tshernikhovsky's translation, this formal choice was not by any means a given in either earlier Hebrew *Iliad* translations nor, more important, in the Russian and German translations that Tshernikhovsky (and Weinreich) would have known.[31] Their attempts to capture the formal feel of the Homeric poetry thus reflects a very considered choice of form over "meaning" (or rather, a rejection of any such distinction in the name of a sovereign logic of poetry). Equally consonant with the sensibilities I have outlined was the translators' deployment of language organically related to existing registers yet distant from any particular spoken or textual register, which served to make the poems simultaneously compelling yet profoundly strange aesthetic objects. Thus, for instance, for the "many-fished sea" of book nine, Weinreich offered the syntactically natural yet stylistically alien "filfishikn fantos." In Tshernikhovsky's case, this involved trying to avoid the biblicization that characterized all previous Hebrew translations of Homer from that of the maskil Meir Halevi Letteris (1800–1871) to the 1898 attempt by Dovid Margolin.[32] As Dikman notes, to turn Greek epic into biblical epic was the culturally obvious choice for Hebrew translators (Erich Auerbach's famous emphasis on their difference notwithstanding) *if* one regarded translation as cultural mediation. Tshernikhovsky's decision to avoid it—and his efforts more generally to escape the gravity of any of the literary languages of the many-layered Hebrew textual tradition[33]—bespeak a will not to mediation but to the preservation of the aesthetic object's strangeness.[34] Tshernikhovsky and Weinreich sought instead to insert belated foundation stones beneath the rising edifice of modern, expansive Hebrew and Yiddish literary languages.

This concern about literary language was, in turn, part of a more global agenda that explains the concern to translate whole swaths of the European literary tradition (rather than selecting those works specially suited to some perceived need of the literary language): the desire to remake Hebrew or Yiddish literature as typical European literatures. For some, this may have had strong nationalist symbolic valence. The Hebraist patron and publisher Shoshana Persits entertained "an aspiration to see Hebrew culture in all of its manifestations stand on a level at least equal to the cultures of the great nations," as one source puts it.[35] Similar concerns seem to have animated Moyshe Kulbak's assertion that successful translation of Homer was not merely a vehicle for the maturity of a "*kulturshprakh*," but also a sign of "a certain spiritual maturity on the part of that nation" (any nation) which translated it.[36]

But, more important, there was a concretely literary goal: the translation programs of the day reflect the conviction that the creation of a compensatory literary tradition through translation was essential not merely as a point of pride and civilized status but as a means to make Jewish literature itself part of a shared, ever-more universal European literary culture. Thus, Litvakov's surprisingly catholic translation efforts were intended to transform Yiddish literature into "a big-city-universalist literature, with inclinations and orientations toward taking a place in world literature," not by emphasizing one particular aesthetic line but precisely by endowing it with world literature's entire panoply of forms and "fundamental motifs and moods, visions and images, symbols and figures, legends and myths."[37] Litai, Litvakov's polar opposite in political and linguistic-political terms, shared precisely the same vision of what literature was, how it worked, and what Jewish literature should be. He imagined the relationship among fully developed literatures like those of England, Germany, and Russia as a constant process of "mutual influence" through which these literatures "renew themselves and enrich themselves from day to day." To Litai, it was self-evident that "our literature," which by "a European measure is only at the beginning of its development," should aspire to join this company, and only programmatic translation could provide the necessary "universal" fundament.[38]

Whereas each individual translation of merit might help transform Hebrew or Yiddish into more flexible literary languages, global translation was to bring about this transformation in the first instance by (re)educating the Jewish writer. Needless to say, none of the champions of translation hoped for a flood of imitations. On the contrary, they no doubt shared the hopes of another advocate of large-scale translation, Frishman, who maintained that such a body of translations would serve not as a source for mechanical imitation—indeed, he believed that only by translating these works accurately and making them an "integral part of Hebrew culture" could imitation be avoided—but provide inspiration, benchmarks, and an aestheticizing and Europeanizing influence on Hebrew writers.[39] Litvakov articulated a similar mechanism: "Should the future and even present Yiddish writer cleave spiritually and psychically to this wonder-world of great artworks, if he should reforge them in the flame of his intuition, our literature's 'Pale of Settlement' will be perforce abolished."[40]

Translation was thus not pro-forma—a matter of appearances—nor mere raw material; the European classics had to become central generative influences in Jewish literature by refining both the literary language and the authors who employed it. In a narrow sense, each individual translation had to be a genuine literary achievement. Although these critics were well aware of the formal challenges inherent in translation, they did not produce technical guides to translation like the 1919 *Printsipy khudozhestvennogo perevoda*[41] (Principles of artistic translation) of their Russian counterparts in Maxim Gorky's grand translation program (see below) or penetrating philosophical meditations on language and translation like those of the Russian Symbolists before them or Benjamin and Buber-Rosenzweig after them;[42] whether due to lack of resources, talent, or leisure, these critics came at the issue piecemeal in individual reviews.[43] One more potent means by which they hoped to overcome this challenge was harnessing the most talented Jewish writers themselves to translation. In the name of all Hebraists who wished for "the revival of our language," Litai hoped Bialik would undertake to translate "the classic foreign works."[44] Independently, David Frishman and the publisher-patron Avraham Yosef Stybel plied Bialik with requests that he translate *Evgenii Onegin* on the grounds that he was the "only one" who could do a good translation.[45] These hopes reflected a wholly Romantic notion of literature and authorial genius: as editor and children's writer M. Ben-Eliezer put it, "For a translation of a classic work of poetry, he only is qualified who is himself a poet and who has in his soul traces of the soul of the poet he is translating."[46] In a more global sense, foreign literature could only have the requisite impact if imported whole, as a set of canons and genres, so that the Jewish writer might internalize the whole embodied history of a putatively universal literary development.[47] Hence the disgust of critic Ezra Korman with an anthology that purported to offer translations of the most important modern European poetry but merely proffered an unsystematic smattering organized not by national literature but by the Yiddish translator![48] Hence too the oft-repeated desire to see translation organized in some central fashion.

As the repeated references to the Stybel publishing house suggest, these visions were not confined to the realm of intention. This same conception of translation guided the grand program of this publishing house from its inception in Moscow in 1917. Its founder, the newly minted millionaire Hebraist Avraham Yosef Stybel, was utterly devoted to Hebrew literature and willing to expend a considerable part of his own fortune on the support of Hebrew writers materially and on the transformation of Hebrew literature itself.[49] When in 1917 he placed the press with its million-ruble endowment entirely in the hands of his long-time hero, the Hebraist aesthete Frishman, he signaled his full agreement with Frishman's particular vision for Hebrew literature. Frishman and Stybel shared the view that Hebrew literature could not confine itself to any Jewish form of expression but must instead strive to be part of a posited universal literature, and that translation of the sort that intellectuals like Litai[50] and Litvakov envisioned was the key means of facilitating this development.[51]

Guided by Frishman and Stybel, the publishing house undertook a massive program of translation from European and world literature. Frishman's conviction that the great works of literature were unique and unclassifiable expressions of a timeless human genius yielded an eclectic list of commissioned translations[52] spanning genres and millennia. The unifying principle of this list, though, was the supposed power of each work to jumpstart a worthwhile Hebrew literature. The translations were to be done by writers, not mere translators—Stybel's first assistant, the newspaperman Ben-Tsion Katz, made particular efforts to recruit Tshernikhovsky (a doctor) to work full-time for the press; Frishman and at times Stybel himself solicited the participation of dozens of Hebrew writers both in revolutionary Russia and abroad.[53] Within roughly a year of its founding, the press had published five translated literary works, fifteen more were in production or ready to print, and over forty had been commissioned; translations also assumed a central place in the Stybel quarterly *Ha-tekufah*. The range of works included a strong selection of Russian classic prose and poetry (Pushkin, Lermontov, Tolstoy, Dostoevsky, Chekhov); other giants of nineteenth-century prose (Dickens, Flaubert, Zola) and poetry (Mickiewicz, Heine); a strong representation of fin-de-siècle work (Wilde, Maeterlink, Ibsen, Hamsun, Przybysweski, France, Strindberg); and the Greco-Roman tradition.[54]

The distinctive features of the translation program collectively imagined by this disparate collection of Hebraists and Yiddishists may be thrown into sharper relief by comparison both to previous translation tendencies in Hebrew and Yiddish literary life and to contemporaneous tendencies in its coterritorial Russian literary sphere. First, the insistence that translation be organized primarily around the perceived formal needs of Hebrew or Yiddish literature themselves marked the triumph of a principle that had never been absent from Jewish literary life but that had been largely subordinate to conceptions of translation as a means for the direct (re)education of the Jewish *reader*. This held true for Hebrew literary life until the readership crisis of the first decade of the twentieth century—thus, Ben-Avigdor's pioneering conception of translation, though certainly concerned with the needs of Hebrew literature, was framed by a desire to leaven his readers' Jewishness with a putatively universal human wisdom (*klaliut*)[55]—and even afterward in some quarters.[56] Translation into Yiddish was, naturally, even more tied to models of readership needs. The existence of a substantial popular market in Yiddish brought a flood of desultory translation-adaptations for a popular readership,[57] and Warsaw and New York publications of fashionable, accessible contemporary European prose writers (Hamsun, Maupassant, Chekhov) seem to have been linked to an as-yet unstudied middlebrow Yiddish readership akin to the emergent urban, middlebrow Russian readership analyzed by Jeffrey Brooks.[58] More ideologically driven translation orientations were no less readership-centered: above all, translations produced within the broad range of progressive publishing in Yiddish were chosen according to an educative model. Thus, the Minsk publishing house "Kultur," founded by a left-leaning engineer in 1904, chose writers like Twain, Chekhov, and Korolenko who were of a piece with its diet of popular science, an almanac on "all lands and peoples," and a guide for emigrants by Alexander Harkavy.[59] Only in the last years of the prewar period did the pendulum begin to swing in the other direction, and it is this reorientation that came to full expression in the reemergent Hebrew and Yiddish literary spheres of 1917–19.

This literature-centered translation sensibility also stands in illuminating contrast to its Russian parallel, Maxim Gorky's *Vsemirnaia Literatura* (world literature) project. Founded in September 1918, *Vsemirnaia Literatura* endeavored to create a "foundational library" of 1500 American, European, and Eastern literary works in Russian translation with the support of the Soviet state and with the participation of Russia's finest writers and scholars.[60] This project, undertaken on a scale of which the Jewish champions of literary translation could only dream, was certainly intended on some level to serve Russian literature itself. In technical terms, the *Vsemirnaia literatura* project was more sophisticated than the visions of the Jewish cultural activists. Beyond the technical primer on translation by the Acmeist Nikolai Gumilev and the future dean of

Soviet translators Kornei Chukovskii, it established a special poetic collegium, and conducted an ongoing practicum for its writer-translators. But the goals of its founder, Gorky, were first and foremost reader-centered: this *osnovnaia biblioteka* was meant to instill an internationalist humanism in the relatively educated Russian reader (it was paired with a *narodnaia biblioteka*, or folk library, aimed at the uneducated reader).[61] Hence, Gorky pressed his translators—who included Russia's leading avant-garde writers—to serve a non-elite readership, and attacked some of their introductory essays as inaccessible.[62]

Thus, strangely, the concerns of these Jewish champions of translation, all of whom were nationalist and radical activists by no means indifferent to the needs of the masses, bore less affinity with the sensibilities of the near-universally admired Gorky than they did with the most unabashed aesthetes of Russia's prewar Symbolist community.[63] Yet here, too, there was an illuminating difference. On the whole, the Symbolists and Decadents of the Russian fin-de-siècle sought to parley creative engagement with idiosyncratic assemblages of foreign cultural sources into literary fusion primarily *in and through* their own literary production, though some of them were also serious translators.[64] The Jewish translation advocates of the 1917 moment demanded something both less and more ambitious: not the slow, careful *processing* of foreign influences, but their brute insertion *en bloc* into the literary tradition.

In all these ways, as well in other tendencies out of step with the times (the concern, for instance, to have only literary writers do translations rather than professional translators),[65] the Jewish discourse on translation at this juncture smacked of a previous age: the Russian and German literary spheres of the previous century—which Litvakov and others like David Frishman[66] quite penetratingly invoked—with their multi-decade quest to master the literary powers of their neighbors to the west and the Western classical tradition.[67] Even as individual Hebrew and Yiddish writers like Der Nister or Avigdor Ha-Meiri carried out creative recastings of external influences in ways no less sophisticated than their European counterparts,[68] the revolutionary-era Jewish advocates of translation were concerned not to enrich Hebrew or Yiddish literature but to *refound* it. Their vision was part of a self-consciously belated program of culture-building. Despite deep ideological differences, they shared a notion of a universal (or pan-European) Literature with a single if evolving structure of genres, styles, and sensibilities that Jewish literature in Hebrew or Yiddish had to encompass through translation (in part so that they would be able to grow beyond these). In so doing, Hebrew or Yiddish literature would necessarily emulate "all the young literatures which maintain themselves from translations."[69] M. Ben-Eliezer captured this sensibility in language drawn from the realm of capital: world literature in translation was "spiritual capital [*hon ruhani*]" that "the young peoples take on credit from their older neighbors" and that served "as the basis for the building of their national literature."[70] This figuration of literary translation as a form of capital investment is profoundly revealing: literature may be qualitatively unique and irreducible, but it can also be transformed through translation into a form of reproducible capital that can be employed universally and serially by any investor nation.

These conceptions of literature stemmed not from naivete nor lack of sophistication but, on the contrary, a firmly historicized and even coldly analytical perspective on what made for a strong national literature. These champions of translation saw that Russian and German literatures (the non-Jewish literatures they knew best) had become the distinctive literatures they were precisely and paradoxically through translation, and they saw similar practices among other young literatures. Furthermore, the modernism-inclined among them, like Litvakov, knew that literary revolutions were only possible when modernists could counterpose their literary experiments to a stable canon. And they knew that they were embarking on this project late, at a modernist moment when the very notion of a single Literature was under attack; but they saw this belated translation project as a necessity, even if it sat ill with their otherwise fairly radical cultural politics.

The Deparochializing Imperative

Running through some of these arguments for systematic, programmatic translation was a radical de-Judaizing strain. Some proponents of translation framed it not as an important supplement in the building of Jewish culture but as the sharp wedge of a larger effort to deparochialize it—to do away with any delimitation of Jewish literature in terms of some posited Jewish thematics or sources and to make it as encompassing of human experience as any other literature. It was this stance that Shteynman assumed when he declared that the massive importation of world literature would play a critical role in bringing Hebrew literature "off its narrow path, its side-track."[71] Tshernikhovsky, long identified with such pagan sensibilities, drily noted in his translation of Anacreon's poems that "there is no cultured nation which does not have in its literature something from those poems which are called Anacreonic. . . . These poems, poems of the pleasures of life . . . are entirely absent only from our literature."[72]

The same assumptions drove many critics' evaluation of translations in terms of their implied reader. It was a given for most critics of the period that a translation had to assume and thus help construct not the (existing) parochial "Jewish reader" but a mature modern reader who could occupy any reader-position demanded by a work. Klausner praised Taviov in his review of the latter's *Dorian Gray* for making no cuts or changes reflecting assumptions that certain things would not be interesting to the Hebrew reader and could therefore be cut out, "as were wont to do even the 'Europeans' among our translators up to the present day."[73] Shteynman poured scorn on prewar Hebrew publishers who, unlike Stybel, shaped their programs based on "their assumptions" that the needs of the Jewish reading public were "somehow special."[74] Litvakov put these sentiments more programmatically: the confidence to reject any sharp division between "'Jewishness-literature' and 'humanity-literature'" was the mark of a "living people, which speaks and thinks in a living language."[75]

In his essay on translation and elsewhere, Litvakov insisted that contemporary Yiddish literature had to grow beyond its intimate attachment to Jewish folk culture. "Our literature," he wrote, "has by now almost entirely exhausted the spring of its traditional, national-Jewishy [yidishlekhe] themes and motifs, thoughts and feelings." What had been a necessary "small-town-provincial [kleynshtetldik]-nationalist phase" in the development of a modern Yiddish literature was now at an end—not because external circumstances (like the Revolution) dictated it, but because the literature itself had "exhausted" the specifically literary value of folk culture and its conceits and was left with mere folk "ornamentalism." Systematic, massive, and rapid translation, Litvakov argued, had proven its capacity in the German, Russian, and even Hebrew cases to drive a national literature beyond parochialism; it would now provide Yiddish literature and its future authors with a way out of their own literary-cultural dead end.

Strikingly, these and other radical advocates of deparochialization-through-translation tied their translation discourse to open rejections of the romantic-populist valorization of pre-modern Jewish folk culture or traditional culture as the essential basis of the new Jewish culture. Thus, Litvakov's aggressive vision of translation's task went hand in hand with a denigration of the place of folk culture in the new Yiddish culture that he hoped would come into being. The "emancipatory national-secular content" that Litvakov sought and found in Yiddish literature emerged precisely through its evolution beyond folk culture toward the self-consciously literary expression of the modern individual consciousness: it was not the folk but "individual creators and poets" who were the "fathers of the new tradition which has come to itself."[76] This model captured a sensibility arguably more prevalent in the Yiddish cultural sphere (certainly the Yiddishist avant-garde) of the day than the valorization of Yiddish folklore as the fundament of Yiddish literature by figures like An-sky or the radical Nokhem Oyslender. Litvakov's colleague Dobrushin, while embracing the significance of folklore for children's books, saw the use of such elements in art-literature as a stage to be over-come.[77]

Reflecting a parallel logic vis-à-vis *kinus* of classic Hebrew texts, one writer in the 1919 Hebrew literary anthology *Erets*, writing under the pseudonym Aleph (perhaps Eliezer Shteynman), directly attacked Bialik's and Ahad Ha'am's elevation of the classical Hebrew tradition over modern Hebrew literature. Where Bialik found artistic greatness in the Talmud and midrashic tradition, Aleph saw only crippling diminution in the interpretive rather than authorial-creative stance dictated by tradition: "We created 'Talmud,' which we called a sea—and we were lost among its waves; in our hands [we hold] many pearls and gems which are essential to no nation or language, and in a short while we too will not understand their language. Because we were merely interpreters. And this is our punishment."[78] Contemporary Hebrew writers had to demonstrate creative plenitude, not assume the stance of commentators; to pull the new literature not from the past, but "out of their finger," as Bialik had mockingly put it.

Those who clamored to free Jewish cultural creativity from the confines of privileged folk or classical sources were themselves responding to sallies by champions of the indigenizing strategy, especially Bialik. In the years before the Revolution, Bialik had repeatedly charged his contemporaries with abject internalization of pan-European conceptions of aesthetic value and a consequent failure to achieve a distinct Jewish national character in Jewish literature. Responding angrily to what he saw as his contemporaries' dismissal of the Jewish tradition's cultural richness, he insisted that "our poverty [lies] not only in what we *lack*, but in the fact that we do not properly use the possessions that we *do* have."[79] Only a grounding in the indigenous tradition would allow modern Hebrew culture to cease "feeding on its own flesh" (dwelling on its own expressive dilemmas) and render it strong enough to absorb foreign works (like the translations that Bialik himself commissioned for Moriah) without being overwhelmed: "The language will 'make national' everything that it is given and all that enters its bounds."[80]

Bialik revisited these charges in his epochal "Halakhah ve-aggadah," delivered as a lecture in Odessa and Moscow in 1916–17 and then published in both Hebrew and Russian in 1917–18.[81] In the section of the essay devoted to drawing out the meaning of these two multilayered terms for modern Jewish literature specifically, Bialik challenged contemporary Hebrew writers to turn rabbinic cultural sources into epic: "a true artist, one who does not seek to draw 'the divine spirit' out of his thumb or from licking the dishes of an alien table, but draws it from the fathomless depths of the nation's soul and the mystery of its life—a true artist will find no insuperable difficulty in producing something great even from material such as this, if only the greatness which is in his own soul."[82] Immersion in classical texts, Bialik suggested, might allow Jewish artists to produce a distinctive "national epic" in place of "borrowed vessels and feeble imitation of ready-made alien forms."[83]

Bialik's preeminent status ensured respectful attention to "Halakhah ve-aggadah," though contemporaries differed wildly on what this fertilely ambiguous essay meant.[84] But at least for this important subset of actors in the Jewish cultural sphere, by 1917 it had come to seem that not Bialik but another veteran cultural figure, Frishman, had his finger on the pulse of his generation. Frishman had long held that the Jewish tradition, with the partial exception of the Bible and the aggadic literature, offered only life-denying tendencies in the Nietzschean sense that were precisely to blame for the stifled creativity of the Jewish people. What Hebrew literature needed in order to become a contributing part of universal human civilization was not an imported European literary tradition *in addition to* but rather *instead of* a reworking of Jewry's own traditions. In 1913, he had dismissed Bialik's faith in the power of Jewish classical sources to compel the engagement of Jewish youth, who, he argued, were not ignorant of traditional Jewish genius, but rather saw it as having no bearing on "whether we still have the power to give birth."[85] The much younger cohort of critics who echoed these ideas in 1917 seemed themselves to bear out his claim. M. Ben-Eliezer, who fell somewhere between these two poles, nevertheless respectfully rebuked those who "say . . . that we do not need to bring within our literature the 'offspring of aliens,' and that just as the Hebrew people did not exert itself to bring in converts, so it is fit that our Hebrew literature keep distant these creations which did not issue from the source of Israel." On the contrary, he insisted, there was no road to literary development except through translation: "But those who believe in the revival of Hebrew literature and its development, and see a great necessity in this, must follow after all the young literatures which maintain themselves from translations."[86]

Deparochialization in Cultural Practice

How representative or influential were these attitudes about translation and deparochialization in the cultural sphere as a whole? We find striking resonances and repercussions of these attitudes in three central sites: the burgeoning critical discourse on Jewish literature overall; literary creativity itself; and the realm of literary publishing.

A survey of the vast corpus of frankly prescriptive literary criticism which flooded the Hebrew and Yiddish cultural sphere in the 1917–19 period reveals that the operative cultural principles of the translation proponents extended well beyond their circle. Broad swaths of the literary intelligentsia across all spectra issued parallel calls for deparochializing and Europeanizing Jewish literary expression. In Kiev's Yiddishist circles, Litvakov—who even dared to question the continued significance of Y. L. Peretz on the grounds that he had posthumously "perhaps against his will" become a point of departure for "regurgitated old-Jewishy feelings, experiences, and images"[87]—was more the norm than the exception. While Nahman Mayzl and Nokhem Oyslender both articulated suitably radical versions of folklorism as a Yiddishist cultural strategy, most of Kiev's Yiddishists, it seems, shared Litvakov's impatient sense that Yiddish literature needed to move beyond such parochialism. Not just Litvakov but many Yiddishist critics (Dobrushin, Ezra Korman, one P. Reyland) hailed the cohort of Yiddish modernist poets who made their debut in the literary circles of Kiev in 1918–19 as pioneers of a new epoch in Yiddish literature in large part because much of their poetry seemed refreshingly free of Jewish themes and intertexts. Critics praised these poets for their "wantonness," their seemingly un-Jewish embrace of nature, their demonstrative inattention to the Jewish past and embrace of the here and now, and their invention of a wholly personal poetic persona in place of the conventional national elegist or folk voice.[88] In a typical move, Dobrushin contrasted the love poetry of Dovid Hofshteyn with that of the more veteran Yiddish poet Dovid Eynhorn and with Bialik.[89] Whereas Eynhorn's love poetry depended on Jewish folk motifs and Bialik's couched the speaker's erotic appeal in a language redolent of biblical love poetry, Hofshteyn transcended these parochial limitations: "I saw her in the naked joy of her flesh,/ in the disheveled crown of her fragrant hair,/ I heard from the depths of age-young years:/—This is what one calls a wife!"[90] Significantly, Dobrushin attributed this capacity to Hofshteyn's mastery of what was "for us a new, truly European emotion-culture."

In a very different corner of the literary world, the noted Russian (ethnically Jewish) aesthete M. O. Gershenzon declared that Bialik's younger Hebrew contemporaries had already surpassed him because they had embraced a modern, universal voice while Bialik was "still almost entirely absorbed in Jewish matters—to him, it has still not been granted to go forth into the expanse of human freedom."[91] It is perhaps unsurprising that an outsider to Jewish national cultural concerns like Gershenzon should take this stance. But strikingly parallel contentions can be found in the works of unvarnished cultural nationalists, and in fact predominated in contemporary *Hebrew* criticism across the political and aesthetic spectrum. Thus, Klausner demonstrated no less of an obsession with overcoming the supposed parochialism of Jewish literature in the name of "universal" literary value and chose the same target. Insisting that "every true poet is also a pantheist," Klausner compared Bialik unfavorably to Shakespeare, Goethe, and Pushkin because whereas these "world-embracing spirits" had drawn on all materials of world civilization to address "truly great and deep general-human problem[s]," Bialik (ostensibly) remained mired in parochial Jewishness.[92]

Klausner had propounded these views, and distinguished himself with them, before the war. But by 1917, they had become the dominant stance in the Hebrew literary sphere as a whole. Almost all the younger Hebrew poets and literary critics who staked out a stance in the period argued that Hebrew literature had to break decisively with the "parochial" and "Jewish" conventions that had defined modern secular Hebrew poetry since its birth in the nineteenth century, such as foregrounding themes of national destiny and structuring the poem in creative tension with biblical and talmudic texts. Many echoed Klausner's attack on their beloved Bialik in these very terms. Tellingly, even some of those who defended Bialik's literary preeminence actually shared the same set of anti-parochial standards. In *Ha-tekufah*, Natan Grinblat (later Goren) attacked those who claimed that Bialik was "more Hebrew that European" and that "a book of Bialik's poems is not a *sefer hitzoni*"—i.e., those who praised Bialik for the very obdurate Jewishness that drove critics like Klausner to distraction. Grinblat insisted instead that Bialik's poetry was in its "very essence . . . none other than that art which is entirely '*hitzonit*' [foreign to the Jewish tradition]," that is, modern European lyric poetry.[93]

The younger Hebrew writers of the day cast about for more suitable canonical forebears and lodestars. Tellingly, numerous Hebrew poets and critics across the political and aesthetic spectrum hailed the "pagan," "European" Tshernikhovsky as the new fundament of Hebrew literary and cultural consciousness. Eliahu Meitus declared that whereas Bialik had "opened windows to the sun for us," Tshernikhovsky "brought us outside and gave us the sun and the moon and the stars . . . and taught us to love—to love everything . . . to love man, and to love life, the world and all it contains, without any accounting."[94] This claim was echoed with little variation by many of his contemporaries.[95] Even the hard left Zionist Sh. Tsemah posited Tshernikhovsky as the "the necessary and logical phenomenon who shows the way which we have traversed and reveals also the new life and the new heavens stretching before us."[96] What all found compelling about Tshernikhovsky was an apparent literary-cum-psychic wholeness that inhered especially in his rejection of any distinction between Jewish and non-Jewish culture. As Klausner put it, "the main thing" was that Tshernikhovsky was a *Euro-*

pean poet who attained to "a level on which stand the more perfect poets of Europe"; yet Tshernikhovsky's very Europeanness and humanism were not at odds with a poetry of Jewish revival, but in fact represented it in the fullest sense as an incarnation of what the nation had to strive to become. Tshernikhovsky was "a poet who is himself entirely Revival [*meshorer, she-hu kulo tehiyah*]."[97]

For all this talk about "Judaizing" and "Europeanizing" tendencies in literature, we might well ask whether these sentiments found any purchase in the arts themselves. Many writers of the day moved fluidly between these ostensibly opposed tendencies, including those who insisted on the central importance of translation. Thus, Moyshe Kulbak became one of his generation's most creative manipulators of folk sources and motifs in a modernist literary framework. None other than Frishman produced during this period a cycle of stories set against the biblical narrative of the Israelites' desert wanderings and the theophany, *Ba-Midbar*; that one of the stories was closely modeled on Anatole France's *Thais*, a work Frishman himself had translated into Hebrew previously, suggests not opposition but complementarity between these imperatives.[98] This interpenetration holds all the more for music and the plastic arts in this period, where the very project of a "Jewish music" or "Jewish art" seemed to imply some kind of fusion between indigenous and pan-European traditions.

Yet in the post-1917 moment, the discourse of deparochialization did in fact find strong echoes (and spurs) in the arts themselves. As Seth Wolitz and other students of Yiddish modernism have shown, if we focus on those who sought self-consciously to be the next wave in Jewish culture (outside the visual arts), we find a broad emphasis on consciously displacing, decentering, and in some cases completely effacing obtrusively "Jewish" elements in their art. In theater, while the Vilna Trupe and Ha-Bimah sought distinctively "Jewish" work,[99] the fledgling theater troupe that would eventually become GOSET initially aspired to a "European" Yiddish theater freed of any "specific repertoire" and sharing the "tasks of world theater."[100] In the Yiddish literary realm, the Kiev Grupe poets made their mark, as I have said, in good part because of their efforts to craft a lyric persona, voice, and set of themes freed of what Litvakov, one of their champions on this score, called "Jewishy" associations (and especially freed of the indigenous-folkloristic elements so integral to the poetry of many of their predecessors as well as contemporaries). It was no accident that in Markish, Litvakov saw proof that Yiddish literature too was finally on the cusp of being able to express the undetermined, all-embracing, and individual voice that was the supposed seal of modern "universal" literature. This attitude was epitomized for Litvakov in what he saw as Markish's typical phrase: "*stam in velt arayn"* (simply out in the world; out in the world without pretense or identifying mark).[101] It resonated in much of Markish's early verse, perhaps most famously in the following 1917 lyric:

> Don't know if I'm at home
> or if I'm afar [*tsi in der fremd*]—
> I'm running! . . .
> my shirt's unbuttoned,
> there are no reins on me,
> I'm nobody's, I'm unclaimed [*hefker*, also translatable as wild,
>   licentious],
> without a beginning, without an end . . .[102]

More systematically, Markish's older Kiev contemporary Dovid Hofshteyn devoted much of his poetic effort in the 1917–19 period to developing a lexicon of imagery and poses unfettered by any identifiable Jewish determinants. Speaking, like Markish, in an anti-typological first-person voice, he depicted his poetic self in poem after poem as a lone wanderer on an open road unbound to anything but the beauties of a universal nature (Yosef Tchaikov's cover for Hofshteyn's 1919 book *Ba vegn* depicts this wanderer, dressed as a dandy in cloak and walking stick). At one point, Hofshteyn's poetic self appeared clad in a most un-Jewish coat of knightly mail: "Today the sun to my new armor/ lent the last golden shine/ and mixed for me of enchanted wine/ a cup of joy." This stood in stark contrast to the strategy of Hofshteyn's best-known prewar poem "In vinter farnakhtn," which still represented a modern Jewish self through a tension between a dreamy Jewish youth and his traditional Jewish home and calendar. Now, no longer bound to any Jewish referent, Hofshteyn's poetic self and his poetry could venture "girded with sunshine . . . without fear into all the black caves/ of world and being."[103]

Having groped for the literary means to depict his own poetic self independently of a reflexively Jewish vocabulary and emancipated from his parental home's all-encompassing Jewishness, Hofshteyn pursued this conscious elision of Jewish elements in a more sophisticated series of poems about children and childhood. In "Vi troyerik-zis iz mentsh tsu zayn" (How sadly sweet it is to be human) he turned to an infant's first moments of self-consciousness, where he could experiment freely with the representation of a completely pre-Jewish self. At the close of the poem, Hofshteyn found a concrete referent for his contemporaries' cherished hope that such a literature of the individual voice could lead alchemically to a "universal" literature:

> . . . and suddenly, in the deep of late at night
> to feel a hidden quiver of the soul

and without moving, suddenly awake
with every atom sense
how eternity's wings are moving
and bitterly to know so little
yet to know, for instance,
that the clock now reads two, perhaps three.
And lying still in the hot glow, in the sweet pain
with every heart-thread violently yearn
that every human brother should know this pain
that every human brother should possess this joy:
how sadly sweet it is to be human![104]

In a more directly confrontational (and perhaps humorous) move, Hof-shteyn's "Vig-lid" (Lullabye) cunningly edited Avrom Goldfaden's pseudo-folk classic "Rozhinkes mit mandlen" to yield a poem that exploited the original's folk rhymes and images but completely denuded them of Jewish figures. As in the contemporaneous prose of Der Nister, the "tsigele" remained (in a direct quote of the Goldfaden original: "a klor vays tsigele"). But Shulamis and the Temple had disappeared; in their place, Hofshteyn offered an unmarked individual lulling his similarly unmarked child: "I rock your cradle/ and sing in your ear/ a little bolt/ has closed a gate there."[105]

Of course, as critics recognized to their dismay or delight, Hofshteyn himself was by no means uniformly committed to the complete elision of the Jewish element in modern Jewish poetry.[106] In other poems, in fact, he thematized the very demand for the "universal" in Jewish literature as a productive problem, subtly asserting the value and perhaps the inescapability of Jewish associations as one element in any universe of aesthetic expression by a Jewish individual.[107] In this, he was typical. *Mutatis mutandis*, the same respect for the aesthetic value of indigenous sources coupled with an impatient desire to grow beyond them characterized the Kultur Lige's music section, which in 1919 declared its commitment to "move beyond the narrow confines of the folk-primitive, build up larger and more complicated forms—to join the modern musical arts in such a way that the national spirit will nevertheless remain whole."[108]

Yet the point remains: by 1917, for growing numbers of artists, the problem of how to move beyond the "narrow confines" of a posited Jewish aesthetics was a motivating, productive artistic problem. It is telling that champions of the *indigenizing* move like Bialik or An-sky themselves clearly felt that this drive to produce a Jewish literature more closely and intimately linked to a posited shared European or universal literature was already ascendant, even a majority commitment. As early as 1897, in a letter to the era's preeminent champion of an anti-parochial stance,

Micha Yosef Berdyczewski, Bialik expressed a sour skepticism about what he saw as the increasingly popular notion "that the translation of the poetry of the prophets of the nations will save Israel from all of its sufferings and woes";[109] An-sky attacked this stance in Yiddish literature in 1908.[110] Bialik's essays of the immediate prewar and wartime period did not present his proposal to build the new Jewish culture from "authentic" Jewish sources as a self-evident starting point for Jewish culture (as is often presumed) but as an explicit *counter* to the "European" drive in a cultural project already well underway, as we have seen.

Finally, we may move from this most hermetic sphere of cultural creativity to the most material: the realm of publishing. I have already alluded to the astonishing resources, effort, and planning that publishers and other cultural institutions invested in translation in the 1917–19 period. Alongside Stybel's press, the two other leading Hebraist presses of the day also made a place for translation. Moriah sought translations of Homer and Shakespeare from Tshernikhovsky and Grimm's fairytales by Frishman.[111] Moscow's Omanut press under the Hebraist-Zionist patrons Hillel Zlatopolski and his daughter Shoshana Persits focused most of its efforts on literary publishing for children. It laid particular emphasis on translations from European children's literature, producing an impressive array of "storybooks and tales for children from the best of world literature."[112] This emphasis was also evident in the press's 1917 Hebrew journal for young adults, *Shetilim*, which placed work by Hebrew writers like Bialik, Tshernikhovsky, Yaakov Fichman, and Shteynman alongside translations of Wilde, Mickiewicz, Daudet, and even Korean folktales.[113] It was paralleled by the program of another Hebrew publishing house founded in Moscow in 1917 in honor of Bialik by Hebraist patron-admirers, the children's book publisher Ahinoar, which planned to publish some 150 children's books drawn mostly from world literature.[114] Litvakov's call for a grand translation program into Yiddish—no doubt inspired in part by the competing Hebraists' leap forward and perhaps by *Vsemirnaia literatura*—came against the backdrop of a similar explosion of translation in the reemerging Yiddish publishing sphere. The Yiddishist-radical Kiever Farlag with which Litvakov was linked made a strong place for translation in its efforts to reshape Yiddish art-literature as a whole, publishing Andersen, Tolstoy, Pushkin, Ivan Franko, Wilde, Longfellow, and Daudet. Other smaller Kiev Yiddishist houses published Andersen (Onhoyb press) and Byron (Dorem-Farlag). The publishing houses Literatur in Odessa and Universal in Warsaw both initiated a "universal-library" series modeled on similar endeavors in other European languages.[115] Kharkov Farlag "Idish" planned a "folks-bibliotek" of Yiddish and translated works including Byron, Jack London, and Knut Hamsun.[116] The small Moscow publishing house Khaver produced an anthology of European poetry, *Fremds*, as well as translations of Tolstoy, Kuprin, and Maupassant.[117] The most ambitious and well-funded private Yiddishist publishing ventures of the day, Kiev's Folks-Farlag and Kultur-Lige, both made translation from world literature a central aspect of their self-declared (and competing) mission to guide the reemergent Yiddish cultural sphere as a whole.[118] The Folks-Farlag was founded by Yiddishists more politically and culturally moderate (though no less culturally ambitious) than those of the Kiev-Grupe; among its central figures were moderate socialists like Moyshe Zilberfarb and Folkists like Zeev Latski-Bertoldi, Shtif, and Zelig Kalmanovitsh (the latter two in charge of its translation division). Like Omanut, the Folks-Farlag's division for children's literature emphasized translation of "the classic works of world-literature which usually comprise the reading material for youth." Its division for art-literature aimed to translate "the classic works of the European novel-literature" and "modern lyric poetry" (as well as translations from modern Hebrew literature—a different though no less interesting topic).[119] Ben-Tsiyon Dinur, who worked for the press, recalls that in its brief existence (founded in late 1918, it dissolved in the drastically altered circumstances of Bolshevik Kiev by 1921), its translation division "prepared translations of the writings of Tolstoy, Chekhov, Byron, Flaubert, Maupassant, and many, many more. And it announced that it planned to translate a selection of the works of Shakespeare, Ibsen, of Goethe and Schiller."[120]

By mid-1919, in turn, the more radical wing of Kiev's burgeoning Yiddishist world was poised to pursue a grander publishing program through the richly endowed, commandingly positioned Kultur-Lige publishing house. The Kultur-Lige Farlag declared its intent to focus (besides its educational publishing) on the publication of "classic works, original and translated."[121] The Yiddishists affiliated with the Kiever Farlag and the Kultur-Lige found themselves catapulted into a position of potential cultural authority with the arrival of Soviet power in Kiev in 1919; by mid-1919, the Jewish Section of the All-Ukrainian Central Publishing House (VseIzdat), charged with publishing "art-literature for adults and children in Yiddish" at the state's expense, came under control of Yiddishists affiliated with the Kultur-Lige like Noyekh Lurie, A. Litvak, and Litvakov himself.[122] Under their guidance, the Jewish Section did not so much change as expand previous plans: it planned to publish not only original Yiddish works but also translations of European writers, books on "the theory and history of art and literature," and, for children, collections of folktales from around the world and literary translations.[123]

Finally, a parallel emphasis on translation from European literature and plans of similar scope characterized the newly emergent Yiddish art-theater sphere as well. By 1920, with new Yiddish art-theater studios and troupes already active in Moscow, Kiev, Warsaw, and beyond, the Folks-Farlag announced that it had a full hundred plays ready to print, "especially European repertoire."[124] When the Jewish Section of the Soviet All-Ukrainian Theater Committee and the closely linked Kultur-Lige Theater Section moved aggressively to create "a modern Yiddish dramatic theater," they commissioned ten translations of European repertoire and sponsored the reediting of existing translations that were, they noted, often "beneath criticism."[125]

When we seek to adduce the ideological motives behind these publishing programs, we face a number of serious challenges. Most of these publishers did not offer (or I have simply not found) the kinds of explicit ideological statements about the meaning of translation that were the stock-in-trade of critics like Litvakov; hence we must reason inductively from the content and practice of these plans, aided by scattered clues to the publishers' own ideologies. Moreover, most of these publishing houses involved congeries of actors with different views and intentions. Furthermore, as Litvakov, Litai, and others complained, some of their publications were not the product of any systematic plan, but rather individual initiatives that had simply come to hand[126] and which often stemmed at least as much from the individual literary interests of individual author-translators as from any overarching logic of translation on behalf of the literature as a whole. Moreover, there was a significant market for translations, and many of these publishing houses, particularly the Yiddish ones, may have had quite practical reasons for their translations; one report suggests that Warsaw Jewish publishers began to prepare Yiddish translations of European authors during the war with the expectation of strong demand afterward.[127] The sorts of authors selected by some of the smaller publishers like Warsaw's "Universal" or even Moscow's "Khaver"—prose writers like Tolstoy, Kuprin, Hamsun, and Maupassant—were the mainstays of middlebrow literatures across Europe, and were of a piece with the market-driven translation publication evident in prewar Warsaw and New York.

Yet when we consider at least the largest and most significant publishing houses (besides Stybel's)—namely, the Folks-Farlag, Omanut, and the publishing houses of Kiev's Yiddishist radicals—we find clear parallels to the ideas propounded by the champions of translation and good reason to posit a shared set of sensibilities. First, market- and demand-oriented explanations cover scant ground for these presses. Although Hebraist publishing houses like Moriah could, it seems, make a profit even at this juncture,[128] profit was manifestly not the goal of the Omanut or Stybel publishing houses. Although these presses sold their works on the market and clearly hoped that their books would find readers who might not otherwise have put their Hebrew to literary uses, both presses produced physically deluxe works[129] in runs far larger than they could hope to sell and, as contemporaries recognized, they certainly expected substantial loss.[130] There is no reason to assume that translation marked an exception to this more general pattern of what one contemporary called "patronage-national" motives, by contrast with prewar Hebrew publishing ventures that received help from patrons but depended ultimately on market success to sustain themselves.[131] Although there was certainly a greater potential market for Yiddish translations, it was not profit but cultural-ideological vision that shaped the publishing choices of the Yiddishist publishing houses in question. The Folks-Farlag, though a stock company that did aim for profit, subordinated the concerns of its investors to its own sense of Yiddishist mission; deeming one of its tasks the material support of Yiddish writers as such, it apparently offered to pay them as much as they needed.[132] More generally, the Folks-Farlag, the Kiever-Farlag, and many other Yiddishist publishing houses ceded exclusive distribution rights to the Yiddishist Kultur-Lige, which used its near-monopolistic market power not to maximize profits but to achieve Yiddishist goals *against* the natural tendencies of the wartime Ukrainian Yiddish book market itself.[133] Committed to the widest possible distribution of Yiddish books at a moment when "the broad masses" were utterly impoverished, the Kultur-Lige sold its books at close to cost and even sold older stock at its nominal cost despite the staggering inflation of the period.[134] In order to ensure that books in limited supply would reach publicly oriented Yiddishist institutions like libraries and clubs: it offered such non-profit organizations a set of "the better books" for 50 percent down before making them generally available.[135]

Granted that these publishing houses were driven by Yiddishist and Hebraist ideological visions more than material motives, it is more challenging to parse the relationship between reader-oriented educative sensibilities and concerns to shape Jewish literature and culture itself. Some of the Yiddishist and Hebraist publishers evidently did see translation, at least in part, as a direct service to readers. More than Litvakov and other critics, they seem to have cherished the hope that there would be strong popular interest and that these translations would serve to directly reshape the Jewish identity of readers assumed to be less educated and cultural flexible than the intelligentsia itself. The Khaver anthology *Fremds* declared that its goal was "to acquaint the Jewish reader with the best and most important creations of European poetry," which its editor seemed to define as Russian Romanticism, French Symbolism (Baudelaire and Verlaine), and a dash of Decadence (Balmont).[136] Speculatively, we might say that this sort of publication balanced unsteadily between a literary-educative mode and a more subtly market-oriented effort to cater to a prospective middlebrow audience of Jewish readers who, like their prewar Russian counterparts, were increasingly open to once-scandalous Decadence (Wilde, Balmont, Kuprin) and who may have sought a sort of cosmopolitan respectability.[137] It may be that Stybel's physically beautiful and anachronistically thick publications—critics were astonished and slightly disgruntled at the 600-plus page length of *Ha-tekufah*—enacted a similar desire for middle-class distinction; Stybel himself was a former clerk of provincial origin only recently made good.[138]

A more purely ideological, reader-oriented sensibility expressed itself in the substantial concern of the Omanut publishing house, the Folks-Farlag, and the Kiever Farlag with providing literary translations for children and for Yiddish and Hebrew secular schools. Leavening original Jewish works, these translations would forge a harmonious modern (i.e., European) Jew—one for whom the pull of Jewish and European identities would not leave the proverbial "rip in the soul" that so many of the translators and teachers themselves carried with them. The rich body of translations offered by Omanut's *Shetilim* speaks to the journal's overarching desire to simultaneously allow its young reader to "find himself in his Hebrew newspaper in his own world and not in a foreign world" while simultaneously bringing him "out of his narrow world."[139] According to one account, Omanut's emphasis on translations for children more generally reflected a recognition that Hebrew alone lacked the standard international canon of youth literature "from which all the peoples of Europe drew sustenance."[140] A similar sensibility informed the Kiev Yiddishist children's journal *Shretelekh* (1919), where readers could find Rudyard Kipling and a Japanese fairytale alongside Hofshteyn and Der Nister.

Yet the publishing programs developed by the Folks-Farlag and, apparently, by the more radical Yiddishists around the Kiever Farlag and the Kultur-Lige also seem to have been inspired by the sorts of ideas about reshaping Hebrew and Yiddish literature themselves propounded by Litavkov, Stybel, Shteynman et al. They seem to have aimed for the encompassing, catholic character that was the hallmark of this conception. The Folks-Farlag program described by Dinur speaks for itself. As for its production of numerous theatrical translations, there was no doubt a market in the proliferation of Yiddish theater groups; but it may have also reflected the widely shared desire among Yiddish theater activists, in the words of the Petersburg Jewish Theater Society's literary director M. Rivesman, to "refresh the dirty, moldy Yiddish repertoire and illuminate it with masterful translations" alongside "truly literary, original dramatic works."[141] The culturally and politically radical Yiddishist cultural producers who gathered around the Kiever Farlag and its flagship journal *Bikher-velt* were under Litvakov's strong influence[142] and shared much of his basic vision. In turn, the Kultur-Lige's vague proposals coupled with the translation plans of its more radical successors suggest a desire to see a body of translated European "classics" serve as no less a fundament of modern Yiddish culture than the Yiddish classics themselves. On the Hebraist side, Persits, the guiding figure of Omanut, seems initially to have envisioned a grand translation program like that the Stybel press would take up; at one point, she invited Bialik himself to serve as the chief editor for a series of "translations from the best of world literature."[143] She may have dropped it because Stybel himself undertook it in so grand a fashion or because she saw a need to focus on children's books; but the very fact of her commitment to a similar catholic literary vision is significant.

It is difficult to move from these affinities of practice to any more concrete claims about the attitudes of individual actors toward translation in particular and where they fall on the spectrum of attitudes about indigenizing as opposed to universalizing strategies. Persits was evidently committed to endowing Hebrew literature with a "European" profile; this seems to reflect both a notion of national respectability, a concern for *appearances*, and an inner-directed conviction that Jews were Europeans and should shape their culture and psyche accordingly. Yet she also showed a lifelong engagement with traditional Jewish texts[144] and supported An-sky's projected album of Jewish folk art even as she founded Omanut.[145] Her father and partner in Omanut, Hillel Zlatopolski, was the most avid early enthusiast of An-sky's *Dybbuk*; indeed, he worked hard to convince Bialik to translate it for Ha-Bimah.[146] The Folks-Farlag, the work of many hands, presents a still more complicated picture. At least one of its leading figures, Latski-Bertoldi, sympathized with the more radical Litvakov's call for a deparochialized Jewish culture, even chiding Litvakov for giving too little credit to the ways in which modern *Hebrew* literature—including "Tshernikhovsky's Hellenism and Shneur's simple *goyishkayt*"—had contributed to this process.[147] But Kalmanovitsh and Shtif certainly numbered among those who hoped that modern Jewish culture would build on internal Jewish traditions at least as fully as European *fremds*; the Folks-Farlag in general, evidently under their influence, made a substantial place for translations from the Hebrew, which had the former, altogether different ideological valence.

In short, many of these figures saw great value in the indigenous sources of Jewish culture. Yet in their capacity as activist-publishers, they, like their more radical counterparts Litvakov, Shteynman, or Frishman, also perceived a particularly pressing—perhaps more pressing—need for a massive infusion of non-Jewish culture by 1917.

The Sociology of the Deparochializing Imperative

This split between cultural ideology and practice held true, tellingly, even for the most vociferous critic of Europeanism in modern Jewish culture, Haim Nahman Bialik himself. In 1917, laying out his vision for the future of Hebrew culture at the founding conference of the Hebraist Tarbut organization, Bialik grouped "translations of the works of the world geniuses—Shakespeare, Goethe, Heine" among the essential tasks that Hebraists would have to carry out if they had any hopes of transforming East European Jewry.[148] Bialik had long acknowledged the importance of translation, despite his criticism of excessive Europeanism in Jewish cultural life. He had taken a leading role in the prewar Turgeman publishing imprint for children's book translations[149] and made a place for the world classics in his agenda-setting 1913 disquisition on "The Hebrew Book." Yet he had always—indeed, increasingly—insisted that translation be accorded a strictly subordinate place relative to the indigenous tradition. It is against this backdrop that his speech at the 1917 Tarbut conference is so remarkable, for it did not hedge the call for translation with such critical animadversions. Another remarkable deviation offers an essential clue: Bialik, perhaps the most famous skeptic among his generation of Hebraists about reviving *spoken* Hebrew, embraced even this idea fully in this speech. Both of these (temporary) deviations from his ideological stance resonate with the overriding concern of the speech for "our nationalist youth," who despite their national commitment "do not belong to us in their heart and soul, but to other worlds . . . to Tolstoy and to Turgenev and not to Isaiah and Ha-Levi." This concern with a generation slipping away suggests a line of analysis that will help us understand the motives of those writers, critics, and publishers who did not share the radical antagonism to indigenous sources but nevertheless laid heavy emphasis on translation at this moment.

In particular, let us turn our attention back to a hitherto neglected feature of Litai's March 1917 essay on translation. Litai framed his translation program as the only way out of an intolerable choice between "mental abstinence or assimilation." This striking phrase was in fact the title of the article,[150] and was repeated verbatim in his later essay for *Hashiloah* on the Stybel press: "The literature of the world . . . God Almighty! Is this not the thing longed for by the soul of all those Hebrews who aspire to spiritual wholeness, all those for whom it is hard to bear both intellectual abstinence and the intellectual assimilation which comes through perusal of books written in foreign tongues?"[151] Litai's potent rhetoric, like Bialik's turnabout, reflected a third and still more urgent motivation for wholesale translation: not merely to reshape the literature itself or to properly educate Jews as moderns, but to prevent the defection of the Hebraist (and mutatis mutandis, Yiddishist) *intelligentsia* from Jewish cultural engagement.

Concretely, Litai contended that modern Jews, however strong their national cultural commitment in general and commitment to Hebrew in particular, could not be expected to confine themselves solely to the existing corpus of works in Jewish languages. Yet the obvious recourse to co-territorial non-Jewish languages—particularly Russian—for access to world literature and thought virtually guaranteed linguistic and cultural assimilation. Litai invoked a previous generation's experience as proof and warning: "The maskilim, that is, those who apart from their knowledge of Hebrew attained for themselves general education to a certain degree and mastered one of the culture-languages—these abandoned Hebrew literature because she could not satisfy their mental and spiritual needs."[152]

This argument for translation transposed the issue from one of cultural ideology to one of sociology (and from the needs of literature itself back to the reader, albeit in this case, the intelligentsia reader him- or herself). For Litai, translation had great practical importance for the consolidation of Jewish national culture, not only because it would expand Jewish literature but because it could (he hoped) eliminate this tension. Rather than Judaizing foreign works or seeking to keep them out by cultural *herem*, it would bring them within the linguistic horizons of Jewish national culture as part of a cosmopolitan Hebrew culture.

Litai's anxious argument suggests that we think about the entire emphasis on translation and Europeanization of Jewish culture not merely as reflecting a particular vision of what Jewish culture itself should be but also as a strategic response to an emerging sociological reality. All the actors in question knew from their own experience that the new breed of Jewish readers and *intelligenty* would not and could not limit its own intellectual horizons in the name of Jewishness, and that any version of Jewish national culture that staked its existence on some delimited, "authentic" Jewishness would simply not prove satisfying to people with ever greater unmediated access to the riches of metropolitan cultures unconstrained by such concerns.

Certain aspects of translation practice in this period reflect these concerns. Arguably, the widespread emphasis on translations from European literature for children that I have hitherto treated as a mode of cultural education was also driven by a more anxious recognition that only a Hebrew or Yiddish children's literature which could compete with the attractions and expansiveness of the much more developed Russian (or Polish) children's literature would secure the allegiance of a new generation of Hebrew or Yiddish readers (and writers). One historian of Hebrew publishing suggests that Shoshana Persits's concern for providing Hebrew translations of the standard European youth canon was driven in part by a recognition that Jewish young people sought these works in "foreign languages" (i.e., Russian).[153] More broadly, contemporaries' preoccupation with the fact that the books for children and for adults produced by the Stybel and Omanut presses matched or surpassed the physical beauty of Russian books suggests not only pride but also a deeply felt sense that in the competition for the cultural allegiance of Jewish youth, "Europeanness" even in form was essential.[154] As one source puts it, Persits felt "the need to publish Hebrew books for students, youth, and the people that could compete from the standpoint of form and content alike—and especially from an aesthetic standpoint quite neglected in Hebrew books—with the best of literature in foreign languages."[155]

In a different vein, the hitherto-neglected issue of translation of Jewish literature *into* Russian suggests a similar set of concerns. The relatively little translation of this sort that did take place in this period was intended almost exclusively to acquaint Russified Jewish readers with Zionist ideals and, not least, contemporary Hebrew culture. This was an explicit principle for Leyb Jaffe of Moscow's Safrut publishing house, the publisher of almost all such translations at the revolutionary juncture, who declared the Russian-language Jewish book merely a substitute "intended for those circles of readers who lack Hebrew."[156] In that sense, the ideological valence of translation from Hebrew *into* Russian at this juncture was the diametrical opposite of the translation praxis hitherto examined: translations of Hebrew poetry carried in the press's *Sborniki "Safrut"* or in its 1918 *Evreiskaia Antologiia: Sbornik Molodoi Evreiskoi Poezii* were intended to Judaize the reader rather than Europeanize him further (much less to deparochialize Jewish literature in Russian, a phenomenon that by definition could only be "Jewish" if it was marked by concretely Jewish referents). Yet strikingly, the latter anthology presented a cross-section of contemporary Hebrew poetry that highlighted its most cosmopolitan, unparochial thematics. This was what Gershenzon found in this poetry and stressed in his foreword: whereas the "old Hebrew poetry" (including Bialik) spoke only about "Jewry, like a sick person who speaks without cease about his own sickness," the "young Hebrew poets love like the youth of all countries, and clearly and resoundingly sing out their love; the natural world is open to them, and they depict it lovingly. " When they did turn to Jewish matters, they did so as "men, entirely free men."[157] An anthology like the *Sbornik Molodoi*

Evreiskoi Poezii could render Hebrew literature respectable to Jews schooled in Russian literature precisely by presenting it as equally expansive.

This strategic calculus no doubt pushed activist-publishers to focus on translation. But it was not merely strategic: it both addressed and bespoke the ever-deepening internalization of schemata of appreciation and reception that dictated for the actors in question whether a work of art was experientially compelling (i.e., good art) or not. Among the many sources that exemplify this subtle but critically important process are the comments of the journalist Sh. Tshernovits (Sfog) on the newly formed Ha-Bimah theater troupe in 1917. By no means hostile to "indigenizing" sensibilities—Tshernovits played a role in convincing Bialik to translate that most "indigenous" of contemporary works, An-sky's *Dybbuk*, for Ha-Bimah[158]—Tshernovits offered a word of warning to the troupe. Whereas ten years earlier, Hebraists had thrilled to see any sort of Hebrew onstage, now they were familiar with the best of Russian theater and would settle for no less on the Hebrew stage. Ha-Bimah had to "remember that their audience will not come now to see 'the great wonder' of people performing in Hebrew, but rather to enjoy an artistic performance, and thus it is incumbent upon the managers [of the company] to endeavor both to enrich the content of the plays and to beautify the external aspect, the artistic aspect, of the performers in the plays."[159] Standards of taste, in other words, were being dictated by growing familiarity with metropolitan, especially Russian, literature. And in order to be compelling, Jewish culture, whatever the content, had to satisfy these metropolitan standards.[160]

A Different Jewish Cultural Nationalism

The ideal of a "universal," Jewishly unmarked Jewish culture enjoyed an ambiguous fate in the years that followed. Certainly, translation does not seem to have forestalled cultural-linguistic assimilation in any obvious way (though forestalling effects are, of course, hard to measure), at least in Eastern Europe; in the emerging Hebrew-speaking community of Palestine, it may well have had that effect for the younger generation.[161] As for the idea of a universal Jewish culture itself, its fate differed in accordance with the larger differences in the political and cultural conditions of the various interwar Jewish communities. In the Soviet Union of the 1920s, it gained in force—albeit in tension with acceptably radical and anti-religious versions of folklorism—but it was harnessed ever more tightly to new political demands of the Revolution and thus profoundly distorted. Litvakov and Dobrushin understood deparochialization dialectically in the service of a new, better national culture, but the Bundist turned Bolshevik Moyshe Rafes would have the last word when, in 1919, he warned them that "we Jewish Communists are the great broom which will sweep off the Jewish workers' street all your Mendeles, Peretzs, Sholem Aleichems, your whole petit bourgeois culture."[162] Tellingly, literary translation itself would come to serve in Soviet Yiddish culture less as a culture-building strategy than as a tactic of retreat into a neutral sphere by writers unable to toe the literary-ideological line.[163] In freer interwar Poland, the notion of a universal Jewish culture resonated with modernists like the Khalyastre group in the early 1920s (though modernism as such could also valorize indigenous sources) but then arguably fell victim to the more general structural and ideological pressures that, as Seth Wolitz has shown, frustrated any attempt by Jewish national artists to enjoy "personal aesthetic freedom without compromising [their] national identity."[164] The creative revision of indigenous sources remained (or rebounded as) the organizing principle of many key works of the era,[165] though the anti-parochial commitment remained potent in other loci like the poetics of the American In-zikh group or Meylekh Ravitsh in Poland. Programmatic translation remained a central feature of Hebrew and Yiddish publishing alike in Poland; but with the exception of the Stybel press in the early 1920s—about which one Warsaw writer could enthuse that it had conquered "Japheth in his tent" and created a new "bookshelf" that "Jewish fathers will bequeath to their sons"[166]—the grand visions of 1917–19 found no purchase in Poland. This contrasted notably with the *yishuv*, where the consolidation of a Hebrew society and state in the making laid the groundwork for the routinization of an open Jewish literature—a notable fact given the current romance in some quarters of the Jewish academy with the ostensible freeing effects of deterritorialized "diaspora culture."

But the explosion of debate and activity around programmatic translation in 1917–19 is important not only for whatever lasting effects it might have had but as an expression of larger cultural developments in the national intelligentsia's project to create a modern Jewish culture. The intellectuals, writers, and publishers who focused so much effort on systematic, rapid translation in this period sought to create a compensatory literary tradition of universal scope that would reshape the sensibilities and orientations of Jewish writers and thus of Jewish aesthetic culture itself. This was, for many, a means to protect the fledgling modern Jewish culture itself against the far more powerful metropolitan cultures. At the same time, for some it was also an end: the creation of an adequate modern Jewish culture through a programmatic embrace of its stylized opposite, the "European" or "universal."

The historian might protest that the pursuit of so-called Jewish and so-called universal cultural strategies are not inherent opposites but two moments of a single process of cultural creation. Yet contemporaries felt these orientations to be opposed in terms of their practical sense of what Jewish culture as a whole needed most and in which direction it ought to develop. Indeed, we might follow Dan Miron in positing this tension as a generative principle or recurrent structuring tension of the modern Jewish cultural undertaking as a whole. The famous confrontations of the 1890s between the *tseirim* and Ahad Ha'am over the issue of Jewish content and the alien "beauty of Japheth" in Hebrew literary expression, or between Ben-Avigor's Tushiyah publishing house and the Hibat-Tsion Ahiasaf over the place of belletristics and non-Jewish writing on the Hebrew bookshelf, were merely the most public manifestations of an ever-stronger countercurrent within the emerging East European Jewish cultural sphere; this countercurrent is evident too in the recurrent invocations of Hellenism analyzed by Yaacov Shavit, in Yosef Klausner's praise for Peretz's imitative 1894 Hebrew love poetry as a step toward the Europeanization of Jewish literature, and even in Bialik's plaintive private admission in 1892 that much of his poetry was not national.[167] By 1917, when it seemed both possible and pressing to provide a solid institutional, social, and ideological foundation for the new Jewish culture, a more concrete facet of this tension displayed itself: the very practical question of cultural resources. The Jewish intelligentsia was well aware of the gap between its vision of massive cultural revolution and its own limited cultural and material resources; hence the allocation of these resources to one strategy of culture-building over another assumed a zero-sum logic. Litai's reaction to Bialik's decision to translate An-sky's *Between Two Worlds* is illustrative: he lamented that Hebrew's greatest writer should squander time on this "completely mediocre" play about "'dybbuks'" rather than furthering "the redemption of our language" through translations from world literature like the *Quixote* he had previously begun.[168]

More broadly, by 1917, this countercurrent had become a flood. The urge to reconcile a commitment to Jewish identity with a universal cultural orientation had become, as opponents and proponents alike recognized, a decisive fact within the national camp itself. In light of this fact, programmatic demands for deparochialization were not peculiar deviations from Jewish nationalism but, firstly, far-seeing efforts to come to grips with real cultural change in ever-broader parts of the Jewish population. Moderate advocates of translation and the champions of a more radical deparochialization alike[169] recognized the impossibility of turning these tides back through any sort of willed self-restriction—what Litai called "intellectual abstinence."

More important, we must recognize that such demands were themselves expressions of Jewish nationalism. It is a revealing fact that even the radical universalizers examined here were by no means opposed to the development of specifically Jewish idioms of expression in modern Jewish literature. Indeed, these figures cherished the hope that their engineered deparochialization might lead dialectically to new and distinctly Jewish literary works. Klausner, Shteynman, and many of their contemporaries repeatedly invoked the hope that "the most universal poet" would also give birth to "the most national" poetry (many accorded Tshernikhovsky this laurel);[170] in this, they paralleled a trope common to Russian nationalist literati from Dostoevsky's famed effusions about the uniquely absorptive capacities of Russian genius to Evgeny Anichkov's summation of the Russian Silver Age as a triumphant rechanneling of Western literary trends, though with none of the same confidence about the advantages of cultural underdevelopment.[171] Yiddishists like Dobrushin aspired to see Yiddish poetry rise to the same "national-classical heights" as that attained by Byron, Pushkin, Verlaine, and Bialik, and to "elevat[e] modern Jewishness to an artistic *Weltanschauung*."[172] And none other than Litvakov held out the hope that through Europeanization, Jewish literature would "not los[e] but perhaps, on the contrary, [deepen] its uniquely national character."[173]

More telling still is the simple fact that even those who most fervently advocated this deparochialization did so explicitly in the name of revitalizing modern Jewish national culture no less than their indigenizing opponents. After all, the point of their undertaking was to strengthen self-sufficient modern Hebrew and Yiddish cultures despite their own sense that these cultures were, as yet, quite inferior to those around them—arguably, the very essence of East European cultural nationalism. Whereas Bialik and others in his camp insisted that Jewish writers and readers compel themselves to work with their own literary "possessions," these figures acted on the view that a modern Jewish national culture could only be truly worthwhile and compelling if it was completely universal in its potentials. Although individual works of such a culture might make use of Jewish realia, symbols, and so forth, there could be no predetermined Jewish limits because that would virtually guarantee stagnation—a stagnation that the radical champions of translation already clearly felt in the Hebrew or Yiddish literature of their own day. Only one limit could not be compromised because it was enabling: the limit of language itself. It is no accident that the most radical advocates of deparochialization numbered among the most fervent monolingualist Hebraists and Yiddishists of their day. Though perhaps only the authorizing power of the state could consecrate a piece of art or music as national, the fact of language alone rendered a work of literature or theater part of an ongoing, open-ended national tradition. With a universal fundament gained through translation and sustained by constant interchange with other literatures, a culture might be as wide as humanity but also self-contained and self-sustaining.

Though the efforts of Jewish cultural nationalists to create an encompassing Jewish culture have enjoyed some penetrating scholarly attention, our regnant historical account of Jewish culture and Jewish cultural nationalism remains on the whole resolutely focused on the dynamic of Judaization in its various forms. Yet the will to an unmarked, encompassing Jewish culture must be accorded descriptive and explanatory centrality in our study of Jewish culture and Jewish nationalism both. For it expressed perhaps the most central desire of modern Jewish cultural nationalism: the desire to be both moderns and Jews—to be, as the Yiddishist Latski-Bertoldi put it in a telling recasting of Y. L. Gordon's famous formulation, "honest and whole everywhere, on the street and in *the home.*"[174]

Notes

My thanks to Olga Borovaia, Jeff Brooks, Marc Caplan, Marcus Moseley, Anne Eakin Moss, Ben Nathans, Gabriella Safran, and Steven Zipperstein for comments and suggestions.

1. A. Litai, "Perishut sikhlit o hitbollelut," *Ha-am,* 10 March 1917.

2. See the thumbnail sketch in Dan Miron, *Bodedim be-moadam: Le-deyoknah shel ha-republikah ha-sifrutit ha-Ivrit bi-tehilat ha-me'ah ha-esrim* (Tel Aviv, 1987), 35–36.

3. Uriel Ofek, *Gumot He'N: Poalo shel Bialik be-sifrut ha-yeladim* (Tel Aviv, 1984), 65–69. See also Zohar Shavit and Yaacov Shavit, "Lemale' et ha-arets sefarim: Sifrut mekorit le'umat sifrut meturgemet be-tahalikh yetsirato shel ha-merkaz ha-sifruti be-erets yisrael," *Ha-sifrut* 25 (1977): 48–51, for the case in the *yishuv.*

4. See Eliyohu Shulman, "Di tsaytshrift '*Di Yudishe (idishe) velt,*'" in *Pinkes far der forshung fun der yidisher literatur un prese* 1 (New York, 1965), 146–47.

5. Yehuda Slutsky, "Ha-pirsumim ha-ivriim be-verit-ha-moatsot be-shanim 1917–1960," in *Pirsumim yehudiyim be-verit ha-moatsot, 1917–1960,* ed. Yitshak Yosef Kohen (Jerusalem, 5721 [1961]), xiv–xxiii.

6. For this process, see Kenneth Moss, "'A Time for Tearing Down and a Time for Building Up': Recasting Jewish Culture in Eastern Europe, 1917–1921" (Ph.D. dissertation, Stanford University, 2003), chap. 1; this will be superseded by a forthcoming monograph, tentatively entitled *Jewish Renaissance, Russian Revolution.*

7. "Me-et Tarbut," carried in *Ha-am* 15–16 (22–23), 28 April 1917; *Di grunt-oyfgabn fun der "Kultur Lige"* (Kiev, 1918), 5.

8. Mark Kiel, "A Twice Lost Legacy: Ideology, Culture, and the Pursuit of Jewish Folklore in Russian until Stalinization (1930–1931)" (Ph.D. dissertation, Jewish Theological Seminary, 1991), 150ff.; Moss, "'A Time for Tearing Down,'" 103–18; Adam Rubin, "From Torah to Tarbut: Hayim Nahman Bialik and the Nationalization of Judaism" (Ph.D. dissertation, UCLA, 2000).

9. See the articles and catalogue in *Tradition and Revolution: The Jewish Renaissance In Russian Avant-Garde Art 1912–1928,* ed. Ruth Apter-Gabriel (Jerusalem, 1988), esp. Seth Wolitz, "The Jewish National Art Renaissance in Russia," and

John Bowlt, "From the Pale of Settlement to the Reconstruction of the World," 21–60.

10. See, on Yiddish literature, David Roskies's influential formulations in *A Bridge of Longing: The Lost Art of Yiddish Storytelling* (Cambridge, Mass., 1995) and "Rabbis, Rebbes, and Other Humanists: The Search for a Usable Past in Modern Yiddish Literature," in *Studies in Contemporary Jewry 12: Literary Strategies*, ed. Ezra Mendelsohn (Bloomington, 1996), 55–77. On the search for a Jewish idiom in the plastic arts, see Wolitz, "The Jewish National Art Renaissance"; Bowlt, "From the Pale of Settlement"; and Hillel Kazovski, *Khudozhniki Kultur-Ligi/The Artists of the Kultur-Lige* (Moscow/Jerusalem, 2003). On the fusion of competing modernist modes of stagecraft with "Jewish content" in the Vilna Trupe, GOSET, and Ha-Bimah, see respectively Michael Steinlauf, "*Dybbukiada*: An-ski's Polish Legacy," forthcoming; Jeffrey Veidlinger, *The Moscow State Yiddish Theater: Jewish Culture on the Soviet Stage* (Bloomington, 2000); Vladislav Ivanov, *Russkie sezony: Teatr Gabima* (Moscow, 1999). On the conceptual and institutional underpinning of these folkloric or *kinus* efforts, see Kiel, "A Twice Lost Legacy," and Rubin, "From Torah to Tarbut."

11. By non-adaptive translation, I mean to distinguish an attitude toward the text as an integral unit and work of art from translation-as-adaptation, in which the alteration of contents (especially "Judaization") and even defining generic features was a matter of course. See Olga Borovaia, "Translation and Westernization: *Gulliver's Travels* in Ladino," *Jewish Social Studies* n.s. 7, no. 2 (Winter 2001): 149–68, for a ground-breaking account. The kind of translation I am dealing with is a polar opposite formally and, even more important, ideologically, as we shall see.

12. A. Ben-Moshe [Litai], "Sifrut ha-olam," *Ha-shiloah* 34, nos. 5–6 (April 1918): 540–46.

13. Frishman to Bialik, 9 June 1917, *Keneset: Divrei soferim le-zekher H. N. Bialik* 5 (1940): 26.

14. Shtif to Shmuel Niger, 13 June 1922, Shmuel Niger Collection, Record Group 360, file 203, YIVO Archive [hereafter RG 360: (file number), YIVO].

15. Ben-Moshe, "Sifrut ha-olam" and A. B. M. "*Ha-tekufah*," *Masuot* (Odessa) 1 (1919): 601–16.

16. In short, I take the reemergent Russian Jewish cultural sphere of February 1917 as an iteration of prewar Jewish culture only marginally reshaped by immanent cultural-revolutionary drives, and then dramatically transformed by the triumphant Revolution between 1919 and 1921. This argument is made at length in my *Jewish Renaissance, Russian Revolution*.

17. This seems the place to note the almost universal devaluation by the Jewish nationalist intelligentsia of Russian as a *target* language of Jewish cultural life in this period, even as the larger process of Russification continued apace. See my "'A Time for Tearing Down,'" chaps. 1, 4, 6. On Russian-language Jewish cultural publishing, see below.

18. The most cogent and encompassing account of Jewish culture in these terms can be found throughout Benjamin Harshav's writings, especially *Language in Time of Revolution* (Berkeley, 1993). Also of note are Yaacov Shavit, *Athens in Jerusalem* (London, 1997), especially chap. 8, and Seth Wolitz, "The Kiev-Grupe (1918–1920) Debate: The Function of Literature," *Yiddish* 3, no. 3 (1978): 97–106; Wolitz, "*Di Khalyastre*: The Yiddish Modernist Movement in Poland: An Overview," *Yiddish* 4, no. 3 (1981): 5–19; Wolitz, "Between Folk and Freedom: The Failure of the Yiddishist Modernist Movement in Poland," *Yiddish* 8, no. 1 (1991): 26–42.

19. Moyshe Litvakov, "Di sistem fun iberzetsungen I," *Bikher-velt* 1 (January 1919): 9–12, and "Di sistem fun iberzetsungen II," *Bikher-velt* 4–5 (August 1919): 37–44.

20. Litvakov, "Di sistem fun iberzetsungen II," 37, 41.

21. Ibid., 42–43.

22. Litvakov, "Di sistem fun iberzetsungen I," 10; see Litvakov, "Di sistem fun iberzetsungen II," 37, 41.

23. L. Gomlen, "Kritik un bibliografye: Poezye un beletristik: *Himel un erd*," *Bikher-velt* 2–3 (March 1919): 42.

24. E. Shteynman, "'Hotsaat Stybel'" in "Maamarim u-reshimot," in *Erets: Measef le-sifrut yafah u-livikoret* (Odessa, 1919), 29–30. On *Erets*, see Yehoshua A. Gilboa, *Oktobraim ivrim: Toldotehah shel ashlayah* (Tel Aviv, 1974), 17–19, and my "'A Time for Tearing Down,'" 215–16 and 314–17.

25. A. Ben-Moshe, "Sifrut ha-olam," 543.

26. N. Oyslender, "Henry V. Longfellow: *Dos gezang fun Hiavata*," *Bikher-velt* 2–3, 41.

27. Yosef Klausner, "Keren-zavit: nitsahon," *Ha-shiloah* 35, nos. 3–4 (September-October 1918): 344.

28. Moyshe Kulbak, "Dos yidishe vort," *Der veker* (1918); reprinted in *Di goldene keyt* 43 (1962): 238–42. See Shavit, *Athens in Jerusalem*.

29. Sh. An-sky to Bialik, 10/23 April 1918, in Moshe Ungerfeld, *Bialik ve-sofrei doro* (Tel Aviv, 1974).

30. Citations from first lines of *Iliad*, Book 9. I am citing from Tshernikhovsky's translation as it appeared later in book form, *Sefer Ilias* I (Vilna, 1930); Weinreich cited from Shulman, "Di tsaytshrift '*Di Yudishe (idishe) velt*,'" 147–48. I am of course trying to approximate Tshernikhovsky's Ashkenazic pronunciation; thus "oto ha-yam" becomes "oyso ha-yom," etc. My thanks to Daniel Moss for his attempted guidance on the intricacies of meter in quantitative and accentual-syllabic verse.

31. Aminadav Dikman, "Homeros shel Tshernikhovsky," in *Shaul Tchernichowsky: Meamarim u-te'udot*, ed. Boaz Arpali (Jerusalem, 1994), 429. Dikman's article offers a detailed assessment of Tshernikhovsky's translation in relation to the original Greek, previous Hebrew translations, and the contemporary Hebrew literary "horizon of reception."

32. Ibid., 447–55.

33. Of course, this could only be a relative escape. Dikman notes many structures and forms reminiscent of biblical, rabbinic, and liturgical corpi in Tshernikhovsky's translation. The key point here, however, is intentionality and the product it yielded: a translation in which what Dikman calls Hebraization was "immeasurably less than that in the translations of his predecessors and was not the guiding foundational principle in the translation." Ibid., 456.

34. Ironically, Dikman suggests that Tshernikhovsky believed—or came to believe—that in fact his translations recovered a historically real "Canaanite" affinity between ancient Greek and ancient Israelite culture. Ibid., 463. But this does not alter the affinity of his translation technique to the larger non-Judaizing agenda examined here.

35. "Shoshana Persits," in David Tidhar, *Entsiklopedyah li-halutse ha-yishuv u-vonav* (Tel Aviv, 1947), 7:2825.

36. Kulbak, "Dos yidishe vort," 238.

37. Litvakov, "Di sistem fun iberzetsungen II," 37–38, 43.

38. A. Ben-Moshe, "Sifrut ha-olam," 541.

39. Iris Parush, *Kanon sifruti ve-ideologiyah leumit* (Jerusalem, 1992), chap. 12. Here, I disagree somewhat with Parush, who argues that Frishman hoped that translation would transform Jewish cultural consciousness but had no particular hope to transform Jewish literature directly. Yet clearly, Frishman's translation praxis at times reflects the hope that translation might indeed have a direct influence on Hebrew literature, for instance generically—Frishman's preoccupation with translating great examples of the modern novel can hardly have been unconnected to his desire to see novels of "genius" in Hebrew literature, and translation was clearly intended in part to transform *writers* themselves.

40. Litvakov, "Di sistem fun iberzetsungen II," 38.

41. *Printsipy khudozhestvennogo perevoda: Stat'i K. Chukovskogo i N. Gumileva* (Petersburg, 1919).

42. My thanks to Ben Nathans and Gabriella Safran for this comparison.

43. See Ezra Korman's formal comments on poetic translation in "A. Pushkin. *Poltava,*" *Bikher-velt* 4–5, 54–55.

44. A. B. M., "*Ha-tekufah,*" 605.

45. Frishman to Bialik, 15/28 April and 11/24 May 1918, *Keneset: Divrei soferim le-zekher H. N. Bialik* 5 (1940): 34–35; Stybel to Bialik, 27 April 1918, File Sh-219, Correspondence Collection, Beit Bialik, Tel Aviv.

46. Ben-Eliezer, "'Al ha-targumim," 320.

47. Writing in the *yishuv* in 1919, Yaacov Steinberg voiced a similar notion of "gaps" in a putative universal literary structure. See Shavit and Shavit, "Lemale' et ha-arets sefarim," 55.

48. E. Korman, "*Fremds,*" *Bikher-velt* 4–5, 56.

49. Amichay-Michlin, *Ahavat 'I''Sh: Avraham Yosef Stybel* (Jerusalem, 2000), 37–65.

50. In fact, Litai criticized many of Frishman's specific choices as too much "cake" and not enough bread; in particular, he was unhappy that some of those he considered truly "universal" writers and works were being neglected in favor of writers who were merely "national" (like Chekhov!), and he was also irritated by the number of Decadent works being translated. See Ben-Moshe, "Sifrut ha-Olam," 542–43. But in so doing, Litai affirmed the larger shared principle of a "universal" literary substratum that had to be translated into all languages.

51. On Stybel's "European" inclinations and commitment to translation, see Yohanan Tverski, "Avraham Yosef Stybel," *Ha-tekufah* 32–33 (1948): 14–18, and Amichay-Michlin, *Ahavat 'I''Sh.* Frishman's investment in translation as a cultural strategy was part of a tightly linked set of convictions about the nature of literature, culture, and humanity as such centering around a transhistorical humanist conception of art implying a single universal though open literary canon. See Iris Parush's painstaking reconstruction in *Kanon sifruti,* esp. 40–49, 70–75, 94.

52. Though a variety of factors seem to have gone into the Stybel press's choice of writers, the list was strongly shaped by Frishman's distinctive vision of the European literary canon. Among those writers actively distributed for translation in the publisher's first year, Dostoevsky, France, Heine, Homer, Ibsen, Pushkin, Tolstoy, Wilde, and Zola occupied a central place in Frishman's canon; the press's call for translators who "know their strength" and were capable of translating Shakespeare, Goethe, Schiller, and Byron as well as the great playwrights and poets of ancient Greece and Rome also reflected Frishman's sense of what Hebrew literature truly needed, while Frishman himself had already undertaken Tagore and the Brothers Grimm. See Parush, *Kanon sifruti,* 47–48, 146, and 146–47 n. 5; "'Hotsaat Stybel' be-arikhat David Frishman" (announcement), *Ha-tekufah* 2 (Nisan-Sivan 1918): back matter.

53. Yehuda Slutsky remarks that virtually every Hebrew writer in Russia took part in this endeavor in some way. Slutsky, "Ha-pirsumim ha-ivriim," 25–30.

54. "'Hotsaat Stybel' be-arikhat David Frishman" (announcement), *Ha-tekufah* 2 (Nisan-Sivan 1918): back matter.

55. Ben-Avigdor, "Ha-ivriut ve-haklaliut be-sifrut ha-ivrit," *Ha-melits*, 21 and 23 April 1895; on his reader-orientation, see Miron, *Bodedim*, 33–35.

56. E.g., the Ha-Poel Ha-Tsair publishing house La-'am; see the description in Shavit and Shavit, "Lemale' et ha-arets sefarim," 48.

57. Chone Shmeruk, "Le-toldot sifrut ha-'shund' be-Yidish," *Tarbiz* 52, no. 2 (1983): 345–46.

58. A. Litvak, "Di farshpreytung fun yidishe bikher in Amerike," *Bikher-velt* 1 (1919): 13; Jeffrey Brooks, "Readers and Reading at the End of the Tsarist Era," in *Literature and Society in Imperial Russia, 1800–1914*, ed. William Mills Todd III (Stanford, 1978), 102ff., 114ff.

59. *Zamelbukh "Kultur"* (Minsk, 1905). On the publishing house and its founder, see Avrom Reyzen, *Epizodn fun mayn lebn* (Vilna, 1935), 85–86.

60. Ol'ga D. Golubeva, *Gorkii—Izdatel'* (Moscow, 1968), 96–99; A. D. Zaidman, "Literaturnye studii 'Vsemirnoi Literatury' i 'Doma Iskusstv' (1919–1921 gody)," *Russkaia literatura* 16, no. 1 (1973): 141–42.

61. Golubeva, *Gorkii—Izdatel'*, 100.

62. Ibid., 110.

63. As a model in the most general sense, Gorky's undertaking was no doubt of interest to these Jewish champions of translation (though many of the proposals and undertakings discussed here, especially the Hebrew ones, predate it). I have seen no reference to it except by Vladimir Jabotinsky, who held it up as a model for a national translation program in the *yishuv*. See Shavit and Shavit, "Lemale' et ha-arets sefarim," 54.

64. See the insightful formulations of Rachel Polonsky, *English Literature and the Russian Aesthetic Renaissance* (Cambridge, 1998), 1–22. Maurice Friedberg suggests that the Symbolists' shared conceptions of language saddled some of them with doubts about the possibilities of satisfactory translation as such and drove them toward either hyper-literal translation poetics or a tendency to remake the target poet as a Symbolist; Friedberg, *Literary Translation* (University Park, Pa., 1997), 63–64.

65. On the mid-nineteenth-century transition from writers-as-translators to professional translators in the Russian literary sphere, see Friedberg, *Literary Translation*, 38, 48, 60.

66. In his *Mikhtavim hadashim al devar ha-sifrut* (Berlin, 1922/23), 6–7.

67. For a suggestive consideration of literary translation and its place in the formation of a national (but also imperial) literary sphere in early nineteenth century Russia, see Monika Greenleaf and Stephen Moeller-Sally, "Introduction," in *Russian Subjects: Empire, Nation, and the Culture of the Golden Age*, ed. Greenleaf and Moeller-Sally (Evanston, 1998), 2–8. Thanks to Anne Eakin Moss for bringing this source to my attention.

68. E.g., Nister's negotiation of Andersen or Ha-Meiri's relationship to Hungarian Decadent Endre Ady. See Roskies, *Bridge of Longing* and *Erets*, respectively.

69. Ben-Eliezer, "'Al ha-targumim," 319.

70. Ibid.

71. Shteynman, "'Hotsaat Stybel,'" 30.

72. Shaul Tshernikhovsky, preface to *Shirei Anakreon* (Warsaw, 1920), 3.

73. Klausner "Keren-zavit: nitsahon," 343. See also Ben-Eliezer, "'Al ha-targumim," 319–20.

74. E. Shteynman, "'Hotsaat Stybel'" in *Erets*, 30.

75. Litvakov, "Di sistem fun iberzetsungen II," 42.

76. Litvakov, *In Umruh*, (Kiev, 1918), 76, 98.

77. Y. Dobrushin, "Kunst-primitiv un kunst-bukh far kinder," *Bikher-velt* 4–5 (August 1919): 16–23; Y. Dobrushin, "Dray dikhter," in *Oyfgang* (Kiev, 1919), 73–98.

78. Aleph (A-L-F), "Genizah ve-hatimah" in "Maamarim u-reshimot," *Erets*, 28–29.

79. Haim Nahman Bialik, "Tseirut o yaldut?" in *Kol kitvei H. N. Bialik* (Tel Aviv, 1950), 218–19.

80. Bialik, "Ha-sefer ha-ivri," in *Kol kitvei H. N. Bialik*, 210–17.

81. In Bialik's own *Keneset* and in the Moscow Safrut publishing house's *Sborniki: Safrut*, vol. 1 (1918).

82. Bialik, "Halakhah and Aggadah"; I cite from Leon Simon's translation in *Revealment and Concealment*, ed. Zali Gurevitch (Jerusalem, 2000), 79, with modifications based on *Kol kitvei H. N. Bialik*, 228.

83. Bialik, "Halakhah and Aggadah," 80. Of course, in many respects this essay can be read as a rejection of the very category of art-literature; I develop this argument in my forthcoming monograph.

84. See David Shimoni on the "tremendous impression" the talk made on the mostly student audience in Petrograd, 1917, in his "Hashpoes," *Di goldene keyt* 16 (1953): 14. For the line of response relevant here, concerning *kinus* and more broadly Bialik's general claims about how art-literature could and should serve the nation see, among others, D. A. Fridman, "Ba-mish'olim II," *Ha-tekufah* 1 (Moscow 1918): 640–41.

85. David Frishman, "Al ha-sifrut ha-yafah," in *Kol kitvei David Frishman*, vol. 8 (Warsaw–New York–Tel Aviv, 1932), 57–58; Parush, *Kanon sifruti*.

86. Ben-Eliezer, "'Al ha-targumim," 319.

87. Litvakov, "Di sistem fun iberzetsungen II," 37.

88. Wolitz, "The Kiev-Grupe (1918–1920) Debate"; P. Reyland, "Bibliografye: Yung Treyst," in *Baginen* 1, no. 1 (1919): 115–17; M. Lit (Litvakov), "Kritik un bibliografye: *Eygns*," in *Bikher-velt* 1, no. 1 (January 1919): 24.

89. Dobrushin, "Dray dikhter," 94–95.

90. The poem cited by Dobrushin is available in translation by Chana Kronfeld in her book *On the Margins of Modernism: Decentering Literary Dynamics* (Berkeley, 1996), 214.

91. Gershenzon, "Predislovie," *Evreiskaia antologiia: Sbornik molodoi evreiskoi poezii* (Moscow, 1918), viii.

92. Klausner, "Sifruteinu 4: Al Bialik," *Ha-shiloah* 32, no. 4 (April-June 1917): 453.

93. Natan Grinblat, "Reshimot sifrutiyot: *Olameinu*," *Ha-tekufah* 1 (Tevet-Adar 1918): 673.

94. Eliyahu Meitus, "Ha-'ahavah' be-shirateinu ha-tseirah (masah sifrutit)," *Ha-Shiloah* 33, nos. 2–3 (August-September 1917): 255–71.

95. See the articles by Y. Elsharif, Y. Karni, and others in *Ha-shiloah* (*Hoveret-Tshernikhovsky*), 35, no. 2 (August 1918). Ironically, Tshernikhovsky was at this very moment working on one of his most evocative portraits of traditional Jewish life, his "Hatunatah shel Elka."

96. Sh. Tsemah, "Shaul Tshernikhovsky," *Masuot* 1 (1919): 581.

97. Yosef Klausner, "Ha-hidah 'Tshernikhovsky,'" *Ha-shiloah* 35, no. 2 (August 1918): 104–5.

98. David C. Jacobson, *Modern Midrash: The Retelling of Traditional Jewish Narratives by Twentieth Century Hebrew Writers* (Albany, 1987), 83; David Frishman, *Bamidbar: Maasiot bibliot, sipurim, ve-agadot* (Jerusalem, 1990).

99. Thus, Ha-Bimah's Menahem Gnesin justified the choice of Pinski's "Eternal Jew" for a first full-length production with the telling remark that "although it wasn't originally written in Hebrew, it was nevertheless Hebrew through and through and it was deemed very proper for Ha-Bimah to perform it." M. Gnesin, *Darki im ha-teatron ha-ivri* (Tel Aviv, 1946), 132.

100. Aleksander Granovskii, "Our Goals and Objectives" (1919), in *Marc Chagall and the Jewish Theater*, ed. Benjamin Harshav (New York, 1992), 147.

101. M. Lit, "Kritik un bibliografye: *Eygns*," 24.

102. Peretz Markish, "[Veys ikh nit, tsi kh'bin in dr'heym]," in *A shpigl af a shteyn: Antologye*, ed. Khone Shmeruk (Tel Aviv, 1964), 375–76. The translation is by Chana Kronfeld in collaboration with Bluma Goldstein (though I have retained more of Markish's distinctive punctuation), in Kronfeld, *On the Margins of Modernism*, 204; see also Kronfeld's rich close analysis, 204–8. M. Lit, "Kritik un bibliografye: *Eygns*," 24.

103. Dovid Hofshteyn, "[Di zun hot haynt tsum nayem pantser maynem]," reprinted in idem, *Gezamelte Verk*, vol. 1, *Lirik* (Kiev, 1923), 41.

104. Hofshteyn, "Vi troyerik-zis iz mentsh tsu zayn," *Lirik*, 64–67; available in idem, *Lider un poemes* (Tel Aviv, 1977), 1:57–58. Thanks to Marc Caplan for his translation suggestions.

105. Hofshteyn, "Vig-lid," *Lirik*, 63; available in Hofshteyn, *Lider un poemes*, 1:59.

106. Litvakov and Reyland complained of this; Bergelson and Dobrushin praised it. See the sources cited above and Wolitz, "The Kiev-Grupe (1918–1920) Debate."

107. This was particularly true of a third poem centering around his children, "Nemen," which I analyze at length in "'A Time for Tearing Down,'" 202–4.

108. *Kultur Lige: byuleten num. 2* (June-July 1920): 57.

109. Cited in Lahover, *Bialik: Hayav ve-yetsirotav* (Jerusalem, 1956), 247n10.

110. See my "Jewish Culture Between Renaissance and Decadence: *Literarishe Monatsshriften* and its Critical Reception," *Jewish Social Studies* n.s. 8, no. 1 (2001): 169–70.

111. Y. H. Ravnitsky to Bialik, 20 August 1918, File R-206, Correspondence Collection, Beit Bialik.

112. "Shoshana Persits," in Tidhar, *Entsiklopediah*, 2825.

113. E.g., "Mi-sipurei Korea," *Shetilim* 3 (2 August 1917): 40ff.

114. Ofek, *Gumot He'N*, 71.

115. Dobrushin "Universal-bibliotek"; "Literarishe nayes," *Bikher-velt* 1 (1919): 39.

116. M. D., "K. Zingman. *Motl der shnayder*," *Bikher-velt* 4–5 (1919): 53.

117. Donyel Tsharni, *A yortsendlik aza, 1914–1924: Memuarn* (New York, 1943), 227–28; *Shriften: Fremds: Eyropeishe poezye* (Moscow, 19[18?]), inner cover.

118. Ben-Zion Dinur, *Be-yeme milhamah u-mahpekhah: Zikhronot u-reshumot mi-derekh hayim* (Jerusalem, 1960), 404–5.

119. On translation *between* Hebrew and Yiddish (and from Russian "Jewish" literature like the *Dybbuk*), which had a completely different ideological meaning (since it was about incorporating "Jewishness," not "foreignness"), see my "'A Time for Tearing Down,'" 217–30.

120. Dinur, *Be-yeme*, 405; *Idisher Folks-farlag* (Kiev, 1920), 8.

121. *Kultur Lige* 1 (November 1919): 41–42.

122. "Kunst-khronik: Literature," *Baginen* 1 (1919): 85; "Kunst-khronik: Plastishe kunst," *Baginen* 1 (1919): 95. For a fresh analysis of these developments, see David Shneer, *Yiddish and the Creation of Soviet Jewish Culture* (Cambridge, 2004). My *Jewish Renaissance, Russian Revolution* offers a substantially different account of this key transitional period in Kiev and elsewhere.

123. "Kunst-khronik: Literatur," 86.

124. Folks-Farlag announcement, *Vilna Leben* 3–4 (June 1920): 53; see also *Idisher Folks-farlag*, 16.

125. "Kunst-khronik: Teater," *Baginen* 1 (1919): 90.

126. Litvakov, "Di sistem fun iberzetsungen I," 9–10.

127. A. Goldberg, "Der bikher-mark in Poyln," *Bikher-velt* 2–3 (March 1919): 19.

128. See Frishman to Bialik, 11/24 May 1918, *Keneset: Divrei soferim le-zekher H. N. Bialik*, 5 (1940): 34–35.

129. At least some of Omanut's publications for children were beautiful books with lush color illustrations, in sharp contrast to the chapbook format of the Yiddish children's books produced by Odessa's Farlag Blimelekh or the Kiever Farlag. One observer deemed Stybel's books more beautiful than any contemporaneous Russian efforts. Ben-Tsion Katz, "Ke-avor tekufah," *Ha-tsefirah* (4 March 1927), 4.

130. See A. B. M., *"Ha-tekufah,"* 615–16, which refers to Stybel as a publishing house "which is not afraid of material sacrifices, and indeed of the largest [material sacrifices]"; see also Ben-Yishai, "Sifrut ve-itonut ivrit be-rusiah be-tkufat ha-mehapekhah ve-ahareihah," *He-avar* 15 (1968): 172. I have not yet acquired primary sources generated by the presses themselves that shed much light on financial and organizational structure, but have relied on memoir sources including Shmuel Ayzenshtadt, "Moskvah ha-ivrit bi-yeme milhemet ha-olam ha-rishonah," in *Katsir: Kovets likorot ha-tenuah ha-tsionit be-rusiyah* (Tel Aviv, 1960); Ben-Tsion Katz, *Zikhronot* (Tel Aviv, 1964), 246–51; A. Litai, "Ha-'yarid' ha-sifruti-haivri ha-gadol ba-Moskvah," *He-avar* 3 (1956): 55–59; Tverski, "Avraham Yosef Stybel," 20–21. With regard to Omanut in particular, I have had to rely on general descriptions of its work and the patronage of Persits and Zlatopolski in these memoirs and the unreferenced summation of its work in Zohar Shavit, *Ha-Hayim ha-sifrutiyim be-Erets Yisra'el, 1910–1933* (Tel Aviv, 1982), 221–22, who notes that it was founded "on a patronage basis." Shavit's statement that the press did not expect profits and that its patrons could cover its losses refers specifically to its activities in Palestine after 1926, but it seems reasonable to infer that the same situation obtained in the even worse economic conditions of revolutionary Russia. On Persits's continued willingness to operate at a loss in the 1930s and beyond, see Yohanan Pograbinsky, "Le-toldot ha-molut ha-'ivrit," *Jewish Book Annual* 9 (New York, 1950–51), lv.

131. Ben-Yishai, "Sifrut," 168.

132. Nokhem Shtif to Zalman Reyzen, 9 August 1920, RG 3: 3035, YIVO.

133. M. Katz, "Di Kultur Lige in Ukraine," 185; and Kalmanovitsh to Vayter, 3 September [1918], RG 360:34, YIVO. As of early 1919, the publishing houses in question included the Kiever Farlag, Kletskin's Vilna Farlag Ukraine branch, the Folks Farlag, Di Velt, Onhoyb, Der Hamer, and Odessa's Blimelakh. See Kultur Lige to the Ministry of Jewish Affairs of Ukrainian People's Republic, undated [probably January 1919], TsDAVO, f. 2060, op. 1, d. 4.

134. *Kultur Lige* 1 (1919): 39–42. Kultur Lige to the Ministry of Jewish Affairs

of Ukrainian People's Republic, undated [probably January 1919], TsDAVO, f. 2060, op. 1, d. 41, l. 13–14.

135. *Grunt-oyfgabn*, 32.

136. *Fremds*, back cover.

137. See Brooks, "Readers and Readership," 112 for suggestive comments.

138. The relevant body of literature is rooted in Pierre Bourdieu, *Distinction* (Cambridge, Mass., 1984). Of course, the literary intelligentsia's more rarefied taste enacted a no less interested form of distinction.

139. "Shetilim" (advertisement) in *Ha-am*, 16 July 1917; Slutsky, "Ha-pirsumim," 32ff.

140. Pograbinsky, "Le-toldot ha-molut," liv.

141. M. Rivesman, "The Past and Future of Yiddish Theater," in *The Yiddish Chamber Theater*, 145.

142. See the acid comments of Y. Hirshkan to Sh. Niger, 21 October 1917, RG 360:167, YIVO.

143. "Shoshana Persits," in Tidhar, *Entsiklopediah*, 2825.

144. Pograbinsky, "Le-toldot ha-molut," lvi.

145. Persits donated 2,000 rubles; Stybel was also a donor, as was one of the founders of the Yiddishist Folks-Farlag. See subscription list, 1917–18, Rossiiskii gosudarstvennyi arkhiv literatury i isskustva (RGALI), An-ski Collection, Fond 2583, op. 1, d. 8.

146. Sh. Tshernovits to H. N. Bialik, 3 November (?) 1917, Box T-92, Correspondence Collection, Beit Bialik.

147. Z. Latski-Bertoldi, "*In Umruh*" (review), *Bikher-velt* 2–3 (March 1919): 29–30.

148. For Bialik's speech at the Tarbut conference, see Zerubavel, "Ha-veidah ha-rishonah," *Ha-am*, 17 April 1917.

149. Ofek, *Gumot He'N*, 65–69.

150. Litai, "Perishut sikhlit."

151. A. Ben-Moshe, "Sifrut ha-olam," 540.

152. Litai, "Perishut sikhlit," 9.

153. Pograbinsky, "Le-toldot ha-molut," liv.

154. Katz, "Ke-avor," 4; Shteynman, "'Hotsaat Stybel,'" 29.

155. "Shoshana Persits," in Tidhar, *Entsiklopediah*, 2825.

156. Leyb Jaffe, opening statement to *Sborniki "Safrut"* 1 (1918). On its founding, see Brian Horowitz, ed., "Pis'ma L. B. Yaffe k M. Gershenzonu," *Vestnik Yevreiskogo Universiteta* 2 (18) (1998): 216–17. Safrut's publications did provide a venue for Russian "Jewish" writing by writers like An-sky and Andrei Sobol; but, founded by the Zionist-Hebraist activist Jaffe and the "committed Hebraist Fayvl Shapira," Safrut was a Hebraist institution explicitly dedicated to the supersession of Russian-language by Hebrew culture. Ben-Yishai, "Sifrut," 170.

157. M. Gershenzon, "Predislovie," vii.

158. Sh. Tshernovits to H. N. Bialik, 3 November (?) 1917, Box T-92, Beit Bialik.

159. Sfog, "Ha-Bimah" in *Ha-am*, no. 4/11 (27 January 1917), 7.

160. If any proof was needed, by 1919–20 these figures could look to the beginnings of the end of what had been a promising synthesis in the Jewish plastic arts between modernism and Jewish folk culture. Even as Abram Efros was hailing the discovery of Jewish "primitive" figures in *pinkasim* and on synagogue walls as an epoch-making event, the most talented practitioners of this synthesis like El Lissitzky were already turning their backs on any such delimitation and moving along

lines of aesthetic logic dictated by their alliegance to avant-garde art itself. The same brief flirtation would play itself out a few years later with Polish-Jewish modernists like H. Berlewi. See Bowlt, "From the Pale of Settlement," 56; Wolitz, "Jewish National Art Renaissance," 40; and Wolitz, "Between Folk and Freedom," 34–36. In the era of the nation-state, museums enshrine these artists as Russian and Polish, respectively.

161. Amichay-Michlin, *Ahavat 'T'Sh*, 296.

162. *Kultur-Lige* 1 (1919): 4; A. Litvak, "Literatur un lebn" in *Baginen* 1 (1919): 99; Kazdan, "Der lebns-veg," 114.

163. Irving Howe and Eliezer Greenberg, "Introduction: Soviet Yiddish Literature," in *Ashes Out of Hope* (New York, 1977), 14.

164. Wolitz, "Between Folk and Freedom," 26.

165. The definitive study for the Yiddish case is Roskies, *Bridge of Longing*, chaps. 7–9.

166. Quoted in Amichay-Michlin, *Ahavat 'T'Sh*, 203.

167. Miron, *Bodedim*, 35–38; Khone Shmeruk, *Peretses yiesh-viziye* (New York, 1971), 7–8, esp. n. 9; Lahover, *Bialik*, 244–45, 247.

168. A. B. M, *"Ha-tekufah,"* 604, mistakenly numbered 694 in original.

169. Frishman, "Al ha-sifrut ha-yafah," 57–58.

170. Yosef Klausner, "Ha-hidah 'Tshernikhovsky,'" *Ha-shiloah* 35, no. 2 (August 1918): 104–5.

171. For Dostoevsky, see the translation in Sona Stephan Hoisington, ed., *Russian Views of Pushkin's Eugene Onegin* (Bloomington, 1988); thanks to Ben Nathans and Gabriella Safran for noting the parallel. On Anichkov, see Polonsky, *English Literature*, 20–21.

172. Dobrushin, "Dray dikhter," 94–95.

173. Litvakov, "Di sistem fun iberzetsungen II," 37. Although for some on the left, like Litvakov or Dobrushin, the radicalizing Revolutionary process itself no doubt lent momentum to their emphasis on the universal moment in Jewish culture; it was not the determining factor. These figures remained outspoken nationalists in their rhetoric well beyond 1919 and, conversely, others in the same left circles like Oyslender pushed the folkloristic line albeit in secularized fashion, demonstrating that the Revolution could authorize either move.

174. Latski-Bertoldi, *"In Umruh* [review]," 31.

Chapter 9

Beyond the *Purim-shpil*: Reinventing the Scroll of Esther in Modern Yiddish Poems

KATHRYN HELLERSTEIN

In interwar Poland, four Yiddish poets wrote poems that dramatized characters from the biblical Scroll of Esther. In choosing to retell a traditional story in modern Yiddish verse, these poets stepped outside the conventions of the poetry of their day, a poetry defined more by the contemporary political, national, and cultural conflicts of Jews in the larger world than by the sacred Hebrew texts that had anchored traditional Jewish life for over two thousand years. Although this movement back to the sources seemed unfashionable at the time, it served two purposes central to the construction of a modern Jewish culture. First, the framework of the Scroll of Esther, commonly known as the Megillah, provided a range of masks or dramatic personae through which a poet could speak about difficult issues for Jews in politically complex times. Second, it allowed poets to reconnect their work to the traditional texts of East European Jews, from which modern Yiddish writing had torn itself, and thus to reaffirm the Jewish nature of secular Yiddish culture. In their Esther poems, Moyshe Broderzon (Moscow, 1890–Warsaw, 1956), Miriam Ulinover (Lodz, 1890–Auschwitz, 1944), Roza Yakubovitsh (Prashnits, Protsker Province, Poland, 1889–Auschwitz, 1944), and Itsik Manger (Czernowitz, Rumania, 1901–Tel Aviv, 1969) worked out various ways that a modern Jew could balance the individualist demands of art with the communal responsibilities of belonging to the Jewish people.

One can easily understand why the Scroll of Esther would have especially appealed to secular Yiddish writers. Unlike the other books of the biblical canon, the Scroll of Esther is a secular celebration of Esther and Mordecai's saving the Jewish people from Haman's plot, with no clear divine intervention. In fact, the Megillah does not mention the name of God at all.[1] Purim—the holiday that commemorates the events narrated in the Megillah—is itself not a solemn day of piety but a carnivalesque occasion, whose purpose is to reverse the order of things (*v'nahafokh hu*, Esther 9:1, 22) with the help of costumes, noisemakers, schnapps, rowdiness, and cross-dressing. Unlike the other holidays in the Jewish calendar, which mark the Jews' covenantal connection to Torah, Zion, and the Temples in Jerusalem, Purim celebrates the survival of Jews in the Diaspora and fantasizes revenge against their persecutors.

The anomalies of the Scroll of Esther and the Purim holiday became institutionalized in Jewish writing, especially in Eastern Europe. Beginning in the Middle Ages, Jews composed chronicles that imitated the story of Esther by describing the salvation of their communities from Haman-like destroyers or disasters, such as a flood or a plague. One of the earliest surviving Yiddish poems by a woman, in fact, comes out of this tradition. Published in Prague and composed by Toybe Pan, probably in the late seventeenth or early eighteenth century, this long poem is entitled "Eyn sheyn lid naye gimakht/ beloshn tkhine iz vardin oys gitrakht" (A brand-new beautiful song/ composed in the tkhine-tongue).[2] Unlike most *tkhines*—supplicatory Yiddish prayers for women to say individually—Toybe Pan's poem seems to have been intended for public recitation, by men as well as women, at a particular moment of communal crisis. The poem asks God to rescue the Jews of Prague from a plague afflicting their region and invokes sacred history in order to persuade God to intervene. Citing many biblical examples of appeals for God's mercy, including Abraham's attempt to save Sodom (Genesis 18:22–32) and King David's Psalms, Toybe Pan also invokes Queen Esther. By alluding to the two months of Adar that occur in the Hebrew calendar's leap years and explaining that the present year is, in fact, such a leap year, Toybe Pan reminds God that Jews customarily celebrate Purim in the second Adar:

> *Oder iz dokh on greyt.*
> *Fun ershtn iz givezn eyn groyse tsure*
> *Der nokh iz droyz givorn eyn groyse freyd.*
> *Zolstu hitundert in der tsayt akh gidenkn.*
> *Un lozn oyf hern ale krenkn:*
> > *Foter kinig. [31]*

The month of Adar approaches.
In the beginning, there was a great distress,
And afterward, a great joy came out of it.
May You now in this time also remember.
And let all the sicknesses cease:
> Father King.[Stanza 31]

Asking God to recall that ancient Adar in Shushan, which began in "a great distress" and ended with "a great joy," the poet begs God to apply that paradigm to the present Adar in Prague:

> *In den oder hobn mir akh groyse layd.*
> *Es zol bald droyz vern eyn groyse freyd.*
> *Kleyn purim zol groyse simkhe droyz vern.*
> *Un loz liber her got ale krenkn oyf hern:*
>> *Foter kinig. [32]*

In *this* Adar we also have great suffering.
Soon from this shall come a great joy.
From the "Small Purim" a great celebration shall come.
And, Dear Lord God, let all the sicknesses cease:
> Father King. [Stanza 32]

Compounding this mention of the leap year's doubled month of Adar, the poet promises God that for His intervention, Prague's Jews will celebrate a *"kleyn purim"* or *"Purim katan,"* a second, "small," or "minor," Purim, to commemorate the community's salvation from the plague.[3] The poet then goes on to explain why she, rather than the community's cantor or rabbi, entreats God for salvation:

> *Mir betn dikh der baremiger foter.*
> *Makh unz di tsore poter.*
> *Vi mir azoy shver beladn zayn.*
> *Liber her got helf unz oys dizer payn:*
>> *Foter kinig.*

> *Vayl hayor iz iber*
> *Iz layder gishtorbn unzer shaliakh tsiber.*
> *Zind unzer liber rebe iz gishtorbn.*
> *Zenen mir kh"v [khas vekhalile] shir far dorbn.*
> *Fil guts zoln mir der verbn:*
>> *Foter kinig.*

> *Vi unzer liber rebe iz givezn af der velt.*
> *Iz er givezn far unz gishtelt.*
> *Ay di tsore iz gikumen.*
> *Hot in HSh"y [HaShem yisborekh] fun unz vek ginumen.*
> *Fil gizunt zol oyf unz kumen:*
>> *Foter kinig. [33–35]*

We pray to you, Merciful Father.
Relieve us of our distress.
As we are so heavily burdened
Dear Lord God, save us from this pain:
        Father King.

Because this year is a leap year.[4]
Alas, our Cantor has died.
And since our dear Rabbi is [also] dead,
We are, God forbid, nearly starved.
May we inherit many good things:
        Father King.

When our Dear Rabbi was in this world,
He stood up for us [defended us].
Then the suffering came upon us.
God took him away from us.
Let much health come to us:
        Father King. [Stanzas 33–35]

The poet explains that before the plague, the rabbi had defended the congregation from adversity. Now that he is gone, she, the poet, must step in to ask for God's help.

In her appeal, Toybe Pan places herself in a role analogous to that of Queen Esther. In the Scroll of Esther, the queen, discovering Haman's plot to annihilate the Jews of the Persian kingdom, risks her own life by approaching her husband, King Ahasuerus, when she has not been called in order to reveal the plot to him. Toybe Pan's plea to God suggests that she, by speaking to God for her community, in the absence of the cantor and the rabbi, takes on risks comparable to those of Esther speaking unbidden to the king. In the story of Esther, and the observance of Purim, Toybe Pan finds canonical support for her own unorthodox action of writing a poem that addresses God on behalf of her community in a crisis.

The Prague crisis posed political as well as bodily dangers to the Jews. Like the Megillah's Esther, who approaches the king with political acumen to save the Jews, Toybe Pan addresses the problem of Jews at the mercy of a gentile ruler. The poet asks God to consider the Jews' "good acts of learning" as insurance against the emperor believing malicious accusations that the Jews had caused the plague:

Az mir zoln gefinen kheyn vekhesed in kayser oygn.
Ale di beyz oyf unz reydn zol ers nit gloybn: [23]

So that we may find grace and mercy in the Emperor's eyes.
May the Emperor not believe all the evil spoken about us: [Stanza 23]

Like Esther, Toybe Pan requests mercy for the Jews, although she addresses God, not the gentile ruler. The poet asks God to ensure that the emperor "shall be merciful to the unfortunate community" (24) and prays for the long life and health of the emperor, the empress, their son, the prince, and "all who speak well of the unfortunate community,/ Let no illness come into their houses" (25). According to the Scroll of Esther, a woman should not address the king unless invited. In Jewish Prague, women prayed to God privately, individually, and often silently. By advocating publicly and politically on behalf of her entire community, like Esther, Toybe Pan moved beyond the customary roles of Jewish women.

An unconnected, second tradition, that of the Esterke story, linked the Scroll of Esther to a specific phenomenon in East European Jewish history—the legend of the love affair between the fourteenth-century Polish king Casimir the Great and a Jewish woman, Esterke, and the subsequent privileges granted to the Jews of Poland. Both Polish and Jewish writers—from a fifteenth-century anti-Semitic Polish tract by Jan Długosz (1415–80) to Aaron Zeitlin's 1932 Yiddish drama, *Esterke,* which he called "a Jewish-Polish mystery play"[5]—invoked the Esterke story. According to Chone Shmeruk's study of the Esterke story, works by Jews as early as David Gans's 1595 Prague Hebrew chronicle *Tsemaḥ David* (Shoot of David) and Menakhem Amelander's 1743 Amsterdam Yiddish chronicle *She'eris Yisroel* (Remnant of Israel), and as late as Shomer-Shaykevits's 1884 Warsaw Yiddish novel *Di yidishe kenigin* (The Jewish queen), linked the Esterke-Casimir story to that of Esther and Ahasuerus.[6] Discussing how Heshl Eppelberg's Yiddish drama *Esterke* (Warsaw, 1890) reflected both the Jewish and the Polish Esterke traditions, Shmeruk mentions a late nineteenth-century variant on the traditional *purim-shpil* (Purim play) that went so far as to replace the ancient Persian Ahasuerus and Esther with the medieval Polish Casimir and Esterke.[7]

This cross-cultural tradition of a story in which a Jewish woman's sexual attachment to a gentile king saves or privileges the Jewish community resonated deeply with the Jews of Poland. Shmeruk traces the ways in which this paradigm came to symbolize the cultural interaction between Jews and Poles, especially for modern Yiddish writers, an interaction that is romanticized in a drama by Sholem Asch and challenged or problematized in works by Isaac Leybush Peretz, Joseph Opatoshu, Zusman Segalovitch, and Samuel Jacob Imber.[8] Significantly, though, the long poems (*poemes*) by Segalovitch (*In Kazerch: Poeme* [Warsaw,

1912]) and Imber (*Esterke: Poeme* [Stanislawow, 1911; Vienna and Brno, 1919; Vienna, 1921]), which focus on Esterke as a symbol for the danger of Jewish assimilation into Polish culture, contain "no biblical allusions or parallels" and make "no mention . . . of the king's bounty to the Jews."[9] For Yiddish writers before World War I, the Esterke story provided a simple but compelling foundation myth through which to explain the place of Jews in Polish culture and the place of Poland in Jewish culture.[10]

In contrast, Yiddish poets writing after 1918 may not have needed such a myth. On the one hand, the devastation of the First World War and the pogroms following it may have burst apart hopes for assimilation. On the other hand, the end of the war brought with it a resurgence of Yiddish literary and cultural life in Poland, and this revitalization of Jewish culture in its own language may have diminished the need for symbols of cultural symbiosis. For example, the Esther poems by Broderzon, Ulinover, Yakubovitsh, and Manger deliberately focus on the biblical text and its enactment in a Jewish cultural context in Poland and make no allusion to the Esterke-Casimir story.

This focus on the scriptural text also distinguishes these four poems from most contemporary Yiddish poetry. As other studies of this period have shown, twentieth-century Yiddish poetry anchors itself in Jewish tradition less through the Bible than through occasional ironic reference to the liturgy or, more frequently and mischievously, to folk forms, such as the ballad or the lullaby.[11] The fact that these four Esther poems call upon the biblical text suggests that they are doing something new. Unlike Toybe Pan's seventeenth-century, scripture-laden appeal to God, these four poems address no divinity. Unlike the modern Esterke poems, their subject is not Jews in relation to gentile history, but Jews in relation to Jewish culture. In their Esther poems, these four poets attempt to define a new kind of Yiddish poetry and a new place for the Yiddish poet, outside the ideological force field of interwar Poland and in defiance of the political, cultural, religious forces inside and outside the Jewish community that threatened to silence the Yiddish poet's voice.

The first of these poems, "Ikh, a purim-shpiler" (I, a Purim player), was written by Moyshe Broderzon, an avant-garde Yiddish poet in Moscow and Lodz[12] (and, in the 1930s, a popular Yiddish cabaret songwriter in Poland),[13] probably just before he returned to Lodz from Moscow in 1918, at the end of World War I.[14] Broderzon dedicated this poem, a Purim actor's lament, to the Russian Jewish modernist artist Eliezer Lissitzky, with whom he had collaborated in 1917 on "the first modernist Yiddish art and literary text, *Sikhes kholin* (Small Talk)."[15] This earlier work was a mischievous verse narrative "based on an entry in the chronicles of the Jewish community in Prague."[16] Indeed, in its physical form, *Sikhes kholin* resembles a Scroll of Esther in several ways. Like a Megillah, Broderzon's text was not set in type, but inscribed by hand by either a *sofer* (Jewish scribe) or by Lissitzky himself.[17] Some 20 hand-colored copies of the 110 published in a limited edition were presented "in scroll form in an oak casket like a Scroll of Esther."[18] And Lissitzky illustrated *Sikhes kholin* with pen and ink drawings of elongated figures in exotic Jewish garb, peacocks and other symbols from Jewish folk art, and scenes from both the shtetl and the orient, all stylized in the visual vocabulary of both "traditional Scrolls of Esther and Art Nouveau."[19] In their collaboration, the visual artist and the poet juxtaposed ancient, medieval, and modern literary and visual forms. By presenting a modern Yiddish verse parody of a medieval Jewish chronicle in the physical form of an ancient Hebrew sacred text, Broderzon and Lissitzky initiated a new kind of Jewish modernism, recasting the sacred as secular and the traditional as modern in order to tell a new Jewish story.

The story of Purim became central to this avant-garde endeavor. In 1918, a year after the publication of *Sikhes kholin,* Broderzon composed "Ikh, a purim-shpiler" in the voice of an actor in a traditional Purim play. In the same spirit in which *Sikhes kholin* parodied both the Prague Jewish community's chronicle and the Scroll of Esther, Broderzon based "Ikh, a purim-shpiler" on the *purim-shpil,* a form of Ashkenazic folk theater presented by masked and costumed actors, often yeshiva students, as monologues or skits at family Purim feasts, originating in or before the sixteenth century. Characterized by conventional prologues and epilogues, vulgar language, eroticism, and a traditional narrator—called a *loyfer* (runner), *shrayber* (writer), or *payats* (clown)—the *purim-shpil* in its original form commented humorously on contemporary Jewish life and included popular tales, including the Esther narrative. Later versions of the genre, known as the *Akhashverosh-shpil* (Ahasuerus play), presented extravagantly farcical versions of the Scroll of Esther, as well as other biblical episodes, such as *The Selling of Joseph, David and Goliath, The Sacrifice of Isaac, Hannah and Penninah,* and *The Wisdom of Solomon.*[20]

In Broderzon's dramatic monologue, the Purim player gazes out at the world—palaces, houses, seas, rivers, roofs—"from his round mask holes" and, thus disguised, begins to "joke with my friends and foes," plucking thorny roses, tickling "every dream-desecrator," and offering "pagan wine to Satan," while he calls for drink, song, and bells so loud that "the dead shall rise," because "Haman's gone to hell/ And Mordecai—on his horse!"[21] (Broderzon, "Ikh, a purim-shpiler," 1–16).

Behind a Purim mask, the speaker can safely criticize his milieu. Broderzon uses the Purim farce as a platform from which to assess the complex political situation of 1918—the Polish-Russian conflict, the ravages of the Great War, and what scholars recognize as the growing Bolshevik "control of Yiddish and Hebrew expression."[22] Ordering his "toothless, dried-up, bony" listener to "laugh," to ignore "*di frume kdoyshim un di khushim-prushim*" ("pious martyrs and imbecile-scholars," 18), to refrain from shouting out antiquated superstitions ("the world is flat"), and to whirl the *grogger* ("And—crash—kerr-ra-rash!—," 22), the speaker seems to embrace a new era of springtime, sunshine, and freedom. However, the sarcastic voice of the Purim player weights the politically loaded diction with irony, so that his words come to mean the opposite of what they say:

> And if you don't see differently, just close your eyes:
> And—crash—kerr-ra-rash!
> Of course, there's peace and tranquility in the world!
> It's already brightening up; a new spring-sun wells up,
> And folks hug and kiss in the free country,
> And peoples are clothed in new spirits,
> And Jerusalem, too, has been built and rebuilt! (Broderzon, 21–27)

Although these lines seem to praise the Bolshevik Revolution, their context renders them ironic, even sarcastic. The poem's speaker jibes that if his reader is fool enough to believe him, then the world in 1918, the year after the Bolshevik revolution and the final year of the Great War, is, in fact, filled with "peace and tranquility," "a new spring-sun wells up," and all the peoples (*felker*), decked out in a "new spirit," express only affection and good will toward one another "in the free country." However, he asks, who would be fool enough to believe the words of a Purim player? Further deflecting the temptation to read these propagandist clichés literally, Broderzon ends the stanza with an equally sarcastic line echoing the Zionist slogan, celebrating the nationalist hopes generated by the Balfour Declaration in 1917.[23] For Broderzon's Purim player, all the competing ideologies of the day—traditional Judaism, socialism, and Zionism—are poison. The Jewish artist, Broderzon intimates, must attempt to carve out a space outside the ideological force field

Mimicking the Megillah's description of the Jews' reversal of fortune (*v'nahafokh hu*), Broderzon's poem, like a *purim-shpil*, reverses the order of everything and applies this reversal to the Megillah's own characters. The Megillah's virtuous, brave queen becomes the butt of a sexual joke. The Purim player lewdly praises her as "*Esterl, mayn shvesterl*" (little Esther, my little sister) for her feminine imperialism in acquiring a kiss from the king (*a melekh-kush*), along with the trifle (*kleynikayt*) of a kingdom that stretches the breadth of Xerxes' ancient Persian empire, from

India to Ethiopia, half of which she gained while the king "amuses him-self with his rod of gold." With the phrase "*Esterl, mayn shvesterl,*" Brod-erzon quotes a Purim song, and with the line "*Nor oysgetrakht hot vashti es, az du—du bist a grine*" (Only Vashti dreamed it up that you—you are green), he alludes to the *purim-shpil* tradition, in which Esther's face is painted green,[24] as well as, perhaps, to the antics of the Russian Futurists Vladimir Mayakovsky and David Burliuk, who often painted their faces for effect. He was also anticipating Jewish modernist artworks, such as Chagall's 1920 green-faced violinist in *Music* (1920) and Lissitzky's green-faced father in the first plate of his graphic interpretation of the Passover song "Khad gadya" (One kid, 1919).[25] The poet manipulates these allusions to the Yiddish customs of celebrating Purim and to mod-ernist art, as well as the accusation that the horned Vashti is jealous, to serve as diversions from the matter at hand.

The matter at hand is Haman, the traditional villain, who proves to be the key to Broderzon's reversal of the Esther story. Haman appears in a stanza that seems almost an afterthought, punctuated by the cacopho-nous whirling of the *grogger*, which may also be the sound of the world banging apart, conveyed in the onomatopoeic line, "*un—trakh—tra-ra-rakh!*" (And—crash—kerr-ra-rash):

Un homen? Homen oykh, der durkhgetribener, der alter homen,
Hot umgebitn itst zayn klingendikn nomen,
Farkirtst, fartsoygn im af 'Homo,"
Un ayngekneytsht, fareydlt di neshome—
Er iz der eyntsiker, der trayer af der vakh,
Vos kekhlt zayn mizinikl Vayzose . . .
Un—trakh—tra-ra-rakh

And Haman? Haman too, the banished one, the old Haman,
Has now changed his resonant name,
Shortened it endearingly to "Homo,"
And crumpled, ennobled his soul—
He is the only one, the loyal one on guard,
Who pampers his youngest son Vaizatha . . .
And—crash—kerr-ra-rash! (Broderzon, 28–45)

Broderzon's Haman is a changed man. No longer banished and evil, he now possesses an ironically "ennobled" soul. Haman's new nickname, "Homo," printed in Latin within the Yiddish text, signifies "mankind," civilization itself, and echoes ominously the optimistically universalizing Yiddish words of socialism, "*mentshn*" and "*felker*" (lines 25–26). Broder-zon has turned the biblical tale in which Esther and Mordecai save the

Jews from a wicked villain into the story of a Haman, disguised as the urbane, modern, universalized civilization into which the avant-garde Jewish artist longs to fit. Haman is no longer the Megillah's lone, scheming, ancient anti-Semite. Broderzon's smooth operator now seems to point to all of humanity, which, in the bright light of 1918, appears to have set out to destroy the Jews.

Out of this topsy-turvy order come lies that are true and truths that are false. Sarcastically, the speaker proclaims that the First World War is benign, but ends his rant with exclamations of the actual consequences of the war—hunger and agony:

> Who says there is now a war in the world?
> A lie! No one has profited!
> Unhappily-undeniably—only blood has spilled!
> And tears flow beyond all measure!
> It's a great life! It's joy and jubilation!
> And somewhere need and hunger rule?!
> And somewhere there rampages a storm of agony!! (Broderzon
>   48–53)

In the end, the real victims in Broderzon's poem are the traditional Jew, whom the Purim player impersonates in his "wide white *kitl*" and the avant-garde Yiddish poet himself, "a Jew, a young man," who "speaks so modern and endearingly" yet who cannot undo the world's misery:

> *Oy, haynt iz purim,*
> *Un haynt bin ikh a yid a yunger—*
> *Un s'shmeykhlen trern af di umetike oygn!*
> *Un kh'reyd azoy modern un fartsoygn,*
> *Un eydlartik tsu dem erev-rav geboygn . . .*
> *S'bahalt di maske—funem likht*
> *Mayn blas un oysgepaynikt yung gezikht,*
> *Fun blikn lesterdike umgerikht . . .*
>
> *Un ver es zet, derkent in mir—pierro,*
> *Vos otemt mit dem tsufeliker khay-sho;*
> *Un kh'gey arum, kh'shpatsir arum in vaysn, breytn kitl,*
> *Un kh'zukh a lustikn, b'simkhedin milt*
> *Tsu oysshpotn fun faynt un fraynd,*
> *Vayl . . . kh'bin nisht mer—*
> *A stam bekhinemdike trer,*
> *A voyler yung, a purim-shpiler haynt!*

Oy, today is Purim,
And today I am a Jew, a young man—
And tears smile in my cheerless eyes!
And I speak so *modern* and endearingly,
And bow so nobly to the riffraff . . .
The mask hides my pale and anguished young face
From the light,
From gazes blasphemously unaware . . .

And whoever sees it, recognizes in me Pierrot,
Who breathes with the chance pleasure of the moment;
And I walk around; I stroll around in a wide, white *kitl*,
And I seek a happy, pleasurable means
To mock foe and friend,
Because . . . I'm nothing more—
Only a pointless tear,
A nice young man, a Purim player today! (Broderzon, 56–69)

By depicting the Purim player, "a Jew, a young man," as one who hides his "tears" and "anguished young face" behind a mask of the "*modern*" (italicized in the Yiddish) to protect him from the uncomprehending "gazes" of the "riffraff," Broderzon's penultimate stanza suggests how deeply alienated is the Jewish artist from the community he inhabits. The tone of this and the final stanza pulls the reader in two directions— both to take literally the statement of the speaker's sadness and to regard it with a measure of irony.

In the end, the actor's jokes and mockery are as irrelevant as the "pointless tear" of a Pierrot, the silent, sad French clown, an image that recurs in other modernist Yiddish poems of the time. But Broderzon's Jewish artist is not disempowered by his irrelevance. Rather, his disjuncture from the world around him allows the artist to write his "pointless" poem. Costumed as a traditional Jew in his "wide, white *kitl*," the speaker finds in the "chance pleasure of the moment" the "happy, pleasurable means/ To mock foe and friend." The guise of the traditional Purim joker gives the modernist Jewish artist the latitude to write, in a setting of competing ideologies, poetry that adheres to none at all. The Purim player becomes the perfect role for the Jewish modernist, who, in retelling the story of how Esther saved the Jewish people, finds his own salvation. The repetition of *haynt* (today, now) throughout the poem reverses the Megillah's old tale to replace the Jews' diasporic triumph through the agency of the heroic Esther with the *purim-shpil's* and the modernist's parody.

The second Purim poem is by Miriam Ulinover, whose works Broderzon likely encountered in the 1919 and 1920 issues of a Lodz provincial publication, *Gezangen* (Songs),[26] to which he contributed after his return from Moscow in 1918.[27] Miriam Ulinover's 1922 poem, "Ester hamalke" (Esther the queen), appears in the context of her sequence, "Kaleyorn," in which the narrator is a "marriageable"[28] girl who (here) takes on the dramatic persona of Queen Esther in order to understand her hoped-for and socially decreed status as a bride, even though she lacks a *khosn* (bridegroom). While she observes other girls and their intended bridegrooms with curiosity and a touch of envy, she prefers to commune with the trees. Purim provides this poetic loner with the opportunity to imagine herself in a different role and a different world:

Klapt un roysht der greger,
M'hert a vort koym-koym,—
Nisht fertriben vet ir,
Mentshn, mir mayn troym!

S'falbt mayn sitsen-kleydel
Zikh aher-ahin—
S'vert derfun anekhter
Breyter karmazin . . .

S'shmole royte bendel,
Vos fershleyft mayn tsop,
Nemt mir kroynen herlikh
Sharlakh-royt dem kop;

Epes vert mayn ponem
Kheynevdik un shvarts . . .
Vi di malke ester!—
Shmeykhlt shtil mayn harts.

Un kh'bli-oyf in shenkayt,
Un mayn kholem oykh,—
Malke bin ikh, malke!
Un far mayns a hoykh

Git avek der melekh
Itst a halben land,—
Kh'bin di malke ester
Untern purpur-band!

When the grogger knocks and rattles,
You can hardly hear a word—

I won't allow you people
To chase away my dream!

My skirt, plain calico,
Swaying to and fro—
Turns into actual
Crimson frill and bow.

The thin red ribbon
Looped around my braid
Will with royal scarlet
Crown my head.

Somehow, my face grows
Charming and dark . . .
Like Esther the Queen!—
A still smile in my heart.

And I blossom forth in beauty,
And my dream comes true—
I am the queen, the queen!
I wink, that's all I do,

And now the king bequeaths me
Half the kingdom's land—
I am Queen Esther
Beneath the purple band.

This poem, like Ulinover's other poems, is predicated on a deliberately constructed naiveté that conveys the contrast between the folk culture of a shtetl grandmother and the urbane literary culture of Ulinover's readers. Whereas Broderzon wrote his Purim poem from an explicitly avant-garde stance, Ulinover pushes the modernist voice into the background of the poem, making it nearly inaudible. She creates a speaker who appears to be part of a seamless pre-modern traditional shtetl culture. In contrast to Broderzon's fractured *purim-shpil*, "Ester hamalke" is written in ballad-like trimeter rhymed quatrains and takes place supposedly while the Megillah is being chanted in synagogue. As Ulinover's narrator speaks her lines, the noise of the *groggers* threatens to drive off her fantasy of herself as Queen Esther. Inside her head, her calico skirt becomes a swath of royal crimson and her plain red hair ribbon, a regal scarlet and purple band. As she envisions her own face transformed into the "charming and dark" visage of the exotic Esther of the Megillah, the speaker herself "blossom[s] forth in beauty." Alienated within her environment, alone in the crowd, this speaker, who in other poems has defined herself as a plain Jane without a suitor, exults in the status that her daydream imparts to her, as "The king now bequeaths [her] / Half a kingdom" out of his love for her.

In this poem, the synagogue reading of the Megillah provides the speaker with the occasion to transcend her life by exercising her imagination. This act of imaginative reading (or listening to a text being read) brings the speaker close to the act of imaginative writing, that is, the act of the Yiddish poet who encounters and transforms the traditional text.

In Ulinover's poem, as in Broderzon's, the point of reading tradition is not to illuminate Jewish sacred history, but to shed light on the speaker's world. While Broderzon's dramatic persona is an avant-garde Jewish poet riding the turmoil of revolutionary Russia with a cynical eye to both religious tradition and current ideologies, Ulinover takes on the persona of a shtetl maiden. But this girl, living in an old-fashioned Jewish town, is no less estranged from her community and its noisy celebration than is Broderzon's urbane young man from his. Although Ulinover's poem seems to evoke a circumscribed shtetl, uninterrupted by modernity, in fact it subverts the modern poet's place in that world.

Unlike Toybe Pan, who spoke confidently, if unconventionally, for the Jewish collective, Ulinover's narrator negotiates an uneasy relationship between her desires and the community's expectations. When the congregation's *groggers* drown out Haman's name, they threaten also to efface the girl's dream of her own power, suggesting that an individual who dares to imagine is as destructive and dangerous to the Jews as one who would annihilate them. Even though she dreams herself into the traditional story, in the very act of imagining, Ulinover's speaker transgresses that tradition. In her dream, the girl escapes the shtetl that has not provided her with a bridegroom by marrying a gentile king, a solution that hardly conforms to traditional Jewish mores! Moreover, in her role as Queen Esther, the girl does not rescue the Jews from Haman but rather acquires beauty, wealth, and power for herself. Ulinover's girl is not cynical or sophisticated, yet she in her shtetl synagogue, like Broderzon's Purim player in Moscow, poses a threat to the reigning orthodoxies when she attempts to speak out as a Jewish artist.

Both Broderzon and Ulinover set their poems in the dramatic situations of Polish Jews' celebrations of Purim—a *purim-shpil* and a Megillah reading. In contrast, the third poet, Roza Yakubovitsh, returns the character of the biblical Esther to the ancient Persian setting of the Megillah itself. Yakubovitsh, whose poems were published alongside Ulinover's in the "Froyen-motivn" (Women's motifs) section of the April 1918 *Yugnt: Zamelheft far shener literatur un frayen gedank* (Youth: Collective book for fine literature and free thought),[29] included a sequence of dramatic monologues in the voices of biblical women in her 1924 book *Gez-angen*.[30] Perhaps Yakubovitsh composed these poems in answer to I. L. Peretz's 1910 call that Yiddish writers should "go back to the Bible . . . the most reliable point,"[31] and thus infuse their works with "tradition"[32] and "Yiddish and Hebrew"[33] in order to write "as . . . human being[s]" "on a Jewish path."[34] Or, perhaps, Yakubovitsh had something else in mind. The final poem in this sequence is "Ester" (Esther):

Purpur un goldgeveb, af alabaster-shangen
Oyfgetsoygn, vehen unter perlmuter-vent,
In kenigs-hoyz di freyd halt bald baym end;
Es klingen nokh di zaratustra-loyb-gezangen.
In lustgortn nemt mikh arum dos shtile benken
Tsu mordkhis shtubele, vu kh'hob mayn ru derkent,
Vu kh'hob gelezn, af shteyner-tovl oysgebrent,
Af felzn oysgekritst, vi s'iz mayn folk dergangen.
Es falt a sod, ver hot es eygehoykht [ayngehoykht?] mayn hartsn?
Ver hot dermont a mamen on ir farlozn kind?
Mayn folk, ikh veys, badarf mayn hilf atsind,
Di shushn-shtot ikh ze, iz ayngehilt in shvartsn,
Gey, mordkhe, mentsh fun folk, tsu alemen tsu visn;
Fun ale shuln zol a vey-geshray aroyf tsu got,
Un ikh—vel mit vayber-shmeykhl geyn un betn gnod,
Baym kenig akhashveresh, faln im tsu fisn.[35]

Purple and gold-weave, raised on alabaster beams,
Blow beneath mother-of-pearl walls,
In the king's house the joy is coming to an end:
The Zoroastrian praise-songs still resound.
In the garden of desire, I am embraced by the quiet longing
For Mordecai's little house, where I knew my rest,
Where I read, branded on stone tablets,
Engraved onto boulders, how my people arrived.
A secret occurs; who breathed it into my heart?
Who reminded a mother of her lost child?
My people, I know, now requires my help,
The city of Shushan, I see, is wrapped in darkness;
Go, Mordecai, man of the people, let everyone know;
From all the synagogues let a shout of pain rise to God,
And I—with a womanly smile will go and beg for mercy
From the King, Ahasuerus, falling at his feet.

Unlike Broderzon's "Ikh, a purim-shpiler," which filters the Megillah
through the Purim plays, Yakubovitsh bypasses the carnivalesque, the
subversive, and the satiric. Unlike the shtetl dreamer of Ulinover's
"Ester hamalke," Yakubovitsh's character decides to act in the world to
effect change. Transporting herself into the psyche of the ancient
Esther, the poet imagines the Jewish queen's situation at the moment
she decides to follow Mordecai's orders (through Hatakh, the king's
chamberlain) that Esther should "go to the king and . . . appeal to him
and . . . plead with him for her people" (Esther 4:8).[36] In the traditional
Megillah, Esther takes full measure of the solemnity of her charge, its
dangers, and of Mordecai's reminder that she cannot escape her identity
as a Jew:

> Do not imagine that you, of all the Jews, will escape with your life by being in
> the king's palace. On the contrary, if you keep silent in this crisis, relief and
> deliverance will come to the Jews from another quarter, while you and your
> father's house will perish. And who knows, perhaps you have attained to royal
> position for just such a crisis. (Esther 4:13–14)[37]

However, when Yakubovitsh's Persian Esther translates these feelings
into a statement of her responsibility to her people, she draws not on the
Hebrew Megillah, but on the Yiddish devotional texts that Polish Jewish
women read. Like a woman reciting a *tkhine* (supplicatory prayer) that
appealed to biblical figures in recognizable, everyday terms, Yakubovitsh's Esther describes how she feels an outsider in the king's palace, how
she longs for her Shushan Jewish home, and how she feels like a mother
to her "*farlozn*" people (line 10), whose exile from Jerusalem to Persia
is recorded in a *new* set of covenantal stone tablets.

The model for Yakubovitsh's *tkhine*-reciting Esther is the *Tsenerene*
(Rabbi Yaakov Ashkenazi's Yiddish compilation of the Bible and Midrash for women), where a sixteenth-century Esther prays to God on the
third day of the Jews' fasting, before she approaches the king unbidden
(5:1). With the queen's supplications, the *Tsenerene* makes explicit
Esther's connection to the covenant of the patriarchs and links the Diaspora story to the central tradition:

> She placed the crown upon her head and then prayed: "O great God of Avra-
> ham, Yitzchak and Yaakov, God of Binyamin my father! Although I have no merit
> before You, I go for the sake of Your people Yisrael, lest they be doomed. For if
> they are destroyed, who shall say before You, three times a day, three times Holy?
> Just as you helped Chananiah, Mishael, and Azariah in the fiery furnace, and
> Daniel in the lions' den, help us also. Let me find favor in his eyes."
> She said these words with tears in her eyes, and then continued: "I beg you,
> my God, hear my prayers. If it has been decreed upon us that the warning in the
> Torah is to be visited upon us—that we will be sold as slaves and no one will even
> want to buy us, and if it has been decreed that we die because of our sins . . .

then remember, Master of the World, how Avraham our father took hold of the neck of his son Yitzchak with his left hand, and with his right hand took the knife to slaughter him, just for his love for You. He fulfilled Your commands: heed our pleas! . . .

"We are like a woman in the severest throes of childbirth. Help us out of our plight and remove it from us."[38]

Invoking the patriarchs, the trials of Mishael, Azariah, and Daniel, Joseph sold into slavery by his brothers, and the Binding of Isaac, as well as the verse "Holy, Holy, Holy," in the *Kedushah* prayer of post-biblical liturgy, Esther of the *Tsenerene* resembles not the circumspect Esther of the Bible but the seventeenth-century Toybe Pan, who entreated God to save the Jews of Prague in verses sung to the melodies of Yom Kippur prayers. The resemblances circle back upon each other, though, for Toybe Pan had compared herself begging for divine help to the biblical queen pleading with Ahasuerus! Interpolating dramatic action—Esther places the crown on her head before beginning to pray and says "these words with tears in her eyes"—the *Tsenerene* appeals to sentiment and alludes to the conventions and tenor of the *tkhines*.

Like the author of the *Tsenerene*, Yakubovitsh presents an Esther modeled upon contemporary literary sources, which include, contradictorily, both the *Tsenerene* and modern Yiddish poetry. Her poem echoes other free-rhythm modern Yiddish poetry of the late 1910s and early 1920s in its genre—a dramatic monologue—and its metrical and stanzaic form—six and seven beat lines with varying numbers of syllables, arranged in quatrains, rhymed *a-b-b-a*.[39] Yet as in the *Tsenerene*, Yakubovitsh makes her character appeal to the contemporary world of her readers: the poet evokes the Jewish queen's state of mind and spiritual dilemma through Esther's own sensuous description of concrete things. These descriptions in the Yiddish poem remind the modern reader that the Megillah itself contains lavish imagery—the purple and gold cloth, the alabaster pillars, the mother-of-pearl walls (Esther 1:6).[40] In addition, Yakubovitsh reminds her Polish Jewish readers that like them, Esther lives in the Diaspora, surrounded by the religion and poetry of the Gentiles, for the Persian king's palace resounds with "Zoroastrian praise-songs" (4).

The pagan worship evoked by this phrase leads Esther to remember the history of her own people:

In the garden of desire, I am embraced by the quiet longing
For Mordecai's little house, where I knew my rest,
Where I read, branded on stone tablets,
Engraved onto boulders, how my people arrived. (Yakubovitsh, 5–8)

In the image of the "stone tablets" and the phrase "how my people arrived," the speaker alludes not to the Ten Commandments and the forty years of wandering in the desert but rather to what would have been the historical explanation of how Esther herself came to live in Persia—the destruction of the first Temple in Jerusalem and the subsequent exile of the Jews into the Diaspora.

In the poet's choice of the neutral Germanic term *tovl* (tablet) in the circumlocution *"vi s'iz mayn folk dergangen"* (how my people arrived [on foot, after some difficulty]),[41] and in her avoidance of the religious Hebrew terms—*lukhes ha-bris* (Tablets of the Covenant) and *goles* (Exile)—one can surmise that, after years in the king's harem, Esther has forgotten the story of the Jews. Esther longs not for Zion but for the quotidian "little house" of her uncle Mordecai. Modest as that refuge is, it connects Esther to the arc of Jewish history. There, she "knew [her] rest" (6) and there, too, she read the chronicle of her people (7–8). The inscribed stone tablets, which she once read in the Jewish home of Mordecai, collapse into a single, potent image: the commandments God gave to Moses and a chronicle of the exile of the Jews from Jerusalem, the event that brought Esther herself to the king's garden.

The realization that she belongs to that history and an intuitive, inner voice lead Esther to act: *"Es falt a sod, ver hot es eygehoykht [ayngehoykht?] mayn hartsn?/ Ver hot dermont a mamen on ir farlozn kind?"* (A secret occurs; who breathed it into my heart?/ Who reminded a mother [repeatedly] of her lost child?) (9–10). The strange question about a mother and her lost child makes sense only when we hear its echo in the *Tsenerene*, when Esther likens the Jews in Persia to a woman in labor: "We are like a woman in the severest throes of childbirth. Help us out of our plight and remove it from us."[42] But while in the *Tsenerene*, Esther will deliver the Jews from Haman, as God will deliver the woman of her child, Yakubovitsh's Esther—an orphan and, according to tradition, never a mother[43]— comes to understand that what she must do for her people is more complicated. She will not fulfill the biblical commandment to bear children, nor will she pray in the Jewish way. Unlike Esther of the *Tsenerene*, who addresses God directly and repeatedly ("O great God of Avraham, Yitzchak, and Yaakov, God of Binyamin my father!"; "I beg you, my God, hear my prayers"; "then remember, Master of the World"), Yakubovitsh's Esther instead commands "Mordecai, man of the people," to lead all the Jews in solemn prayer to God. In contrast, she must prepare to prostrate herself and supplicate before the gentile king. She takes on the more dangerous tasks of a woman who must subvert the power of a man and of a Jew who must confront gentile political power. Speaking for the people's sake but apart from them, Esther, in her singular act, represents another version of the modern Yiddish woman poet, whose voice comes out of but remains apart from the tradition.

Yakubovitsh, like Broderzon and Ulinover, found in the story of

Esther an occasion to assert the cause of a secular Yiddish poetry. Although her representation of Esther may seem the most literal and traditional of the three, Yakubovitsh's poem is actually the most literary. Whereas Broderzon revised the *purim-shpil* and Ulinover, the synagogue chanting of the Megillah, Yakubovitsh subverted the *Tsenerene* itself. Anticipating Itsik Manger's *Megile lider* of 1936, these three poets contributed to the formation of a modern Yiddish literary tradition by drawing on a canonical source in untraditional ways. These poems reveal how Yiddish poets in Poland between the wars balanced Queen Esther's daring political action against the demands of making art. Invoking a canonical text of the Diaspora and the institution of Purim—that epitome of Jewish reversal—Broderzon, Ulinover, and Yakubovitsh turned the Megillah into poems about the poet's imagination and transformed Esther herself into a *tkhine* writer and poet. Reimagining Esther in their own image, these Yiddish poets composed a model for modern Jewish artists in a gentile world.

I conclude by arguing that Itsik Manger, the most famous of the four poets considered here, built upon the ground established by Broderzon, Ulinover, and Yakubovitsh. While it is well known that Manger based his retelling of the Purim story on old Yiddish sources, Manger's place in the mini-tradition of modern Esther poems has not been discussed. Manger's best-known work, the *Megile lider* (Megillah poems), was first published in Warsaw in 1936 and, in the 1960s, translated into popular Hebrew and English musical stage productions.[44] In this sequence of twenty-nine poems, Manger retold the story of Esther, drawing upon "forgotten literary traditions," such as fifteenth- through seventeenth-century Yiddish paraphrases of the Book of Esther, rediscovered in the scholarly works of Max Erik and Max Weinreich in the late 1920s.[45] He also drew on the folk traditions of the later type of *purim-shpil*, the more elaborate Ahasuerus play.[46]

On the other hand, Manger also interjected modern elements into his poems, including an invented romance between the maiden Esther and Fatrigosso, a basting stitcher who belongs to a radical tailors' union. Madly in love, Fatrigosso is so distraught when Esther marries Ahasuerus that he tries to assassinate the king but fails. This addition serves both comic and political ends. Manger transformed the Megillah's victorious salvation of the Jews into the failed revenge of an underdog lover and recast the canonical text as a melodrama. However, in the political subplot of Fatrigosso—which is based, some argue, on Hirsh Lekert, the Jewish Labor Bundist who tried and failed to assassinate the governor of Vilna on 5 May 1902—Manger intimates the increasingly desperate situation of the Jews in Europe in 1936.[47]

Whereas Toybe Pan used the paradigm of Esther's original Purim to justify her sincere actions on behalf of the contemporary Prague Jewish community, Manger transgresses the order of time and history with anachronistic wit. The maiden Esther, "getting ready for the king," as her uncle Mordecai scopes out the terms of the beauty contest, is at once of the modern and ancient worlds, in Leonard Wolf's translation:

> Slim Esther stands at her mirror
> In her blue velvet dress.
> It's dusk, and at her throat
> Her pearls are luminous.
>
> She murmurs, "The Purim players
> Mock me and say I'm 'green.'
> Enough! I know I'm beautiful—
> I wonder what they mean?"[48]

Manger's Esther lives both within and beyond the Scroll of Esther. She wears modern clothing—a velvet dress and pearls—and inspects herself in a modern mirror with modern self-doubt. In Manger's trademark narrative gesture, the characters have also read the ancient text that tells the story that they enact. Esther is aware of the holiday of Purim and the Polish Purim players even before the events they commemorate have occurred. Manger's deliberate anachronisms and metatextual narrative play bring the ancient story into the modern world.[49]

Ahasuerus, too, knows the story of Purim. In Manger's poem "The King Ahasuerus after the Assassination Attempt," the monarch expresses his own, irrational anti-Semitic sentiments as he deliberately signs Haman's deadly decrees:

> He shudders. "That Haman is right.
> Get rid of them all this time.
> Tomorrow I'll send off the letters
> At a quarter after nine.
>
> Let the kikes understand that I mean it.
> It's not just a Purim play. . . ."
>
> He sits at his desk. He spits in
> The inkwell and takes a deep breath.
> Then signs, page by page, the decree
> That will send the Jews to their death.[50]

Manger's emphasis on the foolish king's active participation in implementing Haman's anti-Semitic decree points the reader toward recognizing the anti-Semitism in 1930s Europe. In the original Scroll of Esther, the narrative reaches its climax at this point, where Ahasuerus signs the death decree for the Jews. Immediately afterward, Esther and Mordecai devise their plan to save their people, Mordecai's earlier good deeds are fortuitously brought to the attention of the insomniac king, Esther carries out her daring plan to entrap Haman, the Jews are saved, revenge is taken, and Mordecai is elevated to a position of power.

In contrast to this fast-paced drama and its triumphant ending, Manger's cycle submerges the main actions by the heroes Esther and Mordecai within lesser events. This oblique approach to the story culminates in the final two poems, each describing how Manger's invented characters respond to the unfolding of history. In the penultimate poem, the master tailor Fonfosso presides over a Purim banquet, at which his old-maid daughter Hannah-Dvoyre serves fish and poppyseed hamantashen, the holiday pastry named after Haman's pocketbook. The bespectacled Fonfosso gloats over the punishments of boiling asphalt and whippings, which "that wicked Haman," who dared to "pick on" "the Jews and their mighty God," must endure in Hell. He toasts "the innocent Esther" and "the king, that simpleton-bear"[51] and calls for the Purim play to begin. Intertwining the sacred Scroll of Esther with Yiddish Purim celebrations, Manger foregrounds the European Jewish cultural observance of Purim until it eclipses the Purim story.

In the final poem, Manger reduces the triumphant Purim narrative to a mere mention. Fastrigosso's old mother lights a memorial candle on the year's anniversary of the execution of her son, the would-be assassin of the king. As she weeps, the mother calls for the death of "That whore, that Esther, that queen" who had never even inquired about her imprisoned suitor, the incomparable "gem" Fatrigosso, and berates Mordecai, "the rich man, the entrepreneur," wishing upon them "a desolate Purim."[52] By ending the *Megile lider* with a distinctly Yiddish curse upon Queen Esther and Mordecai—in fact, by reducing these characters to a bitter reference in the mouth of a survivor of his revised Purim narrative—Manger focuses on the situation of his Jewish audience. The central characters of these last two poems—an aging father and an elderly mother—are simple people who speak in uneducated dialect. These parents can anticipate only a limited future through their children who, unmarried or dead, are both fatalities of their own romantic dreams. The settings of both poems—the tailors' Purim feast and widow's kindling of the *yortsayt* candle—point to the past. Like Broderzon's Purim player, who ends his monologue comparing himself to "a pointless tear," Manger's poem ends in tears, too. But where the tear allows Broderzon's Purim player to assert the viability of modernist Jewish art, the

bereft mother at the end of Manger's poem simply weeps with a finality
that eludes translation:

Fatrigoses alte mame
Shteyt farn yortsaytlikht
Un groyse, heyse trern
Rinen iber ir gezikht.

Fatrigosso's old mother
Has hot tears on her face
As she lights the memorial candle
And puts it back in its place. [trans. Leonard Wolf][53]

For all its literary pyrotechnics and wit, Itsik Manger's Megillah foretells
the coming darkness.

Ulinover's "Queen Esther" posits a Purim in which an artist can
dream her way into the modern world. In its intertextual literary form,
transposing Yiddish devotional sources seamlessly into a modern dramatic voice, Yakubovitsh's "Esther" points ahead to Itsik Manger's metatextual *Megile lider*, where the characters have read the story in which
they play the role of saving the Jews from their persecutors and take
revenge, thus reversing the order of power (*venahafokh hu*). But these
modernist poets, having lived through World War I, are too knowing.
They know that the order of power in their world has not been reversed.
Rather, it is the victorious paradigm depicted in the Scroll of Esther that
has been overturned. These poems comprise an unsacred parody of a
sacred fantasy of Jewish triumph over adversity. Revising the Scroll of
Esther to reflect the uncertainties and dangers for Jews in the early twentieth century, these poems become the archetypal modernist Jewish
texts.

Notes

I am grateful to the following people, whose insights, suggestions, corrections,
and sources helped me as I worked on this essay: Hamutal Bar-Yosef, Kenneth
Moss, Benjamin Nathans, Anita Norich, Gabriella Safran, Anita Shapira, Kurt
Stern z"l, and especially David Stern.

1. The Book of Esther and the Song of Songs are the only two books of the
Hebrew Bible that do not mention the name of God. Louis Ginzberg, *Legends of
the Jews* (Philadelphia, 1968), 6:481, n193.

2. Toybe Pan, "Eyn sheyn lid naye gemakht/ b'loshn tkhine iz vardn oys
getrakht," in *Yidishe dikhterins: Antologye*, ed. Ezra Korman (Chicago, 1928),
7–17. In transliterating Toybe Pan's poem, I have modified the standard YIVO
system to reflect the archaic Yiddish orthography preserved by Korman. See also

the text in Jerold C. Frakes, ed., *Early Yiddish Texts: 1100–1750* (Oxford, 2004), 834–42.

3. Jewish communities and families observed the custom of celebrating Purim Katan ("minor Purim") to mark the anniversary of their escape from destruction by a specific pogrom, famine, or plague. They would recite special prayers, read the story of the personal or communal salvation from a scroll (like the Scroll of Esther), enjoy a festive meal, and give charity to the poor. Often a fast day (like the Fast of Esther) would precede Purim Katan. On Purim Katan, see "Purims, Special," *Encyclopaedia Judaica*, CD-ROM ed., 1997.

4. Chava Turniansky has suggested that at the time this poem was written, there may have been a superstition about leap years.

5. Chone Shmeruk, *The Esterke Story in Yiddish and Polish Literature*, trans. Paul Glikson (Jerusalem, 1985), 13–14.

6. Ibid., 37–38.

7. Ibid., 55–57.

8. Ibid., 60–82.

9. Ibid., 80.

10. Haya Bar-Itzhak, *Jewish Poland: Legends of Origin: Ethnopoetics and Legendary Chronicles* (Detroit, 2001), 113–32.

11. Kathryn Hellerstein, "The Demon Within: Moyshe-Leyb Halpern's Subversive Ballads," *Prooftexts* 7 (1987): 225–48.

12. "Biografishe shtrikhn," in Moyshe Broderzon, *Oysgeklibene shriftn: Lider, dramoletn, mayselekh*, ed. Shmuel Rozshanski (Buenos Aires, 1959), 9–10. (Rozshanski calls him the "Prince of *Yung-yidish*," the modernist Yiddish literary group and journal in Lodz.) Zalmen Reyzen, "Broderzon, Moyshe," in *Leksikon fun der yidisher literatur, prese un filologye*, 3rd ed. (Vilna, 1928), 1:401–4. Menakhem Flakser, "Broderzon, Moyshe," in *Leksikon fun der nayer yidisher literature* (New York, 1956), 1:429–32.

13. David Roskies, *A Bridge of Longing: The Lost Art of Yiddish Storytelling* (Cambridge, Mass, 1995), 258.

14. Rozshanski, ed., "Biografishe shtrikhn," 8. Broderzon was born in Moscow in 1890, moved to Lodz with his family in 1891, and attended *heder* in Gevishz, White Russia, at age nine. He returned to Lodz to attend business school and became a bookkeeper. In 1914, at the beginning of World War I, Broderzon fled Poland for Moscow; he returned to Lodz in 1918, where he lived until 1938. Although Melekh Ravitch, "Broderzon, Moshe," *Encyclopedia Judaica* (1971), 1:1391–92, states that Broderzon received his "early education" in Moscow and came to Lodz only in 1918, Rozshanski's account contradicts this version. Also Seth Wolitz, "The Jewish National Art Renaissance in Russia," in *Tradition and Revolution: The Jewish Renaissance in Russian Avant-Garde Art, 1912–1928*, ed. Ruth Apter-Gabriel (Jerusalem, 1987), 29, 33 (21–42).

15. Wolitz, "The Revolution and Jewish National Art," 29.

16. Ruth Apter-Gabriel, "El Lissitzky's Jewish Works," in *Tradition and Revolution*, 104. Also see Gilles Rozier, *Moyshe Broderzon: Un écrivain Yiddish d'avant-garde* (Saint-Denis, 1999), 41–48.

17. A sample of the limited edition can be found in the collection of Bill Gross, Ramat Aviv, Israel. One can see that Broderzon's text was originally handwritten, rather than typeset, from the irregularity of the letters—each alef, for instance, is unique. One can contrast the text to the sixteenth-century type of *Paris un vien* (Verona, 1594), in Gilles Rozier, *Moyshe Broderzon: Un ecrivain Yiddish d'avant-garde* (Saint-Denis, 1999), ills. 44–45.

18. Apter-Gabriel, "El Lissitzky's Jewish Works," 104.

19. Wolitz, "The Revolution and Jewish National Art," 29. Also see my facsimile copy of *Sikhes Kholin* (Tel Aviv, 1957).

20. Chone Shmeruk, "Purim-Shpil," *Encyclopaedia Judaica*, CD-Rom ed.

21. Moyshe Broderzon, "Ikh, a purim-shpiler," in *Oysgeklibene shriftn: Lider, dramoletn, mayselekh*, ed. Shmuel Rozshanski (Buenos Aires, 1959), 76–78.

22. Wolitz, "The Revolution and Jewish National Art," 33.

23. "*Livnot v' . . . yerushalyaim.*" About Moyshe Broderzon's resistance to political ideology, see Y. M. Nayman, "Der eksponent fun veltlekher yidishkayt," originally published in *Literarishe bleter* (Warsaw), no. 505 (January 1934). Excerpted in Moyshe Broderzon, *Oysgeklibene shriftn: Lider dramaletn, mayselekh*, ed. Shmuel Rozshanski (Buenos Aires, 1972), 247–49. "Moyshe Broderzon is not ideologically expressive [*oysgeshprokhn*]. He wets his finger in a spring, but he lacks the strength to immerse himself fully. It is simply not his destiny."

24. Esther's green face may variously symbolize her inexperience and youth, or illustrate rabbinic sources that called Esther both "evergreen," like the sweet-scented myrtle denoted by her Hebrew name, Hadassah, and physically ugly, with a "sallow, myrtle-like complexion," but endowed by God with the "grace and charm" needed to fulfill her divine purpose of saving the Jews. Ginzberg, *Legends of the Jews*, 4:384–85; 6:459n.67. Another explanation of the *purim-shpil*'s literal depiction of Esther's face as green can be traced to the Septuagint, in which the word "pale" is translated as "green," or ugly, and thus supports an interpretation of the verse "For the maiden was of beautiful form and fair to look on" (Esther 2:7), which attributed Esther's beauty not to her native qualities but to the transformative grace of God.

25. Marc Chagall, "Music" (1920), in *Marc Chagall and the Jewish Theater* (New York, 1992), front cover and plate 4; El Lissitzky, "Gekoyft der tate far tsvey gildeyn," in *Had Gadya: The Only Kid, Facsimile of El Lissizky's Edition of 1919*, ed. Arnold J. Band (Los Angeles, 2004), plate 1 (alef).

26. Natalia Krynicka, "Araynfir" (Introduction), in Miriam Ulinover, *A grus fun der alter heym: Lider*, ed. Natalia Krynicka, trans. Batia Baum (Paris, 2003), 18.

27. Reyzen, *Leksikon*, 1:402.

28. Miriam Ulinover, "Far der tir "(Before the door), in *Der Bobes Oytser* (Warsaw, 1922), 80–81.

29. Krynicka, "Araynfir," 17, 78, n. 37.

30. Roza Yakubovitsh (1889–1942), who lived in the Polish town of Kalish until 1939 (then fled to the Lodz Ghetto, where she shared a dwelling with Miriam Ulinover, until she went on to the Warsaw Ghetto, where she died), published her first (and only surviving) book of poems in Warsaw in 1924. *Mayne gezangen* (My songs) ends with a sequence of dramatic monologues in the voices of biblical women—Ruth, Rachel, Hagar, Miriam, Shulamis, and Esther.

31. I. L. Peretz, "What Our Literature Needs," trans. Nathan Halper, in *Voices from the Yiddish: Essays, Memoirs, Diaries*, ed. Irving Howe and Eliezer Greenberg (Ann Arbor, 1972), 31.

32. Ibid., 25.

33. Ibid., 26.

34. Ibid., 31.

35. Roza Yakubovitsh, "Ester," *Mayne gezangen* (Warsaw, 1924), 47.

36. *Esther*, in *The Five Megilloth and Jonah: A New Translation*, 2nd rev. ed., introduction by H. L. Ginsberg, illustrated by Ismar David (1969; Philadelphia, 1974), 97.

37. Ibid., 98.

38. *Tz'enah ur'enah: The Classic Anthology of Torah Lore and Midrashic Comment,* trans. Miriam Stark Zakon, introduction by Meir Holder (New York; Jerusalem, 1984), 2:546–47.

39. Benjamin Hrushovski (Harshav), "On Free Rhythms in Modern Yiddish Poetry," in *Field of Yiddish: Studies in Yiddish Language, Folklore, and Literature,* ed. Uriel Weinreich (New York, 1954), 234–35.

40. Michael V. Fox, *Character and Ideology in the Book of Esther* (Columbia, S.C., 1991), 14. (Esther 1:6 describes "cloths of white, percaline, and violet, bound with cords of linen and purple on silver rods and alabaster pillars . . . on a mosaic pavement of porphyry and alabaster, mother of pearl and dark marble.") See also *Tze'enah ur'enah,* trans. Zakon, 2:537–38. ("White hangings and fine cotton [1:6] Linen, white as pearls, hung from one tree to the next, woven with threads of green, blue, and silk. A hanging of purple encircled it, bound all around with golden chains.")

41. Definition of *dergeyn,* in Uriel Weinreich, *Modern English-Yiddish, Yiddish-English Dictionary* (New York, 1977), 141/652.

42. *Tz'enah ur'enah,* trans. Zakon, 2:546–47.

43. Regarding the traditional views of Esther never bearing children, see Ginzberg, *Legends of the Jews,* 4:388 (Esther never had sexual relations with Ahasuerus, because she was really married to Mordecai); 4:419 (Esther, frightened by news that Mordecai appeared in mourning garb, miscarried); 6:469n.127 (citing the sources for the miscarriage tale as Abba Gorion 35 and Panim Aherim 51, and stating that the latter "contains also another opinion to the effect that Esther took precautions to prevent pregnancy"). In the Talmud, Sanhedrin 74a posits another tradition, which holds that the last Darius was the offspring of Esther and Ahasuerus. Ginzberg, *Legends of the Jews,* 6:460n.80.

44. A popular Yiddish production of Manger's *Megile lider,* directed by Dov Seltzer, was staged in Israel in 1965 and ran for over 400 performances. http://en.wikipedia.org/wiki/Itzik_Manger. An English production, *The Megilla of Itzik Manger,* directed by Shmuel Bunim and starring Michael Burstein, Pesach Burstein, and Lillian Lux, played on Broadway at the John Golden Theater from October through December 1968 and as a return engagement at the Longacre Theater in April 1969. http://www.ibdb.com/production.asp?ID = 3423; http://www.ibdb.com/production.asp?ID = 2863.

45. Chone Shmeruk, "*Medresh Itzik* and the Problem of Its Literary Traditions," in Itzik Manger, *Medresh Itzik,* ed. Chone Shmeruk, 3rd ed. (Jerusalem, 1984), ix.

46. David G. Roskies and Leonard Wolf, "Introduction," in Itzik Manger, *The World According to Itzik: Selected Poetry and Prose,* trans. and ed. Leonard Wolf (New Haven, 2002), xxxii. Also Chone Shmeruk, *The Esterke Story,* nn. 2, 55, and Chone Shmeruk, "*Medresh Itzik* and the Problem of Its Literary Traditions," in *Medresh Itzik,* xxiii, n. 29.

47. Roskies and Wolf, "Introduction," xxxii–xxxiii. Roskies and Wolf argue that Fatrigosso is based on Hirsh Lekert, the Jewish Labor Bundist who tried and failed to assassinate the governor of Vilna on 5 May 1902. That Manger's Fatrigosso might also be drawn from Shomer-Shaykevitch's 1884 novel, *Di yidishe kenigin,* may be inferred from Shemuk, *The Esterke Story,* 41.

48. Itzik Manger, "Esther Getting Ready for the King," in *The World According to Itzik,* trans. and ed. Wolf, 40–41. Itzik Manger, "Ester greyt zikh tsum melekh," in *Medresh Itzik,* ed. Shmeruk, 143–44.

49. Manger drew his literary style from Max Erik's and Max Weinreich's 1926 and 1928 scholarly studies of Old Yiddish texts, such as the *Shmuel bukh,* as well as from quasi-folk ballads by the New York modernists, such as Moyshe-Leyb Halpern. Shmeruk, "Introduction," *Medresh Itzik,* viii–ix, xxi, xxiv–xxv, xxvi–xxvii.

50. Itzik Manger, "The King Ahasuerus After the Assassination Attempt," in *The World According to Itzik,* trans. and ed. Wolf, 54. Itzik Manger, "Der melkeh akhashverush nokhn atentat," in *Medresh Itzik,* 163–64.

51. Manger, "The Master Tailor, Fonfosso, Presides over a Banquet," in *The World According to Itzik,* trans. and ed. Wolf, 68–69. Itzik Manger, "Der mayster fonfose pravet di sude," in *Medresh Itzik,* 185–86. I have slightly altered the translation.

52. Manger, "Fastrigosso's Mother Lights a Memorial Candle," in *The World According to Itzik,* trans. and ed. Wolf, 70–71. Itzik Manger, "Fatrigoses mame tsind on a yortsaytlikht," in *Medresh Itzik,* 187–88.

53. Alternately, "Fatrigosso's old mother/ Stands by the *yortsayt* flame/ And huge, hot tears/ Run over her face" (trans. Kathryn Hellerstein).

Part IV
Memory Projects

Revealing and Concealing the Soviet Jewish Self: The Desk-Drawer Memoirs of Meir Viner

Marcus Moseley

In the preface to his 1903 autobiographical novel, or novelistic autobiography, *Bahoref* (In the winter), Yosef Haim Brenner writes, with shades of Dostoevsky's underground man: "I write for myself and in secret." For Brenner, this was a fiction—part and parcel of the larger rhetoric of authenticity that characterizes his oeuvre. Writing for oneself—and, it should be added, of oneself—and in secret was no fiction for Meir Viner and his literary confreres in the Soviet Union. In this chapter I focus on a text belonging to the unique and complex category of unpublished, or posthumously published, autobiographical writings of Soviet Yiddish writers. These are texts written under the conditions of a totalitarian regime—texts written, some even in hieroglyph, with the specific intention of not seeing the light of day, not, at least, until some unspecified future when the yoke of oppression would have been lifted.[1] The extent of these apocryphal writings—or to use the felicitous term of Eliezer Podriachik, *Genize shafungen* ("buried writings" is an approximate translation)—is difficult to determine. It can, I think, be held in certainty that the trickle of such texts as have reached us represent but a fraction of these underground writings.[2] In his classification of these *Genize shafungen* Podriachik sees their having Jewish national content as their defining category and, more specifically, sympathetic depictions of pre-revolutionary Jewish society and culture.[3] No less central, however, from the evidence of the *Genize shafungen* of Der Nister (Pinkhes Kahanovitsh), Meir Viner, and Peretz Markish discussed by Podriachik in his article, is their autobiographical tenor, their concern with the self.

Soviet conditions were as inimical to the autobiographically constituted, romantic self as they were to nationalist deviationism.[4] This overall negation of the pre-revolutionary autobiographical self manifested itself in Soviet Yiddish literary criticism by a marked hostility toward bio-graphical and autobiographical expressions of identity that did not pro-vide testimony, in Jochen Hellbeck's words, "of the full trajectory of self-transformation from 'human weed' or 'bad raw material,' living in a sim-ilarly unformed or polluted social environment, to conscious, self-disci-plined human beings residing in the well-ordered socialist garden created to an extent by themselves."[5] The first fault, for example, that the "proletarian" literary critic, Avrom Abtshuk, found in Yiddish litera-ture of the late 1920s was that "the writers are cutting themselves off from real life and moving towards individualism and mysticism."[6] A chilling proclamation to the same effect soon to prove tragically pro-phetic was made by Moyshe Litvakov in 1925:

The refined concentration upon the atomized bourgeois individual has become hollow and devoid of content, at a time when collective masses, proletarian and peasants, have begun to reveal in concrete manner their brilliant creative poten-tial. The oneiric, slow-paced individualist-impressionistic style has become a sort of dissonance from the hereafter (*fun yener velt*) at a time when mass-agitation has become the style of the epoch.[7]

Given such hostility to individualist lyrical introspection, backed up as it was by organized state violence and given, moreover, the taboo imposed upon sympathetic, even empathetic, nostalgia evinced by writ-ers for the pre-revolutionary Jewish culture of their parents, siblings, and grandparents, it is no wonder that texts of autobiographical coloration were assigned to the *Genize*. Some writers, indeed, who in Moyshe Litva-kov's formulation "felt the 'worminess' of their petit-bourgeois origins," sought to purge themselves of Jewish nostalgia. Thus Litvakov cites with glee Aron Kushnirov: "In the soul a mouse scratches/ Either Father's or Grandfather's melody [*nign*]"; and Shmuel Rasin: "Perhaps my feet will/ By themselves bring me/ To such a country/ That will in no way remind me/ Of my yesterday."[8] To provide some idea of the critical abuse affectionate and nostalgic Jewish self-accounting could bring upon the heads of its practitioners, consider the following citation from a 1932 Soviet publication, *Problemes fun folkloristik*:

To pogroms of the Black Hundreds, to one of the fighting strategies of decaying tsarism, the An-skys, exactly as did the Prilutskys, Bialiks etc., responded with a nostalgic flight to the putrefied "patriarchal" times, remembering with misty eyes all of their sweet tastes and smells, registering every pure and holy man, every smatter of grease on the old *Kapotes* [gabardines], every surviving trace of the national-religious onion in the holy *Tekhines* [Yiddish supplication literature, especially geared toward women]. . . . Let us recall the old sacred taste of kugel, and the old echt-Jewish foodstuffs imbued with the primeval national spirit, the old *Shtraymls* [fur-rimmed Hasidic hats], *Kapotes*, and *Shterntiklakh* [decorative traditional woman's headgear]. Let's immerse ourselves in the old bizarrely retrograde tales about saints, dibbuks, spirits, devils, miracles, and wonders etc. which provided consolation to our holy great-great-grandfathers in the face of similar pogroms and misfortunes.[9]

The author of the above lines was Meir Viner, the Soviet literary critic whose work has stood the test of time better than any other. Viner thus shared, in his published works at least, the general distaste for both biography and autobiography current in the literary criticism of his time and place. Such distaste made of Shmuel Niger, who more than any other Yiddish literary critic espoused the biographical method, and of Zalman Reizen, precisely on account of his *Leksikon fun der yidisher literatur prese un filologie* (Lexicon of Yiddish literature, press, and philology, published in four volumes from 1926 to 1929) the *bêtes noires* of Soviet literary criticism and foremost representatives of "fascistic Yiddishism and its scholarship." Thus G. Sheinin in his critique of the *Leksikon*:

The methodological foundation of the Yiddishistic literary research is the biographical method, which derives again from the individualistic, idealist approach to history, as if it were the history of heroes. But also the biographical method is taken by the Kasrilevke [Sholem Aleichem's fictional rendition of his hometown Voronke in the Ukraine] researchers *ad absurdum*: they have even begun to seek the secret of the writer's work in his uncles (like Niger, for example, with Sholem Aleichem), or his grandmothers, dining-table depictions etc.[10]

Viner, who referred to Niger as a "nationalist-fascist critic,"[11] speaks in similarly disparaging vein of the two classic Yiddish autobiographical works, S. Y. Abramovitsh's *Shloyme reb khayims* (Shloyme the son of Reb Khayim, 1899) and Sholem Aleichem's *Funem yarid* (From the fair, 1915–16). He views these texts as lamentable manifestations of petit-bourgeois recoil from advanced capitalism that adduces to sentimental nostalgia for childhood and the recent past in the face of the emerging reality of a proletarian-based economy.[12] He lacerates the "bourgeois Yiddishistic" and "philistine" underpinnings of Max Weinreich's biographical introduction to Solomon Ettinger's collected writings[13] and Yitskhok Dov Berkovich's biographical and autobiographical *Sholem aleikhem bukh*—a work he depicts as "saccharine . . . saturated with family-cult."[14] In a work published in 1938, *Lyrik un sotsializm* (Lyric poetry and socialism), Viner characterizes the Yiddish poetry written in the two decades before 1917 in the following terms: "Chewing the cud of the all-important *ego* of the poet and his idle caprices, vacuous posturing of the self, all manner of aimless psychological posturing or formal coquetry."[15]

"I have divided all the works of world literature," writes Osip Mandelshtam, "into those written with and without permission. The first are trash—the second stolen air."[16] Precisely at the time when Viner was, as

Podriachik puts it, "engaged with all his might in the battle for the Leninist process in literary criticism"—the latter half of the 1930s—he was in the midst of writing and planning a wide-ranging autobiographical work, only a small section of which was to be completed, that would encompass his experience from the years of childhood in Krakow (Viner was born in 1893) to the time of his establishing residence in the USSR in 1926.[17] Only in 1969 were the extant sections of the work brought to light and the majority, but not all, published in the journal *Sovyetish heymland* (Soviet homeland). Amounting to some fifty printed pages (large format), these autobiographical chapters were topically rearranged by the two editors into two sections bearing the titles "Der zeyde Binyomen" (Grandfather Binyomen) and "Yugnt fraynt" (Friends of youth).[18]

To my knowledge, this text thus constitutes the most substantial and significant autobiographical manuscript by a leading Soviet Yiddish writer to be published to date. At the time of publication of this work, writes Podriachik, who was responsible for its discovery, Viner's autobiographical revelations and the revelation of Viner's autobiography "astonished those who enjoyed a close acquaintance with Viner."[19] Quite aside from its rich biographical and historical content, Viner's work fascinates in its bearing unmistakable signs of the circumstances of its composition. Any written document, even one destined for the desk drawer, had in the USSR not only to evade the strictures of the external censor but also those of the internalized censor in the mind.[20] Thus the Soviet Yiddish poet and novelist Moyshe Taytsh writes with remarkable frankness to Lamed Shapiro in 1931:

I myself am experiencing a crisis. . . . It was difficult to break myself in two, very difficult. . . . The process has still not ended, but I undergo it with pleasure and enthusiasm. . . . Life has transformed itself for us, so must we transform our perception. For the second generation it will be natural to write in a proletarian manner (and, it goes without saying, think that way also), exactly as for us it was natural to write in a petit-bourgeois manner. The generation of the desert must moreover pay heed and control themselves (it does not always help).[21]

The end result of this process of "self-control" thus yields a document that calls for considerable deciphering. This element of internal censorship is attested to by the generic indeterminacy of the piece: Viner wavers constantly between open first-person autobiographical expression and the third-person pseudonymous protagonist of the autobiographical *Bildungsroman*. The model for such a Yiddish autobiographical *Bildungsroman* may well have been provided him by Dovid Bergelson's *Bam dnieper* (By the Dniepr), the first volume of which, *Penek*, had appeared in 1932. Bergelson, in the latter work, circumvents the autobiographical taboo by endowing Penek, his clearly autobiographical protagonist, with the class-consciousness of a seasoned commissar, and it is through this prism that the familial and social ambience of his childhood is refracted, sometimes cruelly so.[22] Viner thus alternates at random within the text between the narrative perspective of a "Yoyel" and that of "I"/ "we."[23] That Viner himself was aware of this generic indeterminacy is attested to by a revealing aside to be found in the margins of one of the manuscript pages: "Perhaps write the whole thing in the first person."[24] And in one passage he pointedly calls attention to the autobiographical status of the document, lest the reader consider his prior depiction of the banquet furnished by his Grandfather Binyomen to the indigents of Krakow overly novelistic:

I know that many of the people whom I describe here recall in several of their characteristics Jewish beggars as described by other writers from many years back. I swear, however, that all of these people of whom I narrate, really were people that I saw in my own city, that I knew well.[25]

There is again here a fascinating parallel with Mandelstam, the narrator of whose tortuous crypto-autobiographical "The Egyptian Stamp" exclaims: "What a pleasure for the narrator to switch from the third person to the first! It is just as if, after having to drink from tiny inconvenient thimble-sized glasses, one were suddenly to say the hell with them, to get hold of oneself and drink cold, unboiled water straight from the faucet."[26]

There is honorable precedent within the Yiddish canon for autobiography in the third person—Abramovitsh's *Shloyme reb khayims* and Sholem Aleichem's *Funem yarid*. But if the third person is employed consistently within a clearly self-referential text, this makes of the "he" little more than an encoded "I," which is almost automatically "cracked" by the reader.[27] Viner's constant vacillation, to the contrary, between "Yoyel" and "I" suggests a text borne of conflicting motivations, or rather an autobiography that is constantly checked/stifled by opposing forces. That the self-referential, autobiographical impulse is here primary, rather than the novelistic, is borne out by the fact that all other persons depicted in this work that I can identify—including family members and figures of note in East European Jewish intellectual life, such as the neo-Hasidic philosopher Aaron Marcus, the historian and Krakow antiquarian bookseller Fayvl Hirsh Vetshteyn, the Spinozist Maskil Shlomoh Rubin, the rabbinic biographer and bibliographer Menakhem Mendl Krengil, all acquaintances of Viner's grandfather, Binyomen Landau—are depicted by their own names and are drawn, moreover, with an eye to historical and biographical verisimilitude. Viner's concern for historical accuracy is also reflected in the notes contained in his archive pertaining to this work that unfortunately were not published with the text. In these notes, according to Podriachik's lamentably curt depiction, "Viner brings various facts concerning his grandfathers, B. Landau and L. Viner. These notes also contain interesting details concerning Meir Viner's youth and childhood."[28]

At several points in the manuscript, moreover, where names and books are mentioned and Viner is uncertain of their exactitude, he writes as a reminder to himself, "Verify."[29] This is not to say that there are not moments in this work when the hand of the novelist is to the fore; the depiction, for example, of Grandfather Binyomen's beggars' banquet is highly reminiscent of the panoramic crowd scenes in the historical novels and short stories of Yoysef Opatoshu.[30] But since in his nonscholarly writing in Yiddish prior to the writing of this text Meir Viner had applied himself first and foremost to the genre of the historical novel, it would be surprising indeed were not the hand of the novelist to be perceived here.[31]

More problematic than the intrusion of fictional techniques into this narrative—such intrusion having marked a constitutional characteristic of autobiography since Rousseau—is the ever-present ideological interference to be detected in this text. Of course, no autobiography is devoid of the ideological, and the very writing of an autobiography is an implicitly ideological act and thus held in suspicion by many contemporary commentators of more radical persuasion. When, however, the ideology overtly espoused by the autobiographer negates the self/autos and the individual life/bios in face of a determined and determining collective totality, the autobiographer's left hand must constantly be seeking to qualify or erase what his right hand is in the process of inscribing. Thus Evgeny Dobrenko discerns in Gorky's autobiographical trilogy a self-canceling deep structure occasioned by the lack of fit of ideology and genre:

> At the heart of Gorky's autobiography lies an unconditionally anti-autobiographical principle. This is foremost a matter of Gorky's anti-Rousseauianism. . . . Gorky spoke out against individualism, against the . . . "independence" of the individual from class influences and from the conditions of his era, against the cult of "social solitude," and against the idea of an "exceptional personality" as such. . . . All of this could not but be manifested in the Gorkian trilogy: in autobiography the "auto" was called into doubt.[32]

Jochen Hellbeck writes in very similar vein concerning the Stalin-era journals: "Time and again, diarists wrote of their efforts to merge their personal lives with 'the general stream of life' of the Soviet collective. A private existence in distinction or even opposition to the life of the collective, however, was considered inferior and unfulfilled."[33]

Ideological disruption of autobiographical memory in order to appease the external and internal censor is at evidence throughout Viner's text, but nowhere more so than in the sections devoted to his grandfather, a man he clearly loved and admired.[34] Viner no doubt realized that in so affectionate a depiction of a pre-revolutionary patriarchal forebear he was treading extremely dangerous ground—a similarly affectionate memoir by the literary critic Boris Eichenbaum, depicting his Jewish forebears and published in 1929, was singled out for special indictment in the late 1940s.[35] We learn from the memoirs of Esther Rosental-Shnayderman, who worked alongside Viner in the Institute for Proletarian Jewish Culture in Kiev, that Viner was, from the onset of his arrival in the USSR in 1926, markedly "nervous" in his new ambience and highly circumspect in the company of hard-line ideologues.[36] He was composing his memoirs, moreover, in particularly dangerous times: his former colleagues at the Kiev Institute, Maks Erik and Yoysef Liberberg, were arrested in 1936; Erik died in captivity the same year after a failed suicide attempt and Liberberg was shot in 1937;[37] the entire Institute for Proletarian Jewish Culture was liquidated in 1936.[38] Viner, moreover, while a Party member, had much in his past to atone for. The precocious scion of an extremely wealthy family, initially a Zionist,[39] he had already made a name for himself in his twenties as a German writer for his mystical/poetic speculations in the realm of Kabbalah, earning the admiration of Hugo von Hoffmansthal.[40] His books included a reworking of a metaphysical diary in which he formulated a mystical/kabbalistic philosophy, published as *Von den symbolen. Zehn Kapitel uber den Ausdruck des Geistes* (Berlin, Vienna, 1924); an anthology, *Die Lyrik der Kabbalah* (Vienna, 1930); and a collection of poems, *Messias—Drei Dichtungen* (Berlin, 1923), in lavish format with Gothic script and woodcuts, dedicated to Martin Buber.[41] As if this were not enough, in the early 1920s Viner had collaborated with Hayyim Brody, the chief rabbi of Prague and an avowed Zionist, on a Hebrew anthology comprising a selection of poems from the canonization of the Bible to the expulsion of the Jews from Spain—an anthology still considered a classic in the field. He had, moreover, corresponded with Brody concerning a planned second volume that would take the anthology up to the period of the Haskalah, right up to the eve of his departure for the Soviet Union in 1926.[42] His was scarcely a conventional background for a militantly Marxist Yiddish critic; indeed, Viner's intellectual trajectory is, to the best of my knowledge, unique.[43] Even in terms of style and sartorial manner, Viner stood out in the Kiev ambience; his fervent admirer, Ester Rosental-Shnayderman, writes that "from a distance of half a mile he reeked with refined, somewhat degenerate haute noblesse (*aristokratizm*).[44] Viner's "reek" of *aristokratizm*, his—in Soviet terms—highly questionable biography, did not escape the notice of his more sharp-toothed indigenous colleagues. Hence the following characterization, written shortly after Viner's arrival in the Soviet Union, by the Soviet Yiddish poet, Ezra Fininberg:

I actually happen to know this very person—he has been living a while now in Kiev: a "Doctor of Philosophy" [Fininberg spells "Doctor of Philosophy" with manifest malicious intent in Hebrew orthography] from Vienna, a magnate's son, with Hebrew works behind him (inter alia—an "anthology" ["anthology" also spelled in Hebrew orthography]) of mediaeval Hebrew poets, it is taught in all Palestinian high-schools). Became a Party member abroad and with us as you know the powers that be seek out "experts" in literature with a flashlight. They are thrilled with this creature: a European! And a Doctor of Philosophy! . . . It is after all a rare gem! Doctor of Philosophy. . . . Who is our Marxist critic! . . . The "Doctor of Philosophy" (in Kiev, he is referred to as the "nothing with silk underpants") must, all the same, make a career for himself—he changed tracks. . . . One thing is clear Comrade Leyvik: the "Viennese Marxist" will soon meet his dismal comeuppance with us.[45]

Small wonder, then, that Viner had reason to be wary in the writing of his memoirs. Such wary perspicacity is well demonstrated in the following passage in which Grandfather Binyomen's thoughts—and note here the novelistic technique—are arraigned by a process of back-projection to the perspectives of Marxist/Leninist teleology:

Grandfather Binyomen contemplated: Where do we learn from the holy books [*sforim*] that the majority of mankind suffers deprivation through other men? Can this be some sort of new punishment from God? In which case, why is there nothing written concerning this in the holy books? Why is this not so much as mentioned? Why do they all hold their silence and feign ignorance? Perhaps the only people to consult in this matter are the younger generation?[46]

If the ideological superimposition upon Grandfather Binyomen's "contemplations" appears forced and out of accord, moreover, with the more authentic and historically believable image of the grandfather that emerges elsewhere in Viner's text, how much the more so the following "special supplementary note" that Viner had in mind to include in the depiction of his grandfather, as cited by Eliezer Podriachik:

For whole nights long in a separate, unfurnished room in his apartment, Grandfather used to immerse himself in various books. Then he even consulted the Communist Manifesto. . . . Grandfather discovered that his own beliefs and socialism were one and the same thing. . . . Grandfather recited *kaddish* for Naftali Botvin [a Jewish communist sentenced to death in Poland for political assassination], lit a *yortsayt* [memorial] candle for him and told stories about him.[47]

Thankfully, as Elias Shulman notes, Viner's right hand prevailed over the left this time and these episodes, which really strain all credibility,

were not included in the body of the manuscript.[48] Indeed, they are contradicted in the manuscript itself: in one passage, also highly suspect and
tendentious, Viner depicts his father's visit to the library of the "Ezra"
organization, seeking some answers to the ethical dilemma of financial
inequity that plagued him. Having asked the bemused librarian whether
he had any volumes on this topic, the following dialogue ensues:

Librarian: "*Zeydenyu* (Granddad), perhaps you mean socialism?" Grandfather
used to hear that word as a curse upon the dissolute youth. "God forbid [*Khas
vesholem*]!" He shook his head and hurried away.[49]

In the above-cited notes concerning Grandfather Binyomen, autobiographical memory thus appears to submit, whether consciously or not
it is impossible to ascertain, to the distorting imperative of ideological
demands.[50]

It is in the most lyrical and passionate passages of Viner's autobiography—those devoted to the friend of his youth, Yoysi Rotenberg, that we
are witness to a counter-movement whereby autobiographical memory
asserts it own claims in face of ideological revisionism. Here, that is,
autobiographical recollection gives rise to a moment of self-revelation
and assertion of self without parallel in the remainder of the text. The
following citation is not, it is true, entirely free of camouflage—the
oppressive forces, for example, or ideological yoke from which Yoysi
points a way of release are primarily represented in terms of enslavement to "divine powers" and the "kingdom of heaven." And the liberation experienced or longed for by Yoyel/Viner is expressed not directly
but vicariously through evocation of his friend from the past. Nonetheless, it is surely difficult not to discern here the *cri de coeur* of one whom,
as had Viner, experienced the humiliation of a forced confession and
recantation of his former works at an open plenum in Kiev in 1932:[51]

It was at that time that Yoyel liberated himself, not so much through inner waver-
ings and doubts as through well-considered and conscious reflections, from all
supernatural conceptions, and he experienced an extraordinary inner freedom.
There sung within him the song of good, healthy youth, but more than this—the
jubilant song of ecstatic liberation arising from the conviction that man is free.
And it was this that so attracted him to this extraordinarily profound and win-
some man, with whom in time he would form so close a relationship. . . .
Through him he experienced the unbounded and captivating joy of free
thought, of liberating oneself from all inane dogmas, a taste of that philosophical freedom, of philosophy as understood by the thinkers of antiquity—the freedom to cast off the yoke of all the miseries that afflict mankind, from the
oppressive yoke of the kingdom of heaven and divine powers. For Yoysi was
imbued with the joy of free thought which no one can so experience as he whose
thought was at one time imprisoned, with that overwhelming philosophical joy,
as experienced by the man who suddenly looks around him and sees that the

shackles of religion are illusory, that man is free to do as he wishes, free, free, and he sings a song of exaltation. Such was the hymn that was sung without respite in Yoysi's spirit.[52]

The next citation concerns the invitations the *Ile* ("genius/prodigy"), Yoysi Rotenberg—whom Viner compares to the archetypal East European Jewish free-thinker and autobiographer in modern times, Solomon Maimon—received to attend rabbinic institutes of higher learning, with a stipend, including an invitation from Menachem Azariah Callimani to study for the rabbinate in Trieste. The autobiographical investment in the following passage scarcely requires elucidating:

It anguished Yoysi that all types of people, whose opinions were most alien to him, consider him suitable to be an ideological servant, to harness him to themselves in order to provide them with intellectual sustenance. And then he decided to take upon himself a resolution, to indicate to them once and for all, that he does not belong to them, in any manner or form.[53]

The word employed for "harness" in the above passage, *ayntsushpanen,* is of particular resonance. It recalls the 1926 journal *In shpan,* whose programmatic manifesto by Dovid Bergelson calling for a wholesale reorientation of Yiddish literature to the USSR and Soviet ideology provoked considerable controversy at the time. Bergelson stated, inter alia, in this manifesto that the "bygone period"—all that occurred before 1917—can no longer serve as material for Yiddish literature.[54] "The aim of this journal," Shmuel Niger writes, "was to *harness* [*ayntsushpanen,* emphasis in original] the Yiddish writers to the Soviet wagon."[55] Viner, who heeded the call of *In shpan* and immigrated to the USSR in the same year this journal appeared, cannot have been unaware of this resonance. Such intellectual "harnessing" appears to have been precisely the experience of Viner in the Institute of Proletarian Jewish Culture in the Ukrainian Academy of Science, as this is depicted in the memoir of his former student, Esther Rosenthal-Shnayderman.[56]

The manner in which Yoysi Rotenberg and his role in shaping the sensibilities of the young Viner are depicted points to a further significant dimension of Viner's autobiographical work. For any reader of the pages devoted to Yoysi who is well versed in Yiddish literature cannot but detect resonance here of the three classic autobiographical works of Abramovitsh, Peretz, and Sholem Aleichem. In Yoysi Rotenberg we may discern a variant upon a figure that, since Abramovitsh, attains almost archetypal status in Yiddish autobiography: the mentor/muse or Goethean "demon," who awakens or reveals in the child or youth the hidden psychic sources that will be the wellspring of his future vocation.

Almost invariably, this mentor/muse is one who stands on the peripheries of traditional Jewish culture or bears some mark of exceptionality: an orphan, eccentric, artisan/artist/musician, heretic, philosopher manqué, rabbi, or *melamed* (a teacher in a Jewish primary school) who gainsays or transcends the negative Haskalah stereotypes of these professions through innate dispositions of mind and heart that refuse, as it were, to be "civilized." These muse/mentor figures frequently share in the retention of certain childlike or "naive" qualities in Schiller's sense of the latter term: the ability to pierce by a sort of X-ray moral vision the elaborate tapestry of disingenuousness and hypocrisy woven around adult morals and manners; above all the capacity for play, whether in the realm of abstract concepts, the free flight of the imagination in the spinning of fantastic tales, music making, or the creation of plastic art. It is thus that Abramovitsh in his *Shloyme reb khayims* depicts these muse/mentor figures as "grown-up children"—"children they were and children they remained."[57] And thus Peretz's depiction in his *Mayne zikhroynes* of Rabbi Moyshe Wahl:

Children were the love of his life. Whenever he appeared in the street or in the study house, he was immediately surrounded by youngsters, and stood barely taller than them, like a slightly older kid. His childlike trembling voice was like a fine silver bell.[58]

The mentor/muse may of course literally be a child, as Abramovitsh's Ben Tsiyon, the son of one of these "grown up children," Hertzl the carpenter.[59] The purest representation of the child muse is the orphan Shmulik in Sholem Aleichem's *Funem yarid*, whose magical tales open the gates to the protagonist Sholem Nokhem Vevik's rich fantasy world.[60]

It is undoubtedly to this gallery of muse/mentor/demons that Viner's Yoysi Rotenberg belongs. Consider, for example, Viner's initial depiction of this half-blind peripatetic young scholar in Hasidic garb, who appears literally to have materialized out of nowhere one fine day on the streets of Krakow:

One fine morning, there began to appear on the streets of the city a young Jewish man from the provinces, whose appearance attracted the attention of all the passers-by and astonished them. It was apparent that he must have been fairly young, scarcely twenty-five years old. He had, however, a long unclipped mousy blond beard—not at all like a Jew. The whites of his eyes were blue, like those of a child, setting off large black pupils. When he met someone whom he was pleased to see or who exercised his curiosity, his eyes would flicker oddly and light up. He went around dressed in normal Hasidic clothing, like all pious Jews in a long cloth jacket, not an ordinary overcoat, mind you, a long cloth jacket fastened at the waist, and a velvet hat. But for all this without *Peyes*, not a trace of them! His long trousers were tucked into white stockings, as worn by rebbes' children. . . . From these almost blind eyes and from his strange, remarkably beautiful face and the grace of his poise, there radiated such an uncommon, joyful, sincere goodness, naive childishness, kindly disposition, warmth and largesse, that every passer-by could not but immediately discern this and, with a mixture of curiosity and wonder ask himself: "What sort of a man is this? Where does such a man come from? And what is he doing here?"[61]

In the above passage we find all of the key characteristics of the mentor/ muse archetype as developed in the Yiddish autobiographical tradition: an obscurity of origin; familiar yet strange (*modne* [strange] is the constantly recurring epithet in Viner's depiction of Yoysi), he escapes categorization within the familiar taxonomy of East European Jewish culture; the muse is possessed of spiritual and/or physical charisma that exerts an almost magical spell upon all who come within its orbit; and finally it is the naive, childlike quality that draws to the muse adult and child alike. Compare Abramovitsh's "Eizik the Blacksmith," whose innate charisma drew people to him "as if by a magnet," his "friendly smiling face" that affected the young Abramovitsh "like the bright sun emerging behind dark clouds."[62] It is Sholem Aleichem's Shmulik the orphan, however, who provides the closest point of comparison to Yoysi Rotenberg. Just as Yoysi's "shining eyes" exert a special spell upon Viner, so for Sholem Aleichem Shmulik's "dreamy eyes"; like Yoysi, Shmulik's eyes are partially turned inward, "moist, as if covered by a shadowy haze."[63] Both works testify to the most noble and affecting aspect of human capacities—friendship. Viner depicts his relationship with Yoysi Rotenberg, as does Sholem Aleichem his with Shmulik, in terms of a first love; for both writers their choosing of so extraordinary a companion confers in turn upon themselves a sign of chosenness. Thus Sholem Aleichem:

Sholem became attached to Shmulik the moment they met. They shared breakfasts and lunches and became bosom friends—literally one body and soul. . . . Shmulik's dreams about treasures, magic stones and other good things are still ensconced in Sholem's heart—perhaps in another form or guise, but he bears them to this day.[64]

And Viner:

It is no wonder that these two men, so different in rearing age and way of life, embraced one another in a deep friendship, that for the older one was more warm, more moderated, for the younger—passionate love, almost inspired romance, with all the happiness that a love can give.[65]

Nor is Viner's continuity with the Yiddish autobiographical tradition to be perceived in his depiction of Yoysi Rotenberg alone. The sections devoted to Grandfather Binyomen read on occasion like a palimpsest beneath which may be detected the silhouettes of paradigmatic representatives of the traditional world—including the old-style maskil—to be found in the autobiographical works of Abramovitsh, Peretz, and Sholem Aleichem. Of especial import in the sections devoted to Grandfather Binyomen and his ambience is the unmistakable affinity in theme, content, and style with Y. L. Peretz's *Mayne zikhroynes* (My memoirs). Even Podriachik, while writing in the Soviet Union where such comparison would scarcely be construed as complimentary, cannot refrain from remarking upon this correspondence: "Grandfather Binyomen, his thoughts and deeds, provide the impression that he had been reared between the covers of Y. L. Peretz's works."[66]

To take but one example, Viner recounts that one of Grandfather Binyomen's neighbors fell sick and required medical attention. Notwithstanding the fact that it was the Sabbath, Grandfather Binyomen hires a *droshke* to alert a doctor. Returning to his neighbor's house with the doctor he himself helps prepare a fire in the stove which "for him was a far greater act of heroism than risking his life in saving a drowning man."[67] He settles accounts with the coachman not with money but with a silver tobacco box. As expiation for transgressing the Sabbath prohibition on labor, he subsequently "fasts eighteen fasts." Whether this is *Dichtung* or *Wahrheit*, the parallels with Peretz's most famous neo-Hasidic fable, "If Not Higher," wherein is recounted the Nemirover Rebbe's sneaking off incognito at the time of the penitential prayers in order to kindle the stove of a poor Jewish widow, leap to the eye.[68] Viner's indebtedness to Peretz in the framing of his autobiographical work is remarkable in that Peretz, of all the classic writers in Yiddish literature, was accorded the most problematic reception in the Soviet Union. If considerable dialectic ingenuity was required on the part of Soviet Yiddish literary critics in the provision of apologies for Peretz's earlier, more radical socialist-realist works, Soviet Yiddish literary criticism in general held up its hands in despair when confronted with the later "decadent" and "reactionary" period of his writings to which the autobiography belongs.[69] The general consensus of Soviet Yiddish literary criticism was that the late 1890s to Peretz's death in 1915 marked a period of progressive—or rather regressive—decline. Such decline was manifest, according to this scheme of things, in Peretz's petit-bourgeois and ideologically retrograde nostalgia for the pre-revolutionary Jewish past; in terms of his poetics, this decline was reflected in a flight from realism to symbolism, decadence, neo-Romanticism, mysticism. Viner himself was well representative of this tide of Peretz criticism when he declared the sources of Peretz's Hasidic and folkloristic stories: "Dusty old cobwebs with long-deceased spiders, a reservoir of perennial enslavement."[70] These lines were published in *Shtern* in 1935 at the same time that, as Dalia Kaufman points out, Viner must have been considering, if not in the actual process of writing, his thoroughly Peretz-inspired autobiographical work,[71] whose sources could equally be described by a hostile critic as "dusty old cobwebs." What, after all, from such a hostile perspective, could be more "dusty" and "cobwebby" than Viner's sympathetic and affectionate portraits of Grandfather Binyomen's best friends? Take, for example, Viner's depiction of one of these, the traditionalist maskil, rabbinic genealogist, and historian of Jewish Krakow, Fayvl Hirsh Vetshteyn:

The second friend was called F. H. Vetshteyn. He already had a misnagdic, maskil-type appearance. Dressed in a long overcoat, not, mind you, a long jacket, and a top hat. His grey beard was immaculately combed and even very slightly trimmed. This man was a well-known historian of the city of Krakow, and of course of the Jews in Poland. . . . He was a second-hand bookseller in the Hospital Street . . . where the whole road was full of second-hand bookstores and there he had in the fore-gallery to a house his bookstore. He would sit there in a Yarmulke, and students, regular customers and scholars, Jesuits, would rummage in the mountains of books that were strewn around there. Since he was a leading expert in the history of Poland and well versed in Latin documentary material, researchers would come not infrequently to his store with requests that he decipher for them some knotty passage in a historical document.[72]

Nor can Viner have been unaware of his colleague Nokhem Oyslender's article, published in a previous edition of *Shtern* in the same year as his own, that singles out Peretz's *Mayne zikhroynes* for especial obloquy for its nostalgic, idealized, and highly selective "rehabilitation" of the Jewish past.[73] It is a supreme irony that the Yiddish literary critic who, perhaps more than any other, reflected in his scholarly writings the treacherous crosswinds of Soviet literary ideology should have added a link to the Peretzian "Golden Chain," precisely at the point where this "chain" severed its links most decisively with the ideological demands of éngagé Jewish literary criticism of all stripes.

Composed in circumstances that could scarcely be less propitious for the writing of an autobiography, Meir Viner's hidden manuscript testifies to the insistence with which the autobiographical impulse demanded expression on the part of a leading Jewish intellectual of his time and place. No less significant than the will to autobiographical expression is the literary form this expression assumes. For in casting the experience of his early years within the framework of received paradigms offered him by previous Yiddish autobiographers, Viner demonstrates the degree to which autonomous and indigenous conventions for the patterning of the life history had become embedded in Yiddish literary discourse. Viner's right hand continued and enriched the most distinctively Yiddish autobiographical tradition that his left hand would assign to the trashcan of history. The following stanzas of the Soviet Yiddish poet Dovid Hofshteyn capture this tragic dichotomy:

It is difficult to forget the sharp times past
That have incised themselves deep in my flesh
Hearing the call from the depths
Preserve yourselves, endure! . . .
Not easy to forget the sharp times past
Not easy not to repay love with love.[74]

Notes

This chapter is an expanded and slightly altered version of the section on Meir Viner in my book *Being for Myself Alone: Origins of Jewish Autobiography* (Stanford, 2006).

1. Eliezer Podriachik, "Genize-shafungen in der yidish-sovetisher literatur," in *In profil fun tsaytn* (Tel Aviv, 1978), 99–100.

2. Chone Shmeruk, "Yiddish Literature in the USSR," in *The Jews in Soviet Russia since 1917*, ed. Lionel Kochan (Oxford, 1970), 247–48.

3. Podriachik, "Genize-shafungen," 100–101.

4. Insofar as "autobiography" was condoned by the Bolsheviks, it constituted a terrifying travesty of the genre; yoked to a pre-imposed Communist eschatology and widely employed in the assessing of the validity of applications for Party membership, Communist "autobiographies" functioned essentially as inquisitional documents and, as Igal Halfin writes, "a daily means of control of the self." See Igal Halfin, *Terror in My Soul: Communist Autobiographies on Trial* (Cambridge, Mass., 2003), 19 and index under "Autobiographies."

5. See Jochen Hellbeck, "Stalin-Era Autobiographical Texts," in *Stalinism: The Essential Readings*, ed. David L. Hoffman (Oxford, 2003), 188. Thus Hellbeck cites the prospective title of the autobiographical novel that "Stepan Podlyubni, the son of a kulak who lived in Moscow and tried to become a New Soviet Man," hoped to write: *The Life of an Outlived Class, Its Spiritual Rebirth and Adaptation to New Conditions*. See Hellbeck, "Stalin-Era Autobiographical Texts," 202.

6. As cited by Shmeruk, "Yiddish Literature," 249.

7. Moyshe Litvakov, *In umru*, 2 vols. (Kiev, 1919; Moscow, 1926), 2:194; cf. Halfin, *Terror in My Soul*, 59–60.

8. Halfin, *Terror in My Soul*, 96.

9. Meir Viner, "Folklorizm un folkloristik: etlekhe forhanokhes tsu metodologie fun folkloristik," in *Problemen fun folkloristik*, ed. M. Viner (Kharkov, 1932), 83–84.

10. G. Sheinin, "A yidishistisher kolboy," in *Fashizirter yidishizm un zayn visnshaft* (Minsk, 1930), 114.

11. As cited by Elias Shulman in his essay "Meir Viner (1893–1941)," included in his *Portretn un etyudn* (New York, 1979), 87.

12. Viner, *Tsu der geshikhte*, 2:160–61, 247–48.

13. Ibid., 1:208–14.

14. Ibid., 2:235.

15. As cited by E. Shulman, "Meir Viner," 75.

16. Osip Mandelstam, "Fourth Prose," in *The Noise of Time: The Prose of Osip Mandelstam*, trans. with critical essays by Clarence Brown (San Francisco, 1986), 181.

17. Podriachik, "Vegn meir viners avtobiografish verk," in *Sovyetish heymland*,

no. 9 (Moscow, September 1969), 84. The first part of this introduction to the text is written by Podriachik, the second by the co-editor of the text, Moyni Shulman.

18. M. Viner, "Der zeyde Binyomen," *Sovyetish heymland*, no. 9 (Moscow, September 1969); "Yugnt-fraynt," *Sovyetish heymland*, no. 10 (Moscow, October 1969). Even at a remove of some thirty-five years from the writing of the manuscript and its publication, several passages in the manuscript were deemed too ideologically deviant to appear in *Sovyetish heymland*. Podriachik, in an essay written once he had settled in Israel but with the manuscript no longer in his hands, reconstructs from memory one of these passages, in which Viner betrays an overly sympathetic stance toward Zionism. See his "Genize shafungen," 110–11. A section of the autobiography depicting Viner's years in Vienna when he was in his twenties has never been published. See Podriachik, "Vegn meir viners literarisher yerushe," *Sovyetish heymland*, no. 10 (Moscow, October 1969), 10. Only after completing this chapter did I discover that the autograph of Viner's autobiographical text has indeed survived and was brought to Israel by his daughter and donated to the Hebrew University of Jerusalem in the early 1970s. I have not yet had a chance to read this manuscript. See the introduction to a section of the "Grandfather Binyomen" narrative translated—in highly truncated form—into Hebrew by Emanuel Melzer in *Kroka-kaz'imyez-krakov: Mehqarim betoldot yehudei krakov*, ed. Elhanan Reiner (Tel Aviv, 2001), 354.

19. Podriachik, "Genize shafungen," 110.

20. Shmeruk, "Yiddish Literature," 247–48.

21. See Mordechai Altshuler, ed., *Briv fun yidishe sovetishe shraybers* (Jerusalem, 1979), 217–18.

22. On this much disputed text, see Yehoshua A. Gilboa, *The Black Years of Soviet Jewry (1939–1953)* (Boston, 1971), 112–15. Particularly valuable is the assessment of Nakhman Mayzel, since it was he who initially played an important role in encouraging his close friend Bergelson to write autobiographically. Mayzel notes that Bergelson's bitterly sarcastic depiction of his family in this work was the result of ideological superimposition and did not at all correspond to the author's true emotions. See his "Dovid bergelson un der nister" in his *Dos yidishe shafn un der yiddisher shrayber in sovyetnfarband* (New York, 1959), 181–83.

23. Moyni Shulman makes note of this alternation of persona in his section of "Vegn meir viners avtobiografish verk," 85. Interestingly, in the section of the Grandfather Binyomen narrative Viner entitled "Grandfather's Friends," Viner strikes out, in the opening of the first paragraph, the phrase "I shall now relate of them." At the end of this paragraph, however, this first person reemerges: "Now I shall relate who these three friends were." See the page of the autograph as reproduced in Reiner, *Kroka-kaz'imyez-krakov*, 356.

24. Reiner, *Kroka-kaz'imyez-krakov*.

25. Viner, "Der zeyde Binyomen," 111.

26. Mandelstam, "Fourth Prose," 162. For an invaluable decoding of this text see Clarence Brown's introduction, 37–55.

27. In general on the problem of autobiography in the third person see Lejeune, "Autobiography in the Third Person," in *On Autobiography*, ed. and with a foreword by Paul John Eakin, trans. Katherine Leary (Minneapolis, 1989), 31–52.

28. Podriachik, "Vegn meir viners avtobiografish verk," 83.

29. M. Shulman, ibid., 85.

30. Viner, "Der zeyde Binyomen," 107–14.

31. For Viner as historical novelist, see E. Shulman, "Meir Viner"; E. Podria-chik, "Shaynendike shpliters," in his *In profil*, 153–64.

32. Evgeny Dobrenko, "(Auto/Bio/Hagio)graphy: or, Life as Genre: Alesha Peskov—Maksim Gorky—Mark Donskoi," in *a/b: Auto/Biography Studies* 11, no. 2 (Fall 1996): 48.

33. Hellbeck, "Stalin-Era Autobiographical Texts," 206.

34. On the exceptionally close relationship between grandfather and grand-son, see the memoirs of Viner's sister, F. F. Gross, written in 1968: "Mayn bruder Meir Viner," in *Pinkes far der forshung fun der yiddisher literatur un prese*, ed. Hayyim Bez (New York, 1972), 2:158–59.

35. Gilboa, *The Black Years of Soviet Jewry*, 175–76.

36. See Esther Rosental-Shnayderman, *Af vegn un umvegn: Zikroynes, geshee-nishn, perzenlikhkaytn* (Tel Aviv, 1978), 2:192–93, 203–4.

37. Ibid., 234–36, 283.

38. Ibid., 283.

39. For the tensions occasioned between Viner and his father on account of his Zionist leanings see Gross, "Meyn bruder Meir Viner," 552.

40. It was von Hoffmansthal whose recommendation to the rector of the Uni-versity of Basel facilitated Viner's acceptance as a student to the faculty of philos-ophy. F. F. Gross reports that on a visit to Jerusalem, Dov Sadan, whose Jewish genealogical knowledge was formidable, informed her that she and Meir were related to von Hoffmansthal through their mother's family, the Landaus, to which "Grandfather Binyomen" belonged. See Gross, "Meyn bruder Meir Viner," 551.

41. For details of these publications, and for Viner's publications in Buber's periodical *Der Jude*, see Shulman, "Meir Viner," 63–67.

42. The significance of this anthology, *Mivhar hashirah ha'ivrit lemiyom hatum kitvei haqodesh 'ad galut yisra'el me'al admat sefarad* (Leipzig, 1922), is attested to by the fact that it was republished, albeit in somewhat abridged form, in 1963 in Israel. Viner's last preserved letter to Brody, written in Hebrew, concerning the second volume of the anthology was written in August/September 1926, two months before Viner's departure to the Soviet Union. For the publication of Viner's correspondence with Brody and an introduction see Dov Sadan, "Der krokever ile," in *Di goldene keyt*, no. 109 (Tel Aviv, 1982), 138–62.

43. A fascinating exercise in "parallel lives" would be to compare the intel-lectual trajectory of Viner with that of the no less maverick soi-disant Marxist, Walter Benjamin. The two provide a sort of mirror image of each other. Benja-min, too, at an early stage in his career had been singled out as a budding talent by von Hoffmansthal. The two moved in the same intellectual circles and were acquainted with each other, both living in Paris, in 1926. Both traveled to the Soviet Union in that year; while Viner made the leap to Yiddish and Commu-nism, Benjamin recoiled, not without due consideration, both from allegiance to the Party and Jewish linguistic commitment. For Benjamin's encounters with Viner in Paris, see his letter of 29 May 1926 to Gershom Scholem in *The Corre-spondence of Walter Benjamin 1910–1940*, ed. Gershom Scholem and Theodor W. Adorno, trans. Manfred R. Jacobson and Evelyn M. Jacobson (Chicago and Lon-don, 1903), 303. For Benjamin's wavering with regard to pledging his allegiance to the Communist Party see also Benjamin, *Moscow Diary*, ed. Gary Smith, trans. Richard Sieburth (Cambridge, Mass., and London, 1986).

44. Rosental-Shnayderman, *Af vegn un umvegn*, 2:215.

45. As cited from a letter of 14 October 1927 from Fininberg to Leyvik, in

Briv fun sovetishe shraybers. The dangers encountered at the Kiev Institute by Jewish scholars of "alien" class background, especially emigrants whose "digressions" included membership in Jewish nationalist organizations—Bundist or Zionist—prior to their "conversion" to Bolshevism, were considerable; these scholars were especially vulnerable to attacks from within from "insiders," colleagues of equally dubious proletarian status, who may at one time have espoused Jewish nationalist ideologies, and who wished to deflect attention from themselves. See Rosental-Shnayderman, *Af vegn un umvegn* (Tel Aviv, 1982), 3:44–58. Viner's past, I would venture, was more perilous by far than that of any of his colleagues in Kiev. That he survived the various "cleansings" to which this institute was subject is very strange.

46. Viner, "Der zeyde Binyomen," 103.

47. Podriachik, "Vegn meir viners avtobiografish verk," 83.

48. Shulman, "Meir Viner," 101.

49. Viner, "Der zeyde Binyomen," 105.

50. Much of what Nadezhda Mandelshtam writes on this topic is highly germane in the present context. See the chapter "Memory" in her *Hope Abandoned,* trans. Max Hayward (Harmondsworth, 1976), 178–91.

51. E. Shulman, "Meir Viner," 104ff.

52. Viner, "Yugnt-fraynt," 111–12.

53. Ibid., 115.

54. See Niger, *Geklibene shriftn,* 3 vols. (New York, 1928), 1:157.

55. Ibid., 156. See also Niger's open letter to Bergelson, responding to this manifesto in ibid., 121–29.

56. Esther Rosental-Shnayderman, *Af vegn un umvegn* (Tel Aviv, 1978), 2:191–242, passim.

57. Abramovitsh, *Of Bygone Days,* 330, 336. I am using here Raymond P. Sheindlin's translation of Abramovitsh's Hebrew translation of his *Shloyme reb khayims* that he (Abramovitsch) entitled *Bayamim hahem* (Of bygone days), included in *A Shtetl and Other Yiddish Novellas,* ed. Ruth Wisse (New York, 1973).

58. Peretz, *My Memoirs,* trans. Seymour Levitan, in *The I. L. Peretz Reader,* ed. and with an introduction by Ruth Wisse (New York, 1990), 323.

59. Abramovitsh, *Of Bygone Days,* 338–39.

60. David G. Roskies, *A Bridge of Longing: The Lost Art of Yiddish Storytelling* (Cambridge, Mass., 1995), 188–90.

61. Viner, "Yugnt-fraynt," 109.

62. Abramomitsh, *Of Bygone Days,* 329, 330.

63. Sholem Aleichem, *From the Fair: The Autobiography of Sholem Aleichem,* trans., ed., and with an introduction by Curt Leviant (New York, 1985), 10. Here I have modified slightly the fine translation of Leviant, substituting his "slight film" with "shadowy haze"—in the original *"Din roykhl."*

64. Ibid., 9, 13.

65. Viner, "Yugnt-fraynt," 112.

66. Podriachik, "Vegn meir viners avtobiografish verk," 83.

67. Viner, "Der zeyde Binyomen," 97.

68. Peretz, "If Not Higher," trans. Marie Syrkin, in *The I. L. Peretz Reader,* 178–81.

69. For a fine survey of Soviet literary-critical reception of Peretz, see Dalia Kaufman, "Y. L. Peretz in der yidish sovyetisher kritik (1925–1948) un di problem fun der literarisher yerushe," in *Di goldene keyt,* no. 77 (Tel Aviv, 1972), 145–59.

70. As cited in ibid., 153.

71. Ibid.

72. Viner, "Der zeyde Binyomen," 94.

73. N. Oyslender, "Y. L. peretses 'mayne zikhroynes': Tsu der kharakteristik fun letstn period fun peretses shafn," in *Shtern*, no. 2 (Minsk, 1935), 66–79.

74. Dovid Hofshteyn, *Lider un poemes*, 2 vols. (Tel Aviv, 1977), 1:210.

Chapter 11

The Shtetl Subjunctive: Yaffa Eliach's Living History Museum

JEFFREY SHANDLER

The shtetl emerged as a quintessential symbolic locus of Jewish experience once Jews began leaving it.[1] They did so both ideologically—when the Haskalah (Jewish Enlightenment) reached Eastern Europe at the turn of the nineteenth century—and, increasingly, geographically, through internal migration within the Russian and Habsburg empires toward major cities and external migration on a global scale. Over the course of the 1800s, Jews took stock of these journeys away from the shtetl primarily in narrative form, in works of belles lettres, autobiography, and journalism, as well as private correspondence.[2] By the final decades of the nineteenth century, the shtetl figured as the point of common departure for the millions of Eastern Europe's Jews caught up in what Benjamin Harshav terms the "centrifugal trend" of the "modern Jewish revolution."[3]

Subsequently, the shtetl became a prime locus of return—especially in the wake of World War I, which East European Jews widely perceived as an unprecedented watershed. Following prewar literary precedents, the manifold changes in Jewish life wrought by the war and its immediate aftermath were readily mapped onto the shtetl, which demonstrated on a small scale the vast social, political, and cultural disruptions experienced by millions of Jews. At the same time, the interwar years witnessed abrupt shifts in representation of the shtetl with regard to form, content, and agenda.

Symbolic return to the shtetl entailed a number of new cultural practices undertaken in situ as well as a hemisphere away. Ethnographies of shtetl customs and lore were researched by the occasional individual (e.g., Hirsz Abramowicz) and by scholarly institutions (notably the YIVO Institute in Poland, as well as academic centers in Soviet Russia such as the Institut far Vaysrusisher Kultur, which exhorted amateur ethnogra-

phers in 1926: "*Forsht ayer shtetl!*").⁴ Shtetl scenes and types became popular subjects of professional Jewish photographers, notably the work of
Alter Kacyzne, who supplied the rotogravure section of the *Jewish Daily
Forward* with images of Jewish life in Poland during the 1920s.⁵ The
shtetl, actual or fictitious, became a frequent setting for works of Yiddish
theater and film staged in Eastern Europe and the Americas (where
shtetl life was occasionally re-created before the camera on rural lots in
New Jersey or Long Island).⁶ A series of American Yiddish theater songs
revisited the shtetl, sometimes evoking a particular town (most famously,
Jacob Jacobs and Alexander Olshanetsky's 1932 composition "Mayn
shtetele Belts," which spawned several variants, such as "Mayn shtetele
Molif" and "Mayn shtetele Yash"), other times dwelling on the affect of
nostalgia generally (e.g., "A grus fun der alter heym," "Ikh benk un
gedenk nokh mayn heym").⁷

These works of American Yiddish popular culture reflected a signal
shift in immigrant Jews' relationship to their East European hometowns
in the wake of the war's disruption of the steady flow of new arrivals,
followed by restrictive anti-immigrant legislation passed by the U.S. Congress in the early 1920s.⁸ Throughout the period of mass immigration
that had begun in the 1880s, East European Jewish settlers in America
had maintained ties to their hometowns through settlement patterns in
urban enclaves and informal networks, as well as by means of such institutions as the *landsmanshaft* (hometown benevolent association) and
anshey (hometown congregation).⁹ After World War I this relationship
to the Old World grew more attenuated and relied increasingly on childhood memories of prewar experiences. Organized American Jewry also
reoriented its attention to Eastern Europe, centered on providing economic relief to Jewish communities overseas in the wake of the war's
upheavals.¹⁰

For some American Jews, returning to the shtetl in the interwar years
entailed actual as well as symbolic journeys. Jewish immigrants made
trips back to their native towns during the 1920s and 1930s for a variety
of reasons, frequently documenting their travels in written or photographic records.¹¹ In interbellum Poland a shtetl could even became a
tourist site; American Yiddish writer Yankev Glatshteyn noted, on a
return visit to his native Poland in the mid-1930s, that Kazimierz nad
Wisłą seemed like a resort town in the Catskills, filled with vacationers
visiting its picturesque ruins and artists flocking to paint its scenic
views.¹² While many interwar representations of shtetl life were motivated by a sentimental longing for one's past or a communal commitment to preserving East European Jewish heritage, other works,
especially those created during or shortly after World War I, grapple
with the shtetl's breakdown. Powerfully expressionist works such as

Moyshe-Leyb Halpern's poem "A nakht" and Issachar Ryback's album of lithographs *Shtetl: Mayn khorever heym, a gedekhenish* portray the shtetl as a locus of upheaval and destruction.[13]

By the eve of World War II, East European Jewry (including its extensive international network of immigrants) had evolved a complex of practices of shtetl remembrance, linked by a range of symbolic investments in the shtetl as an epitomizing site of a way of life from which Jews were at an ever greater temporal, geographic, and cultural remove—even as millions of Jews still lived in these small towns. As a locus of memory, the shtetl had increasingly become a chronotope—that is, a place understood in terms of its association with time. The shtetl represented a crepuscular culture and, moreover, that culture's dissolution itself. (This can be seen, for example, in playwright and journalist Chone Gottesfeld's memoir of a trip back to his native town of Skała, in southeastern Galicia, in the mid-1930s. Contemplating the face of a man who had been, in Gottesfeld's youth, the town's Lothario—and was now "fierce looking . . . with an enormous beard [who] looked as though he had just stepped out of the jungle"—the author speculates: "Had I remained in Skała . . . I, too, might have looked so wretched and senile.")[14]

The Holocaust provoked a new wave of recalling the shtetl that drew upon this foundation of remembrance, expanding as well as transforming it. No longer a place Jews left behind, whether voluntarily or otherwise, the shtetl was now a communal locus abruptly appropriated from Jewish experience and brutally annihilated. An "eleventh-hour" topos, seemingly on the verge of disappearing for decades, the shtetl's final hour had, apparently, finally struck.

The most extensive of memorial efforts undertaken in the immediate aftermath of World War II are hundreds of *yisker-bikher* (memorial books), which combined remembrance of local shtetl history, personalities, mores, and lore with collective grieving over the destruction of lives and of a way of life. Although they are, as anthropologists Jack Kugelmass and Jonathan Boyarin have noted, inspired at least in part by "the long tradition of Jewish mourning literature," *yisker-bikher* are also very much a response to a particular crisis in remembrance of a specific time and place.[15] They are internal, retrospective works of memory; typically written largely in Yiddish and published by subscription, they were intended for a very limited, intimate audience comprising the books' creators and their acquaintances. In addition to lamenting the demise of particular Jewish communities, these volumes mourn, if implicitly, the loss of personal knowledge of each shtetl as an idiosyncratic, enduring site of Jewish communal life.

In the decades since the end of the Holocaust, the attention of shtetl remembrance has moved beyond its former residents, living or dead, and toward those with no direct experience of shtetl life. This dynamic has inspired new, diverging trends in the practice of memory: On one hand, there has been a greater interest in the physical shtetl, as manifest in the publication and display of prewar shtetl photography, the restoration shtetl architecture (for example, plans currently underway to re-create one of Poland's prewar wooden synagogues, originally erected in Zabłudów, on the grounds of a folk architecture museum in Białystok), and its invocation in postwar building projects (exemplified by the head-quarters of the National Yiddish Book Center in Amherst, Massachu-setts, completed in 1997).[16] On the other hand, post-Holocaust memory projects undertaken for those lacking a direct acquaintance with shtetl life have conceptualized it in highly generalized, abstracted terms, as a pre-modern, comprehensive cultural system. The localized remem-brance of an individual shtetl, exemplified by *yisker-bikher*, has given way to representations in works of fiction, memoir, theater, and what Bar-bara Kirshenblatt-Gimblett terms "popular ethnography." Epitomized by the 1952 study *Life Is with People: The Jewish Little-Town in Eastern Europe*, these efforts represent shtetl life generically as a "timeless" and "hermetic world," dematerialized as a "state of mind."[17]

* * *

As a consequence of these most recent developments in its considerable history of remembrance, the shtetl now demands restoration as a totaliz-ing experience in order to be recalled fully. This is borne out by a grow-ing variety of contemporary memory practices—including tourism, exhibition, music, and theater—that strive toward a restoration of the shtetl by means of performance.[18] Without a doubt, the most elaborate of such efforts is the Shtetl Museum; currently under construction, it is the latest of a series of projects initiated by Yaffa Eliach to commemorate her hometown of Eishyshok.[19] A Jewish Holocaust survivor who became a pioneering figure in Holocaust studies in the United States, Eliach has undertaken more projects, and on a grander scale, to recall prewar Jew-ish life in her native shtetl than any other individual. Her efforts include a massive photo collection, installed in a monumental display in the United States Holocaust Memorial Museum (USHMM) in Washington, D.C.; an eight-hundred-page book that chronicles Eishyshok's Jewish community from the eleventh century to World War II; and participa-tion in an audio documentary for Israeli radio and a documentary film for American public television.[20] These efforts culminate in the Shtetl Museum, described on its promotional web site as "an open-air Museum of East-European Jewish history and culture in the form of a life-size Shtetl."[21] More than a culmination of her singular career, Eliach's latest project makes for a provocative case study of shtetl remembrance. Although it is, as of this writing, years from completion, the Shtetl

Museum already proves an especially rich example of how East European Jewish life of the pre-Holocaust era informs the thinking and practice of contemporary Jewry, serving as a cultural resource that enhances
present sensibilities and, at the same time, as a touchstone against which
these can be evaluated.

Yaffa Eliach (née Sonensen) was a four-year-old resident of Eishyshok
when, on 25 and 26 September 1941, all but twenty-nine of the town's
thirty-five hundred Jews were shot and buried in mass graves by a German mobile killing squad and its Lithuanian collaborators. She and her
immediate family managed to escape this fate; while most of them survived the war in hiding, some were murdered shortly after their liberation in 1944. Two years later, she and an uncle made their way to
Palestine. Yaffa lived in Israel until her marriage to David Eliach in 1953,
when they moved to New York. There she earned a doctorate in Russian
history from City University of New York, writing her dissertation on the
interrelation between the origins of Hasidism and sectarianism among
Russian Orthodox Christians during the eighteenth century.[22]

At the same time, she became involved in the documentation and
teaching of Holocaust history as this topic was beginning to attract significant attention in both the academy and the American Jewish community. Eliach joined the faculty of Brooklyn College in 1969, where she
was a professor of history and literature in the Department of Judaic
Studies until her retirement in 2003. Her research efforts included collecting Hasidic lore related to the Holocaust, the subject of an anthology
she compiled, published in 1982.[23] Eliach was also involved in Holocaust
education for high school students at the Yeshiva of Flatbush, where her
husband served as principal. In 1972 she established the first research
center in the United States specifically devoted to the study of the Holocaust. The Center for Holocaust Studies Documentation and Research
was based at Brooklyn College until it merged with New York's Museum
of Jewish Heritage in 1991 (Eliach also served on the task force and
memorial commission involved in the creation of this museum).[24]

In 1978 Eliach was invited to join President Carter's Commission on
the Holocaust, which was convened to address the question of creating
an American national memorial to the Holocaust; it was this commission's recommendation that initiated the planning and construction of
the USHMM.[25] While serving on the commission, Eliach reports, she felt
compelled to redirect her efforts at memorializing Jewish victims of
Nazism, inspired by her personal remembrance of the Jewish community in her childhood hometown.[26] In multiple accounts, Eliach has
explained that she experienced an epiphany in August 1979 while flying
across Eastern Europe, where she and other commission members were

touring sites associated with the genocide of European Jewry during World War II. She realized that the airplane was passing over Eishyshok:

During my travels I had been struck by the fact that, insofar as the world knew anything about the Jews of Eastern Europe, it knew them as skeletal concentration camp survivors and huge piles of corpses. . . . What kind of memorial could possibly transcend those images of death and do justice to the full, rich lives those people had lived, I wondered. . . .

[A]s I flew over my former home, . . . remembering what I could of the colorful, intricately detailed tapestry of my own family life before that tapestry was so brutally shredded, I suddenly saw that there was a possible answer, and that I might be able to play a role in providing it. With great clarity my mission began to unfold before me: Regardless of what kind of memorial my distinguished colleagues recommended to the president, I decided, I would set out on a path of my own, to create a memorial to life, not to death. Rather than focusing on the forces of destruction as most memorials do, mine would be an attempt at reconstruction.[27]

This revelatory moment—provocatively juxtaposing geographic proximity against temporal and cultural remove—prompted Eliach's first memorial project, an extensive effort to gather photographs of every Jew who had been a resident of Eishyshok on the eve of World War II. Reproductions of some fifteen hundred of these images were eventually selected to be displayed in the USHMM's Tower of Faces.[28] Eliach characterizes the collection as representing Jewish Eishyshok as a self-contained, organic entity that is exemplary yet intimate, describing it as "a typical community . . . a microcosm of life."[29] Within the schema of the museum, the installation of her collection of photographs constitutes "the most important exhibition segment aimed at humanizing the image of the victim," according to Jeshajahu Weinberg, who served as director of the USHMM during its planning phase.[30]

Over the ensuing years, recovering the memory of Jewish life in prewar Eishyshok—a time and place Eliach directly remembers only as a very young girl—has grown beyond a mission that she defines and experiences in personal terms. Eliach describes life in her family home today as a virtual immersion in Eishyshok: "The rooms of our house are filled with photos, documents, books, and memorabilia from Eishyshok, and even the food on our table has sometimes come from Eishyshok, or, to be more precise, from old Eishyshkian recipes that were given to me during my interviews."[31]

At the same time that they are rooted in Eliach's personal ties to a specific place, her memorial projects have grown increasingly paradigmatic. Eliach conceptualizes the remembrance of her native shtetl as having larger implications for Jews generally and even for the world at large. In explaining the rationale for her projects, she asserts the importance of remembering prewar East European Jewish life as an imperative for Jewish continuity. Moreover, she positions her hometown not only as "the very paradigm of the . . . shtetl" but as "a veritable microcosm of Western civilization, and beyond that of the entire family of human-kind," asserting in her book *There Once Was a World* that "there is hardly any major trend in the last nine hundred years of history that did not manifest itself in Eishyshok."[32] As the volume's title indicates, Eliach envisions this "chronicle of the shtetl of Eishyshok" as extending well beyond the conventional scope of local history. *There Once Was a World* integrates her personal story and family history with that of her home-town and situates these narratives within a survey of East European Jew-ish history from the Middle Ages through the Holocaust. Her book also offers a schematic overview of East European Jewish mores (religious life, economy, family life, seasonal holidays, life-cycle events), thereby synthesizing the divergent approaches of the autobiography, the *yisker-bukh*, and *Life Is with People*.

As Eliach has expanded the significance of remembering her home-town, she has also extended the scope of her memory projects, striving toward more complete restoration of pre-Holocaust Eishyshok. In the late 1990s she worked with filmmaker Jeff Bieber on a ninety-minute documentary, *There Once Was a Town*, which follows Eliach and several other Jews who were prewar residents of Eishyshok, as well as members of their families, back to the town. As a memory project, this film com-plements the Tower of Faces. Whereas the photo installation displays the Jews of Eishyshok but not their town, the documentary presents the town but without its Jews. With the Shtetl Museum, which began construction in June 2003 and is scheduled to be completed in 2010, Eliach strives to provide both the town and its Jews in a comprehensive restoration.[33]

Situated on sixty-seven acres in Rishon le-Tsiyon, Israel's fourth-largest city, on land that was at one time intended for a golf course, the Shtetl Museum will, upon completion, comprise a complex of forty buildings, including synagogues, Jewish schools, and private homes.[34] There will also be a Jewish cemetery, a public bath with a *mikvah* (ritual bath), a marketplace lined with shops, and a castle. These structures will be surrounded by a re-creation of the forest and river of Eishyshok. The Shtetl Museum will be inhabited by some four hundred actors imperson-ating the town's prewar residents: rabbis, teachers, merchants, crafts-men, and so on.

The model for this project is the living history museum, epitomized by Colonial Williamsburg in Virginia, which Eliach mentions repeatedly as her paradigm. Other examples include such sites as Plimoth Planta-tion in Massachusetts, Black Creek Pioneer Village in Toronto, and the Famine Theme Park, opened on Knockfierna Hill in west Limerick, Ireland, in the 1990s to commemorate the one-hundred-and-fiftieth anniversary of the Irish potato famine (where, according to promotional literature, " 'it will be possible . . . to experience first hand in this remote area how 1,000 people struggled for survival at the height of the Famine' ").[35] Living history museums are especially complex and provocative works of public culture. Combining elements of the theater, the museum, the lecture hall, the archeological site, the amusement park, and the historical monument, they are, according to Kirshenblatt-Gimblett, "extraordinary experiment[s] in virtuality." While their promise to visitors of complete immersion in the past is unattainable, experiencing the past's elusiveness, the often jarring "intercalation of quotidians (theirs and ours), and the breaking of [contextual] frames," defines, rather than negates, the experience.[36]

Nevertheless, for some the very notion of recalling the shtetl in the form of a living history museum provokes incredulity: "Amerikanischer Kitsch à la Hollywood?" wonders Juri Ginsburg in the *Berliner Zeitung*; "Can a Disneyfied shtetl accurately portray the complex realities of that vanished world?" asks a reporter for the English-language edition of *The Forward*.[37] Indeed, the very notion of such a project can be a byword of maudlin tastelessness. In his unfavorable review of the 2004 Broadway revival of *Fiddler on the Roof*, critic Ben Brantley sniped, "Should the entertainment entrepreneurs of Branson, Mo., ever come up with a pavilion called Shtetl Land, this is what it would be like."[38]

To be sure, realizing the Shtetl Museum's goal of restoring a lost way of life poses challenges that cannot be completely resolved; however, these should be regarded not as flaws in the project but as points of departure for further inquiry. Rather than judging the Shtetl Museum against the actuality of prewar shtetl life, it is more illuminating to consider how the project engages these disparities. It is precisely at these sites of slippage that the Shtetl Museum becomes most interesting, for these reveal its significance as a project of memory culture for Jews at the turn of the twenty-first century, as an effort to negotiate the relationship between the rememberer and the remembered in an especially elaborate, complex form.

As is true of museums generally, the Shtetl Museum is metonymic in nature, relying on fragments to stand in for larger entities.[39] Even though the fragment here is ostensibly an entire town, the Shtetl Museum is, inevitably, a delimited re-creation, and its boundaries—the points at which its representation of the shtetl ends and something else begins—define the project as much as do its contents. These boundaries also reveal the slippage between "here" and "there," "past" and "present," and "us" and "them" most compellingly.

First, consider the geographic boundaries of the site being restored at the Shtetl Museum. Press accounts, as well as Eliach herself, usually characterize it as a re-creation of her hometown. Some elements of the plan, such as the yeshiva Kibbutz Ha-Prushim, are modeled specifically on institutions and other phenomena once found in Eishyshok. However, one of the Shtetl Museum's synagogues is based on a building from the nearby town of Olkenik (hailed for its beauty, according to local lore, by none less than Napoleon),[40] while the castle in the middle of the town is inspired by "the ancient fortified Castle of Trakai, which was typical of four medieval castles of the area." In this respect, the Shtetl Museum's plan resembles synthetic environments built for world's fairs, such as Poble Espanyol, a "Spanish village" that re-creates varieties of traditional architecture from throughout Spain, erected in Barcelona for the 1929 Universal Exhibition. The interior of the Shtetl Museum's castle will not be a re-creation but will house the complex's "main historical center," with a library, an archive, a performing arts center, and a "museum of Jewish life that will feature both Ashkenazic and Sephardic traditions and customs."[41] The Shtetl Museum thus elides the specific with the generic; it represents *a* shtetl as well as *the* shtetl and also uses the shtetl as a point of entry to Jewish traditions and folkways generally. Indeed, the museum is both tied to a particular locale in Lite (Lithuania, as understood in traditional Ashkenazic geography) and emblematic of a universalized diaspora Jewish culture.[42]

Second, consider the temporal boundaries of the Shtetl Museum's restoration. In their efforts to make the past present, living history museums pursue a variety of strategies: Plimoth Plantation annually reenacts the year 1627; Colonial Williamsburg's reenactments are set more generally in the eighteenth century; Strawberry Banke in Portsmouth, New Hampshire, consists of a series of historic houses, each of which restages a different moment in the neighborhood's four-hundred-year history. On one hand, Eliach speaks of Eishyshok as embodying a thousand years of Jewish experience and explains that different sites within the Shtetl Museum will re-create different moments in its history. On the other hand, a number of the Shtetl Museum's planned re-creations—a photographer's studio, a pharmacy, Yiddish theater performances, Zionist youth clubs—suggest that it will largely reenact the shtetl of the early twentieth century or of the interwar years—that is, the shtetl that the last generation of immigrants and survivors from Eastern Europe recalls. Significantly, Eliach insists on the importance of remembering all this history as part of a traditionally Jewish, pan-historical agenda—in her words, "to ensure that the golden chain of Jewish life that stretches from Biblical times to the present remains unbroken."[43]

Third, consider the demographic boundaries for the Shtetl Museum. Its geographic and temporal boundaries have telling implications for its inventory of reenactors. Ideological agendas will also inform the Shtetl Museum's dramatis personae. There will, apparently, be *minyanim* (prayer quorums) worshipping in the synagogues—but will there also be a band of Jewish socialist revolutionaries, who will come along to disrupt them? A Jewish farmer's house, surrounded by fields, as well as a Karaite home (there having been several Karaite communities in the region of Eishyshok), are mentioned among the planned re-creations. However, there is no mention of staging the town's Christian population through display of their homes, professions, or houses of worship. Nor is there any indication that the town's reenactors will include peasants bringing wares to sell in the market or marching in religious processions on saints' days, or a gentile constable, postman, or other municipal officials typical of shtetl civic life. Thus, the Shtetl Museum resembles Eliach's photographic collection displayed in the USHMM's Tower of Faces, which includes images only of Jewish residents of Eishyshok. (Consequently, the Shtetl Museum may wind up unwittingly placing its visitors, at least some of the time, in the position of gentiles, who come to the shtetl from outside to shop in its stores, eat in its restaurants, and otherwise partake of its commercial offerings.)

The apparent absence of representations of Eishyshok's gentiles (who, according to Eliach, composed about one-sixth of the town's population on the eve of World War II) is a significant departure from the shtetl's complete historical actuality. This also appears to be at odds with the protocols of Colonial Williamsburg, Eliach's oft-mentioned paradigm, which in recent years expanded its reenactment of life in eighteenth-century Virginia beyond the colony's white elite to include servants, laborers, and African American slaves; similarly, Plimoth Plantation's reenactors include members of the Wampanoag tribe. And the Shtetl Museum differs from the mission of the Lower East Side Tenement Museum, which is in part a living history museum and is committed to a multicultural representation of immigrant experience in this Manhattan neighborhood.[44]

At the same time, in omitting gentiles, the Shtetl Museum remains true to the conventions of shtetl remembrance as codified in Jewish literature since the mid-nineteenth century. As Dan Miron has observed, in these works the shtetl is configured as a "Jewish polity par excellence"—a self-contained, exclusively Jewish social space, which Miron calls a "tiny exiled Jerusalem, a *Yerushalayim shel mata.*"[45] Indeed, the one vestige of the gentile world in the Shtetl Museum's plan—the castle that dominates its landscape—will apparently not be inhabited by an actor playing the local *porets* (nobleman) but will house a Jewish educational center. (There is, however, potential for a *porets* of sorts: for a donation of $25 million, the castle will be named in honor of the contributor, who will be known as the "Noble Benefactor"—this being the highest of thirteen levels of support listed on the Shtetl Museum's Donation Guide—and the Noble Benefactor's portrait will be displayed in the castle.)[46] The absence of Christians among the Shtetl Museum's reenactors may also be a consequence of Eliach's universalizing of Jewish experience in her approach to shtetl remembrance; by positioning Jews as paradigmatic for all of Western civilization, non-Jewish communities become adventitious.

Fourth, consider how the Shtetl Museum will deal with the boundaries of communication. In Plimoth Plantation, for example, reenactors speak various dialects of seventeenth-century English among themselves and with visitors, and the native American reenactors speak Wampanoag.[47] If the Shtetl Museum seeks to restore a similar linguistic authenticity, then most of its reenactors will speak a Lithuanian dialect of Yiddish most of the time. Most tourists, though, will find this unintelligible. Should the reenactors, then, speak modern Hebrew, the official language of the country in which the Shtetl Museum is to be built?[48] Or should they speak English, which has, arguably, replaced Yiddish as the vernacular most widely shared by Jews around the world today? (According to Eliach, as of December 2003 the issue of language use had yet to be resolved.[49] That this was the case, even as the construction of the Shtetl Museum was already under way, testifies to a remarkable shift in modern Jewish culture, wherein language is no longer a foremost defining issue, its former primacy in modern Jewish life having yielded to the importance of place and of "experience.")

Resolving the issue of language will be tied to the range of encounters envisioned for visitors to the Shtetl Museum. They will be not only observers, but also students (children attending a *heder*, where Jewish children traditionally begin their religious education; adults a yeshiva),[50] consumers (shopping in the market square, eating in a restaurant), interlocutors (visiting the home of the shtetl rabbi for "words of wisdom"), and, albeit contingently, members of the virtual Jewish community of Eishyshok—worshipping alongside reenactors or even celebrating their own life-cycle events at the Shtetl Museum. This array of possibilities extends the protocols of living history in diverging directions: on one hand, the Shtetl Museum will be traditionally didactic (exemplified by the educational displays and resources to be housed in the castle); on the other hand, it proffers a degree of interactivity that will test even the limits of the living history museum as a virtual experience.

These limit-case activities center on ritual and worship: visitors will be able to pray in the synagogues, immerse themselves in the *mikvah*, and participate in memorial services at the cemetery, which will have "tombstones dating back to 1097." According to its web site, the Shtetl Museum will also offer visitors the possibility of celebrating "births, . . . bar and bat mitzvoth, or even . . . weddings, perhaps choosing to follow some of the shtetl wedding customs described in *There Once Was a World*."[51] The Shtetl Museum will then be simultaneously a locus of historic preservation and of invented tradition, just as the celebrants will be both observers and participants, outsiders and fellow Jews. The rituals will be both actual, with real-life consequences (e.g., becoming a married couple), and subjunctive (the wedding staged *as if* the couple were Jewish residents of prewar Eishyshok—or, even more provocatively, a bat mitzvah celebrated *as if* such an event might have ever taken place in a shtetl). Boundaries between categories that are ostensibly discrete—past and present, here and there, tourist and reenactor, actual and imaginary—will all be disturbed through these activities. But these slippages may well be elided—indeed, even go unnoticed—because visitors will encounter them in the course of pursuing a complex of contemporary desires regarding their relationship to the East European Jewish past that are fundamental to the Shtetl Museum's rationale.

Perhaps nothing better illustrates the power of these desires to prevail over the challenges posed by the Shtetl Museum than the decision to build it in Rishon le-Tsiyon, which also complicates its status as a living history museum. (According to one press report, this was "one of a dozen potential sites in Israel and Pennsylvania" considered for the project.)[52] This choice is atypical of living history museums, which tend either to use original architecture, albeit restored, in situ (as in Williamsburg) or are fabrications located close to the original site (as in Plimoth Plantation). Even outdoor museums that collect examples of national folk architecture from across a wide expanse of territory and move them to a central site, such as Skansen in Stockholm or the *muzey prosto neba* (open-air museum) in Pereyaslev-Khmelnitskii, Ukraine, are located in the country whose folkways they commemorate. But the Shtetl Museum is being erected some 1,500 miles from Eishyshok, in a physical environment quite different from that of Lithuania. Moreover, the fabrication of a shtetl in Israel has challenging implications that are not only geographical but also political. (The image of the Shtetl Museum being erected on empty land—" 'Only sand,' says [Rishon le-Tsiyon's] Mayor Meir Nitzan" of the site[53]—both recalls and subverts early-twentieth-century images of Tel Aviv and other projects of the *yishuv* [Jewish settlement in Palestine] that similarly appeared to rise ex nihilo.)

Indeed, a re-created shtetl in the middle of Israel—and moreover, in Rishon le-Tsiyon, founded in 1882, the first settlement established by *halutsim* (Zionist pioneers) from outside Palestine—plays provocatively with the relationship between the Jewish diaspora and the Zionist state.

On one hand, does it intimate that Eishyshok has, in effect, made *aliyah* (i.e., emigrated to Israel)? Does the State of Israel serve as a frame for what will amount to a large artifact, salvaged from exile? (In much the same way, Arnold Eisen has characterized the entrance to Beit Hatefutsoth, the Museum of the Diaspora in Tel Aviv, as tacitly offering visitors the following caveat: "Remember where you stand. Only the Land around you is real. The rest is not. If you come from a Diaspora of the present, know that sooner than you think, your community too will be part of our past, a room in our museum.")[54] On the other hand, does this vision of a shtetl rising up in the midst of a founding locus of the *yishuv* constitute a post-Zionist validation of Diaspora culture par excellence? Does the Shtetl Museum challenge, albeit implicitly, Israeli notions of Jewish indigeneity? ("A different kind of settlement activity," quips Julia Goldman, reporting on the museum's ground-breaking ceremony for *The Jewish Week*.)[55] And, by asserting a historical continuity from ancient times to the present where Zionism insists on rupture, does the Shtetl Museum's mission—to "illuminate the ways in which the legacy of the shtetl continues to play out in the many countries to which the Jews of Eastern Europe emigrated, including, of course, . . . the land of Israel, whose very foundations rested on their labors"—flout the classic Zionist narrative of Jewish history?[56]

The Shtetl Museum's reenactments will further complicate the visitor's sense of relationship between the shtetl and Israel. Among the classes for children to be restaged is the "original hachshara (Zionist orientation) program that prepared Eishyshok youth for immigration to Israel."[57] Also to be re-created is "a small bridge over the river" where "the rabbi blessed people who were departing for Palestine."[58] The Shtetl Museum will thus allow visitors to imagine themselves going back in time to experience the anticipation of *aliyah* and of the State of Israel, but doing so from the subjunctive vantage of its realization in a virtual "future." At the same time that the Shtetl Museum validates Zionism, it is also conceived as offering something remedial to Israeli society, and at least some Israelis who have endorsed the project apparently share this vision. In his praise for the museum, one of the Israeli officials speaking at its ground-breaking ceremony insisted that "a Jewish nation without a past, without roots, cannot exist."[59]

Eliach explains that the Shtetl Museum will present shtetl Jews in "the fullness of their humanity, not simply as quaint characters in a Fiddler on the Roof production or emaciated victims in concentration camp photos."[60] In assailing what are today, perhaps, the two most widely familiar images of East European Jewry, she implicitly critiques their effects—the sentimentalization of Broadway, the shock and awe of Holocaust representation. However, aspects of both these images inform the

Shtetl Museum; indeed, its success with the public will depend to a considerable extent on their enduring appeal.

Should it eventually be completed and open to the public, the Shtetl Museum will doubtless vex some historians, exasperate some Zionists, and pose its share of halakhic (rabbinic legal) conundrums. Nevertheless, it promises to prove popular with visitors, because of its ability to engage them by dint of several subjunctive modes with which they are already familiar: the modern tourist subjunctive, which offers the traveler a contingent immersion in an experience of an exotic way of life; the traditional Jewish subjunctive, exemplified by the Passover seder, during which Jews project themselves back in time and place, thinking of themselves as if they had been among the ancient Israelites freed from slavery and receiving the Torah at Mt. Sinai; and the Zionist subjunctive, the dream of a Jewish homeland, fundamental to Zionist rhetoric (and enduring as a trope after 1948), the realization of this vision reinforced, even as it is ironized, by the ability to re-create a shtetl in the midst of the State of Israel.

There are other modes at work in the Shtetl Museum as well, though perhaps less obviously so. Besides promoting public memory, the museum also engages retribution—"When this is complete," Eliach has said, "I will be able to tell my children and thirteen grandchildren that Hitler lost, and we won"—and it also entails forgetting. There are no Jews left in the actual town of Eishyshok, Eliach reports; its Jewish past has been erased. "In a sense," she explains, "we are closing the door to a vanished past so that we can have a living, breathing town."[61]

That these various cultural agendas are not consistent with those of prewar shtetl life or even with one another is not surprising. Performance theorist Richard Schechner notes that performative restorations "have a life of their own." Their "original 'truth' or 'source' . . . may be lost, ignored or contradicted—even while this . . . is apparently being honored and observed."[62] Should it indeed become "a living, breathing town"—or, rather, a living, breathing reenactment of one—the Shtetl Museum promises to provide rich opportunities to consider the compelling role that engaging their East European past will play for twenty-first-century Jews—even as it renders access to that place and time more complicated for would-be visitors.

Notes

My thanks to Ben Nathans for inviting me to present a version of this essay at the Ninth Annual Gruss Colloquium in Judaic Studies, convened by the Center for Advanced Judaic Studies, University of Pennsylvania, in May 2003, and for his thoughtful suggestions on developing this essay. Special thanks also to

Donny Inbar, Barbara Kirshenblatt-Gimblett, Rebecca Kobrin, Olga Litvak, Deganit Paikowski, Gabriella Safran, and Stuart Schear for their kind assistance.

1. In Yiddish, *shtetl* simply means "small town"; in English, the term is typically glossed as a "small-town Jewish community in E[astern] Europe" (Geoffrey Wigoder, ed., *Encyclopedic Dictionary of Judaica* [New York, Paris, Jerusalem, 1974], 552), exemplifying the added value that the shtetl has acquired with distance.

2. See Dan Miron, "On the Classical Image of the Shtetl in Yiddish Belles Lettres" (Yiddish), in *Der imazh fun shtetl: Dray literarishe shtudyes* (The image of the shtetl: Three literary studies) (Tel Aviv, 1981), 19–138, and Dan Miron, "The Literary Image of the Shtetl," *Jewish Social Studies* n.s. 1, no. 3 (Spring 1995): 1–43; this essay is reprinted in Dan Miron, *The Image of the Shtetl and Other Studies of Modern Jewish Literary Imagination* (Syracuse, 2000), 1–48. See also Ruth R. Wisse, "Introduction," in *A Shtetl and Other Yiddish Novellas* (New York, 1973), 1–21.

3. Benjamin Harshav, *The Meaning of Yiddish* (Berkeley, 1990), 130ff.

4. Hirsz Abramowicz, "A Lithuanian *Shtetl*," in *Profiles of a Lost World: Memoirs of East European Jewish Life before World War II*, trans. Eva Zeitlin Dobkin (Detroit, 1999), 77–98, originally published in *Af di khurves fun milkhomes un mehumes* (On the ruins of wars and turmoil) (Vilna, 1931), 361–84. On YIVO and other interwar ethnographic efforts, see Itzik Nakhmen Gottesman, *Defining the Yiddish Nation: The Jewish Folklorists of Poland* (Detroit, 2003); H. Aleksandrov, *Forsht ayer shtetl!* (Research your town!) (Minsk, 1926). Note that interwar folklorists and ethnographers did not treat the shtetl as paradigmatic for all of East European Jewish life, as would become the case after World War II.

5. See Alter Kacyzne, *Poyln: Jewish Life in the Old Country*, ed. Marek Web (New York, 1999).

6. See J. Hoberman, *Bridge of Light: Yiddish Film Between Two Worlds* (New York, 1991), for discussions of the production of *Yankl der shmid* (Yankl the blacksmith; chapter 19, passim) and *Fishke der krumer* (Fishke the cripple; chapter 22, passim).

7. "Mayn shtetele Belts" (My town Belz) was written for the stage work *Dos lid fun der geto* (The song of the ghetto), libretto by Wm. Siegel; "Mayn shtetele Molif" (My town Mohilev) was written by Chaim Tauber and Manny Fleischman for the stage work *Papirene kinder* (Paper children) in 1936; "Mayn shtetele Yash" (My town Iaşi) was written by Max Kletter in 1935; "A grus fun der alter heym" (Greetings from the Old World) was written by Jacob Jacobs, L. Cohen, and B. Zidman in 1920[?]; "Ikh benk un gedenk nokh mayn heym" (I miss and recall my home) was written by Jacob Silbert in 1930.

8. See Jack Kugelmass and Jeffrey Shandler, "Going Home: How American Jews Invent the Old World" (exhibition brochure) (New York, 1989).

9. See Daniel Soyer, *Jewish Immigrant Associations and American Identity in New York, 1880–1939* (Cambridge, Mass., 1997).

10. On American Jewish philanthropic efforts on behalf of East European Jewry between the two world wars, see Rebecca A. Kobrin, "Conflicting Diasporas, Shifting Centers: Migration and Identity in a Transnational Polish Jewish Community, 1878–1952" (Ph.D. dissertation, University of Pennsylvania, 2002), especially the chapter "'Buying Bricks for Bialystok': Philanthropy, Class and Power in the Trans-national Bialystoker Jewish Community, 1919–1952," 152–214. While Kobrin studies a major city, not a shtetl, the larger issues concerning relationships between American Jews and their fellows in interbellum Eastern Europe as realized through philanthropy are generally consistent for communities large and small.

11. See Daniel Soyer, "The Travel Agent as Broker between Old World and New: The Case of Gustave Eisner," *YIVO Annual* 21 (1993): 345–68; Roberta Newman, "Pictures of a Trip to the Old Country," *YIVO Annual* 21 (1993): 223–40.

12. Yankev Glatshteyn, *Ven Yash iz gekumen* (When Yash arrived) (New York, 1940), 275.

13. Moyshe-Leyb Halpern, "A Night" (Yiddish), in *In Nyu-york* (In New York) (New York, 1927), 181–224; Issachar Ryback, *Shtetl: Mayn khorever heym a gedekhenish* (Shtetl: My destroyed home, a remembrance) (Berlin, 1923).

14. Chone Gottesfeld, *Tales of the Old World and the New* (New York, 1964), 259–60. This text was adapted from Gottesfeld's *Mayn rayze iber Galitsye* (My travels through Galicia) (New York, 1937).

15. Jack Kugelmass and Jonathan Boyarin, eds., *From a Ruined Garden: The Memorial Books of Polish Jewry* (New York, 1983), 6.

16. On shtetl photography, see Jeffrey Shandler, "Szczuczyn: A Shtetl Through a Photographer's Eye," in *Lives Remembered: A Shtetl Through a Photographer's Eye*, ed. Louis Levine (New York, 2002), 19–27. On the re-creation of the wooden synagogue, see "From Memory to Memorial: A Synagogue Rising," *New York Times*, 25 September 2003, F3 (information on the restoration is available at www.zabludow.com). On the architecture of the National Yiddish Book Center's headquarters, see "The New Home of the National Yiddish Book Center," *The Book Peddler/Der pakn-treger* 19 (Summer 1994), 8–30.

17. Barbara Kirshenblatt-Gimblett, "Introduction," in *Life Is with People: The Culture of the Shtetl*, ed. Mark Zborowski and Elizabeth Herzog (New York, 1995), ix, xiv. See also Barbara Kirshenblatt-Gimblett, "Imagining Europe: The Popular Arts of American Jewish Ethnography," in *Divergent Jewish Cultures: Israel and America*, ed. Deborah Dash Moore and S. Ilan Troen (New Haven, 2001), 155–91.

18. Consider, for example, ShtetlSchleppers, a travel service to Eastern Europe in operation since 1999, which guides groups of tourists on "their first steps into the journey of a lifetime," culminating in "four days of visits in your ancestral shtetls, customized just for you! Accompanied by an experienced guide/translator, you will walk on the same pathways in the footprints of your ancestors" (www.jewishgen.org/shtetlschleppers/).

19. Polish: Ejszyszki; Lithuanian: Eišiškės, a town in northeastern Poland, Nowogródek province, during the interwar years, now in Lithuania.

20. *There Once Was a Town* (dir. Jeff Bieber, 2000), a ninety-minute documentary film, was co-produced by WETA (Washington, D.C.) and Noga Productions (Israel). "Grandpa's Stories" (Hebrew), a fifty-minute audio documentary aired on Galey Zahal (the Israeli Defense Force radio station) on Yom Hashoah in 1998, was created by soldier Deganit Paikowsky, the granddaughter of Reuvan Paikowsky, a Holocaust survivor who was born in Eishyshok and a relative of Yaffa Eliach.

21. www.shtetlfoundation.org.

22. Yaffa Eliach, "Jewish Hasidim, Russian Sectarian Non-conformists in the Ukraine, 1700–1760" (Ph.D. dissertation, City University of New York, 1973). See also her essay "The Russian Dissenting Sects and Their Influence on Israel Baal Shem Tov, Founder of Hasidism," *Proceedings of the American Academy for Jewish Research* 38 (1968): 57–83. On the response to Eliach's argument, see Moshe Rosman, *Founder of Hasidism: A Quest for the Historical Ba'al Shem Tov* (Berkeley, 1996), 58–60. Note that, whereas at the start of her career, Eliach focused on the

relationships between Christians and Jews in Eastern Europe, her recent projects devoted to remembering life in the shtetl largely ignore the presence of non-Jews in this milieu.

23. Yaffa Eliach, *Hasidic Tales of the Holocaust* (New York, 1982).

24. See Rochelle G. Saidel, *Never Too Late to Remember: The Politics Behind New York City's Holocaust Museum* (New York, 1996).

25. See Edward T. Linenthal, *Preserving Memory: The Struggle to Create America's Holocaust Museum* (New York, 1995).

26. Yaffa Eliach, *There Once Was a World: A 900-Year Chronicle of the Shtetl Eishyshok* (Boston, 1998), 4.

27. Ibid., 3–4. Eliach relates a similarly revelatory experience upon her first postwar visit to Eishyshok, in 1987, when she stood at the mass grave of the town's Jews murdered in 1941: "'All the Jews in the town were buried there, but I didn't feel like I was standing on a grave,' she recalled. 'They were talking to me. They were saying, show the world that we are normal people!'" (Lisa Keys, "Repackaging the Old World as a Tourist Attraction," *Forward* [English-language ed.], 6 June 2003, 2).

28. This is how the USHMM refers to the installation; Eliach refers to it as the "Tower of Life." See, e.g., Eliach, *There Once Was a World*, 5.

29. Patricia Brennan, "'For the Living': The Holocaust Museum," Washington Post: TV Week (25 April–1 May, 1993), 7.

30. Jeshajahu Weinberg and Rina Elieli, *The Holocaust Museum in Washington* (New York, 1995), 72.

31. Eliach, *There Once Was a World*, xiv.

32. Ibid., 6.

33. On the ground-breaking ceremony marking the beginning of construction of the Shtetl Museum, see Julia Goldman, "A Shtetl Grows in Israel," *Jewish Week*, 6 June 2003; Keys, "Repackaging the Old World as a Tourist Attraction," 2.

34. The Shtetl Museum "is to be built in a special park complex in Rishon Le Zion, Israel, named 'the World of the First Lakes' (Olam Agamai Rishonim)" ("From the Tower of Life in Washington to a Living Shtetl in Israel" (promotional brochure), (New York, [2003?]).

35. As cited in R. F. Foster, *The Irish Story: Telling Tales and Making Up Ireland* (London, 2001), 29.

36. Barbara Kirshenblatt-Gimblett, *Destination Culture: Tourism, Museums, and Heritage* (Berkeley, 1998), 189, 199.

37. Juri Ginsburg, "Ein litauisches Schtetl für Israel—Eine New Yorker Professorin will ihre oesteuropäische Heimstadt wieder aufbauen—ein umstrittenes Projekt," *Berliner Zeitung*, 14 April 2001; Keys, "Repackaging the Old World as a Tourist Attraction," 2. The associations with Disneyland that the Shtetl Museum frequently prompts—perhaps due to its plan calling for a turreted castle located prominently at its center—are noteworthy. Occasional references to Disney in Eliach's memory projects suggest that his theme parks might, to some degree, figure in Eliach's conceptualization of the Shtetl Museum: in the documentary film *There Once Was a Town* Eliach says to her grandchildren about her childhood visits to her grandmother's photographic studio on the town's market place, "This was, for me, Disney World." One of the photos reproduced on the homepage of the Shtetl Museum's web site depicts a Jew from Eishyshok standing with someone in a Mickey Mouse costume. (In a fundraising brochure for the Shtetl Foundation, this photograph also appears, where it is captioned: "Mickey

Mouse, a popular Shtetl celebrity.") Moreover, Eliach's vision of visitors celebrating weddings and other life-cycle events at the Shtetl Museum parallels the practice, since the early 1990s, of holding weddings at Disney theme parks, in which costumed characters (e.g., Mickey and Minnie Mouse), wardrobe (bridesmaids dressed as Tinkerbell), sites (Cinderella's castle), and props (horse-drawn coach and glass slipper) are incorporated into the ceremonies. See Laura M. Holson, "For $38,000, Get the Cake, and Mickey, Too," *New York Times*, 24 May 2003, A1.

38. Ben Brantley, "A Cosy Little McShtetl," *New York Times*, 27 February 2004, E1.

39. See Kirshenblatt-Gimblett, *Destination Culture*, 17–19.

40. Eliach, *There Once Was a World*, 68.

41. www.shtetlfoundation.org.

42. At a public presentation on the Shtetl Museum, convened at City University of New York Graduate Center on 17 December 2003, Eliach explained that the plan of the Shtetl Museum is based on Eishyshok, but individual buildings, designed by architect Shmuel Raveh, represent a greater diversity of shtetl architecture, and the contents of buildings will cover an even broader array of diaspora Jewish culture. One press report mentions that the museum will also represent "Yemenite, North African and Ethiopian" Jewish communities (Goldman, "A Shtetl Grows in Israel"). Another report explains the inclusion of non-Ashkenazic diaspora Jewish culture in the museum "because some Sephardic Jews made their way to Eastern Europe," thereby legitimating this decision by situating Sephardim as indigenous within the nominal geography of the Shtetl Museum (Amy Sara Clark, "Shtetl in the Promised Land," *Jewish Standard*, December 2002).

43. www.shtetlfoundation.org.

44. See Jack Kugelmass, "Turfing the Slum: New York City's Tenement Museum and the Politics of Heritage," in *Remembering the Lower East Side: American Jewish Reflections*, ed. Hasia Diner et al. (Bloomington, 2000), 179–211.

45. Miron, "The Literary Image of the Shtetl," *Jewish Social Studies*, 30.

46. See www.shtetlfoundation.org. To finance the construction of the Shtetl Museum, estimated to cost $100 million, Eliach established the Shtetl Foundation on Chanukkah in December 1999; Elie Wiesel serves as the foundation's honorary president. Eliach reports having received a pledge of $2.5 million from the Israeli lottery and that she donates all the proceeds from her own lectures and books to the project (ca. $1.5 million as of the end of 2002). She acknowledges the challenge of fundraising for the Shtetl Museum currently, noting that "the Sept. 11 attacks and ongoing Israeli-Palestinian conflict have diverted many prospective donors' attention. 'People are focusing more on assisting people who are wounded, on security, and not so much actually for life,' Eliach said. 'I focus on life'" (Julia Goldman, "A Shtetl Grows in Israel").

47. See Steven Eddy Snow, *Performing the Pilgrims: A Study in Ethnohistorical Role-Playing* (Jackson, Miss., 1993).

48. Eliach might make a case for the authenticity of modern Hebrew as the Shtetl Museum's vernacular. She writes in her history of the town that Eishyshkians came from "a fervently Zionist, Hebraist shtetl" and were "long known for the excellence of their Hebrew"—so much so that, upon arriving in Palestine, many Jews from the town "had trouble convincing people that they were new immigrants, fresh off the boat" (*There Once Was a World*, 694).

49. I asked Eliach this question at her presentation at CUNY Graduate Center on 17 December 2003 (see note 42); she replied that it was an interesting question and that "we are working on it."

50. There are plans to arrange longer stays at the Shtetl Museum for children participating in educational programs, thereby further extending the conventional boundaries of the living history museum. Eliach envisions "two- to six-week programs," with students "housed in replicas of the upscale hotels of the resort town of Druskieniki, Lithuania"; she "also hope[s] to add a summer camp program to the project one day" (Clark, "Shetl in the Promised Land").

51. www.shtetlfoundation.org.

52. Goldman, "A Shtetl Grows in Israel." At the public program on the Shtetl Museum held at CUNY Graduate Center on 17 December 2003 (see note 42), Eliach reported that, on hearing of her early plans to establish the Shtetl Museum, friends in Pennsylvania offered her land there for the project. However, she explained, she is committed to building the museum in Israel first and then possibly building another one in the United States.

53. Steve Lipman, "Lithuanian Shtetl to Live Again," *Jewish Week*, 26 May 2000.

54. Arnold Eisen, *Galut: Modern Jewish Reflection on Homelessness and Homecoming* (Bloomington, 1986), 43. Note that, at about the same time that construction on the Shtetl Museum began, Beit Hatefutsoth closed its doors due to governmental budget cuts.

55. Goldman, "A Shtetl Grows in Israel."

56. "From the Tower of Life in Washington to a Living Shtetl in Israel."

57. "Eishyshok, a Shtetl Rebuilt," *Israel Today*, April 2000.

58. Ron Csillag, "Survivor Spearheading Effort to Build Replica Shtetl in Israel," *Canadian Jewish News* (Toronto), 27 July 2000.

59. *The Shtetl: The Living Museum of the Jewish World* (promotional video) (New York, [2003]); translation of remarks, which were delivered in Hebrew, as per the film's subtitles. Eliach screened the video as part of her presentation at CUNY Graduate Center on 17 December 2003 (see note 42). Among those who spoke at the ceremony were Israel's president, Moshe Katsav, and former chief rabbi of Israel Yisrael Meir Lau.

60. Steve Lipman, "Lithuanian Shtetl to Live Again," *Jewish Week*, 26 May 2000.

61. Csillag, "Survivor Spearheading Effort to Build Replica Shtetl in Israel."

62. Richard Schechner, *Between Theater and Anthropology* (Philadelphia, 1985), 35.

Contributors

Hamutal Bar-Yosef is a well-known Israeli poet, a translator of poetry (from Russian, French, and English), and a professor emerita of modern Hebrew literature at Ben-Gurion University, Beer-Sheva. Her main fields of research are the Russian context of modern Jewish culture and Jewish mysticism in modern Hebrew literature. She has published six research books and many articles and edited an anthology of Hebrew literature in Russian translation.

Jonathan Frankel is the Tamara and Saveli Grinberg Professor of Russian Studies and Professor of Modern Jewish History (both emeritus) at the Hebrew University of Jerusalem. He is coeditor of *Studies in Contemporary Jewry*, an annual published by Oxford University Press, and author of *Prophecy and Politics: Socialism, Nationalism, and the Russian Jews, 1862–1917* (1981), *The Damascus Affair: "Ritual Murder," Politics, and the Jews in 1840* (1997), and other works.

Kathryn Hellerstein is the Ruth Meltzer Senior Lecturer in Yiddish and Jewish Studies at the University of Pennsylvania. Her books include a translation and study of Moyshe-Leyb Halpern's poems, *In New York: A Selection* (1982), *Paper Bridges: Selected Poems of Kadya Molodowsky* (1999), and, as coeditor, *Jewish American Literature: A Norton Anthology* (2001). She was also a major contributor to *American Yiddish Poetry: A Bilingual Anthology* (1986). Her poems and scholarly articles on Yiddish literature and, most recently, on women poets writing in Yiddish, have appeared in journals and anthologies.

Marcus Moseley is associate professor of German and Jewish studies at Northwestern University. He has taught Hebrew and Yiddish literature at New York University, Harvard University, and the Johns Hopkins University. He is the author of *Being for Myself Alone: Origins of Jewish Autobiography* (2006).

Kenneth B. Moss is the Felix Posen Assistant Professor of Modern Jewish History at the Johns Hopkins University. He is currently completing a book on the East European Jewish cultural sphere and the interplay of nationalist, revolutionary, and aestheticist ideals in Jewish cultural nationalism, as reflected in Hebrew and Yiddish cultural life during the Russian Revolution. His work has appeared in *Jewish Social Studies* and the *Journal of Social History*.

Benjamin Nathans is the Ronald S. Lauder Endowed Term Associate Professor of History at the University of Pennsylvania. He is author of *Beyond the Pale: The Jewish Encounter with Late Imperial Russia* (2002; Russian edition 2007, Hebrew edition forthcoming) and editor of *Research Guide to Materials on the History of Russian Jewry (19th and Early 20th Centuries) in Selected Archives of the Former Soviet Union* (Russian; 1994), compiled by G. M. Deych. He is currently coediting and annotating the first English translation of Simon Dubnov's autobiography, *The Book of Life*.

Eugenia Prokop-Janiec teaches Polish and comparative literature and ethnology at the Jagiellonian University of Cracow. She specializes in the history of modern literature and literary criticism, literary ethnology, and Polish-Jewish cultural and literary contacts in the nineteenth and twentieth centuries. She is the author of *Polish-Jewish Literature in the Interwar Years* (2003; Polish version *Międzywojenna literatura polsko-żydowska jako zjawisko kulturowe i artystyczne*, 1992) and *Literatura i nacjonalizm* (Literature and nationalism) (2004), an editor of the anthology *Międzywojenna poezja polsko-żydowska* (Interwar Polish-Jewish poetry) (1996), coeditor of *Teatr żydowski w Krakowie* (Jewish theater in Cracow) (1995), and contributor to a wide range of scholarly journals and collective volumes in Europe, North America, and Israel.

Alyssa Quint teaches Jewish literature at Princeton University, where she is the managing editor of *Jewish Studies Quarterly*. She is currently at work on a cultural history of the Yiddish theater.

Gabriella Safran is an associate professor in the Department of Slavic Languages and Literatures at Stanford University. She is the author of *Rewriting the Jew: Assimilation Narratives in the Russian Empire* (2000), coeditor with Steven Zipperstein of *The Worlds of S. An-sky: A Russian-Jewish Intellectual at the Turn of the Century* (2006), and coproducer with Michael Alpert of the compact disc *The Upward Flight/Dos Oyfkumen: The Musical World of S. An-sky*. Currently she is writing an intellectual biography of An-sky.

Jeffrey Shandler is an associate professor in the Department of Jewish Studies at Rutgers University. His publications include *Adventures in Yid-*

dishland: Postvernacular Language and Culture (2005), *While America Watches: Televising the Holocaust* (1999), *Entertaining America: Jews, Movies, and Broadcasting* (with J. Hoberman; 2003), and (as editor) *Awakening Lives: Autobiographies of Jewish Youth in Poland before the Holocaust* (2002).

Michael C. Steinlauf is a historian of East European Jewish culture and Polish-Jewish relations who teaches Jewish history and literature at Gratz College. He is the author of *Bondage to the Dead: Poland and the Memory of the Holocaust* (1997) and the coeditor of volume 16 (2003) of the annual *Polin: Studies in Polish Jewry*, a special issue devoted to Jewish popular culture in Poland and its afterlife. His articles on Jewish theater and culture in Eastern Europe have been translated into Hebrew, Polish, German, and Italian. He is theater editor of the forthcoming *YIVO Encyclopedia of Jewish Life in Eastern Europe* and serves as senior historical consultant for the city of Warsaw's planned Museum of the History of Polish Jews.

Adam Teller is a senior lecturer in the Department of Jewish History at the University of Haifa. He is the author of *Living Together: The Jewish Quarter of Poznan in the First Half of the Seventeenth Century* (Hebrew; 2003) and *Money, Power and Influence: The Jews on the Radziwill Estates in Lithuania in the Eighteenth Century* (Hebrew; 2006). He has written widely in English, Hebrew, Polish, and German on economic, social, and cultural aspects of Jewish history in early modern Poland-Lithuania and is currently working on a history of the communal rabbinate in the Polish-Lithuanian Commonwealth.

Marcin Wodziński is professor of Jewish history and head of the Department of Jewish Studies at the University of Wrocław. He is author of *Haskalah and Hasidism in the Kingdom of Poland: A History of Conflict* (2005; Polish version *Oświecenie żydowskie w Królestwie Polskim wobec chasydyzmu,* 2003), and *Władze Królestwa Polskiego wobec chasydyzmu. Z dziejów stosunków politycznych* (The Authorities of the Kingdom of Poland versus Hasidism; 2007), and coeditor of *Židé ve Slezsku. Studie k dejinám Židů ve Slezsku* (Jews in Silesia: Studies in the history of Silesian Jewry; 2001) and *Małżeństwo z rozsądku? Żydzi w społeczeństwie dawnej Rzeczypospolitej* (Jews in the society of the Polish Lithuanian Commonwealth; 2007) as well as several other works.

Index